There Came A Time ...

Essays on the Great War in Africa

Edited by:
Anne Samson
Ana Paula Pires
Dan Gilfoyle

GWAA / TSL Publications

The Great War in Africa Association

Published in Great Britain in 2018
By Great War in Africa Association, TSL Publications, Rickmansworth

Copyright © 2018 Great War in Africa Association, International Network for First World War Studies

ISBN: 978-1-912416-36-3

The right of the individual authors listed in this publication and the Great War in Africa Association; to be identified as the authors of this work has been asserted by the authors in accordance with the UK Copyright, Designs and Patents Act 1988.

All rights reserved. No part of this publication may be reproduced, stored in a retrieval system or transmitted, in any form or by any means without the prior written permission of the publisher, nor be otherwise circulated in any form of binding or cover other than that in which it is published and without a similar condition being imposed on the subsequent buyer.

Images: courtesy of Kevin Patience and The National Archives, published with permission.

Contents

Foreword	5
Historiography	9

Part 1: Military Aspects

East Africa

How Britain fell into war in East Africa: *Anne Samson*	18
Military overview of the campaign in East Africa: *Harry Fecitt*	23
'Bridging the gap': Exploring the role of the Staff during the 1916 campaign in Tanganyika: *David Boyd*	33
The defence of Karonga and the battle of Kasoa: *Peter Charlton*	55
The Rhodesian Police Units at the front: *Timothy Wright*	60

Some naval aspects

'Strike the Colours': The loss of HMS Pegasus at Zanzibar, 20 September 1914: *Kevin Patience*	82
England expects: Naval action in Nyasaland: *Peter Charlton*	87
'Danes' at war in East Africa: The case of the blockade runner SS *Kronborg*: *Bjarne S Bendtsen*	92

West Africa

The Advent of War: Anglo-African Relations across West Africa: *Nigel Browne-Davies*	109
Nigeria Regiment in Cameroon: *Stewart Hawkins*	114

North West Africa

Northern and Eastern Africa during the Great War: *Harry Fecitt*	142

Part 2 Mobilisation, participants and economics

Mass mobilisation of human resources: *Tanja Bührer*	168
'When two elephants fight it's the grass that suffers.' (African proverb): East Africa during the First World War: *Oliver Schulten*	176

Participants

The Belgian Force Publique in German East Africa during World War I: *Kris Quanten* — 189

I can never say about the men—The Jammu and Kashmir Rifles: *Andrew Kerr* — 214

On Call in Africa in War and Peace - with 3 East Africa Field Ambulance: *Dr Tony Jewell* — 218

Forgotten Citizens and Servicemen: The West African Contribu-tion to the First World War: *Nigel Browne-Davies* — 227

The Germans and British in São Vicente Cape Verde: *Célia Reis* — 255

Diversity in Adversity: The British in Egypt during the First World War: *Lanver Mak* — 271

Economics and politics

The 'other Portuguese Flanders': strategic ambition and operational disaster in the Portuguese Great War in Mozambique: *António Paulo Duarte; Ana Paula Pires; Bruno Cardoso Reis* — 295

War and Empire: Portuguese East Africa and economic warfare (1914-1919): *Ana Paula Pires & Maria Fernanda Rollo* — 311

The Status of the West African Sterling in Southern Nigeria in 1916: *Bamidele Aly* — 327

Part 3: Researching the African Theatre

Researching the First World War in Africa: *Dan Gilfoyle* — 342

The National Archives (London) Collection: *William Spencer* — 356

Bringing African soldiers to life using The National Archives (London) record collections: *Martin Willis* — 360

Let the collection tell its own story: Artefacts of the war in German East Africa in the collections of the Royal Museum of the Armed Forces and of Military History in Brussels: *Jan van der Fraenen* — 380

Citations for military awards: *Harry Fecitt* — 395

Foreword

In 2012 The Great War in East Africa Association, as it was then, held its first conference. Subsequently, under the revised name of The Great War in Africa Association (GWAA) and until 2016, there has been an annual conference in London, Lisbon or Stellenbosch. The Lisbon conference was in partnership with the Institute for Contemporary History at NOVA School of Social Sciences and Humanities who have joined to present this edition, while Stellenbosch was hosted by the Military History Department, Stellenbosch University which produced its own conference publication in 2016. The decision was made in 2017 not to hold a conference as there were too many other events in the UK, in particular, focusing on Africa and the Caribbean during World War One. Rather than over-kill, the GWAA and its members supported and attended these other events.

The increase in events demonstrates the growing interest in the African theatres over the centenary years. Reliance on the Internet for access to material means that many myths and inaccuracies of the campaign are being perpetuated. When many of the popular texts were published, official documents were still closed and few memoirs were in circulation. The result is that many are not able to access archival material for whatever reason and so rely on what is publicly available. Recognising this and that researchers are at different stages of their journey, this compilation seeks to be broad ranging, including military narrative, cultural and social discussions around recruitment, economic aspects and examples of the gems to be found in archives and museums.

The compilation has shortcomings. The most obvious being the limited number of contributions on belligerents other than Britain, the local voice and a bias towards East Africa. There is no apology for this—the compilation reflects the current interests by students of the war in Africa and that in itself provides an important contribution to the historiography of World War One on the continent. The current range of contributions has taken five years to assemble and a perusal of the dates for each submitted chapter provides further insight as to the development of the Great War in Africa.

Feedback on the 2012 conference draft publication intimated that the narrative contributions were out-dated and should not be included in such a publication. There may be some value in such a statement, however, in keeping with the ethos of The Great War in Africa Association whose membership spans the spectrum of all interested in the African theatre, the challenge of accessing narratives of the campaign unless in academic institutions or near a collecting library, the decision has been made to retain these papers as a valuable introduction to the subsequent analysis contained in the more academic contributions. Whilst most narrative is military in nature with many analyses also being military focused, there is a benefit to social and cultural historians in accessing these accounts for detail and connections which is often overlooked in an archive or secondary interpretation. With this in mind, the editors are confident that despite the frustrations some readers might experience, there will be greater value for all in such a compilation.

The volume is divided into three parts: the first dealing with the military aspects of the campaign providing a background and setting the later parts in context for those less familiar with the Great War in Africa. Part Two explores aspects of the war from mobilisation and participants through to prisoners and economics whilst the third and final part contains information on researching aspects of the campaign.

It is unfortunate that as a result of the time taken to publish the collection and the nature of the academic publishing world, a few papers have had to be excluded from the collection. These, however, can be found in book form and are highly recommended for shedding new light on the war in Africa.

Mahon Murphy, *Colonial Captivity during the First World War: Internment and the fall of the German Empire, 1914-1919* (Cambridge University, 2017)

Myles Osborne, *Ethnicity and Empire in Kenya: Loyalty and Martial Race among the Kamba, c1800 to the present* (Cambridge University, 2014)

Daniel Steinbach's book on the German prisoners in East Africa including information on missionaries, is due for publication shortly.

Words of appreciation

Finally, some words of thanks to the British South African Police Association (BSAP) who prompted the idea for the first conference and to Dix Noonan Webb for contributing towards the cost of events. Professor David Killingray, Dr Michael Pesek, Sheila Tremlett, Dr Ana Paula Pires and Dr Dan Gilfoyle who provided valuable comments. All contributors for their patience in seeing this publication come to fruition.

Historiography

The First World War and the impact of the conflict on British Africa[1] has been examined by several historians who have focused on the political, economic and military consequences of the war.[2] Several studies have examined individual campaigns such as South West Africa, Togoland and Cameroon with a particular focus on the military strategies and challenges during the conflict.[3] The most comprehensively covered theatre has been East Africa with works by Edward Paice and Ross Anderson.[4] However, although some scholarly works have examined the African theatre of war, few, if any, of these studies have comprehensively assessed Anglo-African relations at the advent of the conflict, the distinct responses of traditional African communities and the British West African elite to the conflict and the circumstances under which African[5] servicemen were recruited to serve in the conflict.

The official military accounts of the First World War such as the *Military Operations, Togoland and the Cameroons, 1914-1916* by Brigadier-General Frederick James Moberly, *Official History: Military operations East Africa, August 1914-September 1916 vol 1* by Charles Hordern and the *Medical Services: General History* (Volume 1) by Sir William Grant Macpherson, provide detailed accounts of the military

---

[1] Review by Nigel Browne-Davies and Anne Samson

[2] Hew Strachan, 'The Cameroons' in *The First World War in Africa* (Oxford UP, 2004) pp vii-viii, 3-4. Michael Crowder, Jide Osuntokun, 'The First World War and West Africa, 1914-1918' in JFA Ajayi, Michael Crowder (eds) *A History of West Africa* (Longman, 1987, 2nd ed) pp. 546-77

[3] Frederick James Moberly, *Military Operations Togoland and the Cameroons, 1914-1916 (Official History of the Great War)* (HMSO, 1931), pp. 40-60

[4] Edward Paice, *Tip and Run* (Weidenfeld & Nicholson, 2007), Ross Anderson, *The Forgotten Front* (Tempus, 2007)

[5] Refers to all ethnicities unless specified Black, Coloured, Arab, Indian or White.

operations and medical services of the campaign in addition to invaluable statistical data on casualties in the war.[6] Furthermore, the two Official Histories and Sir William Macpherson's *Medical Services* quote from the war despatches and provide unique insight into the military and medical challenges faced by African servicemen.[7] However, although the official histories examine the military and medical aspects of the conflict, these accounts provide little information on the demographic makeup of the Africans who were recruited to serve in the war and the context in which they were recruited to serve. Furthermore, these accounts provide few details on individual African servicemen and their contributions to the conflict. The exceptions are isolated accounts of white soldiers from South Africa and Britain.

Military histories such as Lieutenant RPM Davis' *History of the Sierra Leone Battalion of the Royal West African Frontier Force* and Colonel A Haywood & Brigadier FAS Clarke's *The History of the Royal West African Frontier Force* provide important information on the military campaigns and in particular on the West African Frontier Force who served in the First World War.[8] As historical accounts of the Royal West African Frontier Force and the battalions of the Force, both Davis and Haywood & Clarke emphasise military contributions of the Force that are perhaps less examined in the official military accounts. However, both Davis and Clarke's publications are largely concerned with the military operations of the conflict and therefore neither study provides substantial information on the concerns of British West Africans on the home front. The same can be said about East and Southern African involvement: James Ambrose Brown's *They Fought for*

---

[6] Moberly, *Togoland and Cameroons*, pp. 124, 136, 275-9, 303-7, Sir William Grant Macpherson, *Medical Services: General History: Medical services in the United Kingdom, in British garrisons overseas and during operations against Tsingtau, in Togoland, the Cameroons and South-West Africa*, vol I (HMSO, 1921) pp. 282-4, 288, Charles Hordern, *Official History: Military operations East Africa, August 1914-September 1916 vol 1* (HMSO, 1940)

[7] Moberly, *Togoland and Cameroons*, pp. 136, 426, Macpherson, *Medical Services*, p. 282

[8] RPM Davis, *History of the Sierra Leone Battalion of The Royal West African Frontier Force*, (Freetown, Government Printer, 1932) pp. 89-92, Haywood, Austin Hubert Wightwick & Clarke, Frederick Arthur Stanley, *The History of the Royal West African Frontier Force* (Gale & Polden, 1964) pp. 140-1

King and Kaiser, Tim Wright's *The History of the Northern Rhodesia Police*, Peter Charlton's *Cinderella Soldiers: The Nyasaland Volunteer Reserve* and James Willson's *Guerrillas of Tsavo: An illustrated diary of a forgotten campaign in British East Africa 1914-1916*.[9]

Historical accounts such as Akinijde Osuntokun's *Nigerians in the First World War* and EDA Turay & Arthur Abraham's *The Sierra Leone Army: A Century of History*, provide some insight into the specific experiences of Nigerian and Sierra Leonean servicemen and members of the educated African elite.[10] Turay & Abraham's study largely focuses on the military campaigns but briefly examines the pronounced loyalty expressed by British subjects of African descent in the Sierra Leone Colony.[11] In the chapter, 'The educated elite and the war,' Osuntokun provides an analysis of the conflicting desire of the educated African elite in Nigeria to support the war effort and remain critical of colonial policies implemented by Governor Lugard of Nigeria.[12] Furthermore, Osuntokun outlines the importance of German trade to indigenous communities and the resistance of some communities in Nigeria to the British war effort.[13] However, neither Turay & Abraham's nor Osuntokun's studies analysed the similarities and differences in Anglo-African relations between the experiences of the educated elite and servicemen in Sierra Leone and Nigeria and the inhabitants of other British West African territories.[14]

The closest accounts for East Africa are Michelle Moyd's *Violent Intermediaries* and Myles Osborne's *Kikamba*.[15] Moyd

---

[9] James Ambrose Brown's *They Fought for King and Kaiser* (Ashanti, 1991), Tim Wright's *The History of the Northern Rhodesia Police* (British Empire and Commonwealth Museum, 2001), Peter Charlton's *Cinderella Soldiers: The Nyasaland Volunteer Reserve* (Charlton, 2012, GWAA reprint 2018) and James Willson's *Guerrillas of Tsavo An illustrated diary of a forgotten campaign in British East Africa 1914-1916* (Guerrillas of Tsavo, 2012)

[10] Osuntokun, Akinijde, *Nigerians in the First World War* (Longman, 1979) pp. 21-3, 64-83

[11] Abraham, Arthur; Turay, Edward Dominic Amadu, *The Sierra Leone Army: A Century of History* (Macmillan, 1987) p. 39

[12] Osuntokun, *Nigerians in the First World War* (Longman, 1979) pp. 21-23, 64-83

[13] Osuntokun, *Nigerians in the First World War* (Longman, 1979) pp. 64-84

[14] Osuntokun, *Nigerians in the First World War* (Longman, 1979) pp 21-30

[15] Moyd, Michelle, *Violent Intermediaries* (Ohio UP, 2014), Osborne, Myles *Ethnicity*

focuses on the German askari while Osborne looks at one British-controlled micro-nation. The value of both books is that together similarities and hence inferences can be drawn. In East Africa, there was no elite in the same way there was in West Africa, the influence of western culture had not sufficient time to make its mark by the outbreak of the Great War. Therefore, inferences of West African experiences cannot be drawn across to East Africa, as has been done in the past, particularly with regard to recruitment and local reactions to the war.

Shorter studies briefly examining the roles and responses of West Africans to the First World War include studies by David Killingray and Festus Cole.[16] Killingray and Cole have both examined the contributions of the Carrier Corps to the African campaigns and have analysed the impact of the First World on the Gold Coast and Sierra Leone,[17] however there are few, if any parallels drawn between these territories and the other British West African territories.

Michael Crowder and Jide Osuntokun's chapter, 'The First World War and West Africa, 1914-1918,' provides an overview of the roles and responses of Africans in the British West African territories to the conflict.[18] Crowder and Osuntokun noted the loyalty of the educated African elite to the British war effort and the expectation of political concessions that the British West African elite had during the war.[19] Furthermore, Crowder and Osuntokun also examined the responses of traditional African communities in British West Africa to the conflict.[20] However, the chapter provided only a brief overview

---

and Empire in Kenya: Loyalty and Martial Race among the Kamba (Cambridge UP, 2014)

[16] Cole, Festus, 'The Sierra Leone Carrier Corps and Krio Responses to Recruitment in World War I' in Dixon-Fyle, Mac (ed.) Cole, Gibril Raschid (ed.), *New Perspectives on the Sierra Leone Krio* (Peter Lang, 2006), Killingray, David, 'Repercussions of World War One on the Gold Coast' in *Journal of African History*, Vol 19:1 (1978) pp. 39–50

[17] Cole, Sierra Leone Carrier Corps and Krio Responses, p. 62, Killingray, David & Matthews, James, 'Beasts of Burden: British West African Carriers in the First World War' in *Canadian Journal of African Studies/Revue Canadienne des Études Africaines*, vol. 13:1/2 (1979) pp. 7-23

[18] Crowder, Michael, Osuntokun, Jide, 'The First World War and West Africa, 1914-1918' in Ajayi, JFA & Crowder, Michael, (eds.) *A History of West Africa*, (Longman, 1987, Second ed.) pp. 546-58, 566-75

[19] Ibid. pp. 546-7, 575

of British West African participation in the conflict and did not provide an in-depth examination of the responses of the British West African elite to the conflict.

Geoffrey Hodges has provided the most authoritative account of the carrier in East Africa, although recent investigations of his papers at the Bodleian Library indicate that his published account is rather limited and biased to one view.[21] The South African Native Labour Corps has received a bit more attention in works by Albert Grundlingh and Norman Clothier,[22] while Malcolm Page in *The Chiwaya War* has captured the impact of the war in Malawi (then Nyasaland).[23] Of the East, Central and Southern texts, those by Page and Hodges rely on interviews with local populace. The others are archival based, and as with the West African accounts, little comparison, if any, takes place between regions, or even within national boundaries.

In addition to scholarly works focusing on the military aspects of the First World War, political histories examining British African politics prior to and during the First World War provide some insight into the responses of the educated African elite.[24] Seminal works on British West Africa such as Christopher Fyfe's *A History of Sierra Leone* and David Kimble's *A Political History of Ghana: The Rise of Gold Coast Nationalism, 1850-1928*, briefly examine the tension in Anglo-African relations before the First World War and during the conflict. However, both Fyfe and Kimble's studies largely focus on Anglo- African relations in the nineteenth century and neither work provides a detailed assessment of the responses of the British West African elite to the conflict. Furthermore, both

[20] Crowder & Osuntokun, 'The First World War and West Africa, pp. 546-58, 566-75

[21] Pinfold, John, 'Geoffrey Hodges' collection', *There came a darkness* SCOLMA Conference, 2015

[22] Grundlingh, Albert, *Fighting their own war: South African blacks and the First World War* (Ravan, 1987), Grundlingh, Albert: *War and Society. Participation and Remembrance. South African Black and Coloured Troops in the First World War 1914-1918*, Stellenbosch (Sun Media, 2014), Clothier, Norman, *Black valour : the South African Native Labour Contingent, 1916-1918, and the sinking of the Mendi* (University of Natal, 1987)

[23] Page, Melvin, *The Chiwaya war: Malawians and the First World War* (Westview, 2000)

[24] Fyfe, Christopher, *A History of Sierra Leone* (Oxford UP, 1962) pp. 611, 613-20 Kimble, David, *A Political History of Ghana: The Rise of Gold Coast Nationalism 1850-1928* (Clarendon, 1971) pp. 93-105, 301-13

Fyfe and Kimble's studies focus mainly on the British West African elite, and therefore largely neglect to examine the contributions of West African servicemen to the First World War.25

Anne Samson's *Britain, South Africa and the East Africa campaign* focuses on the relations between Britain and white South Africa over going to war, Edmund J Yorke's study on *Britain, Northern Rhodesia and World War 1* has tended to look at the economics of involvement, as has Jan-Bart Gewald's *Forged in the Great War: people, transport and labour, the establishment of colonial rule in Zambia, 1890-1920*.26 Uganda and Southern Rhodesia have been omitted from detailed studies of their involvement in the wars—politically or otherwise, as have the South African Protectorates of Bechuanaland, Swaziland and Basutoland.

Leo Spitzer's *The Creoles of Sierra Leone: Responses to Colonialism, 1870-1945* and Akintola Wyse's *HC Bankole-Bright and Politics in Colonial Sierra Leone, 1919-1958* briefly examine the response of the Sierra Leone press to the First World War.27 Spitzer examines the responses of the Sierra Leone press to the conflict and the disappointment of the Sierra Leone Creoles to the continuation of British colonial policies following the conclusion of the war.28 Wyse briefly highlights the contributions of Sierra Leoneans to the military campaigns in Africa and the economic and political consequences for Sierra Leoneans following the conflict.29 However, as political studies largely focusing on the perspectives of the elite, neither Spitzer nor Wyse's studies provide a comprehensive overview of the role and responses of West Africans in the First World War. Spitzer

---

25 Fyfe, Christopher, *A History of Sierra Leone* (Oxford UP, 1962), Kimble, David, *A Political History of Ghana: The Rise of Gold Coast Nationalism 1850-1928* (Clarendon, 1971) pp. 313

26 Yorke, Edmund J, *Britain, Northern Rhodesia and the First World War: Forgotten colonial crisis* (Palgrave, 2015), Gewald, Jan-Bart, *Forged in the Great War: People, transport and labour, the establishment of colonial rule in Zambia, 1890-1920* (ASC Leiden, 2015)

27 Wyse, Akintola, *HC Bankole-Bright and Politics in Colonial Sierra Leone, 1919-1958*, (Cambridge UP, 2003) pp. 32-33

28 Spitzer, Leo, *Creoles of Sierra Leone: Responses to Colonialism, 1870-1945* (University of Wisconsin Press, 1974) pp. 154-156

29 Wyse, *Bankole-Bright and Politics in Colonial Sierra Leone*, pp. 32-33

and Wyse examine the Creole responses to the First World War as a backdrop to Anglo-Creole relations in the twentieth century and the formation of the National Congress of British West Africa.[30] Thus, Spitzer and Wyse's studies do not provide an in-depth analysis of the concerns and reactions of the Sierra Leone Creole elite to the First World War, and neither of these works provide substantial information on the service of West Africans in the War.

The role of the press has been addressed in Albert Grundlinghs' *Fighting their own war*, a major source of reaction to the conflict. Bill Nasson has provided an insight to the war as portrayed in the South Africa press in his *The People's War*, a book which has some inaccuracies due to the nature of reporting. Anne Samson looked at the role of the press in recruiting white soldiers and propaganda in South Africa.[31]

Whilst finalising this publication, new studies have come to light which remain to be published. Kyle Harmse has completed an MA looking at the recruitment and experiences of Cape Coloured Battalions especially with regard to the politics and medical implications. He builds on the historical accounts by Ivor Dennis Difford and AJB Desmore.[32] Neil Parsons has explored the role of film and cinema in South Africa; no easy task given that most film was destroyed in the inter-war years as a source of metals.[33]

In West Africa, the Universities of Ghana and Senegal have held conferences covering a range of topics. However, these have not made it into the main-stream academic spotlight for political and institutional reasons. Mainstream publishers do not appear to rate African works unless the authors are linked to western universities, while African institutions are reluctant to publish through other sources for financial and status reasons. The result is that much valuable material remains

[30] Spitzer, *Creoles of Sierra Leone*, pp. 154-161, Wyse, *Bankole-Bright and Politics in Colonial Sierra Leone*, pp. 32-33

[31] Grundlingh, *Fighting their own war*, Nasson, Bill, *World War I and the People of South Africa* (Tafelberg, 2014)

[32] Harmse, Kyle, *The Cape Corps: South Africa's Coloured Soldiers in the First World War* (MA, University of Johannesburg, 2017), Difford, ID, *The story of the 1st Cape Corps 1915-1919* (Hortors, 1920), Desmore, AJB, *With the 2nd Cape Corps thro' Central Africa* (Citadel, 1920)

[33] Parsons, Neil, *Black and white bioscope: Making movies in Africa 1899-1925* (Intellect, 2018)

inaccessible to the majority of researchers. Similarly, the cost of accessing archives and purchasing books remains high, thereby preventing most Africa-based historians and students from obtaining material elsewhere resulting in narrow-focused and often inaccurate accounts of the war in other territories.

Part 1 Military Aspects

Introduction: The campaigns in Africa

The Great War in Africa started on 5 August 1914 when Britain went to war. The first shot was fired on Dar es Salaam on 8 August, German East Africa by the British and on 12 August the first gunshot was believed fired by Lance Corporal Alhaji Grunshi of the Gold Coast in Togoland, West Africa. This was as the first British Expeditionary Forces arrived in Europe on 12 August. Eventually, the war in Africa ended on 25 November 1918 when the German force surrendered at Abercorn, Northern Rhodesia.

There were five main theatres of war on the African continent: in North Africa, Egypt although a military and naval base for the British/Allied powers saw its own action particularly against the Senussi who used the opportunity to assert their claim for independence; in West Africa, German Kamerun and Togoland faced forces from British and French West Africa and Belgian Congo; in southern Africa, German South West Africa was invaded by Union of South African troops supplemented by a Rhodesian Regiment. The conflict in German East Africa, the longest running of all the African campaigns, included over twenty countries and 177 micro-nations.[1] Harry Fecitt provides an overview of the conflict in the lesser-known theatres than the others which feature rather more prominently in this publication.

---

[1] List of countries involved: Angola, Basutoland, Bechuanaland, Belgian Congo, Belgium, Britain, British East Africa, Denmark, Germany, German East Africa, Gold Coast, India, Kenya, Madagascar, Nigeria, Northern Rhodesia, Nyasaland, Portuguese East Africa, Sierra Leone, Southern Rhodesia, Swaziland, The Gambia, Uganda, Union of South Africa, West Indies. The term micro-nation is used by Maathi, Wangari, *The Challenge for Africa* (Anchor, 2010) to describe the various ethnic groupings in Africa including traditional tribes and settled populations which had their own identifying characteristics such as the white Boers in South Africa.

East Africa

How Britain fell into war in East Africa

Anne Samson[1]

The campaign in East Africa was the longest of the war. It started with the bombing of Dar es Salaam (Tanzania) on 8 August 1914 and ended on 25 November 1918 in Abercorn, Zambia. It cost £72million or four times the British War Office budget for 1914 (although what is not clear from this figure is whether it includes the costs of the other Empire countries involved or just the British contribution). Twenty-eight countries were involved in the war although only twenty-three were directly affected by sending troops, supplies or fighting. Most of the fighting forces were volunteers or standing armies whilst the services of carriers and porters varied depending on when they were recruited: volunteers in the early days, coercion in the last. Over a hundred thousand people, including 45,000 black soldiers and carriers, are judged to have lost their lives during the campaign, mostly from disease and malnutrition.[2]

When Britain presented its ultimatum to Germany on 3 August 1914, the British Empire was put on alert resulting in the action on 8 August. This was in accordance with the War Book regarding the destruction of enemy wireless stations when war was declared. The fact that the British Cabinet was still deciding whether or not to declare war in Africa did not feature. Reactions across the theatre were varied, each colony or dependency reacting in an independent and localised manner. South Africa, on deciding to invade South West Africa

---

[1] Dr Anne Samson is Coordinator of the Great War in Africa Association and independent historian of the First World War in Africa. She has published two books on the war in East, Central and Southern Africa and numerous articles. A complete list can be found at www.thesamsonsedhistorian.wordpress.com

[2] Edward Paice, Tip and run: the untold tragedy of the Great War in East Africa (Weidenfeld & Nicholson, 2007) p. 3; TNA: WO 141/30 Pike Report available on www.gweaa.com/medical.

(Namibia), faced a rebellion or civil war which lasted until December 1914. Only then could it focus on the task it had undertaken on behalf of the Empire. British East Africa (Kenya) discovered the colony was at war when a discussion on duck shooting on Lake Naivasha was interrupted to read the recently received telegram.[3]

As the dust around the declaration of war settled, Britain's almost haphazard approach to developing the Empire became apparent. When the decision to launch the November 1914 attack on Tanga was eventually made, four governors were involved (Uganda, British East Africa, Nyasaland, South Africa), one High Commissioner (Southern Africa), four departments in Whitehall (War Office, Colonial Office, India Office and Admiralty) as well as the Viceroy of India. This situation was only marginally improved on 22 November 1914 after the British defeat at Tanga when the India Office was removed from the equation although it remained, until 1916, responsible for supplies. Another change in 1916 was the greater co-ordination of the campaign in the south following the appointment of Edward Northey as commander-in-chief of the Rhodesian Field Force on 12 November 1915. This had been instigated by Lord Buxton in his capacity as High Commissioner and Governor General of South Africa. Buxton greatly felt the need for streamlined communication in the theatres where South Africans could be found. To replace Rhodesians (1st Rhodesian Regiment) who were supporting South Africa in South West Africa, South Africa had sent 200 men to Nyasaland to help defend that border and in 1915 the 2nd Rhodesian Regiment was sent to British East Africa. Buxton, who had only assumed his post on 8 September 1914, was, therefore, responsible for men in eight territories which, in turn, had very little experience in dealing with major wars. South Africa's Defence Force only came into being in 1912 and was still undergoing formation on the outbreak of war.

Greater unity and cohesion of command was achieved in the theatre when Jan Smuts, East Africa commander-in-chief from 1916, and Northey agreed to work in close co-operation, liaising about their movements. On 3 January 1917, the campaign formally came under a single commander. This was to remain

[3] IWM: PP/MCR/150, Norman King diary, 12 Aug 1914; K Forster, 'The quest for East African neutrality in 1915' in *Africa Studies Review* 22:1 (1979) p. 76

the situation until the end of the war. This unification of command had been at the request of Smuts, despite the two commanders working closely together.

One question which has always vexed me about the campaign, is did the war in East Africa need to be fought? My general conclusion is not. This is supported by the fact that Lord Kitchener argued against it. This may appear a rather superficial response, but of the decision makers in London, he was the one who knew something of what he was talking about. Kitchener owned, together with four other men, a large coffee farm—Muhoroni on the Uganda Railway line. He bought this in 1911 when Percy Girouard, a friend, was Governor of British East Africa. Although a mostly absent landlord, he had visited the country in 1908 before his purchase and again in 1911 having spent two weeks trekking around Victoria Nyanza. He planned to retire to Muhoroni during the British winters; the first of which he spent in Britain as Secretary of State for War. The farm, which was within the German raiding distance (63 miles), was clearly important to Kitchener. During the war there is correspondence about coffee beans and improvements to the farm and the day before he drowned he signed a document turning the farm into a limited company. Prior to his land purchase, Kitchener had been involved in the boundary commission which eventually saw Mount Kilimanjaro given to the Germans. In making his recommendations, he had visited the area and as far as can be ascertained, this is one boundary which was not determined by men in London looking at a map (although he was overridden by the negotiating team in London on the Sultan of Zanzibar's territorial claim and probably a few other aspects too).

Kitchener had experience of wars in Africa, including the most recent one in South Africa and was aware of the logistical issues any campaign would entail. He was right. Whether Kitchener was motivated to keep East Africa out of the war for personal or logistical reasons, is immaterial—he felt the loss of life a campaign would entail was not worth the gains which would be determined in Europe by the victors of the European conflict. The decision to go to war must be laid at the feet of the Colonial Office (Lord Harcourt) and the War Office staff. However, actions running their course and the confusion of war were also to blame. By the time the British Cabinet got to focus on events in East Africa, too many violations had taken place for peace to be maintained. The escalation of the campaign in 1916 with the arrival of the South Africans in the theatre is clearly to be laid at the door of Prime Minister Herbert Asquith, who was in charge of the War Office in December 1915 when the decision was made, and the War Office staff. The political conspiracy against Kitchener was ultimately responsible for the destruction of many lives. In this, the British politicians were aided by the South African government of Jan Smuts and Louis Botha (purposefully in that order[4]) which was looking for an outlet for the government-supporting-Boer who would not fight in Europe. South Africa's involvement in East Africa would support the country's case for obtaining Delagoa Bay in Portuguese East Africa, a piece of land the Boers had been after since the 1880s.

Was it worth it? From my assessment of the discussions at Versailles, the only two countries which got most of what they wanted were Portugal and Britain. Portugal got Kionga and Britain was awarded German East Africa minus Ruanda and Urundi. Belgium got more than it bargained for in Ruanda and Urundi but failed to get Kabinda on the west coast which it desired and India was denied an outlet for immigration. South Africa was denied Delagoa Bay which would round off the country to the Zambezi River. Portugal, Belgian Congo and the two Rhodesias were saved from South African expansionist ideas. The one individual to gain was Smuts who ensured his name and legacy would continue through the mandate system and League of Nations; but he lost the election in 1924, giving the Nationalists an opportunity to set in motion their plans for later years.

South West Africa

Before the South Africans became involved in East Africa, they launched a campaign into South West Africa (Namibia) to put the wireless stations at Windhoek and Luderitzbucht out of action. This was partly in response to a request from Britain but also to fulfil nationalist desires to bring the German territory into the Union. The problem South Africa had, was that it could

---

[4] Louis Botha was Prime Minister of South Africa and Smuts his deputy as well as Minister for Defence amongst other roles.

not send troops outside the Union borders without the permission of parliament and that was only to meet on 8 September 1914 when the new Governor General Sydney Buxton arrived.

In the meantime, South Africa undertook its own defence, allowing the Imperial Garrison troops except one battalion to return to Britain. Recruitment was begun with Charles Crewe as director of recruiting and tentative plans laid for the eventual invasion, including notification of German troops having been found on the South African side of the border near Nakob in late August 1914. Following the decision by the Union parliament to send troops into German South West Africa, the Union Defence Force leaders General CF Beyers and Manie Maritz resigned their positions and went into rebellion, the latter taking his men loyal to the Union prisoner and openly siding with the Germans.

Initial incursions had been made into the German territory when the rebellion started, the battle of Sandfontein seeing the South Africans under General Lukin severely defeated. Despite this setback, the South West African campaign was put on hold whilst the rebels were dealt with. By January 1915, the Prime Minister Louis Botha was firmly in control and as head of the Union Defence Force launched the campaign against South West Africa using the railways as far as possible, but also pushing across desert wastes unexpectedly. On 9 July 1915, the Germans surrendered.

In the north of the territory, the Germans had attacked the Portuguese town of Naulila whilst the South Africans were dealing with the rebellion. The outcome of this action was to cause a leadership vacuum in the area which took years to restabilise. However, the town of Shuckmannsburg in the Caprivi Strip surrendered to a Rhodesian force after two hours' discussion on 22 August 1914. The Germans were sent to internment camps in the Union while the Rhodesians moved north to protect their borders against invasion from German East Africa.

Military overview of the campaign in East Africa

Harry Fecitt

This chapter attempts to explain what it was like for the soldiers on the ground. How they fought, how they got their casualties back and how they were supported.

The way to approach this is to look at the shape of German controlled territory in 1914 and see how that changed year by year. It is a visual way of seeing what was happening in the theatre. However, it does not tell you who was winning and who was losing.

1914—German decisiveness versus British lack of preparedness.

The Royal Navy did its own thing and started the war from the sea. The difference between what the Germans did and that which the British and Belgians did was that whilst everyone was unprepared, the Germans were more decisive in making the first moves. So, whilst the British were mobilising and trying to work out what units to have and whether they should be all white or all black, the Germans got cracking and attacked across all the borders, Uganda, Congo,[1] Nyasaland,[2] British East Africa and the neutral border of Portuguese East Africa (for reasons probably associated with the quarrels that white men were having in that part of the world over issues like white ivory). An interesting aspect was the speed with which the Belgians came and supported Northern Rhodesia, but the overall Belgian effort has never been given sufficient credit.[3] As

---
[1] See late papers by Kris Qnatin and Jan van der Fraenen.
[2] See later papers by Peter Charlton and Tim Wright.

Edward Paice said in his book, whatever the Belgians were asked to do, whether it was fighting or coming in from the coast, they did it and they did it well.[4]

In British East Africa, the Germans seized a little town called Taveta (just south of Mount Kilimanjaro), but they failed on the coast at a place called Gazi (near the German border) and they failed at Kissi (near Lake Victoria, southwest of Kisumu). So the Germans attacked but did not make much headway. And when you look at the tactics, I don't think von Lettow-Vorbeck, the German commander, had his A-team running these attacks. But of course, a lot in this theatre of the war was dependent on luck. Were you in the right place at the right time? Because you never, or rarely, knew where the enemy was. If you just happened to be in the right place where you could hit him, as at Karonga (at the head of Lake Nyasa), then you could win. So you needed luck.

In Uganda, on the Kagera River front, a region that does not get talked about often, the British advanced and took some German territory, resulting in a loss to the Germans. One of the first main events was the landing in British East Africa of Indian Expeditionary Force C—the first Indian Army response to reinforce British East Africa, which was one of the Indian war roles.[5] The Germans scored a victory in Zanzibar harbour by sinking HMS *Pegasus*,[6] but then Indian Expeditionary Force B arrived and tried to take Tanga (a difficult battle to get your head around). I believe in short that the Germans won at Tanga for four reasons:

1. More machine-guns and better machine-gunners—they were all Germans.

2. Britain failed to use its artillery and naval gun-fire effectively.

---

[3] See paper by Jan van der Fraenen in this edition. Belgian involvement is starting to be recognised, although very little is yet available in English: Jeannick Vangansbeke, *Monnaie d'echange? Belgisch-Congo en Centraal-Afrika in de international politiek, 1909-1919* (Nieuwpoort, 2012), Georges Delpierre, 'Tabora 1916: de la symbolique d'une victoire' in *BTNG/RBHC*, XXXII (2002) pp. 351-381 and J de Waele, 'Voor Vorst en Vaderland: Zwarte soldaten en dragers tijdens de Eerste Wereldoorlog in Congo' in *Militaria Belgica* (2007-8)

[4] Edward Paice, *Tip and Run* (2007) chapter 7

[5] See paper by Andrew Kerr in this edition.

[6] See paper by Kevin Patience in this edition.

3. Britain failed to use reconnaissance properly because if Britain had reconnoitred professionally they would have realised they could have stayed in Tanga.

4. And the last one was British command failure.

After Tanga Indian Expeditionary Force B sailed away voluntarily and reinforced troops in British East Africa. So the Germans remained pretty much intact apart from a little scrap on the Kagera front.

1915—Consolidation and skirmishes

The most important battle in 1915 started in January at a little place called Jasin (on the Indian Ocean coast at the border point between German and British East Africa territory) where, if you read von Lettow's book *Reminiscences*,[7] although the Germans won, they lost a lot of white men and this was mainly due to the Indian Mountain Artillery targeting machine-gun posts and knocking out a few. The result was two-fold: the whites following the euphoria of Tanga became more unsettled about taking casualties after Jasin. Von Lettow lost a number of his good officers whom he had no means of replacing, so at that point he changed his strategy to go onto the defensive and suck in as much of the allied war effort as he could. In British East Africa, the railway from Voi to Taveta was started and that determined British strategy from then on. The Allies were going to advance down the railway which eventually took them to German East Africa near Moshi.

The first German blockade runner arrived in 1915. This was a welcome boost for German morale. Interestingly, if you read *Wind of Morning* by Hugh Boustead,[8] he was a petty officer on the British ship that had been given intelligence to intercept that blockade runner, he says about ten minutes before the blockade runner was due to arrive the navigator realised the British naval vessel was many miles away from where it should be. By the time they got to Mwanza bay north of Tanga, the blockade runner was in, had devised a deception plan and was able to deliver its cargo.[9] Further south (on the Northern

---

[7] Paul von Lettow-Vorbeck, *My reminiscences of East Africa: The campaign for German East Africa in World War 1* (Nashville, nd)

[8] Hugh Boustead, *Wind of morning: An autobiography* (California, 2002)

[9] See paper by Bjarne Bendtsen in this edition

Rhodesia and Nyasaland border with German East Africa), General Northey arrived to run this front. He came from the Western Front and introduced, for the first time, some British professionalism to what had really been a colonial and Indian situation. At the end of 1915, British naval activity began on Lake Tanganyika.

1916—Encircling attempts versus German rearguard actions

Early in 1916 the British Navy obtained control of Lake Tanganyika. When the Navy got its act together as it did on Lake Tanganyika or going after and defeating the *Königsberg* (in the Rufiji River delta), it was good. It concentrated its resources and did its job well. In blockading the German East Africa coast, the Navy was not successful—but it was an immense task given the number of ships available to attempt the blockade. It also required good intelligence of blockade runners arriving.

There was a battle in early 1916 in British East Africa at a place called Salaita, near Taveta. It was the South Africans' first attempt at bush warfare and was a chastening disaster for them. They had to face the reality that they could not stand up against attacking German East African Askari, even though the Askari were black and had been rather ridiculed up to that point. Then, in early 1916 just after the battle at Salaita, General Smuts arrived and took over the plans that were already in existence and the whole shape of German East Africa began to change. In 1915 it had stayed intact and this allowed the Germans to do a lot of things and to mobilise all the resources they wanted within the country. They had a very good research station at Umani (on the border inland from Tanga) where they produced quinine and similar products. If you read von Lettow's book,[10] they were very focused on health sufficiency and achieved it very well. The British spent eighteen months without really making a dent into German East Africa territory; the shape stayed the same. But then, not concurrently because of different climatic conditions, but more or less in the spring of 1916, things began to change quite rapidly on all fronts.

---

[10] Paul von Lettow-Vorbeck, *My reminiscences*

The British came in with a major attack from British East Africa. There was a major battle at Kahe, just south of Moshi, which was probably the most important battle of 1916. The South Africans failed to encircle and that was the Allies' last chance that year of wiping out the *schutztruppe*, von Lettow-Vorbeck's army.

The Portuguese, Britain's Allies did their bit. They seized the Kionga Triangle (the most southern part of the German coastline) and a bit later in the year they moved further north to Newala but lost the fighting. This gave the Germans as many munitions as a third blockade runner would have done. That was unfortunate for the Portuguese, as not all of them ran away—some of them died fighting.

The British seized Kondoa-Irangi, a place southwest of Mount Kilimanjaro. The Belgians came in from the Ruanda area and also from across the lake. So, the whole shape was changing. In the south, Northey's force was making incursions. Its initial four-pronged attack did not work out as well as had been wanted because the Germans in the south knew how to evade encircling movements. However, Northey's force was in German East Africa and stayed for the duration of the war; expanding its activities in two regions.[11]

The British having expected the Germans to move westwards, now had to follow them south-eastwards down the Usambara Railway from Moshi to Tanga. From here the Germans were in the driving seat as the British could not dictate where the battlefield would be. The Germans withdrew onto ground of their own choice that they had prepared with defensive works. They could do this because they had a large percentage if no all the manpower of German East Africa still under their control; so digging trenches and other labour was not a problem for the Germans. They simply told the village chiefs: 'we need 600 men tomorrow morning at dawn' and they got them.

The Belgians moved towards Tabora (on the Central Railway west of Kigoma on Lake Tanganyika), the South African mounted troops moved south from Kondoa-Irangi, while the British started moving down the coast taking the coastal towns as they went. By the end of 1916, the British were on the Mgeta

---

[11] See paper by Tim Wright in this edition.

River just north of the Rufiji but they had not really beaten anybody, they had just moved. The British had extended their own supply lines which were dependent on manual labour, making a massive administrative task for them that General Smuts always refused to comment on or discuss or debate. He was not interested in logistics: He was going to defeat the Germans within six months using encircling tactics. He failed. The Germans were in a better position at the end of 1916 as they were withdrawing onto prepared lines of communication, with supply dumps. They had district commissioners and others actively getting crops laid and lifted and brought to feed the *schutztruppe*. So, the Germans were working on interior lines of communication and strengthening their position really, whereas the British were extending themselves and running into all kinds of difficulties with men sometimes down on quarter rations, and this resulted in massive debilitation due to disease.

1917—Allied pushes whilst Germans withdraw and dictate the pace of events

General Smuts moved onto greener pastures (in London) and very misleadingly made it look like the theatre was under British control. The South Africans thinned out dramatically, most of them went back, but one or two units stayed. The Rufiji River, the main water obstacle, was crossed. The British introduced two new regiments: The Nigeria Regiment and Gold Coast Regiment. They came fresh from campaigning in Cameroon in West Africa where they had won, and were a very useful counterbalance to the loss of the white South African troops. Now I do not want to knock the South Africans too much but it would be very nice if some academic could look at the number of South African troops, the amount of support they needed and what they achieved, because they lost men mainly through indiscipline as this was an amateur army. They lost men to disease at a vast rate.[12]

The West Africans, including a Gambian company and very good porters from Sierra Leone, moved in as did more professional Indian units which were sent from the Western

---

[12] David Katz is researching aspects of South African involvement in East Africa during World War 1.

Front and Egypt. An interesting fight occurred north of Kilwa at Kibata (which I visited in 2011 and experienced the black cotton soil which they write about. I went in through the clinging mud with my sandals on, not boots, and thought of the men with their packs and rifles on reduced food. They did not have the rotation system as happened on the Western Front—where the British soldiers had seven nights in the trenches and then a week out. That just did not happen here.)

Kibata was the first time real trench warfare occurred in the theatre when the Germans tried to shell the British out of the base. There had been a massive stone fort there but in the end the Germans moved away and carried on moving south. They had the enormous ability to bypass the British and keep moving south because they knew the terrain; they could mobilise porters from any area they controlled and headmen who showed a bit of reluctance to support the German point of view were swinging on a rope very rapidly; the next headman changed his opinions very quickly to support the Germans. Whilst we can criticise the Germans for that kind of brutality in a 2012 context that was the way it was, and it happened then, and we must not kid ourselves that the British did not put the boot in hard at places like Kissi, where the locals ran riot after the battle. Both sides were brutal when it was needed to create an effective situation.

On the command front, a General Reginald Hoskins had replaced General Smuts. Hoskins had been the Inspector General of the King's African Rifles before the war, so he knew what he was talking about. He immediately told the War Office the truth—that he needed a massive amount of support to complete the campaign. The War Office did not want to hear, and it is believed that General Smuts agreed—he was now a big number in London—and put in his old friend, General Jaap (Jacob) van Deventer. So, a South African General came back in for political reasons. I can understand that because without the massive support coming from South Africa in many ways, not least a big medical recuperation facility for the British troops, the British effort would have withered on the vine.

One very interesting operation that happened in 1917 was the Wintgens-Naumann raid[13] and it showed what the Germans

---

[13] See Tim Wright's paper in this edition.

could achieve. Starting from near Songea east of Lake Nyasa, Max Wintgens, who had been running the Ruandan front and who did not particularly get on with von Lettow-Vorbeck because he liked doing his own thing, took off with a few companies and one or two artillery pieces and went back up north. Wintgens got very badly ill before they got to the Central Railway. He was left behind and taken prisoner. His number two, Heinrich Naumann carried on and these raiders under Naumann, a hard man, got up to the Lake Victoria area, where they raided Kahe station right next to British East Africa, shot a few trains up, killing some passengers, and took some British officers prisoner. Naumann and his men, now joined by former German Askari living locally, rampaged around until about six months later when the Cape Corps from South Africa, tough Cape Coloured lads, captured him.

Naumann's achievement was an example of what you can do in Africa if you have the ability and determination, and you are ruthless: you will steal a village's food and you do not care if the villagers die because your men are fed.

Hector Duff, who was in the government in Nyasaland after the war,[14] acknowledged that both sides lost thousands and thousands of porters, but this was war, total war.[15] You were fighting to win and if you did not win then you lost, and in that context the black carrier and black village became expendable. It is not nice to talk about in the sentiments of 2012 but that was the way it was. When we make judgements we must always try and put ourselves back there—you were the guy on the ground; you want your company fed; what are you going to do? Well, we all know what we would do.

By the end of 1917, the Germans were at Lukuledi River, southwest of Lindi, and still controlling the proceedings. The British were on the coast but the Germans were effectively blocking them. There were some Germans under Theodor Tafel on the Mahenge Plateau, northwest of Lindi moving down from the western end of the Central Railway, but von Lettow-Vorbeck with his main force was at the Lukuledi River where the biggest battle of the war took place at Mahiwa. It was a four-day battle and both sides exhausted themselves but the

---

[14] During the war he was Northey's political officer.
[15] Hector L Duff, *African small chop* (London: Hodder & Stoughton,1932)

Germans recovered more quickly. The Germans then moved up the Lukuledi River, turned and went onto the Makonde Plateau where von Lettow-Vorbeck had a big sort out. He got rid of everyone who was both medically unfit and did not have the determination to carry on. This meant that a very streamlined *schutztruppe* proceeded to Portuguese East Africa. Tafel moved to join Lettow-Vorbeck. He got across the river, but he had problems along the way, poor discipline and low morale, so went back to German East Africa and surrendered. Von Lettow-Vorbeck was in Portuguese East Africa.

1918—a merry chase around the northern parts of Portuguese East Africa

The Germans split into three columns to live off the land. As one of them commented in his diary,[16] they never had it so good. They actually paid the natives for the food they took from them with cloth they had taken from the Portuguese posts they had captured. For once in the war, indigenous inhabitants preferred German rule, but that was a result of the Portuguese way of operating in their colonies.

The British came in from the coast and Nyasaland in columns. At this point, there was only black infantry in the field. The white infantry had withdrawn. There still were a number of white troops in units like the service corps driving supplies south, and you will see if you walk around the cemeteries in that area the large number of white men who died in the area in 1918, but that was from disease. And now, some South African specialists came into their own. The British adopted the German tactics of 1914 and put a lot more white men into their black battalions, particularly on jobs such as Vickers and Lewis machine-gun operating. A lot of South Africans volunteered for this and they were good chaps. They were not upset by working with black troops.

The British followed von Lettow-Vorbeck on a convoluted route around northern Mozambique, where there were several battles. Some were close but the British never knocked the Germans out. Extraction of their forces, even if they had not won a battle, was always possible for the Germans so long as they stayed away from the urban areas. The British never

---

[16] P von Lettow-Vorbeck, *My reminiscences* (nd) p. 234

delivered the knockout punch. Von Lettow-Vorbeck went back to German East Africa, almost to the southern end of Lake Tanganyika, and down into Northern Rhodesia where he completely fooled the British who had nobody there to stop him. Where was von Lettow-Vorbeck heading? My guess is Portuguese West Africa, Angola, where he could have lived very well by capturing Portuguese camps. But the armistice came, the war ended and a lot of good men who had survived it died from Asian flu which was very terrible. Interestingly, von Lettow-Vorbeck said that when he surrendered he expected his Askari to dissent but they did not. The dissent came from the whites and I can understand this. They had lost so much, why give up? You have got Africa in front of you, who is going to stop you? The British would have had to sail round the coast. But German discipline prevailed and they surrendered on 25 November 1918 at Abercorn (Mbala) in Northern Rhodesia.

'Bridging the gap': Exploring the role of the Staff during the 1916 campaign in Tanganyika

David Boyd[1]

Background and Abstract

One of the significant outcomes of the 1916 campaign in Tanganyika was its effect on the career of General Jan Smuts, who drove the Germans out of most of Tanganyika but did not decisively defeat them; the campaign continuing until the Armistice in 1918.

There has been significant research and analysis of Smuts' general-ship and recognition of his strategy of manoeuvre, focus on the front line and disregard for logistical considerations. There has been less focus however on the role and performance of his staff — the group of men on whom he relied to sustain his strategy and to support his front-line units.

This paper therefore explores this diverse group of characters and offers some insights into the way in which they 'bridged the gap' in their Commander-in-Chief's (CiC) experience as a general. The paper examines their experience and expertise, their relationships with Smuts and with each other, and assesses how effectively they delivered for him in the 1916 campaign.

---

[1] David Boyd is an independent researcher whose initial interest in the East African campaign was due to a family connection with Brigadier John Anderson Dealy, who served on Smuts' staff as officer Commanding Royal Engineers (CRE) in East Africa from January 1916 until invalided back to India in February 1917. David currently works as a specialist financial consultant for major public companies and lives in Berkshire. He spent his childhood between 1966 and 1979 living in Kenya, Uganda and Swaziland.

It argues that they were a generally competent and effective group and that overall they performed well for their Commander-in-Chief, successfully mitigating the risks inherent in his aggressive strategy. His subsequent career therefore owed much to his staff's efforts in 1916.

Introduction and context

For many years following the end of the First World War the campaign in East Africa was overlooked by historians. It was seen as an exotic side-show, a subject more for the attentions of novelists and film-makers than for serious research and analysis. This was understandable—on the day that the East African force resumed its advance towards the Central Railway in Tanganyika, the British army in France launched its attack on the Somme. The total British ration strength in East Africa was around 45,000 troops.[2] On the first day of the battle of the Somme the British suffered nearly 60,000 casualties, including 20,000 men killed. So however arduous life felt to the men struggling through the bush in Tanganyika on half rations, they were indeed not participating in events that would shape the outcome of the war.

They were however participating in a campaign that has been discovered again by modern historians, in both Europe and Africa, with a wide range of well-researched work published in recent years, covering many political and military aspects of the Great War in Africa. It is well beyond the scope of this paper to make full use of all this work, but it is worth trying to draw out some high-level thoughts about the relative importance of the campaign in East Africa, and to reflect on one particular outcome, and how this was achieved.

That outcome was the impact of the campaign on the future career of General Jan Smuts, who was the General Officer Commanding from early 1916 to early 1917. Indeed, it can be argued that the main direct beneficiary of the war in East Africa was Jan Smuts. At the start of 1916 Smuts was one of the principal political and military figures in the new Union of South Africa. Highly intelligent and educated (Cambridge double-first) with an early career in law and Boer politics, he had been a successful commando leader during the Second

---

[2] Paice, *Tip and Run* (2007) p. 195

Anglo-Boer War and subsequently a senior cabinet minister in the new South Africa, having been one of the main drafters of the Union's constitution. So, he arrived in East Africa at the start of 1916 already a distinguished and successful soldier and politician. However, he left East Africa in 1917 well on his way to being one of the major world figures of the first half of the twentieth-century. He joined the Imperial War Cabinet, was then a signatory to the Treaty of Versailles, served as Prime Minister of South Africa for 14 years, led South Africa during the Second World War and was a signatory of the Charter establishing the United Nations.[3] A trusted confidant of both David Lloyd George and Winston Churchill, he became a UK Privy Councillor, a Companion of Honour, a member of the Order of Merit and a Field Marshall with medals and decorations from ten countries. He also ended up being a Freeman of 18 cities with honorary degrees from 29 universities.

It is highly unlikely that Smuts' subsequent career would have been quite so glittering had things gone differently in East Africa in 1916. For example, if von Lettow-Vorbeck's attack on van Deventer's force isolated at Kondoa had succeeded in May and the South African positions over-run, Smuts would have faced some very searching questions from both London and Pretoria. Instead he emerged from his year in command having driven the Germans out of most of the Tanganyikan territory, avoided the large-scale battle casualties seen in other theatres, and impressed those around him with his personal leadership qualities. He was seen a thruster and a winner, in contrast to the old-school Generals commanding in other theatres, this impression reinforced by his declaration shortly after leaving East Africa that the campaign there was as good as over, with just some mopping up remaining to be done.

The reality of course was that there were two more years of chasing and hard fighting to be done. Smuts had never succeeded in bringing von Lettow-Vorbeck to a decisive battle and the German's fighting strength in the field at the end of 1916 was not substantially less than it had been at the start of the year. Smuts' army on the other hand, although still much larger than von Lettow-Vorbeck's, was not in such good shape,

---

[3] Smuts was involved in writing both the charters for the League of Nations and the United Nations, and formulating the mandate system which was overseen by the League of Nations.

with units decimated by disease and insect infestation and suffering the effects of long periods in the field on short rations. Smuts' own departure from East Africa was the signal for the start of the withdrawal of most of the South African contingent, to be replaced for the most part by troops recruited locally and from other African colonies. Smuts therefore left behind a lot of unfinished business in Tanganyika, but often it can be observed in any enterprise that a leader's success or failure depends to a large extent on their knowing when and how to move on.

Smuts as a General

The general-ship of Jan Smuts has been analysed extensively and it is beyond the scope of this paper to re-visit all of the arguments about his qualities and shortcomings. A good recent summary of the research and analysis to date can be found in a paper by Shaun Corrigan, who reviewed a wide range of contemporary sources as well as work by recent historians, and concluded with a balanced assessment of Smuts' general-ship.[4] He highlighted three major aspects of Smuts as a General about which there seems to be broad agreement. Firstly, Smuts was undoubtedly an outstanding leader of men, inspiring great respect from those with whom he came into contact, including the contemporaries who were critical of his strategy and tactics. There is little doubt that he was brave and tough, with enormous energy and charisma. Second, his strategy of manoeuvre, avoiding frontal assaults against strongly-held enemy positions, was at least in part influenced by his desire, and the political necessity, to avoid excessive battle casualties among his South African troops. He did not want to return to South Africa with the nickname 'Butcher Smuts'.[5] Third, he was undoubtedly deficient in the management of supply and logistics, a persistent feature of his general-ship being 'the almost total subordination of logistical to strategic demands'.[6] This had a major impact on the effectiveness of his fighting

---

[4] Corrigan, S, The Generalship of Jan Smuts during the First World War. *The British Empire at War Research Group* (2014) (https://britishempireatwardotorg.files.wordpress.com/2012/09/the-generalship-of-jan-smuts-during-the-first-world-war2.pdf)

[5] Meinertzhagen, R, *Army Diary 1899-1926* (1960) p. 166

[6] Corrigan, Generalship of Jan Smuts (2014) p. 24

forces and on at least two occasions almost led to disaster, when supply lines were stretched nearly to breaking point.

One aspect of Smuts' general-ship and of the campaign overall on which there has been less explicit focus in the research and analysis has been the role of the staff, and the dynamics both within this group of officers and between the staff officers and Smuts himself. Given Smuts' lack of staff training and experience, and his refusal to allow logistical considerations to constrain his strategic priorities, the role played by both the General Staff and ancillary services heads around Smuts and administrative staff back at base responsible for supplying the force is an area that merits further research. This paper therefore explores this diverse group of characters and offers some insights into the way in which they 'bridged the gap' in their CiC's experience as a general. The paper examines their experience and expertise, their relationships with Smuts and with each other, and assesses how effectively they delivered for him in the 1916 campaign. Just as much as his front-line officers, it is argued that if these men on the staff had not performed well for Smuts, he would not have accomplished what he did in 1916, with all that would have implied for his future career. Jan Smuts owed a lot to the group of mainly British officers around him in East Africa in 1916.

Research sources

There are three main primary sources about the campaign and the men who led and participated in it. The first are the published memoirs by participants, and three members of the British staff subsequently wrote books about their experiences in East Africa.

The first of these to appear was *General Smuts' Campaign in East Africa* by Brigadier JHV Crowe.[7] Crowe served throughout 1916 as the Commander Royal Artillery (CRA) for the force and as head of one of the main services he was in close proximity to the Commander-in-Chief's staff throughout the campaign. His account was written on the voyage home, Crowe having left East Africa at the same time as Smuts in early 1917, and published in mid-1918 (i.e. before the war was over). Crowe gives a detailed, factual account of the campaign, but also at the

---

[7] JHV Crowe, *General Smuts' Campaign in East Africa* (J Murray, 1918)

start makes some comments about the composition of the staff which had been assembled, and this is the one area of his narrative where an element of criticism can be detected. Otherwise, his is a largely uncritical account and he is a great admirer of Smuts and his achievements during 1916—as one would perhaps guess both from the title of his book and the fact that Smuts contributed a lengthy introduction to it.

The second book to appear was *The East African Force 1915-19* by Brigadier CP Fendall, which was published in 1921.[8] Fendall served as Assistant Adjutant and Quartermaster General, effectively the deputy head of the administrative staff, and his book is an altogether more critical account of the campaign and many of the participants. It is a somewhat frustrating account, however, as it is clear that Fendall is pulling a lot of punches, and not naming names. He served in East Africa until the Armistice, stepping up to the top administrative job in 1917, and was the last of the senior staff of 1916 to leave the theatre.

Crowe and Fendall were both professional senior staff officers who arrived in East Africa in early 1916 as part of the force that had been assembled to finally go on the offensive in East Africa. The third memoir was published by an altogether different character, Richard Meinhertzhagen, who had arrived with Indian Force B in late 1914 as a junior general staff officer (GSO3) and participated in the disastrous landing at Tanga. He had previously served in Kenya with the King's African Rifles from 1902-1906 and with this local knowledge he gravitated towards Intelligence work, which service he set up and ran until late 1916 when he was invalided home. His book *Army Diary 1899-1926* was published in 1960,[9] 45 years after the events it described and with all of the senior participants long dead. His account is highly critical of the majority of his colleagues, in one way or another, and the book is filled with colourful, usually unflattering anecdotes. Meinhertzhagen's reliability has been called into question, however, with a number of stories relating to his own actions now claimed to be fabricated.[10] It is therefore

---

[8] CP Fendall, *The East African Force 1915-1919: an unofficial record of its creating and fighting career; together with some account of the civil and military administrative conditions in East Africa before and during that period* (HF & G Witherby, 1921)
[9] Richard Meinertzhagen, *Army Diary 1899-1926* (Oliver & Boyd, 1960)
[10] B Garfield, *The Meinertzhagen Mystery: the life and legend of a colossal fraud* (Potomac, 2007)

likely that he exaggerated his own role and importance during the events of 1916, and some of his comments at the time could well have been altered later with the benefit of hindsight. In spite of this, it would be a mistake to discard him completely as a source—it is just necessary to be a little cautious about some of his observations, particularly when these reflect well on him.

The second primary source about the campaign and the staff are the official papers. The most interesting and useful are the War Diaries in the *WO 95 East Africa series*. The commanding officer of each unit kept a record of the unit's activities and while many of these documents are sparse or uninformative, some are extensive and provide valuable insights into the workings of the staff organisation and the management, and sometimes mismanagement, of the available resources.

The third primary source consists of unpublished papers, by far the most important and interesting of which is Fendall's private diary, a typed copy of which is lodged in the National Archives in *CAB 45/44*. In contrast to his book, in the diary Fendall pulls no punches and does name names. The diary includes his impressions of around 25 of the officers on the staff, recorded on the ship on the way out from London to East Africa and updated ten months of campaigning later. He admires Smuts as a man and as a fighting soldier, and came to admire van Deventer too when he took command from mid-1917, despite earlier misgivings about him. He is scathing, however, about some other South African commanders and their troops, in particularly the mounted brigades. Several of his colleagues on the staff also come in for strong criticism relating both to their professional competence and to their character.

Smuts' own views about the staff do not seem to be particularly well documented. His telegrams to the War Office, *WO/33 858*, give some insight into his priorities and judgements, as do his official dispatches in the *London Gazette*, with some staff officers specifically thanked and praised for services performed well, while others were just included the general list of 'Mentions'. (All his senior field commanders were specifically thanked and praised.) His Foreword to Crowe's book makes great play of the difficulties encountered and overcome but is not specific about how this was done or by whom—the only person mentioned by name being van Deventer. There are also some relevant anecdotes about the campaign in the biography published by his son in 1952, *Jan Christian Smuts by his Son*,[11] although his account of the campaign mainly repeats verbatim what Smuts had said in the Foreword to Crowe.

The composition of the staff

When the East African force was being assembled in late 1915 the command was initially offered to Smuts who declined it,[12] primarily due to domestic political uncertainty in South Africa. The command was then given to General Horace Smith-Dorrien, a very senior and highly experienced regular soldier, who had served in Africa and India during his career, and had commanded a Corps in France before being sacked following clashes with his CiC. Smith-Dorrien set about assembling a full staff, including officers with experience in East Africa as well as India and other colonial theatres. This large group sailed from England on Christmas Day 1915 and having called at South Africa to consult with the authorities there, including Smuts in his role as Minister of Defence, set up supply chain arrangements, disembarked at Mombasa in late January 1916. They arrived without Smith-Dorrien, however, who had become ill on the voyage and had to remain in South Africa. It quickly became clear that his health meant he would be unable to take up the command and this time Smuts agreed to take on the job, arriving in East Africa on 19 February 1916.

There is some disagreement among historians about the extent to which Smuts retained and utilised the staff assembled by Smith-Dorrien. Smuts' son reports that 'his staff he took over without change from Smith-Dorrien'.[13] Paice says that Smuts 'did not tinker with Smith-Dorrien's headquarters appointees but rather circumvented them by appointing his own parallel staff'.[14] Strachan says that Smuts 'albeit gently, dismantled the body created by Smith-Dorrien', and refers to the Director of Transport as a 'rare survivor from Smith-Dorrien's appointees'.[15] The impact of Smuts' arrival seems to be more

---

[11] Smuts, Jan, *Jan Smuts. By his son JC Smuts* (Cassell, 1952)
[12] Strachan, Hew, *The First World War in Africa* (Rhaniket, 2004) p. 134; Smuts, *JC Smuts* (1952) p. 163
[13] Smuts, JC, *JC Smuts* (1952) p. 164
[14] Paice, E, *Tip and Run* (2007) p. 195
[15] Strachan, H, *The First World War in Africa* (2004) pp. 135-136

complicated than any of these comments suggests and it is necessary to distinguish between the General Staff, the heads of the Services (Engineers, Artillery, Intelligence, Signals, Medical, etc.) and the Administration branches (including supply and transport).

In respect of the General Staff, Smith-Dorrien's Chief-of Staff, Brigadier Simpson Baikie, followed him back to Britain. In his place the War Office proposed that Smuts appoint Brigadier AR Hoskins, a trained staff officer who had previously been Inspector General of the King's African Rifles. Smuts however insisted on appointing his own man, Brigadier JJ Collyer, who had served in a similar capacity in the campaign in South West Africa and Hoskins went instead to command the 1st (East African) Division. Collyer brought with him onto the General staff several other South African officers, and while Smuts retained the junior general staff officers appointed by Smith-Dorrien it does seem likely that he relied more on his South African appointees to communicate with the units in the field, in particular with his South African commanders. However, it was noted at the time that it was not unusual for newly appointed Commanders-in-Chief to bring their own senior staff with them.[16] He made no changes to the heads of ancillary services or in the Administration branches, most of whom served through 1916 and beyond and a number of whom received high praise in his dispatches.

When all the various appointments had been settled after the reorganisation in late March the staff consisted of: the General Staff, led by Collyer and including both the other South African officers who had accompanied Collyer and the several British officers who had been appointed by Smith-Dorrien; the heads of the services—Artillery, Engineers, Signals, Medical, etc.—all of whom had either come out as part of Smith-Dorrien's staff or had already been doing their jobs before 1916 (including Meinhertzhagen); and the Administrative staff, which also included a mix of senior professionals brought out by Smith-Dorrien and locally appointed officers, including men who had never previously been soldiers. This composition remained largely unchanged through 1916.

---

[16] Fendall, CP, *The East African Force* (1921) p. 58

Experience of the staff—was this adequate for the task?
Crowe and Fendall both summarise the composition of the staff and comment on their expertise and prior experience. Crowe comments that 'of the General Staff, not an officer had ever previously filled an appointment on the General Staff with troops. The greater number of supply and transport officers were settlers, who had never had any previous military training'.[17] He extends his comments about lack of training to some of the heads of services (which we can infer included Meinhertzhagen in Intelligence), and while acknowledging that Chief-of-Staff Collyer had served in a similar role in the South West African campaign, notes that the conditions there were very different. There is a clear implication in Crowe's remarks that while there were a number of experienced professionals on the staff, himself included of course, there were also a lot of amateurs involved which, Crowe implies, made Smuts' successes in the field all the more remarkable.

Talking specifically about the General Staff, Fendall was impressed by Smuts' appointments: 'I like the three fellows he has brought with him [Collyer, Van der Byl and Nussey]'[18] and throughout 1916 Fendall's comments about Collyer are generally more favourable than those about many of his other, British, staff colleagues.

Fendall also relates a story that demonstrates that Smuts had not completely side-lined his British General staff officers but, ever the politician, used at least one of these men very shrewdly. This was Captain Henry Guest, known as Freddie, a scion of a British establishment family who after service in the Second Anglo-Boer War and various other colonial adventures became a Liberal Member of Parliament, serving as private secretary to Winston Churchill (who was his cousin) and as a government whip. When war broke out he re-joined the army, serving on the staff in France before joining Smith-Dorrien's staff. In August 1916 Smuts sent Guest to solicit the support of the Governor of British East Africa and the War Office for his proposal to offer terms to the Germans, as had been done in South West Africa.[19] Smuts therefore did not hesitate to use the

---
[17] Crowe, JHV, *General Smuts in East Africa* (1918)
[18] Fendall, CP, Diary 18 Feb.
[19] Ibid 18 Aug.

well-connected British politician on his staff for a mission for which he was well qualified. Guest also seems to have accompanied Meinhertzhagen on a number of the latter's trips into the field and they were together in Kondoa in May.[20]

Fendall had retired in from the Army in 1911 as a full Colonel after 32 years' service, had been awarded the DSO in Burma in 1887 and mentioned in dispatches three times.[21] Probably partly because of this, he comes across in his private diaries as a slightly detached observer—he was back in uniform to get a job done, not to advance a career or collect more medals. On the ship out to East Africa he had made brief assessments of his companions, around 30 officers in all. About the senior officers he had the following impressions.[22]

Brigadier RH Ewart (DA & QMG, i.e. head of the Administrative branch) was 'capable but modest; still feeling his feet, will probably strengthen a lot as he goes on'. Ewart was a 31-year veteran, whose career had included Supply Corps roles in India, where had won a DSO in 1895.[23] Before East Africa he had been serving on the staff in France.

Colonel PO Hazelton (Director of Transport – a specialist from the Royal Army Service Corps) 'knows his work well and will stand no nonsense'.

Brigadier JHV Crowe (Commander Royal Artillery and a Staff College graduate) was 'level-headed and clever; should influence things a good deal later on, but there may be rows first'.

Brigadier JA Dealy (Commander Royal Engineers) was 'all there as a Sapper, without being tied up in red tape'. When war broke out Dealy had been just about to retire as a full Colonel after a 30-year career as an Engineer in India, but stayed in the army to serve as a Director of Works with the Indian Corps in France.[24]

Two other senior members of the staff were already in East Africa and so received no initial assessment from Fendall—although he had plenty to say about both of them later on

---

[20] Meinertzhagen, R, *Army Diary* (1960) p. 181
[21] O'Moore, Creagh, *The VC and DSO book: Distinguished Service Order 1916-1923* (Naval & Military, 2009)
[22] Fendall, CP, Diary, 8 Feb.
[23] *VC and DSO book*
[24] *The Times* Obituary 2 August, 1935

during the campaign. There was Brigadier WFS Edwards, a former soldier who at the start of the war had been Inspector General of Police in East Africa.[25] His main qualification for the role was 'his knowledge of the country and the natives' rather than any expertise in running lines of communication.[26] The other was Colonel Sir WA Johns who was Director of Railways.

These personal profiles and the assessments of both Fendall and Crowe suggest that the senior staff did on the whole have the expertise necessary to manage the force. There were gaps—the General Staff did not have the training or depth of experience that would have been normal in a British force this size, although Collyer was undoubtedly able. There was strength in the service arms but also clearly some perceived weaknesses, with Edwards in particular being seen as 'an amateur' and 'very fussy and inclined to quarrel'.[27] Johns was also criticised—'they say [the railway] gets on twice as fast when Sir W Johns is not there than when he is, as he is fussy'.[28] The senior Administrative team was strong, although there were definite weaknesses lower down in the organisation, with Hazelton commenting that it was impossible to trust transport formations to 'irregular troops staffed by untrained staff officers'.[29] Fendall and Hazelton both lamented the dire state of affairs that had existed in many areas before they arrived, but it seems reasonable to assert that with the new, experienced arrivals, comprising more than 30 officers in all, the staff as established in March 1916 was sufficiently experienced and capable for the task it had to undertake.

Staff relationships—did they work well together and with Smuts?

As well as having the necessary experience and expertise, to be fully effective a staff must work well together as a team and must also work well with their Chief.

On the first question, on whether they worked well together, Strachan[30] judges the staff to have been pretty much

---
[25] Crowe, JHV, *With Smuts in East Africa* (1918) p. 4
[26] Fendall, CP, *The East African Force* 1921
[27] Fendall CP, Diary, 26 June
[28] Ibid. 30 March
[29] Hazelton, PO, *RASC Quarterly* (October 1923)

dysfunctional, with constantly disputed chains of command—between supply, transport and communications, between the front and the rear echelons, and between the operational General Staff and the Administration branches. This assessment however seems excessively harsh. They were not perfect but they did function.

It is certainly the case that Fendall's comments, in particular, suggest that there were frequent clashes and frustrations. In June he complained that 'in one respect this show is being damn badly run. There is no proper coordination between the General Staff and the rest of the show. Too many amateurs at the head of affairs',[31] and later that 'General Staff has not kept Ewart sufficiently informed'.[32] He also had problems with Edwards, and the relationship between the Supply and Transport branches and the Line of Communication was not always as good as it should have been. A degree of personal antipathy developed, with Fendall talking about Edwards' 'smallness and meanness', his touchiness and inclination to quarrel and his inability to prevent professional disagreements affecting personal relation-ships.[33] In his book Fendall seeks to explain and excuse Edward's behaviour as being out of character and caused by the stress of his job,[34] but in his diary he did not hold back on what he thought about Edwards at the time. He was sometimes dismissive about Johns, 'useless' and 'a pompous ass',[35] but is kinder in his book (referring to him only as Johnnie Walker) as Johns had returned from East Africa in 1918 worn out and died only days later.

Some other insights into the workings of the staff come from Dealy, who complains several times in his war diary about orders being issued directly to Engineer officers by the General Staff, or by Smuts himself, which cut across orders Dealy had already given and duplicated resources. A specific complaint concerned the water supply at Lol Kissale, vital for the supply of Kondoa, when orders from separate sources resulted in four

---

[30] Strachan, H, *First World War in Africa* (2004) p. 136
[31] Fendall, CP, Diary, 24 June
[32] Ibid. 15 July
[33] Ibid. various
[34] Fendall, CP, *The East African Force* (1921) p. 218
[35] Fendall, CP, Diary, 6 April

senior RE officers going there to work on the problem, leaving gaps in other areas.[36] Dealy also clashed with Ewart's organisation over his ordering the Supply staff in Nairobi to purchase all the planking they could lay their hands on for bridge-building, as well as a lot of tools for use in the field.[37] The Administrative branch felt that Dealy was exceeding his authority and this was also the case later on when Dealy ordered a large quantity of supplies for the repair of the Handeni tramway. Fendall notes that Dealy 'had a good try to be more of a boss than he was entitled to be'[38] and Ewart complained in writing to the general staff.[39]

There were probably many other similar clashes between senior staff officers and departments that were not documented, and a huge amount of frustration when Smuts' demands on them far exceeded what the administrative staff in particular thought feasible. On the whole, however, it seems reasonable to claim that if the staff had really been dysfunctional, if they had not communicated effectively, then their performance would have fallen below that demanded by Smuts, and action would have been taken. In his book, Fendall relates a number of anecdotes that demonstrate that the personal relationships between senior staff officers on the whole were cordial.[40]

The second question posed earlier was about the relationship between the staff and Smuts. Strachan refers to the staff who 'lacked authority to exercise initiative'[41] and it does certainly seem to be the case that the staff had little effective input into Smuts' decision-making. Smuts was a fighting soldier implementing an aggressive strategy, and there is very little evidence that he consulted widely about either strategy or tactics. There were indeed a number of occasions on which he completely disregarded the views of his senior specialists and gave orders that were diametrically opposed to the advice they gave him.

---

[36] Dealy, WO 95/5301 9 April
[37] Ibid. 17 March
[38] Fendall CP, Diary, 12 Oct
[39] Ewart, CAB 45/16
[40] Fendall, CP, *The East African Force* (1921) Chapter XIV various
[41] Strachan, H, *The First World War in Africa* (2004) p. 135

As Chief of Staff and Smuts' own appointee, Collyer would have been expected to be the principal adviser and the conduit for the views of the rest of the staff to be fed to Smuts. While generally complimentary about his abilities, however, both Fendall[42] and Meinhertzhagen[43] felt that Collyer lacked influence with the Commander-in-Chief. There were two occasions during the first few months of the campaign when Smuts extended his lines of communication far beyond what the administrative staff felt could be supported. The first of these was pushing van Deventer's division to Kondoa, 160 miles south of the advanced supply base at Moshi. The re-supply difficulties were immense and von Lettow-Vorbeck concentrated his forces to mount a major attack on the South Africans dug in at Kondoa, which he commanded himself. This was the closest that Smuts came to suffering a major reverse—the transport difficulties meant that he could not keep van Deventer's force adequately supplied with food and ammunition, never mind push reinforcements rapidly down to Kondoa. The administrative staff were horrified by the risk that Smuts was taking, Hazelton writing later about his ox transport and reserves being 'knocked to smithereens' by the advance to Kondoa, from which his transport system never really caught up. Fendall however disassociates Collyer from the decision to occupy Kondoa: 'don't think Collyer was at GHQ when the move was ordered. He did not seem keen on such a move when he was here. How much influence he has over his Chief I don't know. Anyhow he is the only man who has any'.[44] This remark does suggest that Smuts was neither a seeker nor a taker of advice, even from his closest associates. About the second decision that stretched the supply chain to breaking point, the move to south of Handeni in July, Hazelton reflected that this advance was made for reasons which were not clear to him and had 'heart-breaking results to the supply arrangements'.[45]

Another case where expert staff advice was over-ruled by Smuts was about keeping the roads open during the heavy rain in April. At a meeting with Smuts, Dealy expressed the view

---

[42] Fendall CP, Diary, 26 June
[43] Meinertzhagen, R, *Army Diary* (1960) p. 192
[44] Fendall CP, Diary, 6 April
[45] Hazelton, PO, *RASC* (October 1923)

that there could be no motor traffic along the Moshi-Arusha road for two months and advised the use of porters to carry supplies. Smuts however ordered the 2,500 available porters to be set to work repairing the road, supervised by the East African Mounted Regiment. Dealy commented in his war diary that this would not succeed, even when the Engineers supplied tools and a transport officer was sent to supervise. Two weeks later the porters were withdrawn from the road and put to work carrying supplies, with Dealy unable to suppress a clear 'I told you so' tone in his reports.[46] Later in the campaign, Dealy complained about Engineering resources being allocated and controlled directly by GHQ and Divisional commanders and not through him. There are also fewer mentions in the war diary about meetings with Smuts, and the impression is of him being side-lined and confined to technical management. Dealy was not thanked by name by Smuts in his dispatches—in fact Smuts made great play of the engineering work done by others such as Dealy's predecessor, by Johns, and even by one of his brigade commanders who was an engineer (Sheppard).[47] Dealy got his DSO and was on the general list of Mentions in Dispatches, but it is hard not to conclude that he was snubbed by Smuts, and indeed this was picked up and commented on by the Indian Army personnel branch when Dealy left Tanganyika in early 1917.[48] Smuts's son also relates an unflattering anecdote about his father's (unnamed) Chief Engineer,[49] which reinforces the view that Dealy had fallen foul of Smuts—probably not just by being right when Smuts was wrong, but by making sure that people knew that he had been right.

Some further insight into Smuts's relationship with the staff officers around him is reflected in Fendall's assessment of Crowe's performance, which was that although Crowe had been with Smuts throughout the campaign he 'had no influence on him. Indeed, they tell me that he bores the Chief very much and doesn't realise that the Chief does not want him to give advice'.[50] It is difficult therefore not to conclude that Smuts always knew

---

[46] Dealy, WO 95/5301 various, April
[47] *London Gazette* various
[48] WO 374/18191 7 Feb. 1917
[49] Smuts, JC, *JC Smuts* (1952) p. 174
[50] Fendall, CP, Diary, 12 Oct.

his own mind, did not seek advice from his senior staff officers even on specialist topics, and when advice was proffered that he did not agree with, had no hesitation in ignoring it.

Performance of the staff—did they deliver for Smuts?
The purge of senior British field commanders in early March 1916 demonstrated that Smuts did not tolerate poor performance and it is certain that major staff failures would have resulted in senior officers being replaced. The fact that all of the senior staff were retained throughout the whole period suggests therefore that Smuts was satisfied with their performance. He did not run the campaign in a way that the trained professional staff officers would have preferred, he did not generally seek or accept their advice, he sometimes vented his frustrations about the constraints that supply and transportation in particular put on his strategic and tactical flexibility,[51] but it is clear that he recognised the job that the staff were doing for him, in GHQ, in the ancillary services and in administration.

Smuts' praise for Collyer and Ewart in the Dispatch in January 1917, which covers the second half of the campaign in the previous year, reveals perhaps what he saw as the real contribution of the staff. Smuts refers to the 'tact and tireless energy with which they have carried out their respective duties, *thereby relieving me of all detail work and leaving me free to devote myself solely to the prosecution of the campaign.*'[52] In other words, the staff got on with their jobs which meant that Smuts could get on with his, which was directing the fighting. As long as he could do that, he was content to leave the staff to do everything else.

This approach worked, in that while there were occasions on which logistics caused delays to the execution of Smuts' strategy there were no disastrous failures, in particular at Kondoa or south of Handeni. In these places men went hungry, exhaustion and disease were rife, ammunition ran short, and pack animals died in their thousands, but the front-line units were not overrun, nor were they forced to either withdraw or surrender. At Kondoa in particular those would all have been distinct

---

[51] Ibid. 15 July
[52] *London Gazette* 17 Jan. 1917

possibilities if supply, transport and lines of communication units had not delivered for Smuts. The Official History[53] describes the heavy strain thrown onto the services—signals, medical, ordnance, transport, supplies—but states that these were 'maintained with undaunted determination in the face of the most trying difficulties and hardships'.

Looking at the opportunities that were missed throughout the campaign to cut off von Lettow-Vorbeck and make him stand and fight a big battle, Fendall and Meinhertzhagen are both strongly of the view that these were due to failings in Smuts' strategy and its execution by the fighting units and their commanders, not by staff failure. Smuts himself obviously did not share their views about strategy and tactics, laying great stress on the difficulties of the terrain and the climate and its effects on men and animals, but he was only full of praise for the way in which these problems were overcome and his army kept in the field. Crowe too stressed these difficulties and although he thought that there were too many amateurs on the staff, he gives the impression that he thought this just made his Chief's success all the more remarkable.

From the perspective of the staff, the view seems to have been that the job could be done and in June confidence was high that the campaign would soon be over—Fendall notes Ewart and Johns laying bets about whether the end would be in mid-August or early September,[54] although several weeks later he is reporting Smuts and Collyer being less sanguine than they were about being able to finish the campaign in six months.[55]

In his assessments towards the end of 1916 Fendall was complimentary about the General Staff under Collyer. They were 'not found wanting on the whole. In fact, they have done very well' and their 'plans have undoubtedly been very good indeed'.[56] Earlier in the campaign, when the transport problems were slowing down the advance, he recognised the problems on both sides, noting that while Smuts and the General Staff would not 'cut their coat according to their cloth'[57] at the same time the

[53] Hordern, Charles, *Official History: Military operations East Africa, August 1914-September 1916 vol 1* (HMSO, 1941) p. 278
[54] Fendall, CP, Diary, 10 June
[55] Ibid. 24 June
[56] Ibid. 12 Oct.
[57] Ibid. 15 July

Administrative branch was guilty of 'not providing enough cloth'—Ewart had to share some of the blame (although the real failure was blamed on the performance of the South African front line commanders.)

Meinhertzhagen complains bitterly about Smuts and his General Staff not forcing the Divisions to share information with him and he is waspish about some senior staff officers (Dealy being described as 'a charming fellow but constitutionally lazy') and their dash for loot when the HQ moved to Dar es Salaam,[58] but the serious criticisms he makes about 1916 are all aimed at Smuts' strategy and the performance of the South African officers in the field. He does not criticise the workings of any other branches of the staff or make anything like the number of negative comments about staff officers than he does about field commanders.

Fendall re-assessed the individual performance of his colleagues in October, nine months after he recorded his initial impressions.[59] He was hard on most of them, although not Collyer, whom he found 'decidedly able . . . reasonable' and judged to have 'had a hard job and done it well'. Another exception was Hazelton, whom Fendall thinks 'came through a harassing time very well; been very reasonable'. Ewart however he judges to be weak and indecisive and 'overall not a success'. Crowe had 'not had too much to do in reality' and his lack of influence with Smuts has already been noted. Dealy had been 'very careful of number one and very jealous of his position of CRE'. Edwards was always 'rubbing people up the wrong way' and earlier Fendall had been very critical of the risks of failure of the line of communications that Edwards took, when he 'only avoided serious disaster by luck'.[60]

However negative these judgements of individuals are, it is difficult not to conclude that the staff as a whole did what it was supposed to and delivered for Smuts. Fendall's comments about the General Staff doing well 'out here'[61] implies a favourable comparison with the performance of the staff on which he had worked in Europe. When Meinhertzhagen returned to the War

---
[58] Meinertzhagen, R, *Army Diary* (1960) pp. 192, 172, 198
[59] Fendall, CP, Diary, 12 Oct.
[60] Ibid. 13 Aug.
[61] Ibid. 26 April

Office he was equally harsh in his assessments of the capabilities and attitudes of some the officers he found there.[62] And Smuts, although seemingly more constrained in dealing with South African officers, had wasted no time in replacing British commanders whom he judged to have failed. He was not universally impressed by all of his senior staff but if there had been real failures which had caused major setbacks in the field, there is no doubt that senior officers would have been replaced by Smuts.

Tensions between British and South Africans

One of the features of the campaign noted by contemporary writers and analysed by modern historians are the poor relationships between the South African contingent and the British and other nationalities. It is beyond the scope of this paper to explore these issues in depth but there seems to be no direct evidence of tension between the South Africans on the General Staff (Collyer and colleagues) and the rest of the staff, who were mainly British.

However, Fendall in his diary and Meinhertzhagen in his book are both highly critical of the South Africans at divisional and brigade level. Criticisms include: a lack of discipline, mainly caused by the poor quality of their junior officers and NCOs; the inability of the mounted units to look after their horses; their disdain for black African and Indian troops; their propensity to loot at every opportunity; and most damning of all, their unwillingness to incur casualties and consequent reluctance to engage in a stand-up fight with the Germans. However, none of these problems seems to have affected the workings of the staff and both writers to a large extent disassociated Smuts personally from these problems.

Summary and Conclusions

After summarising the 1916 campaign in Tanganyika and in particular its effect on career of General Jan Smuts, and then briefly reviewing Smuts' general-ship, this paper set out to explore the role of the staff who served under Smuts during the campaign. It looked at the diverse group of officers on the staff, their experience and expertise, and their relationships with

---

[62] Meinertzhagen, R, *Army Diary* (1960) pp. 206-7

each other and with Smuts. It sought to assess how effectively the staff had delivered for Smuts, and to provide some insight into how successfully they managed to 'bridge the gap' in their Commander-in-Chief's experience, and enable him to focus on what he wanted to do, which was to manage the fighting.

On the question of the experience and expertise of the staff, it can be concluded that when Smuts took over he inherited an experienced group of senior staff officers, who had the ability to undertake the task they had to perform, and that after making some limited initial changes to personnel he left this group intact throughout the whole of the period he was in command. There were certainly officers without the necessary expertise in some senior jobs, and many junior officers doing jobs for which they had had no training, but overall it can be claimed that the staff had the necessary experience.

It can also be claimed with some justification that the group functioned reasonably well together. There were of course tensions between branches, reflected in some unsatisfactory working relationships between individual officers, which were exacerbated by the excessive strain that Smuts' strategy placed on the staff, in particular the transport and lines of communications organisations. It would be a mistake however to label the staff as dysfunctional—had they been, this would have caused major setbacks at the front line when Smuts' strategy pushed the demands on the staff branches to breaking point.

It is clear however that the staff had little or no influence on how Smuts chose to fight the campaign. He seems not to have sought advice nor to have followed specialist advice when it was offered, seeing the staff as being there to take care of the detail so that he could concern himself exclusively with directing the fighting forces in the field. The staff were there for technical and administrative support, to enable the execution of the CiC's strategy, not to participate in any high-level decision-making—that was for Smuts alone.

Overall the staff delivered well for Smuts. Had they not done so it is unlikely that he would have shied away from replacing individuals who were under-performing. He was generally fulsome in his praise in his official dispatches. Participants in the campaign and modern historians have drawn attention to the major flaws in Smuts' strategy and the many opportunities that he missed during its implementation, but these cannot be attributed to staff failings or to a breakdown in staff systems. Smuts' strategic priorities over-rode any logistical considerations and it is greatly to the credit of his staff and the organisations they ran that this never resulted in a major reversal in the field. Jan Smuts owed his subsequent career to the efforts of a diverse group of mainly British officers, who did their difficult jobs well.

References

Corrigan, S, The Generalship of Jan Smuts during the First World War, *The British Empire at War Research Group* (2014)
Crowe, JHV, *General Smuts' campaign in East Africa* (J Murray, 1918)
Dealy, J, *War Diary*, WO 95/5301
Ewart, *Letter,* CAB 45/16
Fendall, CP, *Private Diary* (1915-19) WO 45/44
Fendall, CP, *The East African Force 1915-1919* (1921)
Garfield, Brian, *The Meinhertzhagen Mystery: The Life and Legend of a Colossal Fraud* (Potomac, 2007)
Hazelton, PO, *RASC Quarterly* (October 1923)
Hordern, Charles, *Military Operations East Africa 1914-16* (HMSO, 1941, reprint Naval & Battery 1990)
London Gazette
Meinertzhagen, Richard, *Army Diary 1899-1926* (Oliver & Boyd, 1960)
O'Moore, Creagh, *The VC and DSO book: Distinguished Service Order 1916-1923* (Naval & Military, 2009)
Paice, Edward, *Tip and Run* (Weidenfeld & Nicholson, 2007)
Smuts, JC, *Jan Christian Smuts by his Son* (Cassell, 1952)
Strachan, Hew. *The First World War in Africa* (Rhaniket, 2004)
Times Obituary 2 August 1935
WO 374/18191 Telegrams

The defence of Karonga and the battle of Kasoa

Peter Charlton

Nyasaland (Malawi) is totally landlocked and is surrounded by Mozambique (PEA), Zambia (NR), and Tanzania (GEA). The country geographically is part of East Africa not British Central Africa. It forms the southern end of the Rift Valley and of the whole country, about the size of England, is one-fifth under water. Development at this stage and for quite a long while afterwards was mainly in the south in an area known as the Shire Highlands which was south of Fort Johnston. There was almost no development north of Fort Johnston and as a result, virtually no roads, and with action expected to take place on the border at the north, it was felt very important to get control of the lake. This was the only means of transporting people along the length of the country quickly. Otherwise, everything was carried by head-loads, Tenga Tenga, if you were going by land as because of tsetse fly, there was no horse-drawn traffic.

Malawi was supplied from Chinde on the mouth of the Zambezi River. Coasters crossed the bar, then barged cargo up from there to the confluence with the Shire. From the Shire River, a railway ran into Blantyre. In the early days they actually sailed through Port Herald to Chiroma and Chikwawa and then the rapids stopped further progress and they had to hand carry goods to Blantyre as head-loads.

Control of lake Nyasa was very important. The regular forces of the country were 1 King's African Rifles (KAR). Previously, there had been 1 and 2KAR but in 1911 Britain had disbanded 2KAR for reasons of economy and most of them had gone over the border into German East Africa and joined the *schutztruppe* in Langenberg. There were so many of them that the Germans used English bugle calls and commands to control them. They probably ended up with the ridiculous situation of British Askaris fighting British Askaris in the war and later battles. 1KAR was down to four weak companies in Nyasaland with a further four companies up north on the Jubaland border. Of the Nyasaland units, one was in Mangochi south of the lake and there was another company of fifty men in Zomba and another two companies of 150 men on leave. There were also 158 Reserves and 358 policemen. These policemen were in most cases ex-KAR Askari so were able to fight.

There was also the Nyasaland Volunteer Reserve. There were 181 volunteers at the beginning of the war in Nyasaland when the actual population size was 540 men and during the campaign approximately 540 men actually saw service. The stats are a bit vague as there were troops from the Congo and South Africa but virtually every white man in Nyasaland participated which was pretty impressive. They were armed originally with the Martini Henri rifle and by the time war broke out they were using the Lee Enfield.

Their adversary was the *schutztruppe* under General Paul von Lettow-Vorbeck who was a very keen soldier. His philosophy was to embroil as many allies as he could in the war and was very active in running around the borders, provoking the British into action which might otherwise not have taken place. At the beginning of the conflict he had 14 companies but by the middle of the war he had developed them into 60. These companies were each a little mobile army. They consisted of 150-200 well-equipped, well-trained men who were well paid and disciplined. Their morale was high. There were approximately twenty German officers and NCOs in charge of each *schutztruppe* unit, usually three or more machine-guns. Quite often they had artillery, even their own cobblers, tailors and mobile boats. They were extremely professional. There were five of these companies around the Nyasaland border and which, in theory, could have invaded into the territory. In fact, only two of them were used—1 Feldkompanje (FK) at Iringa and 5FK at Isoka.

The British forces were mobilised and called up under the command of Captain CW Barton who at that stage was in charge of 1KAR. He insisted that Hector Duff (the Chief Secretary) go with him to represent the government. Duff spoke fluent German. Barton was quite a junior officer and so felt Duff would be his line of communication to the Nyasaland government to rubber stamp his decisions.

The British had by then gained command of the lake by the action of the *Guendolen* which subdued the German *Hermann von Wissmann*. Later, General Northey attacking from the south into German East Africa was very hampered by only having five vessels which he could use to get his equipment moved. He was supplied from Europe. The *Guendolen* was initially the only armed vessel with her 3-pounder Hotchkiss canon. Five-hundred men of the King's African Rifles embarked on the vessels and moved up the lake. At the same time the volunteers were put on a proper footing and fifty of them undertook ten days' training at Zomba, marched to Fort Johnston and shipped up the lake to follow the balance of the army. The armaments of the whole force were three maxim guns, which were old fashioned plus four 7-pounder and two 9-pounder muzzle loaders. These were antique and were obsolete by the time of the Second Anglo-Boer War, 1899-1902, but that was the only artillery available to them.

The force sailed out of Fort Johnston and was landed just below Karonga which was not a port as it had shallow water. They marched into Karonga, which was a tiny settlement just south of the German East African border.

German forces were distributed around the base at Tukuyu (Neu Langenburg), which was approximately thirty kilometres from the border. There was a field company at Massoko under Hauptmann Erich von Langenn-Steinkeller and a detachment of 5FK near Iringa under Captain Heinrich Aumann. They were approximately twenty miles from the Songwe River border. There was a little settlement at a place called Kaporo inside Nyasaland. The Germans invaded Malawi with a small force and captured Kaporo on 20 August 1914. They were there as a threat right on the border. They had not realised that the British had managed to mobilise and get troops to Karonga. This whole little action was described by someone as 'an uncanny symmetry of events characterises this forgotten campaign'.[1]

---

[1] Ransford,O, *Livingstone's Lake*, (John Murray, 1971) p. 234

Von Langenn-Stenkeller being a decent person and knowing there was a little settlement at Karonga, sent a warning on 22 August that he was going to attack and his men might get a bit out of control so if there were women and children in the vicinity, they should be removed. This gave the British a bit more warning and they got themselves organised. They did not do very well as there was not very much available to defend. Karonga was just a couple of buildings and a compound used by some traders which was surrounded by a brick wall about five-foot high. This area was about 100 yards by 100 yards square with a couple of buildings inside and was known as the Ross and Adam Compound.

The Germans after sending warnings on 22 August did not do much for about two weeks, until they moved the main force across the border on 7 September. The British started preparing Karonga's defences. They cleared the long grass but thought it was wasteful to destroy the banana plantations so left them. The German main force joined the one at Kaporo where they over-nighted. Von Langenn-Stenkeller then split them into two columns and sent the main force down the main road to Karonga. The other section under Aumann was sent down the Mambande track together with an additional 500 irregular spearmen. Aumann had hoped to attack Karonga from the rear but seems to have been misdirected by a local trader. It appears that he did not even reach Karonga but there are no clear sources about this.

At the same time Barton decided to attack German East Africa and he stripped Karonga of men. He left 11 Europeans and some reservists numbering 70 men. He left two antique cannon which the inhabitants probably did not know how to use. He then split his forces into three columns of about 170 men each. Armed with the two machine-guns and remaining cannons, they marched between these two German forces without realising they were there. Both sides realised there was something happening, but it is remarkable that they did not stumble onto each others' columns.

Karonga was saved as the Germans had not reconnoitred and did not realise what they were up against. Also their attention was diverted. This was due to a vehicle called the *Vera*, a small lake steamer, that was being towed up the lake. As they rounded the point at Karonga the Germans got excited and opened fire on the *Vera* which gave the garrison more warning. The German Askari were out of control, and were looting the *Vera*, so their two guns never made it to Karonga.

About 9 a.m., at the same time that the Germans advanced, PD Bishop, a stores clerk in Karonga, managed to fire the antique cannon. Barton heard the shots and realised he was in trouble. He was about 15 miles away. He turned his force around, got a column to drop its baggage and force march to Karonga. They did the trip in one hour thirty minutes and attacked the Germans in the rear. Barton managed to re-cross the Lufira River. He bumped into Aumann and they had a clash. He continued south and bumped into von Langenn-Stenkeller with the main force at about 11 o'clock. The fighting was at very close range and Barton was lucky as he had the river behind him but was determined he was not going to fall back. He did not know what was in front. The Germans had black-powder rifles which was lucky for Barton as he could see where they were firing from. The action took place at a range of about 100 to 300 yards. Reports that Barton ambushed the Germans are not accurate.

Barton left a very fine account of the action in his diary and the violence really comes through. The machine-guns were manned by Nyasaland Volunteers who were both mortally wounded. The one German gun had two dead Germans lying over it and both the guns were captured. The Germans were demoralised and fled which resulted in Barton winning the battle. At the end of the fight, the British had lost five Europeans and eight King's African Rifles. We cannot get proper figures on the German casualties but it seems they lost at least seven Germans and 51 Askari killed. According to records found later, the German 5FK lost in total 102 out of 142 men.

Tim Wright's narrative of the British South African Police in both Southern and Northern Rhodesia, in East Africa, provides a chronology of events as well as highlighting the interconnectedness of the two territories controlled by the British South Africa Company. For further background, social and economic implications, see Edmund Yorke and Jan-Bart Gewald.[1]

The Rhodesian Police units at the front

Timothy Wright[2]

In the Rhodesias,[3] the Police were the first line of defence. The British South Africa Police (BSAP) in Southern Rhodesia consisted of 530 Europeans, trained, as mounted riflemen, and 600 unarmed blacks. Eight hundred of a white male population of ten thousand were members of the Southern Rhodesia Volunteers with another 1,241 in rifle clubs.

The Northern Rhodesia Police (NRP), 31 Officers and British other ranks and 786 blacks consisted of the Town and District Police and the Military Branch organised in five companies. One company was based at Headquarters at the capital Livingstone, the others at Mongu, Kasempa, Kasama and Fort Jameson (Chipata). There were about 1,000 white adult males in the territory. Membership of rifle clubs was popular but there was no local defence force. In neighbouring Nyasaland there were only some 300 men of 1st King's African Rifles. There were no roads but the railway was complete to the Belgian Congo.

---

[1] Edmund Yorke, *Britain, Britain, Northern Rhodesia and the First World War: Forgotten colonial crisis* (Palgrave, 2015); Jan-Bart Gewald, *Forged in the Great War: people, transport and labour, the establishment of colonial rule in Zambia, 1890-1920* (ASC Leiden, 2015)

[2] Tim Wright, *The History of the Northern Rhodesia Police* (BECM, 2001) pp. 87-155

[3] The Rhodesias consisted of Northern and Southern Rhodesia which were administered by the British South Africa Company (BSA Co) overseen by the High Commissioner of South Africa. Under its Royal Charter of 29 October 1889 the BSA Co was, inter alia, empowered to maintain a police force in its territories but it had no authority to maintain permanent full-time regular military forces.

On 9 August 1914 a mobile column of the NRP, three officers and 80 men of A Company, left Livingstone for Kasama led by Major HM Stennett, Second-in-Command of the Force.

A few weeks after the outbreak of war Colonel Manie Maritz, commanding South African Forces in the Northern Cape, led his men willy nilly into South West Africa. In South Africa rebellion broke out amongst disaffected Boers. This lasted until the end of the year, delaying the invasion of South West Africa. The threat to Northern Rhodesia from the South West remained for nearly a year, a real one.

On 21 September 1914, a detachment of BSAP joined an NRP section at Sesheke. Together they occupied the German Fort at Schuckmannsburg, across the Zambezi in the Caprivi Strip of South West Africa. In October, the main body of B Company NRP from Mongu reached Sesheke by boat. They were followed by Captain JJ O'Sullevan with most of C Company which had marched from Kasempa to entrain at Broken Hill (Kabwe). In view of these reinforcements, it was considered safe to withdraw the BSAP, and wise to do so before the rains set in. On 26 December O'Sullevan and his force, now known as the 2nd Mobile Column arrived at Livingstone to entrain for Sakania in the Belgian Congo, from where they were to march to Abercorn. However, it was still necessary to leave at least one company on the Zambezi.

One-hundred-and-twenty white volunteers, the Northern Rhodesia Rifles, were mobilised at Broken Hill and left to reinforce the police on the Northern Border.

At Bismarckburg (Kasanga), on Lake Tanganyika, only thirty-eight miles from Abercorn, the German fort could easily be reinforced by steamer from Ujiji, the terminus of the Central Railway. At Abercorn there were only 12 district police. On hearing of the outbreak of war, CP Chesnaye, District Commissioner arranged the evacuation of European women and children, and sent out patrols. In late August enemy native auxiliaries began raiding and cut the telegraph line between Abercorn and Fife.[4]

A German force from Bismarckburg with a light gun advanced towards Abercorn, accompanied by irregulars who ravaged the countryside, looting, raping and again cutting the

---

[4] The only line to Kasama was routed along the border and through Nyasaland.

telegraph. Lieutenant JJ McCarthy had just arrived from Kasama with reinforcements from D Company, bringing the garrison of Abercorn up to forty. The gaol, the only suitable building, was put in a state of defence. On 6 September an attack was repulsed but sniping continued until next day when the enemy withdrew.

On 8 September the enemy returned. A request for reinforcements had been sent to Kasama where Major Stennett had just marched in with his Mobile Column. Though they were tired after their four-week trek from Broken Hill, he at once pushed on to reach Abercorn at 3.30 a.m. on 9 September. From 6 a.m. the enemy fired 40 shells, killing privates Chasesa and Madi and somewhat demoralising their comrades. Nevertheless, when the enemy attacked they were driven off. The next day the enemy withdrew. Lieutenant McCarthy attacked at dawn and drove the Germans back across the border.

Patrolling by both sides continued. The telegraph was constantly cut, which meant that it took seven to ten days for messages, carried by runner and bicycle to the line of rail, to reach Livingstone until a new telegraph line was completed to Abercorn from the south.

In late September, a battalion of black troops from the Belgian Congo under Major Olsen, reached Abercorn. On the march the Belgians were hampered by a shortage of water. On hearing of their advance, the Northern Rhodesia blacks took to the bush, leaving the villages bare of supplies. The Congolese had a reputation for cannibalism which persisted into the 1960s. Major Stennett assumed command of the combined forces with the rank of Lieutenant-Colonel.

An old 7-pounder mountain gun was sent up from Southern Rhodesia by rail with Corporal Jack Horton and three troopers of the British South Africa Police, trained gunners, and six BSA Native Police as ammunition numbers. Lieutenant Percy Sillitoe[5] NRP was ordered to leave his civil police duties at Lusaka, meet the gun and crew at Broken Hill and take them north. With the help of the District Commissioner, he assembled 600 carriers with supplies for the 520-mile march to Abercorn. They were ready when the train arrived, and

---

[5] Chief Constable of Chesterfield, Sheffield, Glasgow and Kent and finally Director-General of the Security Services.

completed the trek in thirty days. A carrier normally averaged 15 miles a day with a 60-pound load and needed 2½ pounds of meal a day.

Due to a misunderstanding, the Belgians were recalled to the Congo. The advance party had left when, on 17 November, German troops landed from two steamers at Kituta Bay on Lake Tanganyika, fourteen miles west of Abercorn, and burnt the stores of the African Lakes Corporation. Percy Sillitoe had arrived at Abercorn. He was sent in command of 50 NRP to link up with the departing Belgian company and engage the Germans. They found the enemy gone. Sillitoe returned to Abercorn while the Belgians went on their way.

However, the enemy steamed on another 14 miles to raid Kasakalawe. An allied force from Abercorn came up and engaged them, but the Germans were able to re-embark under cover of the guns of their steamers. Corporal Jack Horton and his gunners could not catch up in time to bring their gun into action.

On 13 December, Colonel FA Hodson, the NRP commandant arrived to take command. There were now six officers, and 14 white volunteers on the border with about 300 black police. To reinforce the Military Branch it had been necessary to denude the districts of civil police.

Until the return of the Belgians on 26 January 1915, little more could be done than defend Abercorn and Fife. The King's African Rifles at Karonga were involved in subduing the John Chilembwe uprising in Nyasaland.[6]

At Fife, E Company NRP from Fort Jameson had reinforced the five district police and 11 of the Native Commissioner's messengers; former policemen who had rejoined for duty.

On 6 December 1914, Fife was attacked by a force with a 3-pounder gun. Private Ndarama was killed by a shell which hit him in the back when he was going through a door. Captain HC Ingles, in command, was impressed by the steadiness of the black police under fire. The enemy retired in the evening.

---

[6] Hordern, Charles, *Official History Military Operations in East Africa*, vol 1 (HMSO, 1941) pp. 179-180; Charlton, Peter, *Cinderella's soldiers: A history of the Nyasaland Volunteer Reserve* (Charlton, 2010) pp. 82-91. Chilembwe, a Nyasalander, had spent thee years at a seminary in the United States of America before building a church at Mbombwe.

On the evening of 27 December, the night piquet reported the enemy returning. Lieutenant Arthur Charles de Cussans led a half company out. They made contact on the west ridge. After a fire fight, Cussans saw he was about to be outflanked and ordered his men to fix bayonets and charge. Under a hail of bullets they cleared the ridge although Temporary Second Lieutenant Ronald Smith was seriously wounded in the back and Private Kanyanla in the shoulder. The enemy withdrew in disorder.

On 3 February 1915, Major O'Sullevan marched into Abercorn with his 2nd Mobile Column NRP. They had detrained at Sakania where the Belgian Administrator provided 700 porters. Belgian officials accompanied the troops through Katanga to the Luapula River where they were met by a Northern Rhodesia native commissioner with fresh porters. The 430-mile march was accomplished in twenty days in heavy rains; swamps had to be corduroyed, and several bridges had to be erected daily to get the mules over the swollen rivers.

The garrisons of Abercorn and Fife, a hundred miles apart, were insufficient to prevent the Germans penetrating into Northern Rhodesia. The return of the Belgians enabled Hodson to send O'Sullevan's Column to Saisi, about thirty miles east of Abercorn.

On 2 February, the Northern Rhodesia Rifles arrived at Kasama. They detrained fifty miles north from Broken Hill. With 16 ox-wagons of supplies, they had cut the first wagon road, despite tsetse fly and the rains. On 4 February, they set out again for Abercorn and Fife without the wagons. All 200 oxen died at Kasama.

In March 1915, there were further fears of an attack from South West Africa. The South African invasion of this territory was now well under way but it was thought that some of the enemy might attempt to break out and make for East Africa. Lieutenant-Colonel Stennett was now in command at Livingstone. The detachments of the NRP at Livingstone and Mongu were strengthened with the last thirty men from Kasempa to watch the line of the Zambezi. However, the authorities in Southern Rhodesia cannot have been too worried about the security of Northern Rhodesia as having sent the newly raised 1st Rhodesia Regiment to South Africa in

November 1914 they now sent the 2nd Rhodesia Regiment to Mombasa.

On 8 July Maritz, the South African rebel was reported moving along the Okavango in the direction of Livingstone. One-hundred BSAP under Major AJ Tomlinson were sent up from Southern Rhodesia. The combined force concentrated under Colonel Stennett at Sesheke until 9 August when it was learnt that Maritz had given himself up in Angola.[7] The German forces in South West Africa had surrendered to General Botha on 9 July. Rhodesia now had only one front.

The majority of the BSAP returned to Bulawayo but some were allowed to join A Special Reserve Company BSAP raised from whites in Southern Rhodesia on a cadre of regular police. Half this company left Livingstone for the north on 18 August 1915 via Broken Hill while the remainder travelled via Ndola. Staggered departures by different routes were essential to ensure sufficient carriers and food supplies after leaving the railhead.

Fighting patrols frequently clashed on both sides of the border. General Major Kurt Wahle took command of German troops on the border, bringing reinforcements. On 28 June he attacked Saisi but was repulsed by O'Sullevan's Anglo-Belgian garrison.

On 25 July Wahle returned and invested Saisi. Fighting went on until 3 August, when having exhausted his supplies, Wahle returned to Dar es Salaam via Lake Tanganyika. The German gun had been put out of action by a direct hit from the BSAP 7-pounder. The enemy had trenches close to the water supplies. Despite this, at night Corporal Chikusi and Private Piyo NRP would creep down to the river each with twenty water bottles often under fire.

For his action at Saisi, O'Sullevan was awarded the Distinguished Service Order (DSO) but was invalided in September 1915; his career in Northern Rhodesia at an end. The successful defence of Saisi stimulated recruiting in Rhodesia and South Africa, especially among troops returning from South West Africa for demobilisation.

---

[2] Hordern, Charles, *Official History* (1941) pp. 195-6; Brelsford, WV, *The story of the Northern Rhodesia Regiment* (Rhodesia Govt, 1954) p. 29

On 4 October 1915, A Company BSAP marched into Abercorn 160 strong. On 18 October B Special Reserve Company marched into Fife from Karonga, having evaded an ambush. Formed at Salisbury, 131 strong, under Major Walter Baxendale, Southern Rhodesia Volunteers, this company had travelled by rail and water via Beira and Zomba. Major RE Murray DCM BSAP was appointed Colonel Hodson's Chief Staff Officer.

The patrol war continued into 1916 after the Belgians had left to take part in an offensive north of Lake Tanganyika in October 1915. On Boxing Day 1915, German naval superiority on Lake Tanganyika ended.[8]

On 29 January 1916, Brigadier-General Northey arrived at Zomba to take command of the Nyasaland-Rhodesia Field Force, in which all the troops at the front in Northern Rhodesia and Nyasaland came under unified command for the first time.

Nyasaland had been reinforced by 5th Field Battery, South African Mounted Riflemen, armed with German mountain guns captured in South West Africa, and the newly raised 1st and 2nd South African Rifles, each of about 500 men.

After working on logistics, Northey set out by motor cycle combination to tour the 250-mile front from Lake Nyasa to Lake Tanganyika.

At Fife, Major Baxendale was in command with B Company BSAP and two NRP companies. Here, Hodson and Murray joined Northey and accompanied him to Abercorn. A Company BSAP and two NRP companies were at Abercorn, with a third at Zombe, nine miles away. Northey criticised the defence works on the frontier for being built too high off the ground. The ration, down to 1½ pounds of meal a day, was insufficient.

On 23 March, Northey returned to Karonga planning to advance as soon as the rains had ceased. He divided his force into three columns:-

- Number 1 Column under Lieutenant Colonel Murray, with the two BSAP companies and four companies of Northern Rhodesia Police, based at Abercorn, was to take Namema 26 miles to the North-East.

---

[8] When Commander Geoffrey Basil Spicer-Simson's African Lake Expedition put the first of the German vessels out of action on the lake. See Great War in Africa Association, *The Lake Tanganyika Expedition 1914-1918: A primary source chronology* (2016)

- Number 2 Column based on Fife under Lieutenant Colonel Rodger, 2nd South African Rifles, with his own regiment and Captain Sillitoe's E Company, NRP, was to take Luwiwa, thirteen miles to the North-East.
- Number 3 Column under the Commandant of 1 King's African Rifles (KAR), Lieutenant Colonel Hawthorn, consisting of 1KAR, 1st South African Rifles, and 150 Nyasaland Volunteers, was to advance from Karonga and Fort Hill.

Two-thousand first line carriers recruited in Northern Rhodesia were to follow Column Numbers 1 and 2. Colonel Hodson took charge of the Lines of Communication in Northern Rhodesia. Charles Briggs of the Southern Rhodesia Public Works Department was supervising the building of the Great North Road from Broken Hill, upon which Major Duly was soon to be ferrying supplies by a new BSAP motor transport unit. Those of the Northern Rhodesia Rifles who remained at the front were absorbed into the other units.

On 23 May, Murray marched out of Abercorn. The enemy eluded him at Namema and Bismarkburg and Rodger at Luwiwa. Two NRP companies were left to clear the country north of Bismarksburg while Murray with the rest of his column joined in the pursuit of the enemy to Iringa which was entered by Captain Dickinson's C Company NRP on 29 August 1916.

The retirement of General Wahle's troops from Tabora and the delays in the advance of Smuts' main army from the north, left Northey's force exposed. However, disaster was averted by Murray and Hawthorn's victory over Major Georg Kraut at Mkapira and their rapid deployment to relieve Malangali and Lupembe.

The BSAP and NRP with a company of the newly raised Rhodesia Native Regiment went on to force Oberst-Leutnant Huebner to surrender at Ilembule in November.

With the whites and Indians of the main East Africa Force debilitated by sickness and the KAR in the process of expansion, the Nyasaland/Rhodesia Field Force, with the BSAP and NRP to the fore, had to bear the main burden of wearing down the enemy until in February 1917 the actions of Hauptmann Wintgens caused a major diversion.

The return from the pursuit of Wintgens to the return from Mozambique

Having pursued Wintgens almost to Tabora, Murray's Column marched back to reach Rungwe on 14 June 1917 for a week's rest. Fifty-five African police left for Fife to commence three months leave, the first in the campaign. The strength of the NRP under Murray's command was 24 officers and white NCOs, and 515 black police with 24 followers, and 337 carriers. The force was also represented in the Machine-gun Company of five officers, 26 white and 53 black other ranks with seven followers and 265 carriers. The rains had ended and the plan was to drive the enemy into the arms of a British force working inland from the coast.

On 25 June 1917, Murray's Column embarked for Wiedhafen. He established his headquarters at Songea with the BSAP, now only 56 strong, and three companies of NRP as his reserve. Major CH Fair assumed command of the NRP in the field. The Rhodesia Native Regiment under Major CL Carbutt was posted at Kitanda. Lewis guns were now available. Northey decided that the BSAP who were still fit for duty should be trained as Lewis gunners and attached to the NRP and Rhodesia Native Regiment (RNR).

C Company NRP joined E and F at Lupembe all under Captain EG Dickinson, to drive Hauptmann Heinrich Aumann's detachment eastward. By 25 July E Company had driven Aumann across the Ruhuje at Mkapira Drift. On 29 July Aumann drove in the piquet, re-crossed the river and occupied the old Rhodesian trenches at Mkapira. Scouts and one section forced him to disclose his position and after a thirty-minute fire fight, Captain LA Russell and half F Company drove him out at the point of the bayonet. The enemy escaped into the thick grass and reeds of the river bed. Enemy fire prevented Russell crossing in pursuit.

On 7 August, Acting Lieutenant Colonel Fair with A Company NRP, joined 1 Rhodesia Native Regiment which had moved up to attack from the South. On 9 August 1917, Captain Latham in command of A Company, drove in two pickets before assaulting an enemy post at Tuturu. Lieutenant HW Tarbutt, a pre-War BSAP trooper commissioned into the NRP from the BSAP companies, was bayoneted in the throat and fell into the enemy trench. Four black African police were killed, two within five yards of the German trenches. The enemy retired but not before burying Tarbutt. On his grave marker a German wrote: 'In honour of a brave man'.

On 10 August, while F Company demonstrated at Mkapira Drift, Dickinson crossed the Ruhuje with C and E companies by canoe, five miles upstream, despite opposition from a troop of hippo. On 13 August, A Company NRP and the Rhodesia Native Regiment joined Dickinson. Lieutenant Colonel Fair took command.

Aumann was entrenched on a ridge near Mpepo. The NRP dug in within 600 yards of his position while the RNR closed in from the South. Corporal Samsoni and Private Moto came into action with their machine-gun under automatic fire 400 yards from the enemy position. Both were wounded but remained at their posts, bringing the gun out of action when the line retired.

An attack at dawn on 19 August was stopped by machine-gun fire which killed machine-gun Porter Gwalia and wounded three porters and three black police. On 26 August, E and half F Company NRP, under Captains Withers and Russell, rushed Signal Hill, north of Aumann's main position. They beat off a vigorous counterattack by L Field Company. It was police against police again as the enemy charged up to, and at one point, actually penetrated, the NRP's trenches. A German was heard shouting 'Retire! Retire!' in the hope of confusing the NRP. Three of the enemy were killed. Six enemy Askari were taken prisoner together with their Commander, Oberleutnant Bauer, who died of wounds. The enemy were seen to carry off ten wounded. The NRP suffered 14 wounded.

After subjecting Withers' men to heavy machine-gun fire all through 27 August, Aumann abandoned Mpepo that night and broke out north-east to Likassa. Dickinson found him entrenched on a wooded height. There was heavy fighting at close quarters. The enemy counterattacked and the RNR fell back exposing the flank of E Company NRP who withdrew on the local reserve. The Germans continued their desperate attack for two hours right into the lines of the NRP whose ammunition was almost exhausted. The medical staff were swamped. Private PFM Roelke BSAP was killed while clearing a jam in his machine-gun under heavy fire. Night fell with both sides dug in. Next morning Aumann had gone. The fight had been one of the fiercest experienced by the NRP who lost six black Africans killed, and Sergeant F Bainbridge, two other Europeans and 14 Africans wounded. The Germans lost 27 killed and 73 prisoners. For his failure to support the NRP Captain Burke BSAP RNR was sacked. He was later killed in action in France as a sergeant in 1 South African Infantry.

Aumann retreated north-east towards Mahenge. Fair pursued him as far as supplies would allow and on 1 October was twenty-five miles south-west of Mahenge which Belgian troops occupied. Aumann turned south. On 14 October, Corporal Songandewo and his C Company scouts attacked an enemy magazine, captured a German and marched him back cross country wearing only one boot. On 18 October, Corporal Chakanga and ten men of A Company rushed a piquet east of Ngombere held by a German and ten blacks and captured 4 Askari for the loss of Private Chimai, killed. On 25 October, the NRP joined the Belgians in an attack on two enemy companies holding a hill at Sali Mission on the Ruaha. Private Zalile was killed and Lieutenant Latimer and two black police wounded. On 6 November, 145 Germans and 189 Askari, all sick or convalescent, surrendered to Colonel Fair. By the middle of November there were no enemy within reach. Fair was ordered to take over Mahenge.

Meanwhile, civil police elements around Neu Langenburg had been dealing with roving bands of enemy stragglers. On 15 September Fair had been ordered to send 160 of the Rhodesia Native Regiment back to Neu Langenburg to assist. Captain P Graham with B and D companies NRP was watching the Songea Liwale Road. Major JJ McCarthy DSO MC NRP with his Ruga Ruga, in cooperation with 5 South African Infantry was holding a portion of Portuguese East Africa west of the Luchenda River. In October, 54 men of the BSAP had been invalided back to Southern Rhodesia. On 29 October, Lieutenant Colonel Stennett arrived at Mpurukasese to resume command of the NRP. He left there on 15 November with 105 men of the Depot Company and leaving garrisons of twenty men each at Mburugande, Njenje and Mirola, joined Murray on 21 November at Jumbe Faume. There were still detachments of NRP at Ubena, Lupembe, and Muhanga on garrison and police duty.

On 26 November, Murray with B and D companies NRP, and 1/4 and 2/4 King's African Rifles, was around Tunduru with patrols on the Rovuma. Fair remained with A Company to garrison Mahenge while his other three companies were ordered south to rejoin Murray. Murray's task was to prevent Major Theodor Tafel's group of companies, from joining with von Lettow, who was now in the angle formed by the Rovuma and the Indian Ocean. Murray never managed to close with Tafel, but his patrols captured every runner sent by one German commander to the other. Tafel continued south-east through waterless and foodless country. By the time he realised that von Lettow-Vorbeck had crossed his path, making south-west towards the Rovuma, it was too late to avoid van Deventer's columns. On 29 November 1917, Major Tafel gave himself up, together with over 1,300 men.

On 25 November, von Lettow forded the Rovuma at Ngomano. With him were 2,000 troops and 3,000 porters. The river was 1,200 yards wide and chest high. The Portuguese guarding the frontier were scattered by a sudden attack. Hauptmann Goering, with three companies, crossed further downstream.

Murray's task, with the NRP, 1 and 2 Rhodesia Native Regiments, and the Ugandans of 1/4 and 2/4 KAR, was to prevent the enemy doubling back into German East Africa. Posts were established on the Rovuma and patrols roved far to the south. The greater part of the NRP concentrated at Lipumbi. Few of the original British officers were still at duty with the battalion, which was now over 1,000 strong including headquarters staff and the base organisation although five Europeans and 142 black police were sick in hospital. After three years in the field living mainly on corned beef and rice few of either race were regarded by the medical staff as in really good health. Many of the officers were from the BSAP companies, as were almost all the European other ranks. The NRP in the field were now reorganised into a conventional 'Service Battalion' of four double companies, with a machine-gun company and a Stokes mortar company. Web equipment was issued but the belt proved too large for most blacks. By 19 December, the reorganisation was complete and two patrols left for the Luchinga River.

Murray was invalided south as he had developed serious heart trouble. On 27 January 1918, Lieutenant-Colonel Stennett assumed command of the RNR and 3/4 KAR as well as the NRP until Colonel Clayton arrived to take Murray's place. Colonel Ronald Ernest Murray DSO and bar DCM never recovered his health and died in England on 29 June 1920.

On 11 February 1918, the NRP Service Battalion left for Mbamba Bay on Lake Nyasa for a rest. One-hundred-and-sixty-five black police were granted three months' leave. The remainder trained on the new weapons and a number of patrols were sent out. The announcement of a 'War Bonus' was well received, especially as the NRP were the lowest paid black troops.

Back in Northern Rhodesia law and order were maintained by the 120 remaining police, the district commissioners and their messengers.

In March 1917, rebellion broke out in the Tete Province of Portuguese East Africa. The Portuguese administrator from Zumbo fled across the Zambezi to Feira from where the District Police had been withdrawn in 1916. The Native Commissioner, Captain CF Molyneux, an Anglo-Boer War veteran, who had served at the front with the Northern Rhodesia Rifles crossed the river and recovered a quantity of arms which his guest had abandoned and organised a defence force on the Northern Rhodesia side. On 26 July 1917, Lieutenant Castor NRP arrived from Livingstone with a platoon. There were no serious incursions but some 5,000 black refugees sought shelter in Northern Rhodesia where food was already short. In Southern Rhodesia the BSAP faced a similar problem.

In May 1918 Lieutenant-Colonel Stennett was invalided and Major Dickinson assumed command of the Service Battalion. On 6 May, Lieutenant Castor arrived at Mbamba Bay with 72 recruits followed shortly thereafter by Captain Castle with 106 men back from leave, which was just as well. On 27 May the battalion was ordered to join Colonel GMP Hawthorn's column to prevent von Lettow-Vorbeck coming west into Nyasaland. The battalion left Mbamba Bay by steamer for Fort Johnston. They were rushed by motor vehicle to Limbé and then marched into Portuguese territory in order to intercept the enemy commander at Alto Mulocque. They arrived to find that von Lettow-Vorbeck was already far to the south.

In July 1918, Major General Sir Edward Northey KCMG CB left on appointment as Governor of British East Africa. Hawthorn succeeded him in command of Norforce, as the Nyasaland Rhodesia Field Force was known. The NRP Service Battalion joined the pursuit of von Lettow-Vorbeck through Portuguese East Africa to the coast near Quelimane. The enemy doubled back north-east, cutting up 3/3 KAR and moving on to Chalaua He crossed the Mulocque and headed west into the area Ilee-Munevalia. On 8 August the NRP joined 1/3 KAR in Durcol under Colonel CG Durham.

Durcol marched to Alto Ligonha. The situation was confused, but the enemy was apparently moving west. At one stage, the NRP was stranded by lack of food due to a transport breakdown and chicken-pox among the carriers. Durcol was ordered to head off any attempt to make for the Rovuma. The NRP marched through the Inagu Hills and at the end of August was near Maloketera. On 24 August, the enemy successfully engaged half of 2/4 KAR at Namarroe. On 31 August, he was repulsed by 1 and 2KAR at Lioma, but cut through the Inagu Hills. 1/4 KAR and the Rhodesia Native Regiment attempted to bar his passage of the Lurio River and all three battalions of 2KAR (Kartucol) were in hot pursuit. On 11 September, the NRP was ordered to march back to Fort Johnston. In three months they had marched 900 miles, without supply columns, living as best they could, and for much of the time in the sweltering coastal lowlands.

The end game

On 23 September 1918 the NRP moved across Lake Nyasa back to Mbamba Bay in the Songea District of German East Africa where 700 local carriers joined. Von Lettow-Vorbeck was heading north for his home territory. D Company was first to land and set off for Songea under 2/4 KAR. At 1 a.m. on 4 October the weakened NRP battalion, led by Captain RWM Langham's B Company, was approaching Fusi, 15 miles west of Songea, when Sergeant J Sinclair, on patrol, reported that the enemy could be near. Shortly after being overtaken by a Ford van, Langham heard machine-gun fire. Colonel Dickinson tapped into the telephone line and found that the vehicle had arrived at Songea riddled with bullets. Extra flankers and scouts were sent out and the advance continued for a mile before the line was tapped again and found to have been cut. The battalion formed hollow-square with the hospital, in a gravel pit, and stores and carriers in the centre though most of the local carriers soon decamped. Sergeant HM Greenspan was sent forward with a patrol while the rest of B Company, extended each side of the road at three pace intervals and lay down in the long grass with bayonets fixed. Greenspan's patrol soon made contact and was driven back hotly pursued by the enemy who were repulsed by B Company with rapid fire and the bayonet. The enemy main force came up and his attack continued for five and a half hours. Captain 'ANZAC' Mills' mortars put their bombs down just in front of the forward positions. Under heavy fire Colour Sergeant Tegete walked up and down the line giving the men targets and controlling their fire. Sergeant Chikusi set a fine example to his section under heavy machine-gun and rifle fire, encouraging the young Askari. Lieutenant LJ Champion, a pre-war BSAP trooper commissioned from the ranks of the service companies, died of wounds after this action. Privates Siyeya and Mwanabamba were killed and 12 black police wounded with one British NCO and two first-line carriers. One man was missing.

After dark the battalion withdrew to a stronger position but von Lettow-Vorbeck marched by night round the NRP position and made for Peramiho Mission. Lieutenant Cecil Gardiner was sent out with half C Company to find and follow the enemy spoor. The bodies of four enemy Askari were found and two Germans, nine of their Askari and 51 porters captured. Stragglers captured later said that three Germans and nine Askari had been killed and four Germans and twenty Askari wounded.

2/4 KAR closed up from Songea and set off in pursuit still with D Company NRP under command. The remainder of the NRP marched back to the lake shore as it was impossible to supply more than one battalion moving overland. Unfortunately, one of the three steamers chose this time to break down. The NRP had to wait for the last of 1/4 KAR to be ferried north, but on 20 October they were on board ship bound for the head of the Lake.

2/4 KAR engaged the enemy rearguard south of Ubena where they found General Wahle and other enemy sick and wounded in hospital. Von Lettow-Vorbeck still had 1,600 German East

African porters, mainly Wanyamwezi, renowned as the best porters in Africa. They were also brave fighters, providing a mobile recruiting depot from which to make good casualties among his Askari. Other carriers the German commander conscripted as he went along. Where was he going? Tabora seemed the most likely destination. The troops on the Central Railway were strengthened. 1/2 KAR had been shipped up the coast to Dar es Salaam, and railed west. They were now shipped down Lake Tanganyika to Bismarckburg. The route to Elizabethville was watched by a Belgian brigade west of Lake Tanganyika. Northern Rhodesia was devoid of fighting troops. Two KAR battalions were withdrawn to Lindi, to take ship for Beira and entrain for Broken Hill. Whatever the enemy's destination, it was judged that he would first raid the supply depot at Fife. This was the destination of the NRP.

On 24 October, C company, under Captain Allport, landed at Mwaya. He reached Fife at 8 p.m. on 31 October. Major Graham's company, which had come overland with 2/4 KAR, left that battalion at Neu Langenburg and reached Fife at 2.40 p.m. on 1 November. Von Lettow-Vorbeck attacked at 5.30 that afternoon. Graham and Allport had made good use of the time available for entrenching. Reconnaissance showed the German commander that assault would be too costly. He, therefore, decided to merely shell the position. He opened fire the next morning with a Portuguese field-gun, a mortar, which blew up on its second discharge, and ten machine-guns. The defenders gave as good as they got. Private AG Charters BSAP although under heavy fire continued to search the enemy position with his machine-gun temporarily silencing the enemy's fire. When Sergeant AJ Moffat BSAP's emplacement was destroyed, he moved his machine-gun to an adjacent fire bay, eventually silencing the machine-gun opposite him. Private SG Bouwer BSAP, a telegraphist, had been manning an advanced post. When this had to be evacuated he remained close by, tapping out information until he saw an enemy patrol approaching. He retired three miles to a position overlooking Fife and remained, passing back valuable information.

Von Lettow-Vorbeck said that during this action he had his narrowest escape from death. He lay on the ground for half-an-hour while machine-gun fire almost parted the hair on the back of his head. At midnight the wily enemy commander led his troops off south-west for Kasama. Northern Rhodesia was still virtually defenceless.

On 4 November, Colonel Dickinson was making for Fife, when he was told that the Germans had taken Fife and were en route for Kasama. He started south to intercept them when he met an old headman who told him that Fife had not fallen. Dickinson turned back in the hope of catching the enemy at Fife, but they had already gone.

Captain Russell with B Company NRP had joined 1/4 KAR and now led that battalion into Fife. The two battalion commanders agreed that Captain Castor's company of the NRP should also join 1/4 KAR. By nightfall 1/4 KAR had covered 11 miles to Mandala, where the body of a black policeman was found. The Commanding Officer 1/4 KAR was confident that with six companies he could engage the enemy decisively, but higher authority ordered the return of Captain Castor's company to the NRP, which had been ordered to march to Abercorn. Thus weakened 1/4 KAR caught up with the German rearguard at Tumba on 6 November, capturing two machine-guns. The enemy held the water. B Company NRP from reserve made a successful attack enabling the KAR to camp over the water.

Lieutenant Colonel EBB Hawkins, Commanding Officer 1/4 KAR was lucky to have an NRP company with him as he had no map of the area other than in a small atlas. On 7 November, Russell's company ran into the enemy rearguard in a thunderstorm. Four hours later they had driven them out of Kayambi Mission and secured the ridge beyond. On 8 November Lionel Smith, a farmer, offered his services as a guide. Smith had served as a temporary lieutenant in the NRP in 1915. He was able to lead the KAR down the old mail path, 14 miles shorter than the motor road followed to Kasama by von Lettow-Vorbeck.

At Kasama there was only a supply officer, Lieutenant Leslie, with three lorries, eleven NRP African convalescents and some soldiers serving sentences. On 1 November, the European women evacuated from Abercorn reached Kasama. On 2 November, Lieutenant Sibbold 1KAR came in with some KAR recruits. The convalescents and Askari from the gaol were added to his command.

The Native Commissioner, Hector Croad, sent the white women south by lorry and backloaded all cash and ammunition,

30 miles to Chiwutuwutu. From there much of it was removed by canoe to an island in the Bangweulu Swamps. Having evacuated all military and European personnel and such warlike stores and supplies as he could, Croad employed himself on intelligence.

On 8 November a patrol of Askari under Driver Weitz BSAP Motor Transport engaged the enemy twenty miles north of Kasama. Weitz and Mr Thornton, a farmer who had been given command of a patrol on the Abercorn Road, withdrew on Lieutenant Sibbold's position on the Milima Stream, six miles out, where he had a machine-gun. Sibbold sent word to Leslie to burn all remaining stores. At 5 p.m. Croad and Leslie left by motor car. During the night Sibbold's motley band on the Milima lost their nerve and faded away. Next day he managed to get most of them back together. Having regard to the composition of this force, not much could have been expected of it. Most of those from the gaol had been put there for desertion. The convalescents behaved well when under fire on 11 November.

Von Lettow-Vorbeck arrived at Kasama on 9 November. Next morning Hector Croad drove up in a lorry with Sergeant Rumsey. They were halted by trees felled across the road just outside the town. Croad thought the khaki clad troops he could see were KAR and nearly walked in. Just in time Rumsey noticed a gang of black women being taken to draw water under guard. The two Britons returned to Chiwutuwutu by the new motor road while the enemy advance guard was moving in the same direction by the old track.

As much as possible of the supplies at Chiwutuwutu were sent by lorry or canoe another 24 miles to the Chambezi Rubber Factory.

Croad wrote:

> At dusk on 11th November Mr Thornton, who had taken charge of the invalided Northern Rhodesia Police, fell back on Chiwutuwutu. At about 8 o'clock, having sent off the last lorry with loads, we poured petrol over the rest and set fire to the stores. We walked off to the south as the first Germans came in from the north! At about 1 o'clock we were met on the road by Rumsey with one of the lorries. He brought me a wire from the Administrator in Livingstone informing me of the Armistice, but saying that we were to carry on till General van Deventer wired instructions. On reaching the

Chambezi we found two Maxims placed on the south of the river. On the morning of 13th November the German advance patrol started firing into the factory with Lewis guns. They were met by a quite good rattle from the south side, but the Germans were concealed in the trees. After a quarter of an hour firing ceased. About noon I got a wire from van Deventer for Von Lettow. On the morning of the 14th I met General Von Lettow on the Chambezi. He asked me if I would assure him that van Deventer's wire was authentic, and then said he would carry out the instructions to march his men back to Abercorn and lay down his arms there. Von Lettow wrote out a wire to the Kaiser. I told him that Germany was a Republic and that the Kaiser had fled to Holland. He looked upset at this, but said his government would get it in any case. The white prisoners were to be released in Kasama, and in the afternoon Spangenberg handed over their native prisoners. I then returned to Kasama. The main body of the Germans was spread along the road from Chiwutuwutu to Kasama, Hauptmann Kohl told me they were making for Broken Hill, and that if they had reached the railway line they would have destroyed it and followed it north into the Congo, or if they had met a force north of Broken Hill, they might have turned east to Fort Jameson and Nyasaland. Their information as to the country was wonderfully accurate. Most of the native carriers were armed. Guns and ammunition thrown away along the road were brought into Kasama by our own natives. I found three Maxims in the stream below my house in Kasama. The Germans were well equipped with Portuguese and .303 ammunition. The next dry season, when the grass fires started, was like a small battle round Kasama as the cartridges exploded. 'The African Lakes' buildings in Kasama were destroyed by the Germans, who thought they were Government buildings. They had burnt part of the gaol and had made ready to burn the police camp buildings.[9]

1/4 KAR had reached the Milima Stream on 12 November with B Company NRP as its right forward company. Lieutenant Colonel Hawkins was deploying his troops to surround Kasama when at 11.30 a.m. on 13 November a patrol of Askari on the main road reported that two motorcyclists carrying white flags

---

[9] Letter from Hector Croad OBE published in the *East Africa and Rhodesia* Journal in September 1937 quoted in Brelsford, WV, *The story of the Northern Rhodesia Regiment* (1934, reprint Galago 1990) pp. 60-62

had come from the direction of Abercorn, and, in spite of warnings, had gone forward towards the enemy. At 2.42 p.m. the advance point of the battalion, then four miles north of Kasama, met two German Askari with a large white flag, bearing the telegram received from the motorcyclists, announcing the Armistice.

Von Lettow wrote that he was met by one of the motorcyclists, when exploring the Chambezi River and Broken Hill road.

> Spangenberg's detachment, which was on ahead, had to be told as soon as possible, and I immediately set out on my bicycle after it, taking with me Haouter, a Landsturm soldier. About half-way, Weissmann's cyclist patrol of Spangenberg's detachment met me and reported that Captain Spangenberg had arrived at the Chambezi. Our position was very uncomfortable. We were in a district where there was little food, and were therefore compelled to move on from place to place. This circumstance had already compelled us to reconnoitre the crossings of the Chambezi. If hostilities were resumed we must be certain of a safe crossing. This was a burning question, as the rainy season, meaning a great rise of this river, was near. I had, therefore, much to discuss with Captain Spangenberg and the English officer who would be on the far bank of the river. In any case, we must continue to devote our energies to getting food. I cycled with Weissmann's patrol to Spangenberg's detachment. We arrived when it was quite dark. Spangenberg was away on a reconnaissance, but Assistant Paymaster Dohmen and other Europeans looked after me well. I was able to convince myself that the supply depot of Kasama really existed. I tasted jam and other good things. When Captain Spangenberg came back he told me that he had already heard of the armistice through the English. After I had gone to bed, he brought me a telegram from General van Deventer which had been brought in by the English.[10]

This telegram ran as follows:-

> My conditions are: First: hand over all allied prisoners in your hands, Europeans and natives, to the nearest body of British troops forthwith. Second: that you bring your forces to Abercorn without delay, as Abercorn is the nearest place at which I can supply you with food. Third: that you hand over all arms and ammunition to my representative at

---

[10] Von Lettow-Vorbeck, P, *My reminscences of East Africa*, (Hurst & Blackett, 1920)

Abercorn. I will, however allow you and your officers and European ranks to retain their personal weapons for the present in consideration of the gallant fight you have made, provided that you bring your force to Abercorn without delay. Arrangements will be made at Abercorn to send all Germans to Morogoro and to repatriate German Askari.[11]

Von Lettow-Vorbeck's acceptance was handed to Colonel Hawkins on the morning of 16 November. A few hours later the German column marched through the KAR camp for Abercorn.

1/4 KAR and B Company NRP arrived there on the 24th. The rest of the NRP Service Battalion had been at Abercorn since 9 November. Brigadier General WFS Edwards had also arrived to deputise for General van Deventer at the formal surrender. General Edwards had been commanding the troops on the Central Railway in German East Africa. He had been Inspector General of Police in British East Africa and Uganda since 1908.

At 10.30 a.m. on 25 November 1918 General Edwards inspected a guard of honour formed by 25 men from each battalion on the Boma tennis court. At 11 a.m. Major General von Lettow-Vorbeck appeared at the head of his troops. He read out the terms of surrender in German and English. He offered his sword to General Edwards, who refused it.

The enemy troops then grounded their arms and equipment and stacked their machine-guns and ammunition before being marched off. With von Lettow-Vorbeck at the surrender were Doctor Schnee, the Governor General of German East Africa, 29 officers, 125 white other ranks, 1,168 Askari, 1,522 native carriers and 819 women.

On 26 November the NRP played 1/4 KAR at football. Neither team scored. On 16 December demobilisation commenced.

Von Lettow-Vorbeck embarked for Europe on 17 January 1919. The German commander had spoken highly of the fighting qualities of the Northern Rhodesia Police, or as his native troops had described them to distinguish them from the Rhodesia Native Regiment, 'The Old Askari'.

During the war 1,839 blacks had served with the NRP, of whom more than 100 died including nine between the surrender and 13 January 1919. Northern Rhodesia had provided 1,340 recruits for the KAR and some 260 joined the Rhodesia Native

---

[11] Von Lettow-Vorbeck, P, *Reminscences*

Regiment. In addition, Northern Rhodesia supplied nearly 200,000 carriers. More than 40,000 served outside the territory; 24,000 as First Line Transport. Nearly 9,000 served on the Ndola-Kabunda route and 11,000 women served within Northern Rhodesia. As far as possible no man was kept away from his village for more than six months at a time, but some 2,000 lost their lives and 121 were wounded in action.

© Kevin Patience

SMS *Königsberg*

HMS *Pegasus*

© Kevin Patience

Some naval aspects

'Strike the Colours': The loss of HMS *Pegasus* at Zanzibar, 20 September 1914

Kevin Patience[1]

HMS *Pegasus* was one of a class of ten warships built by a number of shipyards in the United Kingdom in the late 19th century. For some inexplicable reason, the Admiralty gave the builders carte blanche to install boilers of their own design which resulted in some ships suffering from mechanical troubles, such that by 1904 two of the class had been withdrawn from service. I researched the builders, Palmers of Newcastle and discovered that *Pegasus* had been fitted with Reed boilers. This was unusual as most ships at the time were fitted with Thorneycroft or other well-known boilers, but Reed was in fact the chief engineer of the yard. The ship served on a number of overseas stations until 1913 when she was allocated to the Cape Squadron based in Simonstown, South Africa.

Pegasus was the smallest of three cruisers comprising the squadron under the command of Vice Admiral Herbert King-Hall. HMS *Hyacinth* was the largest at 5,500 tons, *Astraea* displaced 4,000 tons and *Pegasus* 2,300 tons. *Hyacinth* was armed with six-inch guns as was *Astraea* on the foredeck with smaller guns on the side. *Pegasus* rated as a Third Class cruiser was armed with four-inch guns. All three were well past their sell-by date and only capable of about 16 knots. In fact, when Admiral Jackie Fisher took command of the Royal Navy around 1904, he put a pen through the names of some of these nineteenth-century ships and said, 'scrap the lot'. However, it

---

[1] Kevin Patience is the author of *Königsberg – A German East African Raider* (Zanzibar, 2001), *Zanzibar and the Loss of HMS Pegasus* (Patience, 1996) and *Shipwrecks and Salvage the East African Coast* (Patience, 2018 reprint)

was pointed out that many of the ships were in foreign stations around the world still doing a good job. It was felt that because these three ships were based in South Africa, that their poor performance was not a crucial aspect of their operation. A strange directive dictated they would burn Natal coal with a high sulphur content which did little to improve performance. An extraordinary situation considering good quality Welsh steam coal was available. They patrolled an area which extended from St Helena around South Africa up the East African coast to Zanzibar and Pemba.

On 6 June 1914, the balance of sea-power in the region changed dramatically with the arrival of the German cruiser *Königsberg* under the command of Fregattenkapitän Max Looff at the port of Dar es Salaam. Its arrival brought thousands of natives to see this sleek three funnelled warship, nicknamed '*Manowari wa bomba tatu*' which translates from the Swahili as '*the warship with three tubes*'. The natives believed that a ship with three tubes had to be better than a ship with two tubes, so it was superior to the twin funnelled *Astraea* and *Pegusus*. Built in 1905 it was armed with ten four-inch Krupp guns with a range of seven miles. The *Pegasus* with almost the same calibre guns only had a range of five miles. The reason, I later discovered following some dives on the *Pegasus* wreck, was the shorter shell cases. The *Königsberg* shell case was at least a third longer.

It was not long after the ship's arrival that Looff took colonists and locals alike on trips to sea for the day as well as visiting the ports of Bagamoyo, Lindi and Tanga. This peaceful existence ended on 31 July while the ship was at sea for gunnery practice. Around midday Looff was ordered back to port to coal. The German admiralty aware of the worsening political situation in Europe decided to send the cruiser to sea should war break out and the ship be trapped in the port. With a full load of 800 tons of coal the ship had a range of around 5,500 miles at 12 knots. However, any increase in speed would result in an enormous consumption of coal and a decrease in range to around 1,500 miles. It was *Königsberg*'s Achilles' heel. That afternoon, Looff left around 4.30 p.m. and headed out to sea and coincidently met HMS *Hyacinth*, *Astrea* and *Pegasus* heading for Zanzibar to coal. Because Britain was not at war the three ships turned and followed *Königsberg*. This was an embarrassing situation as both Looff and King-Hall were aware war was likely. Looff gave orders to the chief engineer to fire up all twelve boilers without making smoke giving him the option of his maximum speed of twenty-four knots. About an hour later Looff called for 'full speed' and at a speed of twenty-four knots, turned the ship through 180 degrees and back-tracked between the three ships. He was partly obscured by a squall at the time and King-Hall was horrified to see *Königsberg* coming towards him at a closing speed of forty knots and disappear into the distance.

The manoeuvre burnt a huge quantity of coal leaving Looff to reduce speed to ten knots while *Königsberg* made its way north to the Gulf of Aden. Here on the evening of 6 August she captured the British ship, *City of Winchester* carrying the first of the season's tea crop from India to London. Its loss not only had a large impact on the tea market, but also alerted the authorities as to where *Königsberg* was. All shipping between Aden and the Sub-continent was halted and Looff was forced to conserve coal while looking for a new victim. Fortunately, the Germans despatched the collier *Somali* to rendezvous with the cruiser off the Somaliland coast. It had crossed Looff's mind that if he ran out of coal his only option was to scuttle the ship and put the crew ashore to become prisoners-of-war. He would not let *Königsberg* fall into British hands. After refuelling, Looff headed south for Madagascar in the hope of destroying French shipping. The port of Majunga was empty and short of fuel, he once again met *Somali* at Aldabra Island and transferred the remaining coal. There was insufficient to continue as a raider leaving him with no option but to seek shelter in the Rufiji River, a hundred miles south of Dar es Salaam.

As far as the British were concerned, the Rufiji River delta was an unnavigable swamp and it was highly unlikely that a vessel of this size could get up the river. Both ships, *Königsberg* and *Somali* anchored at Salale on 3 September where word was passed to Dar es Salaam to supply coal. Over the next two weeks coal was shipped to the cruiser and Looff planned to return to Germany via the Cape of Good Hope and capture allied vessels in order to top-up his bunkers. On the afternoon of the 19th, word was received of a twin-funnelled cruiser at anchor in Zanzibar. Looff knew it would be either HMS *Astraea* or *Pegasus*. Not wishing to miss an opportunity to strike at the enemy he announced they would sail that afternoon for Zanzibar with Captain Herm of the *Somali* acting as pilot. That night they sailed slowly up the coast and arrived in Zanzibar at around 5 a.m.

Long days of steaming on poor quality coal and a problem engine prompted Commander John Alexander Ingles, Captain of *Pegasus* to anchor in Zanzibar for repairs and to also allay the fears of the locals, as Zanzibar is only twenty miles off the coast of German East Africa.[2]

At 05.10 a.m. *Königsberg* opened fire with five guns. The first salvo passed over the ship, the second struck home. Within eight minutes *Pegasus* was severely damaged with two gun crews killed. *Königsberg* was out of range of the *Pegasus* guns although they were of similar calibre. Looff had the advantage of an extra two miles range. What happened next went down in history as Ingles ordered the striking of the colours and the flying of a white flag of surrender. The last time this happened was during the American war of 1812 when a number of smaller British ships surrendered to a more powerful enemy. Although the Germans publicised the event with a number of post cards, a scandal of this nature within the Royal Navy at the time was unthinkable and the British Admiralty quickly portrayed the incident in a different light.

A series of paintings were published in a book called *Deeds that thrill the Empire*,[3] showing a sailor holding the white ensign up. The story was that one of *Königsberg's* shells had ripped the flag off its mast and that a young Royal Marine ran forward and held the ensign up, and when he was shot down, another ran forward and so on. In reality, only three Royal Marines were killed and they were likely to have been gun crew who died during the bombardment.

In the 1970s, I dived the wreck and wrote a letter to the *Navy News* asking for information on the sinking. An 80-year old gentleman, John Williams, responded. He had been wounded aboard *Pegasus* at the time of the sinking. I asked him about the white flag and he responded that it never happened. John went

---

[2] At the time Zanzibar was managed as part of British East Africa (Kenya), along with a strip of coast land the Sultan had agreed to share with the British and Germans respectively.

[3] Various, *Deeds that thrill the Empire: true Stories of the Most Glorious Acts of Heroism of the Empire's Soldiers and Sailors during the Great War* (nd reprint).

to his grave, never telling a soul about the incident. Two days after the event on 22 September 1914 when the crew had all been brought ashore, Ingles told them that nobody was to ever mention the white flag incident.

It took ten years of investigating to find a letter in The National Archives (London) written by Ingles which stated *'Gentlemen, I regret to advise that I struck the colours on the morning of 20 September'*. Under these circumstances a court-martial is held to establish the loss. Ingles was not court-martialled and in due course received a letter closing the matter and was placed in charge of the Zanzibar Defence Force. He had little option with the ship being destroyed around him.

With the departure of *Königsberg*, crews from a neighbouring ship ferried the dead and wounded ashore. That afternoon twenty-four bodies were buried on Grave Island in a mass grave while others were buried in the town cemetery. Later that morning the Port Officer had the *Pegasus* towed from its anchorage towards Malindi Spit where it was going to be beached, but tide and wind delayed the operation and the ship sank at 14.30 leaving its masts above the water.

There is a classic photograph of the *Pegasus* taken about midday sinking by the bows with apparent little damage to the superstructure. This has always led me to believe the ship wasn't as badly damaged as reported in the press. Both funnels and all the engine and boiler room ventilators are still upright and the canvas spray dodger around the bridge is still intact indicating the fire had burnt out without causing serious damage.

In 1971 the Zanzibar government began a building program in town which included a road through the cemetery. The Commonwealth War Graves Commission exhumed all the military burials including those from *Pegasus* and reburied them in the Dar es Salaam war cemetery. The Grave Island burials remain as they were.

After leaving Zanzibar, *Königsberg* had a major engine failure and returned to the Rufiji Delta. Within weeks the cruiser was discovered and blockaded for eight months until a combined naval air and sea operation damaged the vessel on 11 July 1915 and Looff scuttled the ship. All the four-inch guns were salvaged and went on to see action in the land campaign under Colonel von Lettow-Vorbeck.

England Expects: Naval Action in Nyasaland

Peter Charlton[1]

The first naval action on Lake Nyasa took place ten days after war was declared.
An intelligence report of 1912 by Captain Heath noted:

> There is only one German vessel on the Lake, the *Wiessman* [sic]. It would appear imperative to sink or capture this steamer. Although we have a preponderance of ships, the result of a struggle for the command of [the] Lake would depend on whether the armament of the *Weissman* were superior or inferior to that of the British gunboats. If we could retain the command of the Lake we would have nothing to fear from the superior numbers of the Germans.[2]

The lake was an important highway leading from the north to the south of the territory as the road system was poorly developed.

The *Guendolen* had a 3-pounder Hotchkiss gun and two Nordenfelt machine-guns.[3] She was named after Guendolen Cecil, the daughter of Lord Salisbury, a Prime Minister in England just before war.

Commander EL Rhoades of the *Guendolen* was reported as having a good working knowledge of the guns and that fifteen natives had been drilled in the use of the guns and were no longer in the marine department but were living in the area and

---

[1] Peter Charlton is the author of *Cinderella's Soldiers: A history of the Nyasaland Volunteer Reserve, its formation and the part it played in the First World War* (Charlton, 2010, reprint GWAA, 2018)

[2] Heath, Capt LM, An appreciation of the military situation in Nyasaland, 10 October 1912 (National Archive of Malawi, Zomba)

[3] A *Guendolen* gun was recently found outside the Police headquarters in Zomba.

that there were another thirteen who had knowledge of the guns.

Guendolen's adversary on the lake was the *Hermann von Wissmann*. She had a 1-pounder quick firing Hotchkiss gun mounted on the bow and was felt to be more than a match for the *Guendolen* as she had a better field of fire and the gun had a longer range. The *Guendolen*'s gun had a superstructure in front of it so it could only fire one side or the other. The gun from the *Wissmann* ended up on the *Chauncy Maples*, another British boat on the Lake.

GM Sanderson, a medical officer, who actually sailed on the *Guendolen* left a very full account of the action, but he wrote it about forty years later so his memory may have been faulty in places. The account is pretty good especially as you will not find much else on the action. PD Bishop, the clerk at Fort Johnston had a diary which is very disappointing with only a couple of lines about the action. The Official History records that when war broke out, the British immediately called the vessels to the Bar at Fort Johnston as they were concerned the *Wissmann* might capture one or more of them, arm them and use them back against the British.[4] The British vessels were *Pioneer, Queen Victoria, Chauncy Maples* and *Guendolen*.

Fort Johnston is right in the south, in the top right hand corner is the German border and about half way down was the German harbour, Sphinxhaven (Liuli) from where the *Wissmann* sailed. There were very good relationships between the British and Germans working together to transport goods along the lake.

When war was declared, the *Guendolen* was summoned under Rhoades to go up the lake to destroy the *Wissmann*. They had heard that the *Wissmann* was undergoing repairs but were not sure whether these were general repairs or having another gun fitted. In the meantime, they prepared the *Guendolen* to get her ready for war. The first problem they had was that they could not find any ammunition for her at all. Bishop, the Stores Clerk, dug around and eventually found a box marked 'spares' which had some ammunition in. They then had to find someone to fire the gun despite a 1912 report on the Hotchkiss gun which

---

[4] Charles Hordern, *Official History: Military operations East Africa, August 1914-September 1916* vol 1 (1941) pp. 169-170

stated that trained staff were available. The 1912 report indicated that they had 3,920 rounds of ammunition dated 1896 and 1897 which was useless. They had a further 2,800 rounds of black practice ammunition which was unreliable but nothing was done to replace it. Eventually one of the African Lake Corporation employees, a Scotsman called Jock, claimed to know something about guns from service in the Royal Navy so he was employed right away as the gun layer. Twenty-five Askari from the King's African Rifles were designated marines and a few white officers were put on board to go into action with the *Wissmann*.

The orders were quite strange. HG Collins, the King's African Rifles officer, had orders to remove parts of the *Wissmann* but not to destroy her in case they wanted to re-use her later. Rhoades' orders were a classic piece of contradiction.

> The *Guendolen* will proceed with caution and instructions have been issued for her not to risk an encounter which might prove disastrous to her, but if it is ascertained that the *Wissmann* is still undergoing repairs endeavour will be made to put her out of service, unless Sphinxhaven is too strongly defended.[5]

They went up to the top of the lake to Nkata Bay on the English side where Rhoades confirmed that the *Wissmann* was in Sphinxhaven—the rock looks a bit like a sphinx, thus the name. The *Guendolen* sailed on the night of 12 August, two weeks after war was declared. They sailed at half speed to keep the sound down as it travels very clearly across water at night. Sailing down the coast, Jock, the gun layer remarked that there was a multitude of fires along the coast on the German side. It looked as though the whole German army was out waiting for them. They had no idea what to expect. It turned out later that the fires were in native villages where they were burning the debris from harvesting their crops. This had caused concern for the men as their vessels were rather fragile.

As the *Guendolen* arrived in Sphinxhaven at about 4 a.m., they fixed bayonets ready for action. They could see the *Wissmann* on the slipway and attacked her. They later found that she had six plates removed from the base so she could not do anything anyway—she was demobilised, but they had not

---

[5] Duff, H, *African Small Chop*, (Hodder & Stoughton, 1932) p. 63.

known that. They came round and at 2,000 yards opened fire. What rounds were fired that were not dud, with the rolling vessel, went over the boat into the bush behind. At the last minute, Jock managed to land one of the shells on the slipway and at about the same time, a small white dinghy put off from the shore. Rhoades ordered "Ceasefire" and the infuriated captain of the *Wissmann*, clad in a singlet and shorts, stormed onto the *Guendolen's* deck. Shaking both fists over his head he screamed the immortal words "Gott for dam, Rhoades, vos you dronk!' The poor man did not know that war had been declared and was captured there and then along with his German engineer and four Indian artificers who were on the vessel.

The King's African Rifles then picketed the ridge. As there was a little fort above the bay which was not manned, the King's African Rifles fortified it just in case of attack. They then looted the *Wissmann*, taking the engine, her gun and mountings and a few other bits and pieces. They had immobilised her for all intents and purposes and sailed away. Eleven days later Rhoades was removed from command of the lake and the *Guendolen*, probably a little unfairly but he seemed a difficult character. The reason given was that he would not cooperate fully with the military and as they were commanding the operations, they had the final say.

In October, one of the vessels, *Adventure*, steamed into Sphinxhaven and did some more looting and in November, the *Pioneer* did the same.

Shortly after, Lieutenant-Commander Dennistoun came down from East Africa and took over from Rhoades. He had been seconded from the *Fox* which had been blockading the East African coast. He came down with a couple of officers, six ratings and five 6-pounder Hotchkiss guns. The Hotchkiss guns had been taken off the *Pegasus* which had been sunk in Zanzibar harbour by the *Koenigsberg*. Dennistoun had two of the guns mounted on the *Guendolen*. The gun at Fort Mangoche is a *Pegasus* 6-pounder, not the one which fired on the *Wissmann*. The others were mounted on carriages and used in the land battle against Lettow-Vorbeck.

Late in May 1915, a rumour went around that the *Wissmann* was being repaired and a bigger gun being put onto her for re-launching. The lake was the means of communication and would be the highway for Northey when he started his campaign. Loading 200 men from the King's African Rifles and Nyasaland Volunteer Reserve onto the *Guendolen* and *Chauncy Maples*, the British sailed up to Sphinxhaven. They landed about half-a-mile away, stormed up and attacked the harbour again. The fort was in readiness this time and reports later suggest that it was actually manned by a German missionary in the *schutztruppe* and about 13 Askaris. They put up a spirited defence, suffered a couple of deaths and retreated. The troops swarmed over the area, dynamited the *Wissmann* and blew a hole in her hull so she could not be repaired. They also put holes in the slipway so she could not be launched. This was in effect the end of the more important naval actions, but rumours of her repair continued. The British again went up on 27 April 1916. They tried to land troops but were fired upon by a large German contingent so packed their bags and left. About the same time, Bishop was sent to Likomo Island to fortify it as there were rumours that the Germans were building a torpedo boat. This marked the end of the lake campaign as Northey took command and the British occupied the German part of the lake too.

Ironically, towards the end of the war, the *Wissmann* was repaired and served until being scrapped in the 1950s. She was named *George V*. One thinks had the British destroyed her right at the beginning they would have saved much trouble.

'Danes' at War in East Africa: The Case of the Blockade Runner SS *Kronborg*

Bjarne S Bendtsen[1]

Since the German occupation of Denmark during the Second World War, the First World War has been a neglected topic in Danish popular memory and historiography—and the war in East Africa even more so. This general lack of interest in the First World War was, however, not what you found during the war and the interwar era, when numerous books on the topic were published in neutral Denmark: history books, propaganda pamphlets, war novels and poems, and not least collections of soldiers' letters, which were published in many different volumes during and immediately after the war.[2] During the interwar years, accounts of the war in Africa were published in Danish, and one of these was among the most widely-read of the war books: journalist and author Christen P Christensen's *Sønderjyder forsvarer Østafrika 1914-1918* (1937). The book was based on the Schleswig Dane Nis Kock's journals about his experiences aboard the blockade runner SS *Kronborg* and with von Lettow-Vorbeck's troops in German East Africa; a fairly big success with six impressions during the year of its publication. Several other books and articles were published in Danish about 'Danes' serving aboard the blockade runners and fighting for Germany in East Africa. The present chapter tells the story of the *Kronborg* as narrated in *Sønderjyder forsvarer Østafrika* and other books, and examines the way the secret mission was

---

[1] Bjarne S Bendtsen, independent scholar. His first book, *Mellem fronterne. Første Verdenskrigs aftryk i dansk litteratur og kultur 1914-1939* was published in 2018.

[2] The most famous and best-selling example was edited by Harald Nielsen, *Sønderjyske Soldaterbreve* (Copenhagen, 1916) which came in 16 editions. This book contains no letters from North Schleswigers fighting in Africa; quite expectedly, as they were not able to send letters home due to the Allied blockade.

treated in these Danish books and articles as well as in German books on the topic.

The 'Danes' in East Africa

'Danes' is in inverted commas since this largely Danish-speaking crew as well as many other Danish speaking and pro-Danish soldiers in the German army were Prussian citizens at the time. Since the 1864 war between Denmark and Prussia/Austria, which Denmark lost, and which led to the country's cession of Schleswig and Holstein to Prussia, there had been a large Danish minority in what became the German Empire by 1871. This is important background for the somewhat strange story at hand: that quite a number of 'Danes' wound up fighting for Germany in German East Africa during the Great War, even though Denmark managed to remain neutral throughout the war. The 1864 war is certainly not the topic of this chapter, but is an absolutely necessary context to address. Lord Palmerstone's famous anecdote about the situation in the region can be used as a reason for *not* going into any depth of it:

> The Schleswig-Holstein question is so complicated, only three men in Europe have ever understood it. One was Prince Albert, who is dead. The second was a German professor who became mad. I am the third and I have forgotten all about it.[3]

To avoid this complicated situation, a less complicated formula will suffice: because of the Danish defeat in the 1864 war, some 26,000 men of Danish allegiance fought for Germany in the First World War, and about 5,200 of these men lost their lives.[4]

---

[3] See for example the article 'Schleswig-Holstein question' in Nicholas Atkin, Michael Biddiss & Frank Tallett (eds), *The Wiley-Blackwell Dictionary of Modern European History Since 1789* (Blackwell, 2011) 10 May 2013 http://www.blackwell reference.com/subscriber/tocnode.html?id=g9781405189224_chunk_g978140518 922420_ss1-20

[4] Exact numbers for participants and casualties are difficult to calculate – who was 'Danish', who was not, in which contexts? A convincing calculation is offered in Claus Bundgård Christensen, *Danskere på Vestfronten 1914-1918* (2009) pp. 11-2 and fn p. 496, based on Karl Alnor, *Handbuch zur schleswigschen Frage*, vol II (1929) and articles by Jørgen Kühl and Jens Ødegaard, 'Dansksindede sønderjyske krigsdeltagere og faldne i Første Verdenskrig' in *Sønderjyske Årbøger* (1990) and Martin Bo Nørregaard, 'Sønderjyder ved fronterne' in Inge Adriansen & Hans Schultz Hansen (eds), *Sønderjyderne og Den store Krig 1914-1918* (2006)

Nevertheless, 'Danish' could—and should—also refer to actual Danish citizens since a few of these fought on the other side in East Africa: most notably in Belgian Congo, where Frederik Valdemar Olsen, the future General Olsen, led the Belgian troops beating the British to conquer Tabora in the west of German East Africa in September 1916.[5] There was also at least one volunteer for the British: in one of the popular Danish collections of soldiers' letters, you can find a couple of letters from, and about, Jens Peter Jensen from Copenhagen. He was seriously burned in late September or early October 1916 when the Germans had set the bush on fire as Sigrid M Gliemann from the Scandinavian Mission at Limoru, British East Africa, wrote to his parents while he was a convalescent there.[6] And finally, the famous Danish author Karen Blixen transported munitions for the British in British East Africa,[7] where she had found her coffee farm in 1914 before the war broke out. She was, furthermore, a friend of Lettow-Vorbeck's, to make things even more complicated.[8] But Olsen, Jensen and Blixen are not the topic of this chapter.

The adventurous voyage of the SS Kronborg

It is the story of the first German blockade runner SS *Kronborg*'s voyage from Wilhelmshaven to German East Africa in 1915. The *Kronborg*, also known as the British steamer *Rubens*, had been seized by the Germans in Hamburg at the beginning of the war. The voyage and the story of the 'Danes' at war in East Africa has been the topic of a handful of Danish books and articles, on which this chapter is based. A second *Sperrbrecher*, or blockade runner, *Marie*, which in 1916 ran the British blockades used a similar strategy as the *Kronborg*— masked as a neutral Danish merchant steamer—has also been the topic of some books and articles. This chapter will, however, concentrate on the case of the *Kronborg* and two of the Danish-

---

[5] See for example Byron Farwell, *The Great War in Africa 1914-1918* (1987) pp. 286-9, or Klaus Winkel, *Danskere i tropisk Afrika – fra slavehandler til bistandsarbejder* (2011) p. 38

[6] J Ravn-Jonsen, *Danske Frivillige i Verdenskrigen. Soldaterbreve fra Fronterne* (1917) pp. 148-54

[7] Errol Trzebinski, *Silence will speak* (1985) pp. 166-7

[8] See Farwell, *The Great War in Africa*, pp. 105-7, 120

speaking participants aboard the ship on her adventurous voyage, who published memoirs about their war in Africa. The case of the second *Sperrbrecher* will be left for later.

The *Kronborg* left the German North Sea naval base Wilhelmshaven in all secrecy on a foggy afternoon, 18 January 1915. A false wooden funnel and other parts of the ship's construction, meant to mislead possible spies at Wilhelmshaven, were removed in open sea and burned in the boiler; the crew's uniforms, sent back with a torpedo boat returning the pilot who had guided the steamer out of Wilhelmshaven, had been replaced with civilian seamen's clothes in which, Kock remembers, they even found Danish discharge books. There were pictures on the cabin walls of Danish icons such as the castle Kronborg and the Danish king and queen, and thus, the ship now was the Danish steamer SS *Kronborg*[9]—the name of a real Danish steamer present at dock in Copenhagen at the time.[10] The goal of the mission, which had been kept a secret even to the crew, was then revealed by Captain Carl Christiansen: German East Africa with coal and ammunition for the light cruiser SMS *Königsberg* and for von Lettow-Vorbeck's troops.[11]

The course was set due north, along the Danish west coast, and the plan was to run the British blockade going north of the Faeroe Islands.[12] However, the *Kronborg* did not follow the intended route between Iceland and the Faeroe Islands, but went south of the Islands because of a heavy storm off the Norwegian coast that nearly wrecked the ship; a storm that made the British blockade ships unable to keep an efficient lookout.[13] Here, it lost some of its deck cargo—timber disguising the actual cargo carried by the ship—and one of the funnels.

From this dramatic point of the mission, they sailed in calm waters off the normal routes in the Atlantic to avoid contact with other ships. In the Bay of Biscay, however, they met a

---

[9] Chr P Christensen, *Sønderjyder forsvarer Østafrika 1914-1918* (1937) pp. 19-31
[10] See Die Kapitäne Christiansen. *Nach Lochbüchern erzählt* (1933) pp. 124-6
[11] For the content of the cargo, see Farwell, *The Great War in Africa*, p. 139
[12] This route is incorrectly drawn on a map in Anker Nissen, *Sønderjylland Afrika tur retur. Anker Nissens oplevelser som tysk soldat i Afrika under den første Verdenskrig* (1962) p. 24
[13] See Die Kapitäne Christiansen, pp. 126-8

squadron of French destroyers, but passed them without causing suspicion—even saluting with the Danish flag which resulted in considerable amusement among the crew of the *Kronborg* as Christensen wrote.[14] Eventually, they rounded the Cape of Good Hope and reached the waters off German East Africa without being caught by British naval vessels. But then, things went wrong: at one of the Seychelles islands, the *Kronborg* was awaiting a wireless message from the *Königsberg* about where to meet the cruiser in open seas. The British, however, intercepted and deciphered this message and intensified their patrol of the sea off the Rufiji delta, thus blocking the *Königsberg*'s attempt at breaking out and meeting the *Kronborg* in open seas. The *Kronborg* instead steered for Tanga to unload the cargo there, but was discovered and chased by the British cruiser *Hyacinth*, which attacked and destroyed the steamer at Mansa Bay. Yet, either by chance and British negligence or by a cunning scheme of Captain Christiansen's— deliberately sinking the ship in shallow waters by opening the sea cocks while setting the remaining lumber on the deck of the *Kronborg* on fire, and thereby deluding the *Hyacinth* into believing that the steamer had been sunk[15]—most of the valuable cargo was saved. This was quite miraculous, when the quantity of explosives is taken into account: Captain Christiansen mentions the nervousness about being aboard a ship with 100 tons of explosives while being shelled by a British cruiser.[16] But the ship did not explode and during the next couple of months, the crew of *Kronborg*, divers from the *Königsberg* and local porters salvaged the most important goods from the wreck.

Heizer Nis Kock

Nis Kock (1892-1965) came from Sønderborg on the island Als north-east of Flensburg. He had already been through his military training before the war, aboard the SMS *Roon* in 1910-11, and was consequently called up at the beginning of the war. Yet, he was not sent directly to the front. During autumn

---

[14] Christensen, *Sønderjyder forsvarer Østafrika*, pp. 53-4
[15] The latter version can be found in Christensen, *Durch!*, p. 51 and, based on Christiansen's description, Christensen, *Sønderjyder forsvarer Østafrika*, pp. 80-5, whereas the former can be found in Farwell, *The Great War in Africa*, pp. 140-4
[16] Christensen, *Durch!* p. 51

1914, while he was stationed at Kiel, he was worried about being sent to Flanders, where many marine soldiers served. Instead he was picked for the secret mission with the *Rubens/ Kronborg*, or 'Sp A': Sperrbrecher A, as was its initial name, and ordered to leave Kiel for Wilhelmshaven in January 1915.[17]

He was a highly skilled machinist and worked as a stoker aboard the *Kronborg*. After arriving in Africa, and the wrecking of the *Kronborg*, he played an active role in salvaging the munitions from the ship and was eventually transferred to the German *schutztruppe* in East Africa. He was attached to the munitions company, fixing the partly ruined cartridges and grenades salvaged from the *Kronborg* and the salt water of Mansa Bay, altering the size of captured British grenades to fit German guns, and later on he produced improvised land-mines on the march with von Lettow-Vorbeck's troops while they were being chased by the British. He led large safaris, carrying ammunition through the bush and jungle. During the latter part of his participation, he brought a portable lathe for mine production purposes and for altering the size of shells.

After the rough landing at Mansa Bay, he went to Mpapua in the Uluguru Mountains to recover from his first attacks of malaria after working hard on the salvaging of the cargo. Then he spent about a year in Dar es Salaam, after which his safari started: going to Morogoro, Kissaki, Kungulio, and staying with the troops at the Rufiiji delta. Then further south, across the river, to Logologe, Liwale, Nangano, Ruponda, and finally he was left behind at Nambindinga.

Thus, he did not take much part in direct fighting, but nevertheless got wounded when a mine he was assembling exploded in his face which eventually in 1925, resulted in the loss of his right eye. Apart from this, he contracted chronic malaria[18]—as most Europeans did in the unsound Rufiji area, where he spent the winter 1916-17. Malaria, he says, was a much more dangerous enemy than the British,[19] and eventually malaria led to the end of his participation in Lettow-Vorbeck's

---
[17] Kock's story is based on Christensen, *Sønderjyder forsvarer Østafrika*
[18] See Kocks's file from the Danish board for invalid veterans in the German army: Invalidenævnet for De Sønderjyske Landsdele, Landsarkivet for Sønderjylland, Aabenraa: I-akter 1921-1990
[19] Christensen, *Sønderjyder forsvarer Østafrika*, p. 171

campaign when he and a couple of thousand other German soldiers and carriers, wounded or suffering too severely from disease, were left behind at Nambindinga in the south of German East Africa in November 1917 and subsequently became British prisoners. After he was taken prisoner by the British, he was first interned at Dar es Salaam and then, in January 1918, moved to the Sidi Bishr prisoner-of-war camp in Egypt where he was to stay for nearly two years. Here, despite prisoners' complaints about only eating rice and the mentally hard inactivity of the internee, they also managed to do some sight-seeing—to the pyramids and the sphinx—and Kock made friends with a Sergeant Fischer from London, who arranged it so that the two of them could go swimming in the Mediterranean once a week. They even kept in touch after the war.[20]

Upon his and his comrades' arrival in Egypt, in a quarantine camp, they were clad in prisoners' uniforms. Kock's friend and fellow stoker from the *Kronborg*, Peter Hansen, commented on their many instances of slogging during the war:

> Nis, now we are changing our appearance for the fourth time in this war. The first time was when we put on the naval uniform, the second time when we entered the *Kronborg* and changed back to mufti, then when we put on the khaki uniform in German East Africa, and now we are going to wear these most unsuitable prisoner's togs.[21]

During his time in East Africa, Kock won the Iron Cross, second class, as his membership card from the organisation of Danish veterans from the German army, DSK, states.[22] But what seems to have made a far bigger and lasting impression on him was Africa itself: the nature, wildlife and hunting, the people and their ways, exotic things like the rhythmic dancing all night to the monotonous ngoma drum, and especially his loyal 'boys',

---

[20] See Nis Kock, *Sønderjyder vender hjem fra Østafrika. Fra Krig og Fangenskab til Frihed og Fred* (1938) pp. 61,107-8, 113

[21] Nis Kock, *Sønderjyder vender hjem fra Østafrika. Fra Krig og Fangenskab til Frihed og Fred* (1938) p. 52, 'Nis, nu skifter vi for fjerde Gang vort Udseende i denne Krig. Første Gang, da vi trak i Marineuniformen, anden Gang, da vi ombord paa *Kronborg* blev civile igen, derefter i Khakiuniform i Tysk Østafrika og nu skal vi bære et højst uklædeligt Fangekluns.'

[22] Dansksindede sønderjydske Krigsdeltagere (DSK) membership card index, Landsarkivet for Sønderjylland, Aabenraa, DSK Medlemskartotek 1936-1950, archive number: SBAC107/5a

Ramasan and Hassan.[23] Kock's war was, as this brief outline clearly indicates, not at all typical, but it was so adventurous that *Sønderjyder forsvarer Østafrika* became a minor bestseller when it was published in 1937. Nis Kock himself wrote a sequel to the book in 1938, telling the rest of his story from the time of his capture by the British, the internment in Egypt and the voyage back to Denmark in 1919.

A quote from Christensen's preface to *Sønderjyder forsvarer Østafrika* describes Kock's character and the reaction to the war by the Danish minority in North Schleswig—or Southern Jutland as has been the preferred term in Denmark since the armistice and the consequent reunion of North Schleswig with Denmark.[24] Here from the English translation:

> These reminiscences then, tell the story of an ordinary man, and moreover one whose life in East Africa turned out differently from those of the other fifty odd South Jutlanders, but it seems to me to give fine expression to a whole people's courage, devotion to duty and ready sacrifice in the service of a foreign Power.[25]

Sønderjyder forsvarer Østafrika ends with the surrender of Kock and many other German soldiers at the Rovuma River before Lettow-Vorbeck entered the Portuguese colony Mozambique and fought there and in Northern Rhodesia until after the armistice had been signed in Europe. The surrender of the sick German troops is commented in the following semi-gothic way:

> Then one of the sick men raised his head and began to laugh: and more joined in, laughing. 'The General,' shout-ed a voice in broken English, 'the General's gone to hell!' The great surrender at Nambindinga took place on November 18th, 1917. Round about in that huge camp lay many South Jutlanders from *Kronborg*, but we first saw each other many days later on the way to Lindi.[26]

---

[23] Kock published other stories about his time in Africa, eg 'Som Krøsus i Afrika' in DSK *Aarbog 1941*, pp. 66-69, and 'Ramasan' in DSK *Aarbog 1942*, pp. 96-106. DSK *Aarbog* was the annual publication from the veterans' organisation, published between 1941 and 1972.

[24] The 1920 plebiscites about national belonging in Schleswig has been termed a reunion in Denmark; the correct term, as eg professor Uffe Østergaard often has pointed out, is the partition of Schleswig.

[25] Christen P Christensen, *Blockade and Jungle* (1941) p. 9

[26] Christensen, *Blockade and Jungle*, p. 255

In a short postscript, Christensen sums up Kock's story after the surrender in a few lines, and lists the names of the entire crew so that they will not be forgotten—with their real addresses, the author says: as opposed to the ones on the muster roll of the *Kronborg*. Nine of the 31 men aboard had died: three from malaria; two shortly after returning back home, but with no cause of death stated; one during imprisonment in India; two fell in action in East Africa; and one died of a snake bite.

The postscript also mentions that when Kock, at some point after their return home, went to Berlin to have his military papers dealt with the Spartakists shouted 'guardsmen of Noske' at the men who had fought in East Africa. Prior to that, and as a much more positive experience, Kock, Peter Hansen and another 'Dane' Lauritz Hansen were among those who disembarked from the Danish cruiser *Valkyrien* at Langelinie in Copenhagen on 10 September 1919. Another member of the *Kronborg* crew who returned from the war in East Africa and imprisonment in Egypt aboard the *Valkyrien* was Anker Nissen.

Zahlmeister *Anker Nissen*

The second 'Dane' sailing with the *Kronborg*, who published his memoirs of the voyage and his participation in the war in East Africa, was Anker Nissen (1892-1980). Before the war, Nissen worked in a bank in Haderslev, and later became manager of a bank in Graasten. Both Nissen and Kock were reported missing for 3½ years, writing the first letters to their families when they were interned in Egypt. Nissen had managed to meet in secret with his fiancée just before the *Kronborg* departed Wilhelmshaven on the secret mission, and she waited for him for 4½ years, when they got married after his return from Africa. Kock was already married before the war and had become the father of a son just before they departed.

Nissen first published his war memoirs in a long article in the 1928 issue of *Sønderjydske Aarbøger*, an annual publication from South Jutland. With the decennial of the armistice, the editorial board decided to publish a series of narrations from North Schleswig or South Jutland veterans—under the joint title *I Krigens Vold* (At the mercy of the war), which focused on the disbandment of the German army during the revolution and armistice, and the soldiers' long and adventurous journeys back home—as a supplement to the many published letters, which typically stopped when the war stopped. The very first narration of this series was about Africa: Nis Jacobsen's *Under Danebrog til Afrika; tværs over det indiske Hav*,[27] about the second blockade runner *Marie*, and Nissen's *Under Verdenskrigen i Afrika*[28] was the fifth article in the series, making Africa a highly prominent topic among the nine articles printed in different volumes of *Sønderjydske Aarbøger* between 1928 and 1939. Nissen, furthermore, published a new version of his memoirs in 1962: the twenty pages were privately published as *Sønderjylland Afrika tur retur. Anker Nissens oplevelser som tysk soldat i Afrika under den første Verdenskrig*. His experiences in East Africa are not described in as much detail as Kock's are, but nevertheless are a good supplement to Kock's story and a theme he returned to throughout his life.

After the *Kronborg* was attacked and later emptied of its cargo, Nissen, who had been quartermaster aboard the *Kronborg*, was attached to the German staff in Dar es Salaam. Here, he stayed for a year, and then took part in Lettow-Vorbeck's retreating war through the bush. Like Kock, he was left behind at Nambindinga in November 1917 when Lettow-Vorbeck reorganised his troops and crossed the River Rovuma to wage mobile warfare in Portuguese East Africa. In the prisoner-of-war camp at Maadi south of Cairo Nissen acted as the leader of the 'Danes' and, after the armistice in November 1918, managed to contact the Danish consul in Cairo who made the British gather all the 'Danes' at the Sidi Bishr camp, and eventually secured their return home aboard the Danish cruiser *Valkyrien* via Denmark in August/September 1919. Therefore, the 'Danes' did not have to stay in the camp until Germany had signed the Versailles treaty, as most of their German comrades did.

Thereby, Kock, Nissen and about 150 other German prisoners-of-war and civilian internees, of whom about fifty were 'Danes' or North Schleswigers, returned on board the Danish cruiser *Valkyrien*, receiving a heroic welcome in neutral Denmark when they arrived at Copenhagen on 10 September 1919—in time to participate in the plebiscites in Schleswig in

[27] In *Sønderjydske Aarbøger* (1928) p. 43-85. In 1957 the yearbook changed its name to *Sønderjyske Årbøger*. Jacobsen later published an extended version of his story: *Under Dannebrog til tysk Østafrika og Indien. Dagbogsoptegnelser fra Verdenskrigen* (Christiansfeld, 1940)
[28] In Sønderjydske Aarbøger (1929) pp. 48-81

February and March 1920. The arrival of the prisoners-of-war was treated extensively in contemporary Danish newspapers; in *Politiken*, for instance, there was a short notice on the front page of the 11 September issue with a picture of some of the former prisoners and the crowd receiving them, and a long article with more pictures inside the paper.[29] There is a picture of 'a soldier from Sylt of the East African troops', as the caption says; he is described as 'a mighty tall soldier with the boldly upturned African hat, which one knows from the pictures of Lettow-Vorbeck', and he 'is a magnificent specimen of viral power and blondeness'.[30] Interestingly enough, the article—and front page notice—states that of the 165 returning prisoners-of-war and civilian internees, only about fifty are Danish; the rest are German. The German guests are, however, described as polite and highly civilised; some of them insist on speaking the little Danish they know, even though the journalist tells them that he speaks German—it is a matter of returning hospitality, they say.

Aside from the already mentioned 'magnificent specimen' of a soldier, the East African soldiers were not the focal point in *Politiken*'s articles about the visit of the former prisoners-of-war, which rather consist of reports of the compact program that had been put together for the guests: a committee had donated new clothes and boots, in which they were dressed before an official dinner, followed by a visit to the Royal Theatre in the evening etc. Anker Nissen, however, does appear in the article quoted above, thanking their hosts for the welcome on behalf of his comrades—he is referred to as 'the Aaron of the South Jutlanders'.[31] His young fiancée has come to meet him in Copenhagen, the article says; he has been a Prussian soldier for 8½ years and now he is so happy to be free that he can barely believe it.

In an article in *Politiken* on 12 September, when the visiting Schleswigers already had been replaced on the front page by news about the atrocities of the Bolsheviks in Hungary,

---

[29] The article 'Valkyrien' kom i Gaar med Sønderjyderne', *Politiken*, 11 Sep 1919, pp. 10-1

[30] *'En Soldat fra Sylt af de øst afrikanske Tropper'* and *'En mægtig høj Soldat med den dristigt opslaaede afrikanske Hat, som man kender fra Billederne af Lettow-Vorbeck, er et Pragteksemplar af viril Kraft og Blondhed'* in *Politiken*, 11 Sep 1919, pp. 10-11

[31] '[...] de danske sønderjyders Aron' in *Politiken*, 12 Sep 1919, p. 10

Rumanian troops occupying Budapest and other repercussions of the war and placed on page seven, the anonymous reporter quoted the former member of the Reichstag in Berlin and present minister for affairs regarding North Schleswig in the Danish social-radical government, HP Hanssen, during the visit by the prisoners-of-war to Rigsdagen, the Danish parliament. In his speech, Hanssen mentioned that there were many Schleswigers scattered all over the world in prisoner-of-war camps, for instance twenty Schleswig seamen were interned at Java, who sailed with 'an unlucky German blockade runner that sailed under Danish flag and a with Danish speaking crew!'[32]— evidently some of the crew of the *Marie* managed to escape to Java. What is noteworthy in this quotation is the exclamation mark and the reporter's obvious surprise that a German ship sailed under a Danish flag, which would not have been narrated this way had information about the German strategy been known at the time.

The blockade runners in German books

An account of the *Kronborg*'s voyage was, however, already published in 1918 by its captain Carl Christiansen: *Durch! Mit Kriegsmateriel zu Lettow-Vorbeck*. Judging from the text, it clearly came out before the armistice in November, and thus seems to have had certain propagandistic aims. Interestingly enough, and probably in accordance with these aims, Christiansen does not mention that the ship sailed under a false Danish flag—maybe to avoid revealing this successful trick to the Allies, even though they probably would have known already. Or more likely, I believe, to avoid giving any credit for this cunning and heroic action to anybody but the Germans themselves.

In von Lettow-Vorbeck's memoirs of the war, the *Sperrbrecher*'s usage of the Danish flag is not mentioned either: in *Heia Safari! Deutschlands Kampf in Ostafrika* (1920) he writes that it was masked as a Norwegian ship, which could be a mere slip of memory; in *Meine Erinnerungen aus Ostafrika* (1920), in an otherwise parallel passage, no mention of this trick is given

---

[32] 'Et Selskab paa 20 sønderjydske Sømænd sidder [...] paa Java, hvor de er interneret. De var ansat paa en uheldig tysk Blokadebryder, der gik under dansk Flag og med dansktalende Besætning!' in *Politiken*, 12 Sep 1919, p. 7 'Uheldig' means both unlucky or unsuccessful and unfortunate (bad for something) in Danish; here, the latter meaning clearly has to be taken into account.

at all.³³ Von Lettow-Vorbeck's judgement of the value of the blockade runner did not so much focus on the actual munitions it brought—he preferred to capture enemy arms and ammunition—but on the psychological boost it brought to those fighting far away from the mother country: they were not forgotten.³⁴

More surprisingly, the trick with the false Danish colours was not mentioned in a short book about Knud Knudsen's voyage with the second blockade runner, *Marie*, which came out in 1917 as the first eyewitness account of the missions by the, so far, only man who had managed to return to Germany.³⁵ Knudsen was evidently from the Danish minority Schleswig, judging from his name and the fact that Danish speaking soldiers were hand-picked for these missions; his national disposition, however, is not known—he came from Flensburg, and probably stayed there after the 1920 partition of Schleswig.³⁶ The book probably had to serve propagandistic means as well. In KE Selow-Serman's book about the *Marie: Blokade-Brecher* (1917) the German stratagem of using false Danish colours is not mentioned either. This book appeared in a Danish translation as *Blokadebryderen*—published by the German-paid and evidently propaganda-oriented publisher Nordiske Forfatteres Forlag in 1918.

The successful voyages of the two blockade runners were also mentioned in contemporary Danish newspapers. For instance, in *Politiken,* 27 March 1917, in a short article with the headline *Tyske Dampere sejler til Østafrika med Ammunition'* (German Steamers sail to East Africa with Munitions), the stories are told to stress German heroics and focus on the inadequacy of the British blockade—quite predictably when quoting from a telegram from the German Wolff's Bureau. No mention is, however, given of the steamers sailing under the Danish flag,

---

³³ Paul von Lettow-Vorbeck, *Heia Safari! Deutschlands Kampf in Ostafrika* (1920) p. 75, and *Meine Erinnerungen aus Ostafrika* (1920) pp. 60-1

³⁴ Lettow-Vorbeck, *Meine Erinnerungen aus Ostafrika*, p. 61

³⁵ Joh Lensch (ed.), *Knud Knudsens Fahrt nach Ostafrika* (1917). Here, the second edition (1918) has been used. The rather thin book has the long under title: *Wahrheitsgetreuer Bericht über die Hilfsfahrt der* Marie, *Kapitän Sörensen aus Flensburg, mit Munition nach Deutsch-Ostafrika und die abenteuerliche Rückkehr des ersten und bis jetzt einzigen Mannes von der Besatzung über Batavia, den Suezkanal und England nach den Schilderungen des Oberheizers Knud Knudsen.*

³⁶ He does not figure in the aforementioned archive of the Danish Invalidenævn, which, of course, could mean that he had not been wounded or suffering from tropical diseases—the latter option seems, however, highly unlikely.

and only the captains' names: the typical Danish -sen names Christiansen and Sørensen, would indicate this side of the story.

Books were also published in German dealing with the *Kronborg* and the *Marie* in the 1930s: for example, *Die Kapitäne Christiansen. Nach Lochbüchern erzählt* (1933) and Peter Eckart: *Blockadebrecher* Marie. *Abenteure-Fahrten des Kapitäns Sörensen im Weltkrieg* (1937), but in both of these books, the disguise as Danish or other neutral ships is no longer kept secret.

The reception of Sønderjyder forsvarer Østafrika and the legacy of Kock and Nissen's war experiences

Finally, a quick glance at the reception of Chr P Christensen's *Sønderjyder forsvarer Østafrika* in the Danish public and the legacy of Kock and Nissen's war experiences in East Africa. Christensen's version of Kock's memoirs seems to have struck a chord of interest in the Danish public in the late 1930s, when otherwise Nazi Germany loomed as a large threat over Denmark as imperial Germany had done a good twenty years earlier. The book sold remarkably well—it came, as mentioned above, in six print runs in all; it came out in September 1937 and already on 26 November a short notice in *Politiken* stated that the third print run had been sold out and a new one was in print, now comprising 10,000 issues, as opposed to the previous 1,500 per print run.[37] A rather big success for the small Danish book market, as the newspaper notice also says. Furthermore, the book was translated into German in 1938 and English in 1941—hardly the most strategically well-timed year to appear there.

This book was, however, not the most successful publication about the 'Danish' soldiers in the German army and navy: already during the war and in the immediate post-war years, popular writer Erich Erichsen's *Den tavse Dansker* (1916, *Forced to Fight*) had become an unlikely success with 27 editions in Danish, and English, French, Dutch, Swedish, Finnish and other translations: a war novel that combined sentimentalism with a presumably genuine interest for the 'Danes' south of the border. After the war, two memoirs proved very popular: Kristian Tastesen's *En sønderjysk Soldats Oplevelser under Verdens-krigen* (1921), which by 1934 had been

---

[37] *Politiken*, 26 Nov 1937, p. 8

published in seven editions, totaling 32,000 copies, and Martin Feddersen's *Bevægelseskrigens Strabadser paa Vestfronten. Oplevet som søn-derjysk Soldat* (1932), which had been published in eight editions by 1934. But both of these were short and cheap books, unlike *Sønderjyder forsvarer Østafrika* which was published by a commercial publisher.[38]

The reviews of *Sønderjyder forsvarer Østafrika* that I have found are highly positive. In *Jydske Tidende*, 26 September 1937, Kock's fellow veteran from the German army, journalist Morten Kamphøvener, thanked Kock not only for the exciting story, but also for preserving his exceptional experiences of these soldiers for later generations.[39] In *Politiken*, 22 September 1937, an anonymous but equally enthusiastic reviewer called it 'A lovely book, so full of excitement as only the genuine truthful reality can be'.[40] This review incorrectly stated that *Sønderjyder forsvarer Østafrika* was 'the first description [published in Denmark] of this adventurous journey where a crew of Danes aboard a ship flying the Dannebrog tried to come to Lettow-Vorbeck's help'.[41] But of course a peripheral publication like *Sønderjydske Aarbøger* might easily be overlooked in the Copenhagen press. What is particularly interesting in these reviews is that they do not comment on the abuse of the Danish flag for this mission. The fact that the Danes aboard the ship are referred to as Danes as such, without inverted commas or the like, is less surprising nearly twenty years after they had become Danish citizens. But the fact that there does not seem to have been the least critique of Kock and the other 'Danes's' participation in this exotic part of the war, and, most importantly, of the German abuse of the Danish flag, which otherwise could constitute a potentially serious threat to Danish neutrality at a moment when a new war might not have been entirely threatening yet, but definitely in the making, is interesting.

---

[38] See Bjarne Bendtsen, *Mellem Fronterne*, (unpublished PhD thesis, Odense: University of Southern Denmark, 2011) p. 221

[39] 'Paa Krigs-Safari i Østafrika', in *Jydske Tidende*, 26 Sep 1937, pp. 4-5

[40] *Politiken*, 22 Sep 1937, p. 7, 'En dejlig Bog, saa fuld af Spænding som kun den fuldkomment sanddru Virkelighed'

[41] 'Da sønderjyske Soldater forsvarede Østafrika', *Politiken*, 22 Sep 1937, p7, 'Men det er i alt Fald herhjemme den første Beskrivelse, vi faar af dette Eventyrtogt, hvor en Besætning af Danskere paa Skib, fra hvis Mastetop Dannebrog vejede, søgte at komme Lettow-Vorbeck til Hjælp'

Furthermore, *Sønderjyder forsvarer Østafrika* and the other memoirs written by Danish-speaking veterans from the East African campaign do not tell the otherwise by then collectively accepted story of the North Schleswig Danes's participation in the war as a war they had been *forced to fight*, with the English title of Erich Erichsen's aforementioned Danish wartime bestseller. Or, with yet another similar *pathosformel: They fought for a cause that was not theirs*, as this interpretive frame has been formulated on the plaque at the entrance of the official Danish monument for the Danes killed in the war, the *Marselisborgmonumentet* at Aarhus. This interpretation was, however, already in place during or at least immediately after the war—also in relation to these soldiers: When Kock, Nissen and the rest of the prisoners-of-war arrived at Copenhagen, *Politiken* quoted from the speech by Frederiksberg's[42] mayor Godskesen who gave the welcome speech for the veterans disembarking the *Valkyrien*. In this speech, he called them 'those, "who had fought for a cause that was not their own".'[43] Particularly in Chr P Christensen's version of Kock's story no mention of this is given;[44] and Kock himself only criticizes the madness of war in general terms, not the special situation of the Danish minority in North Schleswig. In the short preface to the German translation Christensen even, as the dramatic, action-packed cover illustration of the Danish original clearly hints at, praised Kock's '*unbeugsamen Willen und das starke Blut ihrer Rasse*'—his unbendable will and the strong blood of his race— and thus rather underlines the racial kinship between Danes and Germans than point to their differences.[45]

Christensen's sympathies would, however, soon come out in the open when writing for the Danish Nazi paper *Fædrelandet* (The Fatherland) during the German occupation of Denmark a few years later. Kock, on the other hand, evidently did not sympathise with the Nazis, as he was a member of the

---

[42] Frederiksberg was and is a separate part of Copenhagen with its own government.

[43] *Politiken*, 11 Sep 1919, p. 9, '*dem, "der havde kæmpet for en Sag, som ikke var deres egen"*'

[44] As in the other books in his minor series of retellings of the war experiences of North Schleswigers: *Kejserens sidste Kaperkrydser* (1934), *Fire Aar paa Quiriquina* (1935) and *8 Mand savnet* (1938)

[45] Christen P Christensen, *Nordsleswiger verteidigen Deutsch-Ostafrika* (Essen, 1938)

aforementioned DSK: the members of this organisation were not allowed to participate in German organisations or activities, especially those which turned against the Danish state and king, but were instead obliged to work for a free and independent Denmark. Kock signed his membership card in 1941 during the German occupation of Denmark.[46]

Despite the fate of Christensen's book—and the Danish First World War in general—after the Second World War, Kock and Nissen's stories were not forgotten altogether: in 2009 journalist Peter Tappe wrote a short, slightly inaccurate article about the *Kronborg*;[47] in 2011, Klaus Winkel wrote a chapter about Kock in the book *Danskere i tropisk Afrika. Fra slavehandler til bistandsarbejder*; and in 2012, Rasmus Hundsbæk Pedersen, PhD student at The Danish Institute for International Studies, wrote about Kock in the newspaper *Jydske Vestkysten*.[48] And finally, from a somewhat different cultural sphere but with a much larger audience, Nis Kock and the war in East Africa appeared in Swedish author Jan Guillou's novel *Brobyggarna* (2011, The Bridge Builders)— Kock's name, however, spelt as Nils.

---

[46] See the back of Kock's membership card, Landsarkivet for Sønderjylland, Aabenraa, DSK Medlemskartotek 1936-1950, archive number: SBAC107/5a
[47] In *Sønderjysk Månedsskrift*, no. 5 (2009) pp. 163-8
[48] Rasmus Hundsbæk Pedersen, 'De andres krig', in *Jydske Vestkysten*, JV Magasinet Søndag, 15 Jan 2012, pp. 16-7

West Africa

The Advent of War: Anglo-African Relations across West Africa

Nigel Browne-Davies[1]

At the advent of the First World War, Anglo-African relations across British West Africa had deteriorated as a consequence of the displacement of the colonial elite from the civil service and the establishment of Protectorates over independent African kingdoms. As pseudo-scientific racial theories and the excesses of some educated African civil servants contributed toward the Europeanisation of the civil service, tensions developed in relations between educated Africans and the British colonial authorities.[2] Furthermore, as the British established formal Protectorates over traditional West African societies such as the Ashanti Kingdom and the Sierra Leone hinterland, traditional African societies resisted the encroachment of British rule into traditional African culture. Thus, by the advent of the First World War, tension had developed in Anglo-African relations across the four British West African territories.

In the late nineteenth and early twentieth centuries, some colonial authorities sought to curtail the rights granted to educated Africans on the basis of pseudo-scientific racial theories propagating the intellectual inferiority of Africans. The advent of pseudo-scientific racial theories ushered in an era in

[1] Nigel Browne-Davies is a historian specialising in the study of coastal elites in the Republic of Liberia and the former British West African colonies during the late eighteenth to early twentieth centuries. His articles have been published in several academic journals including the *Journal of Sierra Leone Studies* and the *Transactions of the Historical Society of Ghana*. Browne-Davies is a history graduate of Queen Mary University of London and he is a Fellow of the Royal Society of Arts and a member of the Royal Historical Society. He also serves as a member of the editorial board of the *Journal of Sierra Leone Studies* and is a Diversity Delegate on The National Archives User Advisory Group.

[2] Ayandele, EA, *The Educated Elite in the Nigerian Society* (Ibadan UP, 1974) pp. 21-8

colonial West Africa that prevented promising British West Africans from entering the higher ranks of the civil service or medical or legal professions.[3] Africans were rejected from serving in the high-ranking positions within the civil service and Europeans were recruited to serve in senior colonial positions. Thus, the West African Medical Staff established as the premier colonial medical service in 1902 was restricted to candidates of 'pure European descent.'[4] Thus, racial theories and colonial policies based upon these nascent ideologies contributed to the downfall of the British West African elite in the colonial strata.

The transgressions of a few educated African colonial officials from within the British West African elite further eroded at the privileged position that some members of the elite occupied.[5] Professional misconduct or errors of judgement by African civil servants or professionals tarnished the perception held by British colonial authorities of African civil servants and professionals and further contributed to the Europeanisation of the colonial civil service in British West Africa.[6] Thus, the controversy concerning the service of Dr John Farrell Easmon, the Chief Medical Officer of the Gold Coast and James Hastings Spaine, the colonial Postmaster in Sierra Leone served to undermine the confidence of British colonial authorities in the ability of the educated African elite to serve in positions of responsibility.[7] British colonial officials such as Governor Edward Marsh Merewether of Sierra Leone described educated Africans as incompetent civil servants and professionals and in circumstances where the professional conduct of educated Africans were impeccable, detractors used racial theories to

---

[3] Ayandele, *The Educated Elite in the Nigerian Society*, pp. 21-8. The ethnocentric form of evangelical Christianity that allowed equality for Africans who adhered to Christianity and adopted civilisation' or assimilated into a form of Westernised culture was not as relevant to British colonial policy in the late nineteenth and twentieth centuries as it had been during the nineteenth century.

[4] Patton, Adell, *Physicians, Colonial Racism, and Diaspora in West Africa*, (UP Florida, 1996) pp. 169, 174

[5] Porter, Arthur, *Creoledom: A Study of the Development of Freetown Society* (Oxford UP, 1963) pp. 97-99

[6] Fyfe, Christopher, *A History of Sierra Leone*, pp. 532-4. Patton, Adell, *Physicians, Colonial Racism, and Diaspora in West Africa* (UP of Florida, 1996) pp. 113-21

[7] Fyfe, *A History of Sierra Leone*, pp. 532-4, Patton, *Physicians, Colonial Racism, and Diaspora in West Africa*, pp. 113-121

discredit the abilities of these African civil servants.[8] Thus, although the disinheritance of the elite was largely the result of a new racial ideology, British colonial authorities used the professional failings of a select number of high-ranking African officials to argue that the British West African elite were not capable of serving in high positions of responsibility.

As racial theories were utilised to undermine the abilities of educated Africans, the intimate terms on which the British colonialists interacted with their educated African counterparts decreased as social segregation was implemented in some British West African territories.[9] The social terms that unified the educated African elite and the British colonial Raj were further eradicated by the creation of segregated European commun-ities.[10] As the British colonial civil service expanded, clinical analyses and the discovery of scientific treatments for tropical diseases reduced the death rate in the British West African colonies and allowed the Colonial Office to recruit Europeans for positions within the colonial civil service.[11] Segregated settlements such as Victoriaborg, Accra and Hill Station, Sierra Leone were established for and restricted to European colonial officials. Thus, social segregation began to be implemented in British West Africa, and in territories where intimate social relations and even intermarriage between West Africans and Europeans had been previously overlooked during the nineteenth century.[12]

Although the elite were largely resigned to the changing social dynamics of the relationship between the colonial authorities and educated Africans, British West Africans vehemently opposed the Europeanisation of the civil service and clamoured for self-determination and greater political rights.[13]

---

[8] Cole, Festus, 'The Sierra Leone Carrier Corps and Krio Responses to Recruitment in World War I,' in Dixon-Fyle, Mac & Cole, Gibril Raschid (eds.), *New Perspectives on the Sierra Leone Krio* (Peter Lang, 2006) pp. 54-6

[9] Spitzer, Leo, *Creoles of Sierra Leone: Responses to Colonialism, 1870-1945* (University of Wisconsin, 1974) pp. 59-61

[10] Spitzer, *Creoles of Sierra Leone: Responses to Colonialism,* pp. 59-61

[11] Ibid. pp. 55-61

[12] Spitzer, *Creoles of Sierra Leone,* pp. 59-61

[13] Crowder & Osuntokun, 'The First World War and West Africa, 1914-1918' in Ajayi, JFA, & Crowder, Michael, (eds.), *A History of West Africa* (Longman, 1987, Second Ed) p. 547

The British West African press strongly criticised the perceived shift in British colonial policy and decried the curtailing of the rights that the educated African elite held as British subjects. However, despite the achievements and qualifications of the educated African elite, the colonial authorities did not allow these communities to influence a change in the colonial policies that excluded educated Africans from serving in the upper echelons of the colonial service. Thus, although the educated elite in British West Africa would clamour for a return to fair play and the appointment of Africans to the civil service, racially-based colonial policies continued to be implemented in the late nineteenth and early twentieth centuries.

Traditional African societies and resistance to British rule

The deterioration in Anglo-African relations was not merely confined to the educated African elite in the colony areas and Africans from traditional societies also challenged the extension of British rule in territories adjacent to the colonies.[14] As Anglo-African relations deteriorated between the British West African elite and British colonial authorities, Africans from within the territories declared as British Protectorates also resisted attempts to impose British rule.[15] Thus, as Britain attempted to annexe and govern the Ashanti Kingdom as a Protectorate, a large scale resistance occurred in 1900. In Sierra Leone, the attempts by Governor Frederic Cardew and the colonial authorities to implement the house tax in the hinterland was fiercely resisted by Temne, Mende, and Sherbro leaders and culminated in the 1898 Hut Tax War in the Sierra Leone Protectorate.[16] The resistance of West Africans in traditional societies to the extension of British rule further reinforced the tension in Anglo-African relations in the late nineteenth and early twentieth centuries.

Thus, at the advent of the First World War, Anglo-African relations between British colonial authorities and the westernised British West African elite and indigenous African communities had significantly deteriorated. The British West

---

[14] Fyfe, *A History of Sierra Leone*, 547-553, 588-589
[15] Ibid., 547-53, 588-9
[16] Ibid., 547-53, 588-9

African elite, the traditional allies of the colonial establishment and often the advocates for the extension of the British sphere of influence, were dissatisfied with the increasingly discriminatory colonial policies. Furthermore, indigenous Africans, unassimilated into British habits and customs, similarly rebelled against the extension of British rule into the hinterland of British West Africa. It was at this critical juncture in Anglo-African relations that the First World War broke out in Europe.

The following account by Stewart Hawkins provides an insight into the introduction researchers have to the field of World War 1 in Africa. Most researchers have spent time in Africa, or had a family member involved in the conflict, or read one of the novels such as An Ice Cream War *by William Boyd or* Shout at the Devil *by Wilbur Smith. The search for what happened is similar although unless from a military background, few will know the value of the war diaries, tending to rely more on what is available and the Internet. Stewart compares his experiences as a soldier in Nigeria, 46 years later, with what he discovered about World War 1.*

1 Nigeria Regiment in Cameroon

Stewart Hawkins[1]

The Jewell brothers and sister were publishing the memoirs of their grandfather[2] and were put in touch with me as I had done a similar thing in 2013.[3] Richard Jewell said that they were going to launch it at the GWAA Conference in May 2016. I asked about the Conference and remarked that I had done my

---

[1] Stewart Hawkins served as a National Service officer with the 1st Battalion of the Nigeria Regiment in 1957-58 in between Charterhouse and Balliol College Oxford where he read Arabic and Persian. He was again for a short time in oil in Nigeria soon after independence and has continued to follow the fortunes of Nigeria ever since. After four years in the steel industry he spent the rest of his working life with a computer company. For the last quarter of a century he has lived in the southern Alps. In 2014 he published a biography on the mountaineer and writer Wilfrid Noyce.

[2] Norman Parsons Jewell, *On Call in Africa in war and peace, 1910-1932* (Gillyflower, 2016)

[3] *Far, Far, the Distant Peak: The Life of Wilfrid Noyce, Mountaineer, Scholar, Poet* (2013)

National Service in Nigeria and I knew that the Nigerians had fought in the Great War in Africa. Our exchange of emails involved Anne Samson and I was encouraged to tell the story of the *1st Battalion of the Nigeria Regiment in the Great War* at the Conference.

I knew very little of the subject—I had climbed Mount Cameroon at Christmas 1963 and I had served with the Nigerian soldier. I had my copy of Haywood and Clark's *History of the RWAFF*[4] and started to read that in some detail. I obtained a copy of the War Diary of 1 Nigeria Regiment for 1914-1915.[5] I looked around for other sources and found some books which were mainly about East Africa, with very little on Cameroon.[6] With this sparse resource I teased out the activities of 1NR. The War Diary was invaluable and enabled me to add colour and detail to the narrative. The style of military reporting had not changed through two world wars! One can also see why war is described as long periods of boredom punctuated by brief interludes of intense activity. The names on the nominal rolls of the companies did not seem to have changed much in 43 years. Those and the detailed statistics came from the diary and attachments. By the 50s the soldiers wore boots, in 1914 they were still barefooted, although chaplis[7] came in during the war. Our predecessors walked everywhere in Nigeria and Cameroon, unless there was a train or boat, because there were just tracks in the bush. We walked everywhere because the transport was only sufficient for stores and equipment.

The amazing feature of the Nigerian soldiering in the Great War was the dependence on carriers. A battalion of 700 all ranks had a tail of up to 600 carriers who were effectively part of the unit. On both sides of Africa where vehicles were not available or practicable, the army had thousands of carriers, the Carrier Corps, to maintain the supply chain to the troops at the front. For the 7,000 troops in the Cameroon 20,000 carriers were brought in from other West African territories. When we

[4] Royal West African Frontier Force, composed of the military forces in Nigeria, Gold Coast, Sierra Leone and Gambia, Haywood, Austin & Clarke, FAS, *History of the Royal West African Frontier Force* (Gale & Polden, 1964)
[5] TNA: WO 95/5387/4
[6] For a list of books, articles and publications on the war in Africa, see the Bibliography on www.gweaa.com
[7] A type of sandal of South Asian origin.

went to bush, we were allowed six porters for the company (93 all ranks) to carry company equipment and stores and each platoon took it in turn to act as porters for the company.

> These Africans astound me the loads they carry. All their own kit and arms and a 40lb sack of cassava or rice on their head. It is easy on the flat! But when you see them go up them there hills, it is just fantastic.[8]

In 1914 West Africa was still the white man's grave. The weather in Southern Cameroon was a great deal worse than that in Northern and Western Nigeria, where I was, and the terrain was very unforgiving – thick tropical forest and even mangrove swamp. There were always the diseases and insect life and in 1914 tropical medicine was in its infancy. However, the Nigerians in Cameroon were well supported in terms of number of doctors and medical staff and the Europeans were very resistant to sickness. This was the result of their Principal Medical Officer maintaining that Europeans in the tropics must have a certain amount of kit if they are to keep fit. This had been very conclusively proved in the Cameroon campaign. When they got to East Africa in 1916, they still insisted on the two extra loads each, one a bed, the other a tin-bath filled with kit. As a result they were known as the *Bed and Bath Brigade.*[9]

There was another development over the years. In the Great War all the officers and quite a few NCOs were British and seconded from British regiments. When I joined the battalion in April 1957 we had two African officers in the rank of Lieutenant. They had both been to Sandhurst and had spent time with British regiments. In August 1958 I handed over my company to an African Captain and there were four or five other African officers in the battalion. This trend accelerated with the approach of independence in 1960 and the ending of a supply of National Service officers.

When I went back to Nigeria in 1963 my African colleagues were all COs of battalions or similar units.

The Nigerian soldier played crucial roles in both the West and East African campaigns in the Great War and this paper is the story of the 1st Battalion in the Cameroon campaign in 1914-1916.

---

[8] Author's collection, Letter from bush of 8.12.57
[9] WD Downes, *The Nigerian Regiment in East Africa* (Methuen, 1919) p. 53

The Nigeria Regiment in 1914 was adjusting itself to new situations. Northern and Southern Nigeria had been amalgamated on 1 January and the two regiments, Northern and Southern Nigeria Regiments became The Nigeria Regiment with four battalions totalling about five thousand. The 1st Bn NNR became the 1st Bn NR and each battalion had up to eight companies. They continued to operate largely as they had done before and their duties were essentially keeping the peace or 'in aid of the civil power' although they were well-trained soldiers as we shall see. The companies of the new 1st Battalion were deployed throughout Nigeria, mainly in the North. They were volunteers, predominantly Hausa, but conscription became necessary during the war and this tended to operate through requests to the local chiefs, to which they did not necessarily accede. This was particularly true in the Zungeru area and in Southern Nigeria. The Commanding Officer was Major (local Lieutenant Colonel) JB Cockburn, Royal Welch Fusiliers, originally appointed to command 1NNR on 16 March 1913. His headquarters were in Kaduna.

The declaration of war in early August caused a redeployment of the companies with a greater concentration on the Cameroon border as a defensive measure against any possible aggression on the part of the German troops in Cameroon. Colonel Carter, the Commandant Nigeria Regiment moved up to Kaduna and on the basis of instructions received from London on 14 August ordered the frontier areas to be reconnoitred.

There were two forays into Cameroon in August 1914 by the Maiduguri and Yola columns, in neither of which 1NR participated. The Maiduguri Column made contact with German troops patrolling from Mora, a fortified outpost in the far north of Cameroon, and on 20 August Captain RW Fox with three companies of infantry and one company of Mounted Infantry (MI) established a position at Sava, east of Mora. They made an assault on the German position on the top of Mora mountain and were repulsed. The doctor, two African soldiers (AORs) and five gun-carriers killed, and one machine-gun, one European NCO and one soldier were captured by the Germans. The Yola column reconnoitred and attacked the key German centre of Garua, on the Benue river but were seen off with a total of 63 casualties including four officers killed, one wounded and captured, and two wounded.

Sir Frederick Lugard, the Governor-General of Nigeria, returned from leave on 2 September and the following day received instructions from the Colonial Office that troops were to be confined to the border area. On 6 September Carter was recalled to England and Lieutenant Colonel FJ Cunliffe, Assistant Commandant, Nigeria Regiment, was appointed Commandant.

Early in September the British and French governments decided that they would collaborate in the invasion of Cameroon. This was required as the wireless station at Duala was a key link in German naval and imperial communications. The Kamina station in Togoland had been captured in August 1914. General CM Dobell was appointed to lead the Anglo-French Expeditionary Force with the priority objectives of Duala and Yaunde, the capital of Cameroon.

Leaving Liverpool on 31 August he sailed down the West coast of Africa picking up the contingents from Sierra Leone and Gold Coast and on 17 September arrived in Lagos. By then the Nigeria Regiment had been reorganised and prepared for the invasion of Cameroon. The 1st Battalion's A and F companies were assigned to Dobell Force and moved to Forcados, a port in the Niger delta. The other companies of the original 1st Battalion were deployed as follows, B company at Mubi, in reserve, C company at Lagos, D company at Birnin Kebbi, E company at Sokoto and G company at Lokoja. D, E and G companies were on Internal Security.

Dobell progressed down the coast to Forcados where the companies of 1st Battalion and D and F companies of 2nd Battalion, embarked in the *Niger* and *Lokoja* on 19 September. These four companies became the new 1st Battalion Nigeria Regt (1NR) under Lieutenant Colonel JB Cockburn, At Calabar A, D, E, F companies of the 4th Battalion, section I Battery with four 2.95 inch QF (Quick Firing) mountain guns, embarked in *Boma* and the entire convoy entered the Cameroon river estuary on 23 September and anchored off Suelaba base.

On 24 September there was a reconnaissance patrol on the north bank of the Dibamba River where a small road led to Duala. An attempt was made on the following day to land a force. It was unsuccessful because of the mangrove swamp and dense bush. However, a local resident appeared, KV Elphinstone. He had written a report on Cameroon in 1913, had considerable local knowledge and was recruited to the force as a lieutenant and posted to A company 1NR.

On 26 September Dobell called upon the Germans to surrender Duala, or face bombardment. The following day the Germans blew up their wireless station, hoisted a white flag over Government House and their representative surrendered Duala, Bonaberi and the surrounding area. 1NR disembarked at Duala on 28 September and Dobell established his Headquarters in Government House. The rest of the force disembarked in Bonaberi, across the water from Duala and the start of the railway that went north to Nkongsamba.

The first objective was achieved and the next few days were spent in consolidating the base. The 1NR War Diary reports that on 7 October Lieutenants Elphinstone, Radcliffe, Paul and Schneider were struck off the strength of the battalion being employed in Civil capacities. Later the Diary notes for Elphinstone *Trans Political Kribi*.[10]

First attack on Yabasi, 6-10 October 1914

Early in October north of Duala a German force of about 60 Europeans and 300 natives was reported to be concentrated on the Wuri River about Yabasi and Yamtam. In order to widen his area of manoeuvre Dobell decided to assemble a column under Colonel EH Gorges to attack Yabasi. This was to consist of two mountain artillery sections (Sierra Leone and Gold Coast), the West African Regiment, two companies 1 Nigeria Regiment, half the Pioneers and 680 carriers transported by launches with a naval escort. The Nigerians, the Gold Coast and Sierra Leone troops were mainly in reserve and the result was a failure. The whole force returned to Duala on 10 October.

Second attack on Yabasi, 12-16 October 1914

A fresh expedition under Gorges was organised and left Duala on the 12th by river. The military portion this time was composed of 1 Nigeria Regiment, the Composite[11] Battalion, the Nigerian Battery (less one section), the Gold Coast Artillery

---

[10] Elphinstone was in Nigeria after the war and compiled the *Gazeteer of Ilorin Province 1921*.

[11] Two companies each of Gold Coast Regiment (GCR) and Sierra Leone Regiment (SLR) under Leutenant Colonel Rose

section and 450 carriers.

On the 13th the bulk of the Composite Battalion was landed at Nsake on both banks of the river. By 10.00 hours RA de B Rose had two and a half companies on the left bank and one on the right bank. Officers' patrols got within two miles off Yabasi, finding the enemy holding positions on both banks and that there was dense bush on the left bank. That evening Rose's force on the left bank, half a mile north of Nsaka, had been stopped by an impassable creek. Before daybreak on the 14th this portion was transferred by launches to the northern side of the creek, and at 05.30 hours, covered by the detachments on either bank, the flotilla, in which Gorges had his headquarters, proceeded slowly upstream. At 09.20 hours 1NR (less one company), one section of Pioneers, the Nigerian Artillery section and a Naval 12-pounder, landed on the right bank. A section of infantry and the Gold Coast Artillery section were left to guard the flotilla. A reserve of one company 1 Nigeria Regiment, half a company Composite Battalion and the balance of the Pioneer Company were retained in three vessels to reinforce either bank as necessary.

Gorges then issued his orders for the attack. On the left bank Rose was to assault two factories the enemy was said to be holding. The main attack was to be made on the right bank. Cockburn, with 1NR, the Nigerian Artillery and Pioneers, was to make a turning movement to his left and come in from the west onto the heights above Yabasi. His rear and right flank would be protected by the company Composite Battalion and the naval 12-pounder on a hill near the river.

At 1100 hours the troops on both banks moved forward covered by a gun mounted on one of the vessels. Little opposition was encountered and both banks were cleared before dark.[12]

Two African Other Ranks (AORs) were wounded and CSM Stark of the Pioneer Company died of sunstroke. Ten Germans were taken prisoner. The enemy retreated towards Nyamtam. 1NR were left to garrison Yabasi and the remainder of the force returned to Duala. Early in November the level of the water in the Wuri river went down and the battalion was brought back to Duala before it became impossible to evacuate them by river.

---

[12] Haywood & Clarke, *Royal West African Frontier Force* (1964) pp. 124-125

Operations west of Duala

Attention turned to the west. On 12 November the Tiko Column under Gorges of which 1NR now formed a major part and included two Naval 12-pounders, half the Pioneer company and a company of Senegalese Tirailleurs, a total of 70 Europeans, 1,077 African soldiers and 1,015 carriers. Tiko is on the river Bimba. This column embarked on a flotilla of small steamers commanded by Captain Charles Pipon Beatty-Pownall and headed up the river. It was planned that Victoria, Muyuka, Mpundu and Tiko were to be attacked simultaneously on 13 November with a landing at Bibundi, the other side of Mount Cameroon, to give the impression of a big force. The following day the column advanced on Buea. There was some opposition in Dibamba with entrenchments manned by about 50 rifles and four Europeans. The latter were all captured. Part of the force guarding the flank had been sent off to Boanda which they had reached with slight opposition. The advance continued through very dense forest with sporadic opposition and by 15.30 Gorges was ready to call the Boanda force in and they all bivouacked for the night near Molyko.

Gorges' column entered Buea unopposed at 13.45 on 15 November and the German District Commissioner handed over the keys of Government House. The stay at Buea was greatly appreciated by the troops. At an altitude of 2,850 foot, with a pleasant climate it offered fresh milk, butter, good meat and fresh produce.

The columns all achieved their objectives and by 14 November the area west of Duala was in British hands and communications between Victoria, Buea, Muyuka and Mpundu and Duala were established.

French move into Edea during October

The Royal Navy, after a recce, found the river Nyong to be navigable up to Dehane. It was decided to send the main column of the French contingent of the Expeditionary Force under Colonel Mayer, consisting of a company and a half of the West African Regiment and two French artillery sections up to Dehane whence they followed the road to Edea. At the same time, under Commandant Mathieu, a column of two companies of Senegalese Tirailleurs, a small detachment of West African Regiment and some French artillery and machine-guns advanced along the railway line from Duala and a third thrust was made by the naval flotilla with a West African Regiment escort sailing up the Sanaga river. After considerable opposition all columns finally captured Edea by 26 October. The enemy forces had retreated along the railway to Eseka and Mayer with the French contingent were detailed to hold Edea.

The Northern Railway

Dobell decided that the next objectives were to clear the Northern Railway which ran from Duala to Nkongsambe, a distance of some 75 miles, and link up with the Cross River column coming in from the west under Captain GT Mair. This operation was commanded by Gorges. By 2 December he had assembled a force at Muyuka that consisted of a naval 12-pounder from the *Challenger* and two machine-guns manned by seamen, the Nigerian Battery, a section of Gold Coast Artillery, a Field Section of Royal Engineers, 1NR, 2NR and half the Pioneer Company. The force advanced in three groups, one under Captain C Gibb, on the left flank, following roughly the east bank of the Mungo River, the second on the right flank under Lieutenant RH Poyntz following the Dibomba river, and the main column, which included 1NR, advanced by the railway.

On 4 December the main column camped at Penja station, some 20 miles up the line from Muyuka. On 5 December A company 1NR moving along a path east of the railway tried to surprise an armoured train reported at Lum station, seven miles further on the line. It took them five hours through the dense bush and the train escaped but they did disperse an enemy detachment. At 10.30 the main column bivouacked at Lum. At noon a company of 1NR under Captain JW Chamley, with a party of Royal Engineers under Lieutenant HH Schneider, was sent to reconnoitre the Nlohe Bridge over the Dibombe River, about five miles further north up the line. The bridge had been destroyed and the river appeared unfordable. During the operation Chamley's company fell in to an ambush that was covered by machine-guns on the other bank. Chamley, managed to extract his men with the loss of two killed, including Schneider, and nine wounded, including Lieutenant C Luxford. Another company of 1NR came up to reinforce them and they bivouacked for the night. The enemy did not follow.

During the period 6 to 9 December, the main column crossed

the Dibombe by temporary bridges below Nlohe and reached Manengole after a very hot and trying march of 13-14 miles. They derailed and blew up a dynamite-filled wagon before it could do any more harm and had snipers to contend with most of the way up. The retreating Germans had left behind rolling stock and telephone equipment, which was perhaps a sign that they were becoming demoralised.

On 10 December, the advance continued north with little opposition and at 10.30 a German officer came in under a white flag with a message from Leutnant von Englebrechten surrendering Nkongsamba and the surrounding country as far as Bare, some 13-14 miles further up the line. Gorges then occupied Nkongsamba where Gibb and his column rejoined the main force. Rolling stock and stores and 23 Germans were captured. A week later a locomotive was repaired and a train ran down to Nlohe Bridge. Repairs were completed by 3 January 1915 and the railway was then open all the way to the coast at Bonaberi.

The advance continued and on 11 December Gorges occupied Bare with a small detachment of 2NR, sappers and gunners. Forty Germans were captured and a large quantity of stores. A major find was two aeroplanes, the first to reach West Africa and still in their crates. Bare was the headquarters of a German District and was set on a hill north of the tropical forest belt. It was an ideal place to recuperate after the hard slog through the forest of the previous weeks.

It also provided an opportunity for Gorges to replenish his stores and set up supply depots for the next stage in the advance. He occupied Melong, a road junction 14 miles north of Nkongsamba and established fortified depots there and at Bare.

By Christmas he had gathered enough stores and carriers for the next stage in the advance. It must be remembered that there were no roads—nor any vehicle transport—and there were usually almost as many carriers as soldiers in any column. The next objective was Chang, some 35 miles north of Melong. The force moved in two columns; the main force moved up the Nkam valley while a column under Captain Austin Hubert Wightwick Haywood moved up on the left flank through difficult thickly-wooded country towards Fort Mbo. On 26 December after some skirmishing in the thick grass the main column bivouacked near Fongwang. Haywood's column had met serious opposition and had driven the enemy back at a cost of 12 casualties including one Colour-Sergeant killed.

> An officers' patrol under lieutenants JFP Butler and LS Biddulph, Gold Coast Regiment, sent out the previous day to round up a hostile detachment which had been harassing our right flank, rejoined us in the evening, having successfully carried out its mission. Lieutenant Butler swam the swift unfordable Nkam river under hostile fire to reconnoitre single-handed the enemy's dispositions and numbers, and for this and for other remarkable acts of valour during the campaign this splendid young officer gained the VC. He was killed later in the War, in East Africa, having also won the DSO—one of the bravest of them all.[13]

During this period the enemy was forced out of a series of entrenched positions by both columns without severe opposition, but the country was steep and often heavily wooded, entailing arduous scouting and the picqueting of innumerable hills. While skilfully handling his vanguard at one of these Lieutenant DHS O'Brien, 1NR, was severely wounded. Road repairs and damaged telephone lines (caused by elephants) caused further delays. On 1 January Gorges reached the road junction just south of Chang, and a day later Haywood arrived, having occupied Mbo Fort without opposition the previous day.

Gorges decided to push on to Chang at once. The road lay up a narrow valley, though the country was more open than it had been hitherto. On approaching Chang the column was fired on from neighbouring hills, but after a few rounds had been fired from the naval 12-pounder and the Nigerian guns, a white flag was hoisted on the fort. In spite of this, however, intermittent firing by the enemy continued until the town was occupied by 17.00 hours.

The sudden evacuation of Chang was most unexpected. The enemy had apparently been surprised by the skill with which Gorges had overcome the physical difficulties of the advance.

Dobell had urged on Gorges the necessity of withdrawing to Bare as speedily as possible after destroying the fort. The GOC felt some anxiety for his long line of communications and shortage of reserves and sent Cockburn with a column including 1NR to disperse the enemy who were retiring towards Bamenda. On 5 January Cockburn returned to Chang, and a

---

[13] Brig Gen Gorges, EH *The Great War in West Africa* (Hutchinson, 1930) p. 193

day later Haywood with 2NR and a section of the Nigerian Battery moved south, escorting sick and prisoners. On the 10th the whole force withdrew unmolested to Nkongsamba.

1NR was left to garrison Bare and Nkongsamba, 2NR held the line of communications down the railway to Bonaberi inclusive, while the rest of the Force withdrew to Duala.[14]

During December 1914 and January 1915 Mair's Cross River Column and Mann's Ibi Column came into Cameroon from Southern Nigeria to make the link with Gorges' forces.

For the month of January 1915 most of 1NR were in garrison at Nkongsamba and Bare with the Nigerian Battery under Cockburn. H company were in Northern Cameroon as part of Major WI Webb-Bowen's column encamped at Bogole. Their task was to watch the approaches between Garua and Ngaundere.

In February 1915 there was considerable German activity north of Nkongsamba. They were encamped along the line of Mbureku-Harmann's Farm-Ekom, with headquarters at Melong. Their strength was estimated to be about 50 Europeans and 500 natives, with four machine guns.

On 2 February to clear up the situation and free the railway posts from raids, Cockburn issued orders for an offensive against the enemy's main force. His plan was to carry out simultaneous attacks next morning by a column from Nkongsamba on Mbureku, and another column from Bare on Harmann's Farm under Lieutenant Colonel Newstead.

The first column, commanded by Cockburn, composed of a section of Nigerian Artillery and the total strength of some 400 rifles 1NR, marched by moonlight, hoping to be within striking distance of Mbureku by daybreak on the 3rd. About 03.30, supposing he was some four miles south of the enemy's position, Cockburn was on the point of halting to rest his men, when a rifle shot rang out killing the leading man of the 'point'. A concentrated fire from three machine guns and rifles caught the British front and left flank at close range from the enemy's main position. For a short while there was confusion in the column, much enhanced by carriers dropping their loads and stampeding through the ranks to the rear. High grass and hilly country added to the British difficulties. But the officers, under

---

[14] Haywood & Clarke, *Royal West African Frontier Force* (1964) pp. 134-135

Cockburn's resolute leadership, rose well to the occasion and quickly rallied their men. At this critical stage many distinguished themselves, but Cockburn gives special praise to Captain AH Giles, commanding the advanced guard, also to Sergeant-Major Shearing, whom he sent up with a machine gun to reinforce the advanced guard.[15]

As day broke on the 3rd the enemy abandoned his position, in which was found:

10 Rank and File killed, 2 wounded (1 died)
10,000 Rounds small arms ammunition
2 Boxes dynamite
16 Rifles, various
12 Tents[16]
30 Tents d'abri[17]
3 Horses
1 Cow
60 Goats
6 Boxes Surgical Medicines etc., Personal kit of at least 12 Europeans, Large quantities food supplies for European and Native.[18]

Unfortunately, the British were in no condition to pursue; they suffered heavy casualties. Twelve were killed including Colour-Sergeant HRG Hooker and one carrier and one AOR who died of wounds the following day. The 48 wounded were from all four companies of the battalion and the battery.

While they were re-organising, there was heavy fire from the direction of Harmann's Farm and Cockburn decided to march there via Bare, having detached Number 3 company to escort the wounded back to Nkongsamba. They arrived at Bare at 18.15 on the 3rd.

The Newstead column had advanced on Harmann's Farm and had captured it by 09.30. However, an hour later the enemy, reinforced from Melong, launched a vigorous counter-attack

---

[15] *Ibid.* p. 139

[16] Improvised bivoac shelters from service blankets or groundsheets to form an A shelter (British Field Service Pocket Book, 1914)

[17] Circular tent which could accommodate 1 General or Officer Commanding, or 3 other officers, or 5 female officers, or 7 sergeants or 15 men. [http://1914-1918.invisionzone.com/forums/topic/252797-british-and-empire-tents-and-shelters-of-the-great-war/?tab=comments#comment-2555525]

[18] *War Diary* for 3.2.1915 of 1NR

supported by the fire of two or three machine guns. This attack was met by the Sierra Leone men with steadiness and courage, but they were in an exposed situation and had no machine guns. Consequently, after suffering considerable casualties, they were forced to evacuate the position they had won. The retirement was carried out in good order at noon, but was not followed up by the enemy. Newstead received two messages from Cockburn. The first sent off seven hours previously, arrived at 11.20 hours, asked for assistance. The second received about noon announced his success. Newstead was unable to get into communication with Cockburn and decided to return to Bare, starting at 15.30 hours. His total casualties were 55, including Lieutenant MJ Parker, severely wounded and made prisoner.

Gallant attempts were made by Lieutenant G Dawes and some of his men to carry Parker out of action. But these were abandoned after Parker had been twice again wounded (apparently mortally), and Private Monde Yeraia, one of his rescuers, had been severely wounded. For their gallantry Davies and Monde were awarded the MC and DCM respectively.

Cockburn had difficulties in reorganizing. The rain was incessant; he had lost all his permanent company commanders in 1NR and a large proportion of his men were lame from 'jiggers.'[19]

Dobell at once sent reinforcements to Nkongsamba, also sending Gorges to assume control. In the meantime Cockburn was instructed to keep on the defensive.

> On 10 February Major Coles, 2i/c INR with N°s 2 and 4 companies took the morning train down to Bonaberi. The rest of the battalion took the train four days later. Once down in Duala 1NR was reorganised; Bn HQ and N°s 1 and 3 companies sailed to Victoria. N° 3 company stayed in Victoria and 1/2 4 Company went to Zopo and the other half went to Buea. 2 & 4 companies were dispatched to Kribi, further down the coast, where for two weeks they patrolled the Outpost Line, the border between Cameroon and Rio Muni, Spanish Equatorial Africa. They were back in Duala/Bonaberi by the end of the month.[20]

During March 1915 the two companies of 1NR were at Bonaberi on lines of communication duty which meant safeguarding the

[19] Haywood & Clarke, *Royal West African Frontier Force* (1964) p. 140 The jigger is a flea that buries itself under the toe nail and lays its eggs.
[20] War Diary 1 Nigeria Regiment, 1 March 1915

railway up to Nkongsamba.

The War Office takes over the WAFF

On 1 April 1915 the War Office took over the command and the responsibility for WAFF from the Colonial Office. After discussion with the French it was agreed that the whole of Cameroon was to be taken over and that Yaunde was the next objective. No advance beyond Bare was planned. Patrols continued from there as the Germans still occupied Chang and were active in that area.

Operations in the North

In order to secure Yaunde and the south of Cameroon it was necessary also to neutralise the enemy forces who were in the north of Cameroon. The force was commanded by Cunliffe. Following the earlier débacle Mora was by-passed and attention paid to Garua, further south. By 31 May Cunliffe was ready to take on this key centre. His force now consisted of the following:

British: B and H companies 1NR with H company 2NR, B, D, H companies 3NR, B company 4NR, one naval 12-pounder gun, one Nigerian Battery (three guns), 10 machine-guns, B company Mounted Infantry, a total of 78 Europeans and 1,130 Africans.

French: one heavy gun (95mm, two Hotchkiss, two mountain guns, one squadron cavalry, three infantry companies, two detachments *Gardes Régionnaux*, a total of 46 Europeans and 580 Africans.

As Garua was on the river Benue the 95mm gun had been brought up by river from the rail-head at Baro and put ashore west of Garua. Cunliffe concentrated his British troops some 3,000 yards north of Garua. The French under Captain Brisset were to guard the exits at Nassarao and Bogole to the east. The German artillery opened fire on the Allied position. After four hours with heavy guns the enemy was silenced. The following day, the artillery duel continued and on 2 June the Allies had advanced 1,000 yards. By 6 June supplies to the German garrison had been cut off and four days later the Allies were entrenched 1,000 yards from position north-west of the town.[*]

---

[*] *The Times* - PeriodicalsOnline version: (London) *Times history of the war.* v. 1-22 (pts. 1-273) London, *The Times* [1914]-21 (OCoLC)558550086 Document Type: Book OCLC Number: 642276 Notes: Vols. 1-21 were issued in weekly parts from

At this point Cunliffe learnt that Crailsheim, the German commander, had tried, the previous night, to evacuate all his troops across the Benue, and 15 were drowned. The Allied bombardment was intensified and the troops closed in. At 15.30 a German mounted officer, Captain Wanka, came out with a white flag. Major Wright and French Captain Ferrandi took the surrender. Thirty-seven Europeans and 212 Africans were taken prisoner. The remainder ran away to Ngaundere. The French cavalry pursued them for a bit and then returned to Garua. Brisset then decided to go for Ngaundere with his French force and occupied it on 7 July.

In July and August 1915 while there was a lull in major operations Cunliffe decided to make another attempt to reduce Mora, having come to the conclusion that the best chance of success lay in attacking Dabaskum from Wacheke by night. His dispositions were as follows: Wacheke: HQ; two mountain guns; H company 1NR, D and G companies 3 Nigeria Regiment; and a French company (Captain Remond), for the main assault. Podiko: 95mm gun. Gauala Ridge: A company 1NR. Vami: A French company (Captain Popp). Sava: C company MI (Military Intelligence).[21]

Between 1 and 8 September no less than three attempts to capture Mora failed. H company 1NR gained a footing on

August 25, 1914, to July 27, 1920; v. 22, published in 1921, forms general index. Parts 1-63 have title: The Times history of the war; pts. 64-273: The Times history and encyclopædia of the war. No more published. Description: 22 v. illus. (incl. ports.) maps. 31 cm. Other Titles: Times (London, England), Public Domain, https://commons.wikimedia.org/w/index.php?curid=31392646
[21] *Ibid* p. 155.

Dabaskum and advanced to within 60 yards of the German breastworks before being stopped. Raben, the German commander, paid tribute to the gallantry of these Nigerians. Captain RN Pike was shot dead while leading the attacking force, which incurred 38 casualties, including Captain A Gardner and Lieutenant AJL Cary wounded.[22]

Mora Mountain

After these further débacles, Cunliffe withdrew to reorganise and was told by the Governor in Lagos to support Dobell on the advance on Yaunde. The next main objective was now Banyo, a key German position further south, and a major obstacle on the route to support Dobell.

In early October 1915 there were minor operations at Gandua and Kentu. Captain FJH Pring with three sections of C company 1NR from Gashiga made a surprise attack on the Germans at Gandua killing two Europeans and six Africans. As a result, the German commander at Banyo reduced the post at the pass in the Genderu mountains, facilitating Cunliffe's progress to Banyo.

By 14 October Cunliffe had concentrated his force at Koncha. It then consisted of:
    B coy MI
    1 section 1 Battery
    1 gun 2 Battery
    B & H Coys 1NR
    1/2 C Coy 1NR
    A Coy 2NR
    1/2 C Coy 2NR
    D Coy 3NR
    H Coy 3NR

By the evening of 22 October, the column from Ibi, which consisted of C company 1NR, 1/2 C company 2NR and H company 3NR under Major GC Mann, had reached Gandua and Cunliffe's column was at Mbo. The following day they all advanced on Banyo.

Banyo Mountain

On 24 October the Germans retired to Banyo Mountain. Mann's

---

[22] *Ibid.* p. 155

force occupied the European cantonment at Banyo. Cunliffe arrived an hour later after having marched 445 miles in five weeks.

Banyo Mountain rises as a single feature about 1,200 feet above the surrounding area of broken country. Its slopes are very steep and covered with large boulders, many of which the enemy had linked together in stone breastworks. Altogether some 300 of these had been constructed. In all, immense preparations had been made for a prolonged defence. On the summit, cement reservoirs had been built; brick houses had been made for Europeans, equipped with heavy furniture; cattle and grain had been stored in quantities. It was evident that the place had been intended as a rallying-point for the garrisons of Banyo, Bamenda and Chang. There was complete confidence that it could be held till the end of the war. Cunliffe made careful preparations for his attack. By 2 November his four and a half infantry companies with 10 machine guns were established on the under-features round the mountain; in the plain behind them the MI were dispersed in a wide circle to give early information of any attempt to break through.

Orders were issued for a general attack at dawn on the 4th, the three mountain guns were dispersed north-east, south-west and south. Four companies attacked in a converging movement as follows: H company 1NR from the north-east; B company 3NR from the west, with half G company 2NR as a connecting link; H company 3NR from the south-west and C company 1NR from the south. Companies had orders to act independently, as communication could be difficult, moving steadily and advancing in depth, making full use of cover.

A thick mist enabled progress to be considerable. H company 3NR, in fact, almost reached the summit before being seen by the enemy. It then came under fire from all directions at short range. Bowyer-Smith its commander, and one of the most fearless and dashing officers, was killed and the company forced back some distance. By midday the rest of the attacking infantry had got half-way up the mountain and, in many places, were within 30 yards of the breastworks. While daylight remained, they could do no more than hold their ground. At nightfall the enemy began throwing bombs, a missile to which our troops were unaccustomed. For a time the position was critical. Then, extricating themselves and reorganizing, the Nigerians made a further slight advance.

During the 5th steady progress was made, one breastwork after another being outflanked, till by dusk all four companies had reached to within 100 yards of the summit. At 1900 hours a violent thunderstorm intervened and at daybreak on 6 November the summit was carried. The white flag hoisted but the enemy had fled.

It appears that the German commander, realizing the position was hopeless, at 1700 hours on 5 November had issued orders for the garrison to break away in small parties and rendezvous at Ngambe. Not many escaped, however. Out of a total of 23 Europeans and 200 natives, 13 Europeans and 103 natives were killed, wounded or captured. The commander, Captain Schipper, was killed. A quantity of stores and material were also taken.

The capture of this formidable position was a feat of which Cunliffe and all ranks had every reason to be proud. Skilful planning, resolute and gallant leadership, endurance and courage all contributed to the success. Considering the nature of the position the casualties were not excessive, totalling 60, including Captains CG Bowyer-Smith, LNA Mackinnon and Colour-Sergeant W King killed; Captain G Seccombe and Lieutenant J Chartres wounded.

Extract from a letter of Capt CPL Marwood to a Political Officer in Nigeria 13 November 1915

> We took Banyo after 11 days 'hate', the last two days of which we stormed a mountain 1,200 ft. high, and the men had their first taste of hand grenades—nasty things—but they did splendidly, and we got in at dawn on 6th November. Our casualties Bowyer-Smith, Mackinnon, Colour-Sergeant King killed, Secombe, Chartres wounded; 50 rank and file killed and wounded. We rounded up nine Germans (white men) and killed three or four.
>
> Since then we have been pursuing. Our men have got their tails up and the Huns have got theirs down. I would never have believed before the War that the men would advance within 30 yards of an entrenched position and stay there two days, and then rush—it was raining all the time too.[23]

---

[23] *Ibido.* p. 159

By 3 November British and French columns had converged and occupied Tibati and by 18 December 1915 Cunliffe Force was at a line Ditam-Yoko, well placed to block any attempt by the Germans to escape to the north.

Operations in the South: the advance from Edea as it was in March-April 1915

General Dobell was approached in March by a mission from French Equatorial Africa led by the Lieutenant-Governor of the Middle Congo, M. Fourneau, to collaborate with French General Aymerich in an advance on Yaunde. Dobell was reluctant for two reasons: one, he did not think he had enough troops, and two, the rainy season was already on them and operations would normally be discontinued until September. However, in deference to Fourneau and the advantages of an early occupation of Yaunde, he agreed.

The plan was for one column, British, to follow the Yaunde road and the other, French, to go along the railway to Eseka and to meet up at Wumbiagas. While the other 1NR companies were left in place 2/1NR was dispatched by rail from Bonaberi to Edea on 9 April. On 11 April Lieutenant Colonel Haywood, CO 2NR with one section Nigerian Artillery (two guns), 2/1NR, HQ and three companies 2NR, 1 company SLR (Sierra Leone), the Gambia Detachment and six machine-guns, 600 rifles in total, took the Yaunde road. The 1NR company was the vanguard and encountered opposition all the way. The dense bush and the rain did not help. On the 13th Haywood bivouacked 1,000 yards from the river Ngwe:

> 14/4/15 Sgt. L Everitt with No.3 Section paraded at 4.15 a.m. As support to the guns, Capt. AN Balders, Capt. CJ Maclaverty, C/Sgt. CL Chandless, 50 rifles and the Maxim Gun with Sgt. Prince RAMC in charge of medical arrangements paraded at 5.15 a.m. forming a right flank column in the attack on the German position at the R. NGWE.
>
> No.4 Section remained behind in Camp as baggage Guard. No.2 Coy., No.1/Bn. N. Regt., was ordered to cross the R. NGWE over a ford about 2 miles down stream and endeavour to attack the enemy's left flank while the remainder of the force concentrated their attack against the front. On arriving at the ford we were fired upon from the other side but the Germans soon cleared off and we crossed safely without any

casualties—No.R/421 Pte. Garuba Gaya and No.6282 Pte. Oseni displayed great courage here by volunteering to go across the river to ascertain if the Germans had retired. We had a very tiring march through dense bush—at 10 a.m., we had reached a point about 200 yds, from the main road and here we marched off into the bush at 11 a.m. We came out in sight of the German position. We advanced to within about 150 yds of the position before we were noticed and the enemy opened fire. By that time our Maxim Gun was in a good position on our left flank—we had a fair[l]y warm time for about ½ hour, 2 of our men being killed:- No.6080 Pte Adamu Dorozo and R/429 Pte Musa Kano. The enemy's position was a very strong one, being an excellently prepared Redoubt surrounded by a very strong barbed wire entanglement. About 12 noon we were within 50 yds of the wire entanglement, the enemy was believed to have gone then, an order to fix Bayonets and charge was given—the men went forward splendidly but when we got into the Redoubt we found the enemy had got away. One dead German Soldier also the tripod of their M. Gun, 5 tanels,[24] 3 spare locks and about 300 rounds of Amtn: were found.

No.5232 Pte. Dowdu Darbai No.4 Coy. No.1/BN, attached to No.2 Coy was severely wounded on the head whilst escort to the Guns. MGCs[25] Ari Kukawa and Musa Bauchi did excellent work during the fighting, bringing up reserve Ammunition and distributing it out to the men in the firing line.

15/4/15 Orders received that Column would remain here until the end of the month before moving on. Capt. AM Balders placed on Sick List with dysentery.[26]

The French column under Commandant Mechet left Edea at the same time and on 13 April forced the crossing of the Kele river with 15 casualties. It was not an easy task following the railway as many of the bridges had been destroyed but they finally occupied Eseka on 11 May.

The Haywood column left Ngwe on 1 May with 1NR company in the vanguard and bumped the enemy several times during the day with one German soldier was killed. They reached Nsoga and camped. The following day the pattern was the same although they encountered a position held by 20 Germans on

---

[24] Tanel is Hindi for subway. A T-shaped piece of metal or wood on a boat to which ropes are attached or the protection on the sole of a shoe.
[25] Machine-Gun Carriers
[26] *War Diary of N° 2 Company 1NR* for 14 & 15 May 1915.

the east side of the river Ninupe. The position was taken with one German killed and no Nigerian casualties. On 3 May 2/1NR was Baggage and Rear Guard. One section was escort to the Guns. The column encountered fierce resistance at Wumbiagas on the east bank of the river Mbila. The column fought hard all day and C/Sgt Chandless was very active with 2 Company's Maxim Gun. The column camped half a mile west of the river. The WAFF casualties that day were Lieutenant Martsham Ross, GCR, killed, Lieutenant Beattie (Adjutant), Lieutenant Warren and Colour Sergeant Dwyer severely wounded and 20 AORs killed and wounded.

The following day 2/1NR left the camp at 05.15 to do a recce and try to turn the left flank of the Germans. By the time they reached the German position it had been evacuated and the column camped the night half a mile east of the river.

From 5 to 11 May the column was at Ngwe patrolling in the area and along the Yaunde road. The Germans were sniping continually at the camp. On 11 May a patrol was sent out and discovered that the Germans were 800-900 yards away with 50 soldiers and several Europeans. They fought them all day but with little effect as the bush was so dense.

The following day half the column, including 2/1NR was mobilised to support the French who were having a hard time at the river Kele on the way up from Eseka. They went south through the bush and, having heard from the locals that the French had occupied Eseka, returned to Wumbiagas on 15 May. On 19 May the French column arrived in Wumbiagas and the rains really started.

After resting and reprovisioning the advance continued on 25 May under the command of French Colonel Mayer.

> This column, about two thousand strong with a host of carriers, soon found itself in the grip of the primeval forest through which the men had to hack their way when off the beaten track, often up to their waists in swamp and ever in the face of an enemy disputing every yard of ground in well-chosen and concealed positions, the deluge of rain swelling the sea of trouble. Under such conditions it became increasingly difficult to carry forward sufficient supplies to maintain the force.[27]

The British troops were in the vanguard and 2/1NR were the

---

[27] Gorges, *The Great War in West Africa*, p. 218

leading company. There was opposition all the way and a number of casualties and on the first day they made only two and a half miles, the next days were scarcely better and the French took over the vanguard. By 30 May they were in Ngok some four miles from Wumbiagas and the rain was incessant. The pattern repeated itself over the next four days with the British troops leading the column initially. The French later took over the lead and the column reached Matem a further three miles down the road on 4 June. Over the next eight days despite reinforcements coming up from Duala the force only managed to reach the Puge river some 12 miles from Wumbiagas. They were still 53 miles from Yaunde.

The battle casualties, sickness and the rain had taken their toll of the troops and with the difficulties of supply—the French had lost a major supply convoy to the enemy—Mayer requested Dobell's agreement to retreat. On 14 June the force retired to Wumbiagas and did the 12 miles in five hours, having spent 19 days fighting to get there! They went on back to Ngwe on the 16th.

Meanwhile Battalion HQ and 1 and 3 companies 1NR were around Duala. On 16 June they took the train to Edea and the following day moved up to Ngwe. Cockburn then took command of this garrison which consisted of seven companies, three mountain guns and a Machine Gun section. For the next twelve days the enemy made sporadic attacks on the outposts and then retired.

On 26 June the British units withdrew to Edea and the French took over Ngwe garrison.

At the beginning of July 1915 Dobell had the following troops in Southern Cameroon:

Unit	Effective	Sick	Total	N° Coys
Gambia Detachment	34	27	61	
Sierra Leone Battalion	514	65	579	6
Gold Coast Battalion	789	87	876	5
Unit	Effective	Sick	Total	N° Coys
1 Nigeria Regiment	437	224	661	4
2 Nigeria Regiment	291	286	577	4
West African Regiment	682	34	716	6
TOTAL	2747	723	3470	

These figures show how the two Nigerian battalions had been depleted by sickness.

With the rainy season full on, military operations in the direction of Yaunde were suspended and attention turned to the Germans who were harassing the Nyong flotilla. On 5 July Captain Fell and 122 men of 4 company 1NR left for Dehane. Four days later Major Coles with 3/1NR and 30 from the Gold Coast Regiment left for Dehane. With the reinforcements the enemy camp at Ekjane was occupied and destroyed and the Nigerians returned to Duala on 16 July leaving the GCR detachment as a garrison at Dehane. One man was killed and six were wounded in this operation.

On 20 July, 2 and 4 companies embarked for Nigeria, 2 destined for Kano and 4 for Zungeru. 3 company stayed in Duala. On the 26th, 1/1NR left for Campo with two companies of GCR, 1/2 company of SLR, one naval gun, one sub-section Nigerian Battery as part of the force under Lieutenant Colonel Rose to patrol the border and prevent the German forces escaping to Rio Muni. The SLR detachment stayed as garrison and the rest returned to Duala on 4 September.

Lieutenant Colonel Cockburn was appointed commander of the British Contingent on 31 August.

On 4 September 2 and 4 companies returned from Nigeria and on the 8th, 1 company embarked for recuperative leave in Nigeria. For the rest of the month a base routine was followed and there were various in and out postings of personnel.

The month of October saw the end of the rains and the battalion in garrison in Duala while the remainder of the British force under Colonel Haywood resumed the advance on Yaunde. On the 6th Haywood moved out of Ngwe and the French force moved up the railway line to Eseka. By 9 October Haywood was in Wumbiagas and the French reached Eseka, now deserted by the Germans. Short of supplies until 23 November the French would not move from Eseka. During November lNR were moved up towards Yaunde and on the 23rd the column left Wumbiagas. 1NR under Cockburn was on the right flank and drove the enemy back for some 12 miles.

> Off the road the troops had to work their way through very thick undergrowth covering precipitous hills, while in the valleys they had to wade through wide stretches of swamp, sometimes above their waists. Colonel Cockburn's battalion

of Nigerians bore the brunt of the week's fighting on our right flank, forcing the passage of the Kele river near Lesogs, his losses in killed and wounded bearing witness to its conduct and work in the field and Cockburn's fine leadership.[28]

The casualties in the six days of the battle at Lesogs were three officers and 19 AORs killed or died of wounds and four officers and 76 AORs wounded and by the 28th the well-entrenched Puge river position was captured and Ngung was occupied. Here the fortifications were strengthened and the troops had a few days' rest.

On 7 December the advance to Chang Mangas continued with Haywood in the vanguard. It was still very difficult country and after 10 days hard fighting the column reached the main road one mile east of Chang Mangas and entered the town without resistance. Here was a fort, blockhouses and a hospital. In those ten days 1NR had 32 casualties, more than any other unit. Cockburn's War Diary for November was typed up in Chang Mangas and signed by him on 19 December. The various units carried out routine patrols from there and suffered casualties. Reinforcements were received and preparations were made for the final push to Yaunde.

The French meanwhile had left Eseka on 23 November and in the face of heavy opposition had reached Mangeles on 21 December suffering 175 casualties.

The final advance on Yaunde started on 23 December, Dobell ignoring a request from the German commander for a truce over Christmas. Cockburn and 1NR were in reserve initially and moved up on 27 December, where with the Gambia company, they relieved Haywood and reached Unguot. Three days later they were close to Yaunde with considerable opposition and were relieved by Haywood and his 2NR force. On 31 December Rose's GCR column occupied Mendong on Yaunde-Kribi road.

On 1 January 1916 the Force entered the deserted town of Yaunde and occupied the fort. The Rose column entered the Catholic Mission Station. 1NR were deployed for the defence of the south-west corner of the town. From there they carried out patrols to the south over the next few days and German deserters were coming in giving information. Efforts were made

---

[28] *Ibid.* p. 238

to pursue the German forces and on 8 January Haywood reached Widemenge, south of Yaunde on the Nyong river after overcoming a strong rearguard action. The result of this was that all the allied prisoners of war, including British and French officers, AORs and a few non-combatants were released. All had received fair and humane treatment during their captivity.

On 9 January Cockburn was appointed Commander British Eastern Forces, succeeding Colonel Gorges. Major RG Coles was appointed CO 1NR and took a column down the Kribi road to Ebolowa, consisting of 1NR, Gambia company, one gun of the Nigerian Battery, and the supply column. The armoured car, which had suddenly appeared, joined them later in the day and subsequently returned to Yaunde. On 10 January they met up with the French in Engumo (Ngoumou). They camped there for a few days but by the 15th they were having difficulty getting local produce to feed the carriers and the troops. This was alleviated two days later with the arrival of a supply column.

The Coles column pressed on against considerable opposition at Elabe. Five AORs were wounded before they were able to occupy the town and there they found a German mission with: 13 European men (missionaries?), five women, four cows, five horses, three donkeys etc etc.

On 24 January Coles column arrived at Ebolowa and continued to Ngalan on the Lolodorf road and on the 29th they arrived at Lolodorf. While they were at Ngalan, on 25 January they had been asked to send on an officers' detachment to the American mission two and a half miles from Lolodorf as the American missionaries there were nervous of the natives.[29]

On 31 January the Haywood column was ordered to Kribi for embarkation for Nigeria. Major Coles signed the 1NR War Diary for January at Lolodorf on 3 February and the battalion spent the rest of the month there.[30] It was a centre of activity, the GOC and staff all passed through on the way to Kribi. The Germans, short of food and ammunition, had slipped through the net and escaped to Rio Muni by 18 February.

Early in February Ebermaier, the Governor of Cameroon, and Colonel Zimmermann the overall German commander surrendered to the Spanish authorities. Mora, the German

---

[29] *War Diary of 1NR* for 25.1.16.
[30] War Diary of Lolodorf Road Column [1NR], 3.2.16

redoubt in northern Cameroon finally capitulated on 18 February. There were 11 Europeans, 145 black Africans, four Machine Guns and 183 rifles. The officers were allowed to keep their swords.

On 29 February 1916 1NR and the rest of the column under Major Coles were ordered to Kribi for embarkation to Nigeria.

The casualties of the campaign for the whole of the WAFF were:

	African	European
Participants	5927	864
Invalided out	434	151
Killed or died of wounds	192	24
Wounded	557	30
Died of Disease	84	6

For the 1st Battalion the detailed figures are below.

References

TNA: WO 95/5387/4 Cameroons Headquarters and Troops; 1 Battalion Nigeria regiment, War Diary: September 1914 to February 1916

Haywood, Austen & Clarke, FS, *The History of the Royal West African Frontier Force* (Gale & Polden, 1964)

Farwell, Byron, *The Great War in Africa* (Norton, 1964)

Gorges, E Howard, *The Great War in West Africa* (Naval & Military Press, 2004)

Killingray, David, *The British Military Presence in West Africa* (Oxford: University of Oxford Development Records Project, vol 3, 1983)

Strachan, Hew, *The First World War in Africa* (Rhaniket Press, 2007)

Osborne, Myles & Kingsley, Susan, *Africans and Britons in the Age of Empires* (Routledge, 2005)

Nominal Rolls of September 1914

		Officers	BNCOs	AORs	MG Carriers	Posted in Cam	TOTAL AORs	Killed	Wounded	Invalided out	Disease	Left in Nigeria
	HQ 1st Bn	4	4	19								
1 Coy	A Coy 1Bn	6	2	151	6	81	238	4	37	1	3	5
2 Coy	F Coy 1 Bn	5	3	149	6	72	227	16	25	3		11
3 Coy	D Coy 2 Bn (2 offrs local civilians)	7	2	149	7	65	221	7	17	2		3
4 Coy	F Coy 2 Bn (2 offrs local civilians)	6	2	172	7	63	242	7	42	2	2	13
	Medical Team	4	2									
	Total	32	15	640	26	281	928	34	121	8	5	32
											1 Deserter	

Figures from Original Nominal Rolls marked up at end of Cameroon campaign
Latest date 19.12.1916 at Elabe

	Offrs Personal Servants	42
	Mess cooks	7
	Carriers	176
	44 Europeans at 4 personnel	
1	1 Orderly Room Clerk at 1	1
2	Signalling equipment	6
3	Entrenching tools	50
4	Tents	50
5	G45 R&F and MGCs at 16%	45
6	Company stores	12
7	Battalion records	3
8	Battalion cash tank	1
9	Battalion Armourer's tools	6
10	Medical loads	72
11	Reserve ammunition	60
12	Water carriers	60
13	Total	542

Battalion on move 1566

In addition to the above 16 carriers would be required if one day's ration of 11/2 lbs per man for the battalion Carriers for European food have not been allowed for.

North East Africa

Northern and Eastern Africa during the Great War

Harry Fecitt[1]

The Senussi Campaign

Working from eastern Libya, Sayed Ahmed, known as the Senussi, was the leader of a sect of devout Muslims who as a group took their leader's name of Senussi. His men had been fighting the Italian occupiers of Libya with considerable success. They were trained and assisted by a group of Turkish military officers led by Nuri Bey, half-brother of the Turkish War Minister, Enver Pasha. During 1915 German submarines began supporting the Turkish effort with the Senussi's army by transporting Turks and weapons to Eastern Libya and attacking shipping along the Egyptian coast. The Senussi was at first reluctant to fight Britain, but in the end Nuri Bey persuaded him to join the Turkish Holy War and to invade Egypt. The Allied reverses at Gallipoli doubtless influenced the Senussi's thoughts and actions.

In early November 1915, a German submarine sank the British ships *Tara* and *Moorina* off the western Egyptian coast, and the British survivors of these attacks were handed over by the submarine to the Senussi who arranged their captivity. The Senussi's troops then harassed and fired upon the British outposts at Sollum and Sidi el Barrani. British Headquarters in Cairo decided that a withdrawal was necessary, and all British troops west of Matruh were ordered to move to that location. At Sollum, the most westerly British post, the withdrawal was

[1] Harry Fecitt, MBE, TD, retired from military life in 2002 since when he has been researching and writing about campaigns in Africa and Asia. Many of his articles can be found at www.kaisercross.com with others on www.gweaa.com. He is author of *Sideshows of the Indian Army in World War I* (Vij Books, India, 2018)

effected rather too hastily, as the Egyptian Army garrison of the fort was left behind. During the withdrawal, many Egyptian Coastguards deserted to the Senussi with their weapons and camels. The Senussi's followers now occupied and pillaged all the abandoned British locations.

The British then reorganized their forces and advanced westwards to confront the Senussi. After several serious engagements the British, working in concert with Italians operating from Libyan territory, had by March 1916 cleared the coast and freed the captives held by the Senussi.

But the Senussi moved inland and occupied oases in the Egyptian Western Desert. The British attacked using aircraft and armoured cars and also blockaded the Libyan coast to prevent arms and supplies reaching the Senussi from the Turks. By February 1917 the Senussi had withdrawn to Libya and a peace was negotiated with the British, although Senussi hostilities with the Italians continued until the end of the war.

Sources:
McGuirk, Russell, *The Senussi's Little War: The Amazing Story of a Forgotten Conflict in the Western Desert, 1915–1917* (Arabian, 2007)
Macmunn, G; Falls, C, *Military Operations: Egypt and Palestine, From the Outbreak of War with Germany to June 1917. History of the Great War Based on Official Documents By Direction of the Historical Section of the Committee of Imperial Defence. I (repr 1928. Battery Press 1996)*
Field Marshall Lord Carver, *The National Army Museum Book of the Turkish Front 1914-18.* (Pan, 2004)
Fecitt, Harry. *The 15th Ludhiana Sikhs and the Senussi*
http://www.kaiserscross.com/188001/297622.html

The Darfur Campaign

The Darfur region of the Sudan has been on our news-programme television screens for some time, depicted as a remote desert corner of Africa where raids, rapes and massacres occur, and where child-soldiers are recruited. In 1916 the British Army mounted a campaign against the Ruler of Darfur.

The British had abandoned the Anglo-Egyptian Sudan in 1884 in the face of a revolt that they could not handle. General Gordon stayed on in Khartoum but was killed and beheaded by rebels in January 1885, just two days before a British relief column arrived. Retribution was necessary and General Kitchener gained a decisive victory over the rebels at Omdurman in 1898.

The British, through the Sudan government, then expanded political influence in the Sudan and finally defeated the remnants of religious insurrectionist forces a year later at Umm Diwaykarat. Here the Sudanese insurgent leader, the Khalifa, was killed and his remaining troops wiped out. Hiram Maxim's gun controlled the battlefields, and British fingers and thumbs were firing it.

As Hillaire Belloc wrote:

"Whatever happens we have got
The Maxim Gun and they have not."

Darfur (the land of the Fur people) lay on Sudan's western border with French Chad. Just to the north was the Libyan-Sudanese border and political problems in Italian-run Libya, known as Tripoli, during World War One were to lead to the British campaign in Darfur in 1916.

The leader of the Tama tribe in Darfur, Ali Dinar, had signified his acceptance of Sudanese government authority after Omdurman, and the government appointed him as their agent for Darfur. However Ali Dinar played his own game in his remote unattractive land, gradually distancing himself from British influence. By 1901 he had become the independent Sultan of Darfur, paying nominal tribute to the Governor-General in Khartoum.

Historically Turkish influence was strong, and in fact Egypt and the Sudan were theoretical provinces of the Ottoman Empire until 1914 when Britain declared Egypt a British Protectorate. Sultan Ali Dinar did not like this British move and when Turkey entered the Great War he corresponded with Turkish officers in Libya.

Ali Dinar probably felt optimistic because at that time the Germans and Turks were providing a lot of support for the Libyan leader of the Senussi people who was fighting the Allies. The Senussi leader, Grand Sheikh Sayyid Ahmed al-Sharif, had driven Italian troops back to the Libyan coast, was supporting dissidence against the French in Tunis, had invaded Egypt, and was encouraging Ali Dinar in Darfur.

Ali Dinar, believing Turco-German propaganda promising

that an Islamic state would be created in northern Africa when the European colonisers had been driven out, decided to challenge British authority in Sudan. He had some legitimate grievances, such as British passivity towards French land-grabbing on his western border, and his tribesmen did not want to accept the application of quarantine regulations when selling livestock in other regions of Sudan, but it was the arrival of around 250 rifles and some boxes of ammunition in Darfur, sent by the Senussi in Libya, that tipped the scale and decided British action against him.

The Governor-General of the Sudan, General Sir Reginald Wingate GCB, ordered the mounting of a punitive expedition to Darfur under the command of Lieutenant-Colonel PV Kelly, 3rd Hussars. The force was 2,000 strong and included:

2 companies of Mounted Infantry
2 batteries of Artillery (six 12.5 pounder Mountain Guns)
12 Maxim Guns (half of them British-crewed, with Mule transport)
5 companies of Camel Corps
6 companies Sudanese Infantry (XIII & XIV Battalions)
2 companies Arab Infantry (from the Arab Battalion)
3 companies Egyptian Infantry (from the IVth Battalion)
1,200 baggage camels organised into five Transport Companies plus supporting medical, supply and transport services.

Also, and importantly, Egyptian Army HQ provided a flight of four BE2 aeroplanes of the Royal Flying Corps and eleven 30-cwt motor lorries.

The British Intelligence Officer responsible for Darfur, Captain HA MacMichael, estimated that the Fur Army could put into the field 800 Regular Cavalry, 3,000 Regular Infantry with rifles "but very badly trained and ill-equipped with ammunition", and perhaps up to 2,000 irregular spearmen.

The difficulties of the campaign lay not in the military opposition but in the distance to and remoteness of Darfur, and the shortage of good wells for drinking water between the railhead at El Obeid and El Fasher, the Sultan's capital. El Obeid was 428 miles (690 km) from the military base at Khartoum and El Fasher was 400 miles (650 km) further on from El Obeid.

On 16 March 1916 the British Western Frontier Force, as it was titled (quickly adapted to *Waterless Fatigue Force* by the

British soldiers involved) marched north-westwards from the railhead through desolate scorching country—at one point it is alleged that the water being carried on camels in tins was boiling from the sun's heat!

Whilst the Royal Flying Corps (RFC) flew reconnaissance missions and made a propaganda leaflet drop on El Fasher (one plane being damaged by a Fur bullet-strike on the propeller), mounted troops moved ahead of the main column to seize key water-holes, sometimes skirmishing for them but always being able to deploy more effective firepower than the Fur Army could. The key water-hole of Melit was seized on 18 May after a RFC bombing raid caused the Fur garrison to withdraw. The Force, now considerably fatigued, concentrated at Melit and rested in preparation for an advance south onto El Fasher.

On 21 May the British advance resumed, mounted troops keeping in touch with large parties of Fur horsemen and camel-mounted troops. The following morning saw the British camp struck at 0530 hours and the whole force advance in square formation through large sand dunes that limited visibility. This was one of the last occasions that a large British square advanced to the attack and it must have been a memorable spectacle and experience for those involved.

The Mounted Infantry composed the front face of the square, but because of the proximity of enemy mounted troops four Maxims escorted by a company of Camel Corps were added to this front face. At around 1030 hours the square halted whilst Artillery and Maxims came into action to disperse an entrenched enemy group on the left of the axis of advance. The square advanced again another 800 yards (730 metres) and began to entrench for a rest from the fierce midday heat.

Now the British could see a small village, named Beringia, 500 yards (460 metres) to the front, and ominously a small length of trench containing about 200 men behind the village. This was in fact part of a trench over a mile long containing the main Fur force that was waiting to ambush the British. As his men dug-in Lt Col Kelly planned an attack to be delivered from the left front of his square onto the length of enemy trench that he could see, and he formed-up his assault troops.

However at that moment Major HJ Huddlestone, Dorsetshire Regiment, the Camel Corps company commander in the front face, advanced his company without orders to a ridge to the right front that overlooked Beringia Village. Why "Huddle" as his contemporaries called him, made this move is not known, but perhaps from his elevated seat on his camel he had seen the extent of the enemy trench, and so he determined to seize and fight from what he considered to be vital ground on the ridge above Beringia.

Major Huddleston's move triggered a general Fur attack as they swarmed out of their trench in their brightly-coloured robes, raised their battle-flags and raced towards the hated British infidels. The British infantry on the two sides of the square now swung forward to join the face in one long firing line containing eight Artillery guns, four Maxims and five companies of Infantry.

The Fur warriors displayed tremendous courage in storming forward to attack the British firing line, where Captain Alexander Pott would have been steadying his men and issuing fire orders. Successive waves of attackers were cut down by British firepower, the nearest warriors getting within 10 yards of the line before being killed. After 40 minutes of carnage the Fur finally wavered and fell back. Lt Col Kelly then ordered a counter-attack, and as the Sudanese Infantry trotted forward offering the bayonet and supported by Artillery and Maxims the Fur broke and fled.

Out of an estimated 4,000 attackers the Fur left 261 dead and 96 seriously wounded on the battlefield, and because of their ability to accept wounds that would have immobilized Europeans, probably many more seriously wounded walked or staggered away. The British casualties were three Officers wounded, five Other Ranks killed and 18 wounded. Major Huddlestone's Camel Corps company, which Lt Col Kelly had not expected to survive as it was outside the square, had only four men slightly wounded. That ridge above Beringia obviously was good ground to fight from.

That afternoon at 1600 hours the British Force advanced towards El Fasher, halting and entrenching a few miles outside the capital. Here at 0300 hours next morning 500 Fur cavalry with 300 infantry attacked the British square. The British illuminated the battlefield with star shell and magnesium flares, giving the Artillery and Maxims another good shoot. After ten minutes of heavy defensive firing this attack dispersed. A British aircraft piloted by Lieutenant John Slessor (later to become Air Marshal Sir John Slessor) bombed the Fur assault group as it withdrew towards El Fasher.

At 1000 hours Lt Col Kelly and the mounted troops entered El Fasher, which was inhabited by women, children and old men. Sultan Ali Dinar tried to rally his men for another attack on the British, but his two best commanders had been killed at Beringea and his men started dispersing. John Slessor bombed these dispersing troops at the southern end of El Fasher, but Fur riflemen hit him and his plane. It is believed that as Sultan Ali Dinar withdrew southwards with loyal troops he hit John Slessor in the thigh with a round from a sporting rifle presented to him some years earlier by the Governor-General. The aircraft rudder controls were also damaged, making Lieutenant Slessor's return to base difficult. Because of the impending rainy season the Royal Flying Corps now withdrew to Egypt to repair planes and pilot.

Captain MacMichael explored the Sultan's Palace and reported that it was:

> ... a perfect Sudanese Alhambra ... There are small shady gardens and little fish ponds, arcades, colonnades, storerooms and every type of building. The floors are strewn with fine silver sand ... Trellis work in ebony is found in place of interior walls and the very flooring in the women's quarters, under the silvery sand, is impregnated with spices."

Palace records had been scrupulously maintained and one book, using a page for each lady who bore them, listed the names of about 120 of the Sultan's sons. MacMichael forgot what the number of daughters was.

But Ali Dinar was still alive and so the campaign continued. On 29 May Lt Col Kelly received a letter from Ali Dinar, renouncing his sultanate and requesting that he be allowed to live with his family quietly on his lands. Kelly replied that on his surrender the Sultan would be given safe-passage elsewhere. (He would probably have been sent across the Red Sea to exile in the Hedjaz in Saudi Arabia.) Ali agreed, saying he would come in after the rains, but then wrote again to say he could not convince all his men to surrender. Kelly wrote again, requesting a surrender, but by now the British knew that Ali Dinar was playing for time, and so would have to be killed.

On 7 October Lt Col Kelly sent Major Huddlestone with 250 men from the Camel Corps and XIIIth Sudanese Infantry, Alexander Pott's Battalion, south to establish a fortified post at Kas, east of Jebel Marra (Marra Mountain). Whilst on the march "Huddle" heard that a Fur force under the former Sultan's eldest son Zakariya was at Dibbis, on his flank and threatening the British lines of communication. "Huddle" marched on Dibbis, made a surprise attack on the Fur camp and routed Zakariya and his troops.

Major Huddlestone, realizing that he was now near Ali Din's own camp, requested reinforcements so that he could attack. Both Kelly and Wingate said "No". But as we have seen, "Huddle" was not the kind of chap to let the grass grow under his feet whilst senior officers pondered. Hearing of a Fur camp not far away at Kulme he marched with 100 men on ponies and mules and attacked the camp at dawn. Maxims dispersed the Furs, and whilst most of Huddlestone's men made for the loot and the female companionship in the camp, Huddlestone and a small party chased the best-dressed party of fleeing Furs over a series of ridge-lines, shooting as they pursued.

> ... after about the third rise we came on a thick-built form, with a strong and dignified face marred only by cruel, sensuous lips, with a bullet hole drilled through the centre of his forehead. It was Ali Dinar."

Three of Ali's elder sons, one of them wounded in the leg, waited nearby ready to surrender. The Darfur Campaign was over.

On 1 January 1917 Darfur became a province of the Anglo-Egyptian Sudan under civil administration. Major Hubert Huddlestone, who so ably demonstrated the military virtue of immediately seizing initiatives, went on to become Governor-General of the Sudan between 1940 and 1947. Captain Alexander Pott gained a Mention in Despatches and the silver Khedive's Sudan Medal 1910 with clasp "Darfur 1916". He fought on in the Sudan and earned more clasps.

Sources:
Macmunn, G, Falls, C, *Military Operations: Egypt and Palestine*
Theobald, AB, *Ali Dinar – the last Sultan of Darfur* (Longmans, 1965)
Pott, AJ, *People of the Book* (Blackwood, 1932)
Davis, Reginald, *The Camel's Back*. (J Murray, 1957)
Daly, MW, *Empire on the Nile—The Anglo-Egyptian Sudan 1898-*

1934 (Cambridge UP, 1986)
Herbert, Edwin, *Small Wars & Skirmishes 1902-1918* (Foundry Books, 2003)
London Gazette Issue 29800, 25 October 1916, *Wingates' Despatch*
Keown-Boyd, Henry, *Soldiers of the Nile* (Thornbury, 1996)
Fecitt, Harry. *Darfur 1916,*
http://www.kaiserscross.com/188001/224322.html

The Suez Canal 1914-15

Great Britain and France declared war against Turkey on 5 November 1914. At that time Egypt was theoretically still a province of the Turkish Empire but for practical purposes the country had been occupied and controlled by Britain since 1882. Egypt's strategic importance lay in its possession of the Suez Canal, a waterway regarded with good reason by the Germans as the jugular vein of the British Empire. Britain needed to keep the Canal open to facilitate the transport of troops and mounts from India and Australasia. Also commercial shipping needed the Canal open in order to speedily move the military equipment, food and commodities that originated in British colonies and Dominions in the Far East and which were required in Europe. Germany needed to close the Canal.

The Allied declaration of war resulted in the Sultan of the Ottoman Empire obtaining from the Islamic clergy in Constantinople a proclamation of a Holy War against the Allies. The Sultan himself, as Khalif of his Empire, proclaimed a Jihad (religious war) on all those who were militarily confronting Turkey or her allies. The Khedive (Viceroy of Egypt appointed by Turkey), Abbas Hilmi, had been in Turkey since August 1914; he was actively and openly pro-Turk and he stayed in Turkey where he was used politically by the Central Powers. The British response was to proclaim Egypt a British Protectorate on 18 December 1914. Khedive Abbas Hilmi was deposed and his uncle, Prince Hussein Kamal Pasha, elevated to the Egyptian throne with the new title of Sultan. The British Consul-General, Lord Kitchener (the real power behind the Egyptian throne) was in England in August 1914 and remained there to become Secretary of State for War. He was replaced in Egypt in January 1915 by Sir Henry M'Mahon who held the new title of High Commissioner. In an attempt to reduce tensions in

Egypt where the vast majority of the population was Muslim and where nationalist agitation and hostility to Britain were on the increase, the Egyptians were told that they would not be pressed into fighting the Turks.

The British defence of Egypt

The British peace-time Regular Army garrison in Egypt had consisted of one cavalry regiment, four infantry battalions, one horse and one mountain artillery battery and an engineer field company plus supporting services. In August 1914 these troops were needed in France. The primary task of the Egyptian Army, which contained many British officers, was the defence, and maintenance, of security within the Sudan, and just one field artillery battery, one garrison company and three infantry battalions were located in Egypt when war broke out. They should not have been involved in operations against Turkish troops but British demands of expediency were soon to alter that arrangement.

The Indian Army therefore took over the first-line defence of the Suez Canal, supported by Allied warships. The Lahore (3rd Indian) and Meerut (7th Indian) Divisions passed through the waterway towards France leaving the 9th (Sirhind) Brigade temporarily detached to man the Canal defences. This allowed the British Regular Army garrison in Egypt to also move to France. The Lucknow Brigade was then dispatched from India to relieve the Sirhind Brigade allowing the latter to move on and re-join the Lahore Division. The Egyptian theatre was also allocated an Imperial Service cavalry brigade, composite infantry brigade and the Bikaner Camel Corps (all provided by Indian Princely states), eight Indian Army battalions, and then three all-Indian Army brigades. These troops were organized into two Divisions, the 10th and 11th, and eventually were titled "Indian Expeditionary Force E".

One other British formation had been mobilized in England and sent to Egypt. This was the Territorial Army East Lancashire Division which needed intensive training to reach operational fitness. Newly-raised and mobilised units from the Australian and New Zealand Corps (ANZACs) were also heading for Egypt for war training before deployment to France. The British rather complacently considered the Sinai Desert east of the canal to also be a defence because it was mostly waterless, and to make things even more difficult for any Turkish movement westwards from Palestine a detachment of Egyptian Coastguards destroyed the wells at Nekhl 70 miles east of Suez.

Turkish and German preparations

However there was one man in Palestine who considered that the Sinai Desert was more of a logistical challenge than an obstacle. He was Oberst Freiherr Kress von Kressenstein, a German officer attached to the Turkish Army. Kress had previously reconnoitered into the Desert of Sinai, and after hostilities were declared he headed a German team of six staff officers attached to the Turkish VIII Corps at Damascus.

When a decision was made to attack the Suez Canal Kress became the chief planner of this Turkish operation. In Damascus Djemal Pasha, the energetic Commander of the Turkish Fourth Army, and his German Army Chief of Staff, Oberst von Frankenberg und Proschlitz, organized an expeditionary force of around 23,000 men, nine field batteries of artillery plus a 15-centimetre howitzer battery. The majority of the men to be used in the initial attacks on the Canal came from the Syrian territories of the Ottoman Empire but the force reserve was the 10th Division composed of Turks. Regular cavalry and camel-mounted troops supplemented the Bedouin irregulars who were raised for the operation. Djemal Pasha was hoping to provoke a revolt within Egypt against the British occupiers. Kress was probably more realistic in wanting (he later claimed) to hold the west bank of the waterway for two or three days whilst ships were sunk to cause a serious blockage. Kress' team purchased camels and loaded 5,000 of them with water carriers, prepared roads and brushwood tracks through the Sinai for the artillery, and equipped the two engineer battalions with pontoons.

Meanwhile in northern Sinai the first confrontation between the Turkish and British armies had occurred at Bir El Nuss. On 20 November 1915 a 22-man strong patrol from the Bikaner Camel Corps fought with a group of 200 Bedouins and Turks, losing one Indian officer and twelve men killed and three men wounded. The British patrol commander, Captain AJH Chope, 2nd Gurkha Rifles, returned with an enemy bullet lodged in his saddle and claimed to have inflicted 60 casualties on the enemy.

An Indian Order of Merit 2nd Class was awarded to 1534 Sepoy Ali Khan and an Indian Distinguished Service Medal to 115 Sepoy Faiz Ali Khan. Unfortunately during this patrol several Sudanese members of the Egyptian Coastguard who were acting as guides for Chope allowed themselves to be captured. These men then served as guides for the Turks.

By mid-January 1915 the General Officer Commanding Canal Defences, Major General A Wilson, had allocated his troops into three sectors.

Sector I. (Southern) Port Tewfik to Geneffe.
30th Brigade. 24th and 76th Punjabis. 126th Baluchis. 2/7th Gurkha Rifles. 1 squadron Imperial Service Cavalry. 1 Company Bikaner Camel Corps. A half-company of Sappers and Miners. 1 Territorial Battery Royal Field Artillery. 1 Indian Field Ambulance.

Sector II. (Central) Deversoir to El Ferdan (inclusive).
22nd Brigade (less 3rd Brahmans). 62nd and 92nd Punjabis. 2/10th Gurkha Rifles.
28th Frontier Force Brigade. 51st and 53rd Sikhs. 65th Punjabis. 1/5th Gurkha Rifles. 1 squadron Imperial Service Cavalry. Bikaner Camel Corps (less 3 and ½ companies). The Machine Gun section of the Egyptian Camel Corps. 1 Territorial Brigade Royal Field Artillery. 1 Battery Indian Mountain Artillery. 2 Field Ambulances.

Sector III.(Northern) El Ferdan (exclusive) to Port Said.
29th Brigade. 14th Sikhs. 69th and 89th Punjabis. 1/6th Gurkha Rifles. 3rd Brahmans from 22nd Brigade. A half company of Sappers and Miners. 1 squadron Imperial Service Cavalry. 2 companies Bikaner Camel Corps. 2 Territorial Batteries Royal Field Artillery. 26th Battery Indian Mountain Artillery. An Armoured Train with a half company of Indian infantry. An Indian Field Ambulance.
A Territorial Royal Army Medical Corps detachment.

Other Indian Army and Imperial Service troops secured the Advanced Ordnance Depot at Zagazig, the railway, the Sweet Water Canal and also formed a General Reserve at Moascar. (The Imperial Service Cavalrymen were the Mysore and Hyderabad Lancers, whilst the Rulers of Alwar, Gwalior and Patiala provided the infantry.) Territorial, Indian, Australian and Egyptian sappers, pioneers and military works personnel were given engineering tasks to strengthen the canal defences, which included a few strongly-defended posts on the east bank. British and French planes flew reconnaissance missions whilst British and French warships entered or stood by to enter the Canal to provide fire support wherever required. As the British prepared their defences the Turks advanced in three columns across the Sinai Desert, encouraged by their German mentors.

Initial contacts and British reactions

From 18 January 1915 onwards Allied aircraft began reporting the progress of the Turkish advance and two brigades of British Territorial field artillery were deployed forward into prepared positions west of the Canal. On 22 January the enemy skirmished with British covering forces east of Kantara leading to the 33rd Punjabis and the 4th Gwalior Infantry, both from 32 Brigade, being deployed forward into that sector. The New Zealand Infantry Brigade also moved forward and detrained at Kubri and Ismailiah.

Five days later the Turkish southern column attacked the British Baluchistan and El Kubri posts on the east side of the canal in Sector I. Both attacks were easily beaten off without loss and appeared to be diversionary. The following day attacks were mounted on the Kantara outposts but without conviction. In the belief that Sector II would see the decisive confrontation, 2nd Rajputs from 31st Brigade was sent to reinforce Serapeum. The large Turkish central column was observed in the vicinity of Jebel Habeita and the 5th Battery, Egyptian Artillery was deployed to Toussom. On 1 February troops from the enemy central column advanced northeast towards the Ismailia Ferry post. The British outer screen engaged these troops but the Turks did not press forward and dug themselves in at about three kilometres distance from the British main positions.

Crossing the canal

A decisive Turkish move was made at 0330 hours on 3 February when several pontoons and rafts were launched 1,500 metres south of Toussom. Heavy rifle and machine gun fire from the 62nd Punjabis supported by excellent gunnery from the 5th Battery, Egyptian Artillery, decimated the attackers. But at least two pontoons reached the west bank. The Turks who had crossed the canal could make no headway against determined British counter-attacks and the survivors hid along the edge of the canal. This action was not without British loss as the Turkish covering fire was effective, Mulazzim Awaal Effendi Helmi of the 5th Battery, Egyptian Artillery being killed whilst gallantly fighting his gun under heavy fire at short range. Lieutenant RA Fitzgibbon, 128th Pioneers, who commanded the protection party for the Egyptian battery died of wounds after counter-attacking Turks on the west bank. Two other smaller Turkish landings on the west bank were made nearby but neither progressed far, as Indian troops either killed or captured the enemy who survived the crossing. Whilst this action took place the enemy northern column unsuccessfully attacked the Kantara outposts, losing many men.

As dawn broke the British saw that nearly all the Turks on the west bank had been neutralized but that was not the case on the east bank, where an enemy attack was being launched against the Toussoum post. Turks were occupying trenches around the post and the 92nd Punjabis, supported by naval gunfire and enfilade machine gun fire, successfully cleared this ground during a nine-hour fight. Seven Turkish officers and 280 other ranks were killed or captured. The 2nd Rajputs mopped up the Turkish survivors sheltering along the west bank.

Serapeum post, south of Toussoum, was also under attack. Two companies of 2/10th Gurkhas and six platoons of 2nd Rajputs crossed the canal by ferry where they were joined by two companies of 92nd Punjabis from a post on the east bank. This force advanced north up the canal edge clearing a surprising number of Turks out of broken ground until the enemy 74th Regiment of the 25th Division advanced towards Serapeum. Heavy firing now started and Captain RT Arundel, 2nd Rajputs, was killed whilst moving his men along the canal bank. But with the aid of fire support from two French warships the small British force halted the Turkish regiment about one kilometre away from the canal.

As the unused pontoons lying on the east bank needed destroying, a Royal Navy torpedo boat moved along the canal using its 3-pounder gun to fire two rounds into each pontoon. When the boat commander decided to land in order to use gun cotton against any pontoons out of sight over the canal bank, he almost walked into a manned Turkish trench. During the scramble back aboard the boat the commander and another officer were wounded.

Further north the Turkish 68th Regiment of the 23rd Division advanced against Ismailiah ferry post but the attack halted 750 metres from the British wire. Whilst the enemy infantry attacks had not prevailed, the Turkish artillery fire was effective and the armed Indian ship *Hardinge* had to quickly move after receiving hits from a 15-centimetre howitzer battery. The French *Requin* finally silenced the enemy howitzers. The Turkish southern column made no further aggressive moves. During the night of 3rd March Australian infantry was moved up to support Sector II. This Sector received sniping during the hours of darkness.

As daylight crept across the desert on 4 February the British in Sector II observed that the main body of Turks had withdrawn but scattered groups of enemy remained near the east bank. Captain LFA Cochran, 92nd Punjabis, was in a post on the east bank and was ordered to use two companies to clear the enemy stragglers. Whilst attempting to do this Captain Cochran was killed. A company from each of the 27th and 62nd Punjabis and the 128th Pioneers were now sent across the canal and after an action lasting an hour 298 of the enemy surrendered, 52 of them being seriously wounded. Amongst the 59 enemy dead was the body of Hauptmann von den Hagen, the German staff officer who had supervised the operation to cross the canal.

Conclusion

All three Turkish columns now withdrew eastwards across Sinai. The British failed to mount a pursuit, citing lack of training especially amongst the cavalry, and so the Turkish guns and gunners and the mass of infantry lived to fight another day. Allied aviators did drop some bombs on the withdrawing enemy. The battle was hailed as a British defensive success, which it was, and a Turkish defeat, which it only partially was as the bulk of the enemy forces withdrew in good order along their well-constructed desert tracks. British casualties numbered 163 (ten of them being naval) and Turkish casualties were estimated at over 2,000.

Had Djemel Pasha's dream of an Egyptian uprising actually happened then the British would have been pressed to both maintain internal security throughout Egypt and the Sudan and to defend the complete length of the canal. The Indian Army had fought professionally to hold the canal and Indian and Egyptian Muslim troops had shown no collective desire to be associated with the Turkish Holy War.

Sources:
Macmunn, G; Falls, C, *Military Operations: Egypt and Palestine*
Field Marshall Lord Carver, *The National Army Museum Book of the Turkish Front 1914-18*
Sir John Maxwell's Despatch dated 16 February 1916
Dane, Edmund, *British Campaigns in the Nearer East 1914-1918 Volume I.* (Hodder & Stoughton, 1919)
Duff, REB, *100 Years of the Suez Canal* (Clifton, 1969)
Storrs, Ronald, *Orientations* (Nicholson & Watson, 1945)
Fecitt, Harry, *The Suez Canal 1914-15*
http://www.kaiserscross.com/188001/279622.html

Actions at Shimber Berris, Somaliland
November 1914 to February 1915
Indian Sepoys fighting with the Somaliland Camel Corps

British Somaliland in 1914

During the latter half of 1914 millions of people around the world began to live in a state of war, but this was not the case for the people of the British Somaliland Protectorate. This territory, located 250 kilometres south of the strategic port of Aden, had been enduring savage periods of war for the previous 15 years whilst a renegade named the "Mad Mullah" and his tribesmen-followers fought British troops. However this man was not mad, nor was he a Mullah, but he was an early type of "freedom fighter" who possessed a vicious and cruel streak, particularly towards those of his fellow Somalis who did not immediately and openly support him in his aim of getting rid of the foreigners on Somali soil.

The Mullah's name was Mahomed Bin Abdulla Hassan, a Somali who declared himself to be the expected Mahdi (Guided One) and who declared jihad or religious war against the foreign occupiers of Somaliland. By a combination of strength of personality, military prowess, cruelty and guile the Mullah continued to survive despite five British military expeditions having been mounted against him and his followers who were named Dervishes. In 1910 the British authorities had, in desperation and in order to cut costs in a territory that had no integral wealth, adopted a "Coastal Concentration" policy whereby the Mullah was left to roam the interior at will whilst the British defended the coastal ports with Indian troops from the Aden Garrison.

In 1911 in an attempt to halt the anarchy spreading throughout the Protectorate an armed force was re-constituted, the previous local force, 6th King's African Rifles, having been disbanded in 1910. The new organisation was a local camel-mounted police force named the Somali Constabulary. The Constabulary was not a military unit but regrettably it was used as one against a strong Dervish force in 1913 when the Dervishes killed the British commander and defeated the Constabulary detachment that opposed them in an action at Dul Madoba, south-east of Burao.

The Somaliland Camel Corps

That defeat led to a re-appraisal of what was needed, and a new unit named the Somaliland Camel Corps (SCC) was raised, and was categorised as being a military unit within the King's African Rifles. The SCC was designed to enforce government policies in the interior, and after an attempt to recruit Sudanese and Arab soldiers had failed it was eventually composed of:

- Two 150-man strong companies of camel-mounted Somalis.
- One 150-man company of Somalis mounted on ponies.
- One 150-man company of camel-mounted soldiers seconded from the Indian Army.
- 250 infantry soldiers seconded from the Indian Army and used primarily for garrison duties in the interior.
- The Somali companies had one machine gun each and the Indian mounted company had two machine guns.

The Somaliland Camel Corps garrisoned Burao (military headquarters), Las Dureh and Sheikh. A Temporary Contingent of 150 Sepoys from Aden garrisoned the chief town and port in the Protectorate, Berbera, and one or two of the minor ports. Experienced and proven European and Indian officers were seconded from both the British and Indian Armies.

The soldiers wore a khaki puggree (cloth head dress looking like a turban), a greenish-brown singlet, khaki shorts and blue puttees (cloth gaiters covering the lower legs). Initially the mounted Somalis did not wear boots. This dress provided excellent camouflage in the dry, dusty, thorn-bush scrub that covered much of Somaliland. Somali ponies were used and apart from one company mounted on Arab camels all the other riding camels were Egyptian. The leather saddlery for camels was the Bikaner pattern from India whilst the pony saddlery came from England.

The men were armed with modern short-pattern rifles and extra-long bayonets to compensate for the short length of the rifle. At first rifle magazine-loading was not taught, as single-shot loading conserved ammunition in situations when there were no supply columns to quickly replenish ammunition expenditure. Ammunition was standard British military issue and tampering with the bullet-heads to produce a "dum-dum" expansion effect was prohibited. Each mounted man carried 260 rounds in his saddlebag and another 140 in three bandoliers worn around the waist and across both shoulders.

The mounted men carried a water bottle and animal watering gear; a haversack; two water chaguls (skin or canvas containers – for camels only); a blanket; a waterproof sheet; a Gudimo (bush axe); a hobble; rations for man and beast for five days; and in the bottle and chaguls water for himself for three days. To ensure that the pony men could react and move quickly their reserves of water, food and ammunition were distributed amongst the camels. The Somalis were used to living frugally on camel milk and a few dates if necessary, and when thirsty they often relished drinking spring or well water that was so brackish, saline or polluted by stock that the Europeans could not stomach it.

The forts at Shimber Berris

By 1914 the Mullah was no longer a young fleet-footed hawk of the desert, and he had both physical and mental impairments. It was believed that in his youth the Mullah had received surgery on his head by a tribal doctor, and that resulted in an unsettled temperament; as he grew older a disease such as elephantiasis appears to have afflicted him, leading to obesity. But whatever the reasons, the Mullah had decided to follow a more static and less-mobile lifestyle.

The Dervishes brought over experienced builders and masons from Yemen to construct fortresses that could withstand attacks by the British weapons that so far had been deployed against them. A massive fort was built at Tale, east of Jidballi and near the Italian border, but of more concern to the British were six small but strong forts built at Shimber Berris at the head of the Ain Valley that led into the large Nogal Valley. The stone fort walls were nearly four metres wide at the base and the three largest structures were each up to nine metres high, with overhanging galleries supported by strong timber baulks. These forts were extensively loop-holed to allow defensive rifle fire to cover all the surrounding ground. The forts could each hold 50 or more defenders and were sited to cover the approaches to Shimber Berris. Below the forts was a very steep-sided valley a kilometre wide; at the valley base was the Shimber Berris well and the three smaller forts that guarded it. The steep valley sides were honeycombed with caves that provided good defensive positions and concealment for Dervish snipers.

Shimber Berris was used as a base that allowed the Dervishes to raid the herds of tribesmen friendly to the British who occupied the region nearer the Somaliland coast. On 12 March 1914 a Dervish party even raided the Somali residential and trading area of Berbera, forcing the British authorities to respond.

The first attack on Shimber Berris

In November 1914 a force was organised to attack the Dervishes at Shimber Berris. The British troop dispositions in Somaliland were:

Berbera. Garrisoned by 150 Sepoys of the 75th Carnatic Infantry from Aden (the Indian Temporary Contingent).
Las Dureh. Garrisoned by 100 infantry Sepoys of the Indian Contingent SCC.
Sheikh. Garrisoned by 50 infantry Sepoys of the Indian Contingent SCC.
Burao. Concentrated here were:
- Force Headquarters commanded by Lieutenant Colonel

TA Cubbitt DSO, Royal Artillery;
- 'A' Company SCC – 100 Indian soldiers on camels;
- the two Somali camel companies and the one Somali pony company (a total of 450 men);
- the remaining 100 infantry Sepoys of the SCC as Burao garrison;
- the SCC Depot Company (50 Somalis).

Cubitt's offensive column left Burao on 17 November and two days later was within five kilometres of Shimber Berris before the Dervishes realised that it posed a threat. The column's animals were placed in a zareba (enclosure made of felled thorn bushes) on top of the ridge that was being used for the advance, and a guard of 200 men stayed with the animals. The three larger forts were visible, two on the ridge to Cubitt's front and one on another spur; as yet the British were unaware of the small forts below that guarded the Shimber Berris wells.

Cubitt ordered Lieutenant CAL Howard, 32nd Lancers, Indian Army, to charge the nearest fort with his dismounted 'A' Company Indian Sepoys; this fort was secured, primarily because its standing garrison was taken by surprise and did not man the defences. But the next fort to be attacked, by Captain A Carton de Wiart, 4th (Royal Irish) Dragoon Guards, and his dismounted 'C' Company of Somalis, proved to be a much tougher proposition. The defenders were ready and there was no easy access into the fort. Heavy machine gun fire supported the attackers but three British charges failed to get inside the fort; all the British junior officers joined in the final charge. Carton de Wiart was severely wounded in an eye, which he later lost, and Captain HW Symons, King's Own Yorkshire Light Infantry, was shot dead whilst within a metre of the fort doorway. Major AS Lawrence, 1st County of London Yeomanry, received an arm wound. Throughout these charges the Dervish defenders taunted their attackers.

Cubitt realised that he was under-resourced for this kind of fighting and he withdrew his force and camped at Little Bohotle 13 kilometres to the south. The Dervishes did not interfere with Cubitt's retirement as they were licking their many wounds from the machine gun fire that had entered fort loopholes, and were re-organising themselves. Meanwhile a messenger was speeding to Burao to order that one of the two 7-pounder mountain guns there be despatched as fast as possible to Cubitt's camp. In past encounters with the Dervishes these old guns had been packed on or pulled by camels, and had figured prominently as the only artillery pieces permanently in Somaliland. Why Cubitt, himself a horse-gunner, did not initially deploy one or both guns with his column is not known, but probably he had little idea of the strength of the Dervish forts until he saw them.

From Burao Jemadar Feroze Khan of the 56th Punjabi Rifles, Indian Contingent SCC, rapidly marched a camel-mounted gun and 40 Sepoys to the British camp; the Naik (local Havildar) in charge of the gun was 293 Shan Khan, 76th Punjabis, Indian Contingent SCC. The gun arrived on the evening of 21 November and on the 23rd Cubitt ordered Captain HC Dobbs, 124th Duchess of Connaught's Own Baluchistan Infantry, Indian Army, to attack all three visible forts using the gun and two dismounted SCC Companies. Again the first fort was seized without a fight, and this time the second fort was abandoned after a few artillery rounds had been fired at it from 500 metres range. The approach to the third fort was difficult as a detour of over six kilometres had to be made around ravines, but again a few rounds into the fort walls from very close range, and one through an observation slit, made the garrison flee. Later interrogation of captured Dervishes found that although the artillery rounds hitting the forts were not killing or wounding the defenders, the concussive effects of the bombardments significantly demoralised them. Later the Mullah further significantly demoralised these unfortunates by castrating them for deserting their posts.

The gun then engaged a small fort that could be seen 250 metres below in the valley, and the defenders there fled once Shan Khan started hitting the walls and roof. By now Cubitt had several badly wounded officers and men on his hands but no doctor with him, and he did not have the explosives needed to properly demolish all the forts and blockhouses, so he withdrew his force to Burao. Within two weeks the Dervishes re-occupied all their defensive structures, but the Mullah ensured that only fresh men were in the new garrison. Cubitt had lost one officer and five Somalis killed, and two officers, one Indian Sepoy and 24 Somalis wounded; several of the wounds were serious. Over 21,000 rounds of rifle ammunition, over

10,000 rounds of machine gun rounds and 34 artillery shells had been fired. Cubitt had achieved as much as he could with the resources in his column; in his after-action report he commented that explosives and specialists were needed, and any future attacking column would need to occupy the Shimber Berris area for four or five days in order for all the structures to be effectively demolished.

Awards for the first action

For the gallantry that he had displayed when attacking on 19 November Captain Adrian Carton de Wiart was admitted to be a Companion of the Distinguished Service Order.
Jemadar Feroze Khan and Naik (Local Havildar) Shan Khan both received Indian Distinguished Service Medals. Feroze Khan had been prominent in the seizing of the three forts on 23 November.
Indian Army personnel Mentioned in Despatches were:
Major GH Summers, 26th (King George's Own) Light Cavalry.
Captain HC Dobbs, 124th Duchess of Connaught's Own Baluchistan Light Infantry.
Jemadar Feroze Khan, 56th Punjabi Rifles, and 293 Naik (Local Havildar), 76th Punjabis, both of the Indian Contingent Somaliland Camel Corps.

Preparations for the second move against Shimber Berris

Aden military headquarters was sympathetic to requests made by Cubitt and Captain WAH Bird, 23rd Sikh Pioneers, Indian Army, was despatched to Somaliland with 29 of his Pioneers, gun cotton explosive and hand grenades. Bird and his men arrived at Burao on 29 January 1915, allowing Cubitt to advance a force against the Shimber Berris fortifications on the following day.

This time preparations were made to allow a longer stay on the objective. A Medical Officer, Lieutenant RE Drake-Brockman, Royal Army Medical Corps, accompanied the column; Lieutenant HB Davidson, 10th Goorkha Rifles, Indian Army, was the Transport Officer and Lieutenant GJJ Johnston, 32nd Lancers, Indian Army, commanded the Water Column. Cubitt's principal staff officers were unchanged: Brevet Major GH Summers, 26th (King George's Own) Light Cavalry, Indian Army, and Captain HL Ismay, 21st Prince Albert Victor's Own Cavalry (Frontier Force), (Daly's Horse), Indian Army. His

Majesty's Commissioner and Commander-in-Chief Somaliland Protectorate, GF Archer, accompanied the force.

Cubitt prepared two columns. The Mounted Column of 12 officers, 357 men, five machine guns and five days' rations moved with 388 riding camels and 38 ponies; because of insufficient water on the route the remainder of the Pony Company SCC were dismounted. The Dismounted Column marched with five officers, 324 men, two 7-pounder guns, one machine gun, eight ponies, 222 transport camels (eight of these camels being spares), and six days' rations. As always in Somaliland irregular pony-mounted scouts named Illalos were employed for reconnaissance and flank protection duties. Irregular riflemen from friendly tribes were engaged to garrison staging points and the objective after its capture.

To provide the necessary water at Ber, a staging point about half-way between Burao and Shimber Berris, 18 new wells were dug in advance. The tanks of water carried on the Water Column transport camels each held nearly 38 litres when full but the cans inevitably leaked. The water ration was: British Officers – four to a tank; Indians and Somalis of all ranks – 10 to a tank; ponies – four to a tank. Camels were watered when it was available from wells.

The standard load for a transport camel weighed 145 kilograms; all these camels were hired locally at Burao along with one attendant for each three camels. Six camels (plus two of the spares held ready for emergencies) carried the two 7-pounder guns whilst nine others carried 250 artillery shells; nine camels carried the force reserve rifle and machine gun ammunition and nine other camels carried the Pioneers' explosives and tools.

The second attack on Shimber Berris

On 2 February 1915 Cubitt concentrated his force five kilometres from Shimber Berris. He had to destroy the top three forts before he could go down into the valley below to destroy the small forts near the well; this job was made easy as the top forts were not occupied, but the new foundations of a much larger fort were discovered on the ridge. The Dervishes had obviously hoped that the new fort, when completed, would withstand artillery shells. Whilst the Sikh Pioneers demolished the top forts the Dervishes sniped from caves below the plateau.

The morning of the following day was spent in moving the entire British force around to the other side of the valley in order to use a track that led down to Shimber Berris well. Friendly tribesmen secured the ridgeline and the nearest water holes. Once down in the valley Cubitt could see that two small forts overlooked and flanked the water course and a third central one commanded the far end; Dervish snipers were also manning many of the caves that were now above the British troops on both sides of the valley. Whilst the two 7-pounder guns engaged the central fort the flanking forts were each attacked by a SSC company. Both flanking forts were captured by 1500 hours; they were not destroyed but used as cover for riflemen and machine gunners who supported attacks on the caves that the two attacking companies now made.

By 1600 hours many Dervishes could be seen fleeing from the caves and the remaining fort. Cubitt ordered a company to charge the fort, which it did, but it could not gain access. Whilst the company riflemen and supporting machine gunners provided covering fire the Sikh Pioneers laid charges at the fort doorway. Effective fire came from the fort's remaining defenders making the Pioneers' work extremely hazardous. Two men of the 23rd Sikh Pioneers were later awarded the Indian Order of Merit, 2nd Class, for the gallantry that they displayed:

No 4392 Naik Sher Singh's citation read: *For bravery in action on the 4th February 1915 at Shimberberris, Somaliland. In placing a charge of gun-cotton against the door of a fort, he was knocked over and rendered practically insensible by the discharge of dervish rifles through the door, but after getting clear, he returned and placed the box in the correct place.*

The citation for 4584 Havildar Teja Singh read: *For bravery in action on the 4th February 1915 at Shimberberris, Somaliland. He followed Naik Sher Singh to the door of a fort and coolly placed a charge of gun cotton, arranged fuzes correctly, fired the charge and enabled the demolition to be carried out successfully.*

The effect of the explosives collapsed the top half of the fort onto the bottom half, burying and killing the 10 brave Dervish defenders who had remained to fight it out. Concurrently Lieutenant Howard and his 'A' (Indian) Company SCC were grenading and clearing the caves on the slopes above; whilst engaged in this activity Howard was wounded. Cubitt ordered the two flanking forts to be demolished, and after the dust had settled on those explosions the force withdrew to a zariba.

Whilst the Illalos had behaved as ordered the friendly tribesmen had come down off the ridgelines during the cave clearances in attempts to get hold of Dervish rifles, and the presence of these friendlies had hampered Howard's men. But next morning when the force returned to the battleground all the caves were found to be empty of live Dervishes, although the bodies of 32 men were found there, including those of the Dervish commander and his second-in-command. Cubitt had lost three Other Ranks killed and three officers and ten other ranks wounded. Captain W. Lowry-Corry, 23rd Cavalry (Frontier Force), Indian Army, was one of those severely wounded. Only dead Dervishes remained under the rubble of the demolished forts.

The conclusion of the Shimber Berris actions

Cubitt marched his force back to Burao, leaving a garrison of friendly tribesmen at Shimber Berris. The platoon of gallant 23rd Sikh Pioneers returned to their regiment in Aden. Morale in British Somaliland was now high and groups of determined Illalos prevented the Dervishes from encroaching forward of their position at Jidballi, 100 kilometres to the east of Shimber Berris. The SCC was recognised as being an effectively trained and disciplined fighting force; nevertheless the Indian Contingent was to provide a professional and vital stiffening to the Somaliland Camel Corps for many years to come.

Awards for the second action

Apart from the awards already mentioned, Major and Temporary Lieutenant Colonel Thomas Astley Cubitt DSO, Royal Artillery, was awarded the Brevet rank of Lieutenant Colonel. The Mentions in Despatches for Indian Army troops were:
Captain WAH Bird; 4392 Naik Sher Singh; 4584 Havildar Teja Singh, all of the 23rd Sikh Pioneers.
Lieutenant CAL Howard, 32nd Lancers.
Brevet Major GH Summers, 26th (King George's Own) Light Cavalry.
Captain HL Ismay, 21st Prince Albert Victor's Own Cavalry (Frontier Force).

The Africa General Service Medal

Somaliland was not considered to be a theatre of the Great War, but a new Africa General Service Medal was struck in 1916, with the head of King George V replacing that of King Edward VII; the medal ribbon did not alter. A clasp to this medal titled *SHIMBER BERRIS 1914-15* was authorised for those who had been in the field during Cubitt's actions at Shimber Berris. Of the 821 clasps issued, 306 were awarded to members of the Indian Contingent SCC, indicating the involvement and importance of Indian soldiers in the actions. Today this medal and clasp is sought after by collectors, and is rarely seen at auction.

Sources:
Archer, GF, Despatch 20 February 1915, London Gazette Supplement, Number 29690, pp. 7631-34, 2 August 1916
Archer, Sir Geoffrey, KCMG, *Personal & Historical Memoirs of an East African Administrator* (Oliver & Boyd, 1963)
Carton de Wiart, Sir Adrian: *Happy Odyssey* (Pen & Sword)
Chhina, Rana, *The Indian Distinguished Service Medal* (Invicta 2001)
TNA, WO 106/272, *Digest of History of Somaliland Camel Corps, King's African Rifles*
Duckers, Peter, *Reward of Valour. The Indian Order of Merit, 1914-1918* (Jade, 1999)
Hayward, J, Birch, D, & Bishop, R, *British Battles and Medals* (Spink, 2006)
Ismay, General The Lord, *The Memoirs of General The Lord Ismay* (Heinemann, 1960)
Ismay Papers in The Liddell Collection, Leeds University
Jardine, Douglas, OBE: *The Mad Mullah of Somaliland* (Naval & Military; on-line: https://archive.org/details/TheMadMullahOf Somaliland)
Lucas, Sir Charles, *The Empire at War* (Oxford UP, 1921)
Magor, RB, *African General Service Medals* (Naval & Military, 1993).
Moyse-Bartlett, Lieut Col H, *The King's African Rifles* (Gale & Polden, 1956)
Fecitt, Harry, *Somaliland. The actions at Shimber Berris* http://www.kaiserscross.com/188001/517143.html

Part 2
Mobilisation, participants & economics

Mass mobilisation of human resources

Tanja Bührer[1]

This chapter is about mass mobilisation of human resources within German East Africa during World War One. The majority of black males and almost all of the white population were recruited for service in the army or war economy. In what follows I will focus on the recruitment for service in the colonial troops, the so called *Schutztruppe*.

According to the defence plans for the German colonies in Africa, the colonies would be isolated and thus no supplies or reinforcements from Germany could be expected. As the colonies were strategically, as well as economically, insignificant, any expensive rearmament on the periphery was also out of the question, especially because the Foreign Office feared that such efforts would fuel fears of German ambitions to become a global player.

The colonies thus had to cope with the forces already deployed which, with regard to strength and training, were designed for internal peacekeeping only. From the introduction of conscription for the German settlers in 1913, in the case of German East Africa, a considerable reinforcement could not be expected. Similar to the King's African Rifles, the colonial force consisted of black mercenaries, so called Askari, put under the command of German military officers and non-commissioned-officers (NCOs). German soldiers in the tropics proved to be far inferior to the Askari, especially with respect to orientation, endurance, health, and agility. Thus, to save costs due to health issues and to keep the so-called 'prestige of the white race', only officers and NCOs of the reserve would be conscripted. The other white settlers could be admitted to the troops as

---
[1] Tanja Bührer, Assistant Professor (Oberassistentin) at the University of Berne

volunteers if they did not belong to an opponent of war. But according to a survey among the settler population in 1912, the vast majority were only willing to organise in militias and defend their own land. The limited reinforcement of the leadership at the same time restricted the recruitment of black mercenaries.

However, a large body of troops was not desirable anyway as it would exacerbate the difficulties of supply. The colonial economy was characterised by African cash crop and European plantation economy—both could not contribute much to self-sufficiency as the main products were sisal, natural rubber, coffee and cotton intended for export. Only some depots were established, mainly stocked with medicaments, uniforms, weapons and munitions for about one year. Estimations of how long the different food stuffs would last went from a few months up to a year—in the end it depended on uncertain factors like climate, uprisings, and on whether the adversary would impose a naval blockade or invade the territory.

Only one thing seemed sure: the lack of support from outside combined with limited possibilities of material and human mobilisation within the colony would not allow for waging ambitious campaigns. According to the defence plans, the troops should withdraw into the inaccessible interior to put up resistance through a combination of retreat and guerrilla tactics. They should try to keep a part of the territory under German control until the end of the war and keep the colonial infrastructure intact for the post-war order.

Against this background, it is very surprising that East Africa developed into a considerable side-show of the Great War. About 180,000 soldiers and more than a million military porters were deployed on these battlefields, and the German troops would only surrender when they learned of the capitulation in Europe on 13 November 1918.

The escalation of the campaign was mainly due to the strategic change imposed by the German commander of the colonial troops, Paul von Lettow-Vorbeck. Soon after his appointment in April 1914, he submitted a memorandum that broke with the defensive plan: he intended to concentrate colonial war efforts to relieve the pressure on the fatherland in the main theatre of war in Europe. The best way to achieve this was to relentlessly exploit the colonial economic and human resources and assemble the forces to attack the enemy focused at a sensitive point, thus forcing him to deploy troops to the periphery.

The Governor, Heinrich Schnee, declined von Lettow-Vorbeck's proposals, and a reply from the colonial office was still being awaited when the war broke out. It is unlikely that it would have been approved as it had been contrary to von Lettow-Vorbeck's appointment. Lettow-Vorbeck, in his thinking and behaviour remained a Prussian military officer, but had to conform to the decision-making authority of the military cabinet. However, after his appointment, the commander and his colonial troops were put under civil authority—which meant a considerable break from the tradition of conservative military policy of Imperial Germany. And as there was no response from the Secretary of the colonial office to von Lettow-Vorbeck's memorandum, it was the Governor who had the decision-making authority on strategy.

When the war between Germany and Great Britain broke out, Governor Schnee was relieved that the Commander conformed to his orders and withdrew the troops outside the coastal towns. But in fact, von Lettow-Vorbeck was determined to take control of the war effort on his terms and was only waiting for the Governor to leave to the safe back-country. When, at the beginning of November 1914, a British fleet appeared at Tanga Lettow-Vorbeck ignored all constitutional obstacles, interfered with the negotiations with the British delegates and deployed as many troops as possible to the coastal town. Against all expectations, the Germans defeated the eight-time superior British forces.

The battle of Tanga was a decisive battle in a double sense: The British had to postpone their invasion. Thus, the German territory stayed unoccupied until March 1916 and the war was characterised by skirmishes on the borders. Von Lettow-Vorbeck's triumphal victory also meant a silent military coup, as nobody from among the settlers, the military staff, the civil officers and even the Governor dared oppose the commander's war efforts anymore. Both paved the way for the almost total mobilisation of the human and material resources. At the beginning of 1916, the German troops numbered up to 13,000, which was about eight times their pre-war strength. Two-thousand-two-hundred police Askari were transferred to the *schutztruppe.* They had the same training and many had served in the colonial troops before. In addition, about 600 Askari of the reserve were mobilised. As German rule was uncontested and the country still able to pay wages enough blacks volunteered for military service. Whereas within the old core of the forces steady employment, symbolic rewards, pensions as well as medical and family care enhanced loyalty beyond mere payment, the mass of new recruits had a more materialistic attitude. Many were Wasaskuma and Wanjamwesi; people with a long tradition of wage labour.

Von Lettow-Vorbeck was very keen to recruit among the white inhabitants as he needed more officers and NCOs to train and command the additional Askari companies. He also intended to use the white settlers for mounted patrols on the steppe against the Uganda Railway; the only area where horses survived. About 3,600 Germans, including 312 officers, were recruited which meant almost all the male Germans within the territory, regardless of whether they were fit for service or not. A considerable number of the civil officers were military officers of the reserve whom von Lettow-Vorbeck put under pressure to transfer to military service, arguing honour and duty. In addition, von Lettow-Vorbeck had already, before the war, convinced many of the former soldiers to join the troops in case of a war and support his efforts against the Governor. Some of them, like Tom von Prince, who was a hero of the wars of conquest, had very valuable experiences in commanding Askari. After the battle of Tanga, Governor Schnee no longer opposed the general conscription of all Germans who were fit for service. Many Germans also volunteered out of necessity as companies and plantations could not continue their export business anymore.

There was one non-German group among the settler population which von Lettow-Vorbeck was especially keen to win over for his mounted patrols: the Boers who were superior in their local knowledge of the area and in handling horses. Most of them had migrated from the Transvaal to German East Africa after the South African War (1899-1902). Thus, they were British subjects with an anti-British attitude, which did not mean that they were pro-German. As it was against international law to recruit citizens from an adversary, Governor Schnee applied for retroactive authorisation to naturalise them—the letter of application had to be sent through Portuguese East Africa and it took several months before it arrived in Berlin. Von Lettow-Vorbeck ordered the district officers to encourage the Boers to join the forces. They should be allowed to form patrols on their own around a leader of their choice and would not be submitted to the usual discipline. After the battle of Tanga there was another wave of volunteers from the already interned Boers as they did not want to spend what would probably be a long time behind fences. Some Boers had private contracts with the military command. For instance, a former Boer commander was paid monthly to establish an intelligence service with the Maasai. When they made up stories about a mass invasion of people with slit eyes, the Germans finally found out that the Maasai were double agents. I have not come across any numbers of how many Boers joined the Germans, but it probably was a minority. However, whereas their fellow countrymen who stayed away from war events or joined the British in 1916 were compensated for losses due to the war, they would have a bitter fate after the war: like the 'other Germans' they were interned in Egypt and India before they were transferred to Germany, where they had no means or network and were absolute strangers. While their families remained in East Africa, they were not allowed to return until 1924.

The recruitment of soldiers was thus considerable—but it was nothing compared with the mass mobilisation of black males for carrier service. The rivers within the German territory were not navigable, animal transport was very limited due to a lack of routes and horses in almost all areas died of tsetse fever, and there were only two railways, the northern and the central line. Thus, the troops were dependent on hundreds of thousands of black carriers. On average each soldier was supported by six to ten followers. Whereas before the war about 20 per cent of the black male population worked in the colonial economy, in the course of the war in many areas almost the whole male population was involved in the war effort: the bulk of them as porters. They transported food stuffs from the production areas, often still under civil authority, to the military stations. There the military took over carrier logistics according to the dumping system in which a line had permanent posts every 15 to 20 kilometres, where labour was housed and fed. The lines mainly ran from the central railway to the northern railway in order to supply the bulk of the troops deployed in the northeast. Another group within the military system were the so-called 'company porters' who carried weapons and munitions.

How could such masses be recruited? Carrier labour was from the beginning only partly voluntary. Some migrant labourers still joined to earn money and get away from the restrictions of village life. In addition, about 40,000 to 50,000 contract labourers became redundant when plantations were abandoned and railway construction ceased. Most of them were simply transferred to the carrier service, and not informed of what they would have to expect. Furthermore, the military command put the Governor under pressure to provide labour. The district officer acted according to the partly compulsory pre-war system which depended entirely on mediation with chiefs, who were often paid for each recruit they supplied. In the areas under military rule, already in this first stage, forced recruitment was adopted, often by using violence and taking hostages. After a few months, the Governor had to admit that in the areas under civil authority hardly anybody volunteered anymore. This was mainly due to the fact that the porters involved in the military lines did not return. Many company porters, for example, did not quit service or escape as they feared being conscripted for the military lines where the labour was even more exhausting and subject to strict military discipline.

When the Allied forces started their concentrated attack in March 1916, the Germans waged a war of retreat and finally fell back behind the central line in August/September 1916. The Allies were exhausted and logistically not able to make an immediate pursuit, so the German troops reassembled for a few months in the far southeast of the German territory. When the Allies took up their attack again, von Lettow-Vorbeck left German East Africa with a select fighting force of 2,000 men for Portuguese East Africa. The marauding and raiding column moved to the south as far as the Zambezi River, then back to the former colony in September 1918, and finally forayed into Rhodesia, where they learnt of the general armistice.

With the invasion by the Allies, black cooperation broke away immediately as German acts of retaliation were no longer to be feared. Instead the threats of the new occupying forces already could be felt. The failing colonial state also lost its organised executive power, thus, mass mobilisation of labour was not possible anymore. Instead those already in service of the troops were hit all the harder. Some of the long-serving Askari stayed loyal because their loyalty went beyond mere payment and the company had become their family; some of them may have believed their superiors that the Germans would be victorious in Europe, re-establish themselves in East Africa and pay the overdue wage. But the main reason that kept the majority of the Askari loyal to the Germans at this stage was that they could not escape far from their home countries anymore as the local people considered them part of the detested marauders and were eager for retaliation. This point is confirmed by the waves of desertion: the first one took place when the troops left the north-eastern territories, where many Askari were recruited; another one took place when the troops returned to the former German colony; desertions also occurred when the Askari had opportunities to defect to the adversary. No new recruitment drives were undertaken, the Askari were replaced with followers like boys, male family members or front-line porters and weapon carriers who had already proved themselves and could improve their standing and position within the troops.

Similarly, none of the carriers stayed with the troops voluntarily anymore; the retreat meant a journey into strange countries, with no certain prospect of ever returning. Under such circumstances, sick men lost the will to live—and many became ill. Their labour was very exhausting and their clothing and provision was very poor as they were the weakest link of the already half-starving troops. Already in the Northern area the Germans literally left a trail of death behind—thousands of porters were dying on the road from hunger, cold and illness. Those left behind in the bush often were lynched by the returning local inhabitants. The high mortality rate made new recruitment necessary. They were carried out by raiding villages at dawn, carrying off all people they captured, who then had to walk in chains—pictures that strongly recalled the slave raids and slave trade in the last years of the nineteenth-century—conditions that pro-colonial propaganda used to morally legitimise the German occupation of the East African sphere of interest. Against this background, the moral argument of the Versailles Treaty to justify that the colonies were taken away from Germany is not completely wrong.

References

Anderson, Ross, *The Forgotten Front. The East African Campaign 1914-1918* (Stroud, 2004)
Bührer, Tanja, *Die Kaiserliche Schutztruppe für Deutsch-Ostafrika. Koloniale Sicherheitspolitik und transkulturelle Kriegführung 1885 bis 1918 (Schriftenreihe des Militärgeschichtlichen Forschungsamtes, Bd. 70)* (München, 2011) (Oldenbourg Verlag)
Bührer, Tanja, ‚Die Massenmobilisierung der afrikanischen Bevölkerung. Zwangsarbeit als Militärstrategie während des Ersten Weltkrieges in Deutsch-Ostafrika' in Klaus Gestwa & Kerstin von Lingen (Eds.), *Zwangsarbeit als Kriegsressource* (Paderborn, 2014) pp. 109-26
Farwell, Byron, *The Great War in Africa (1914-1918)* (New York, 1989)
Hodges, Geoffrey, *Kariakor. The Carrier Corps* (Nairobi, 1999)
Lettow-Vorbeck, Paul von, *Meine Erinnerungen aus Ostafrika* (Leipzig, 1920)
Methner, Wilhelm, *Unter drei Gouverneuren. 16 Jahre Dienst in deutschen Tropen* (Breslau, 1938)
Michels, Eckard, *'Der Held von Deutsch-Ostafrika', Paul von Lettow-Vorbeck. Ein preußischer Kolonialoffizier* (Paderborn, 2008)
Moyd, Michelle, '"We don't want to die for nothing": Askari at War in German East Africa, 1914-1918,' in Santanu Das (ed.), *Race, Empire, and First World War Experience* (Cambridge, 2011)
Pesek, Michael, *Das Ende eines Kolonialreiches. Ostafrika im Ersten Weltkrieg (Eigene und fremde Welten, Bd. 17)* (Frankfurt a. M. 2010)
Schnee, Heinrich, *Deutsch-Ostafrika im Weltkriege. Wie wir lebten und kämpften* (Leipzig, 1919)

'When two elephants fight it´s the grass that suffers.' (African proverb): East Africa during the First World War

Oliver Schulten[1]

translated from German by Oliver Seitz

From 1885 to 1917 the present states Rwanda, Burundi and Tanzania used to form the colony German East Africa (German: Deutsch-Ostafrika, hereinafter referred to as DOA),[2] its size as large as the German Empire and France together. There was approximately 7,5 million people, half in Rwanda and Burundi. In the colony 120 languages were spoken. The foreign population comprised 5,336 Europeans and 15,000 Asians. The colony was surrounded by other European-influenced areas: in the north there were the British protectorates Kenya and Uganda, in the west the Belgian Congo, in the southwest the British territories Malawi and Zambia. In the south DOA bordered

---

[1] Oliver Schulten (45) is an expert for African History from Wuppertal, Germany and author of *Bibliography of the First World War in Africa*: http://gweaa.com/wp-content/uploads/2018/01/Bibliography-Africa-First-World-War.pdf

[2] Further Reading: Pesek, Michael, *Koloniale Herrschaft in Ostafrika* (New York, 2005); Okello, Benson, *A History of East Africa*. Pp. 160-6: *German East Africa* (Kampala, 2002), Baer, Martin & Schröter, Olaf, *Eine Kopfjagd – Deutsche in Ostafrika* (Berlin, 2001), Bückendorf, Jutta, *Schwarz-Weiß-Rot über Ostafrika* (Berlin 1997), Moore, Sally, *Social Facts & Fabrications: Customary Law on Kilimanjaro, 1880-1980* pp. 95-110 (Cambridge, 1986), Ssekamwa, JC, *A Sketch Map History of East Africa*. pp. 153-68 (Leckhampton, 1986), Wright, Marcia, 'East Africa, 1870-1905' in *The Cambridge History of Africa 6*, pp. 539-91 (Cambridge, 1985), Temu, AJ, 'Tanzanian Societies and Colonial Invasion, 1875-1907' in Kaniki, MHY, *Tanzania under Colonial Rule*, pp. 86-127 (London, 1979), Raum, OF, 'German East Africa: Changes in African Tribal Life under German Administration, 1892-1914' in Harlow, Vincent, et al., *History of East Africa II,* pp. 163-208 (Oxford, 1965), Ingham, Kenneth, *A History of East Africa*, pp. 191-205 (London, 1963), Brode, H, *British and German East Africa* (London, 1911)

Portuguese East Africa, present-day Mozambique. The islands off the coast were under British control.

Hut- and poll taxes

Since Tanzania was conquered forcibly from 1885 from the coast, the Germans appeared as confederates of the local elites in Rwanda and Burundi. The heavily centralised polity of the Tutsi in this region thwarted further advance. During the following years dubious protection letters were signed with local authorities: mostly the Africans assumed they merely granted rights for settlement and exploitation. The Germans however interpreted these procedures clearly as surrender of all political power plus complete dispossession. In parallel to this the Germans proceeded with armed force against anybody who refused to submit. This and the implementation of hut- and poll taxes provoked massive resistance. Until 1917 the Germans conducted over 80 military pacification campaigns, for example, against the Makonde and Hehe. On account of this over 300,000 people died before the First World War.[3]

Expensive—and no peace

The attempts of the colonial government to prod African farmers to adapt their production for export failed. Hence the governor started to directly settle the land with Europeans. The consequence was protests and revolts against the expropriations. The misery of the indigenous people was further aggravated by tax liability. Since there was limited cash, taxes had to be paid with natural produce or fatigue. By this, mostly young men were forced to work on European plantations. The Germans had access to over 800,000 employable people. Nevertheless, the colony did not pay and it was not possible to pacify. In total the German Empire had to pump 122 million Deutsch-

---

[3] Herzog, Jürgen, *Geschichte Tansanias*, pp. 46-58 (Berlin, 1986); further reading: Kuß, Susanne: *Deutsches Militär auf kolonialen Kriegsschauplätzen: Eskalation von Gewalt zu Beginn des 20. Jahrhunderts* (Berlin, 2012), Klein, Thoralf & Schuhmacher, Frank, *Kolonialkriege: Militärische Gewalt im Zeichen des Imperialismus* (Hamburg, 2006), Seeberg, Karl-Martin, *Der Maji-Maji-Krieg gegen die deutsche Kolonialherrschaft* (Berlin, 1989), Iliffe, John, *A Modern History of Tanganyika* p. 200 (Cambridge, 1979), Gwassa, Gilbert CK, *The Outbreak and Development of the Maji-Maji-War, 1905-1907* p. 389 (University of Dar es Salaam, 1973)

mark into DOA[4]—and until the outbreak of war there still were several districts under military administration.

Land as security

On 5 August 1914 martial law was imposed over DOA. All Germans were called to stand against the Allies. In the same month the British destroyed the Germans' communication channels. The German colonists were isolated. After conquering Togo, Namibia and Cameroon the Allies concentrated on DOA. For the British it was mostly a matter of territorial gains—according to the motto land is security.

Apart from European soldiers, detachments and porters came from 23 countries to East Africa—from Malawi, Zambia, Zimbabwe, Uganda, Kenya, Congo, South Africa, Gambia, Ghana, Nigeria, Sierra Leone, Botswana, Swaziland, Somalia, Mozambique and Sudan. Furthermore, Jamaicans and divisions from Rajasthan, Kashmir, Afghanistan and Punjab.[5] The French in Central Africa supported the Belgians in the Congo with war materials and food and from Madagascar the same supply came to the British in East Africa. The British and South Africans refused help from French troops; they wanted to restrict French influence in East Africa to secure their own territorial ambitions.[6]

---

[4] Gründer, Horst, *Geschichte der deutschen Kolonien*, p. 166 (Paderborn, 2000)

[5] Further reading: Yorke, Edmund: *Britain, Northern Rhodesia and the First World War* (Basingstoke, 2015), Nasson, Bill, *WWI and the People of South Africa* (Cape Town, 2014), Wrangham, Elizabeth, *Ghana during the First World War* (Durham, 2013), McCracken, John, *A History of Malawi* pp. 147-62 (Rochester, 2012), Samson, Anne, *Britain, South Africa and the East African Campaign, 1914-1918* (New York, 2006), Stapleton, Timothy, *No Insignificant Part: The Rhodesia Native Regiment and the East African Campaign of the First World War* (Waterloo, 2006), Smith, Richard, *Jamaican Volunteers in the First World War* (Manchester, 2004), Page, Melvin E, *The Chiwaya War: Malawians in the First World War* (Boulder, 2000), Pradhan, SD, *Indian Army in East Africa, 1914-1918* (New Delhi, 1991), Brown, James A, *They Fought for King and Kaiser: South Africans in German East Africa 1916* (Rivonia, 1991), McLaughlin, Peter, *Ragtime Soldiers: The Rhodesian Experience in the First World War* (Bulawayo, 1980), Page, Melvin, 'The War of Thangata: Nyasaland and the East African Campaign, 1914-1918' in *Journal of African History 19/1*, pp. 87-101 (1978), Downes, WD, *With the Nigerians in German East Africa* (London, 1919)

[6] Strachan, Hew, *The First World War in Africa*, pp. 111-112 (Oxford, 2004), Anderson, Ross, *The Forgotten Front: The East African Campaign, 1914-1918*, p. 58 (Stroud, 2004)

Terrain, rain and malaria

In the beginning the British opted for heavy armament: arms technology, plated vehicles, planes and trucks were supposed to ensure victory. This plan was upset by unclear orders, lack of communication and planning, outdated maps which made it difficult to plan troop movements and mostly the local conditions: the Allies were troubled by rough terrain, two rainy seasons per year and disease. Above all, malaria and sleeping sickness claimed the lives of thousands of men and animals in the shortest time. Furthermore, a functioning infra-structure and adequately trained soldiers were missing. Therefore from 1914 to 1916 the German units were able to carry out successful attacks. Primarily the supply lines and communication routes were preferential targets, i.e. the British Uganda railway.[7]

The end of DOA

The turning point came with the offensive of 1916: the Allies attacked the German colony from Kenya, the Congo, from Zambia and from Malawi at the same time. In parallel to this, the coastal towns on the Indian Ocean were taken over. Thereby German resistance broke down. More than half the colony came under allied control. Therefore, the Germans changed from static to mobile war. Since no reinforcements were to be expected, open battles were meaningless. The Germans were kept alive only by captured food stuffs, ammunition and weapons. The everyday life of the *Schutztruppe*[8] was dominated by harassment, permanent eluding, sabotage and minor attacks. This tactic was not successful though. Through to 1917 the Allies could disrupt the Germans within the colony. All of the important cities and train connections were captured. Yet again,

---

[7] Paice, Edward, *World War I: The African Front*, p. 29 (New York, 2008)

[8] Further reading: Traoré, Mohamet, *Schwarze Truppen im Ersten Weltkrieg* (Hamburg, 2014), Moyd, Michelle, *Violent Intermediaries: African Soldiers, Conquest, and Everyday Colonialism in German East Africa* (University of Ohio, 2014), Shepherd, G, *Conflict in the Colonies: East Africa and the First World War* (Ayrshire, 2014), Bührer, Tanja, *Die kaiserliche Schutztruppe für Deutsch-Ostafrika, 1885-1918* (Oldenburg, 2011), Michels, Stefanie, *Schwarze deutsche Kolonialsoldaten* (Bielefeld, 2009), Morlang, Thomas, *Askari und Fitafita: „Farbige" Söldner in den deutschen Kolonien* (Berlin, 2008), Bechhaus-Gerst, Marianne, *Treu bis in den Tod: Von Deutsch-Ostafrika nach Sachsenhausen* (Berlin, 2007), Lochner, RK, *Kampf im Rufiji-Delta: Das Ende des kleinen Kreuzers Königsberg – Die deutsche Marine und Schutztruppe im Ersten Weltkrieg in Ostafrika* (München, 1990)

German officers surrendered with their troops due to lack of supplies of medicine, weapons, water and food, as well as lack of help by the local population. The German *schutztruppe* had been forced to the south; the colony ceased to exist. At the end of 1917 the DOA became a British protectorate.[9] The German troops had slipped into Mozambique. At the end of 1918 the last Germans lay down their weapons in Zambia—together with 1,300 men, 1,500 porters and their respective families.[10]

'Black' soldiers, 'white' commanders

One thing both war parties had in common was that they used black African soldiers, the so called Askaris, who were commanded by white officers. Many of the German colonial force were former slaves,[11] 'criminals', professional soldiers and mer-

---

[9] Further reading: Reigel, Corey, *The Last Great Safari: East Africa in World War I* (Lanham, 2015), Olusoga, David, *The World's War: Forgotten Soldiers of Empire*, pp. 109-26 (London, 2014), Samson, Anne, *World War I in Africa: The Forgotten Conflict among the European Powers* (London, 2012), Strizek, Helmut, *Geschenkte Kolonien: Ruanda und Burundi unter deutscher Herrschaft*, pp. 144-51 (Berlin, 2006), Baer, Martin & Schröter, Olaf, *Eine Kopfjagd*, pp. 127-41 (Berlin, 2001), Roberts, Allen, 'Insidious Conquests: Wartime Politics along the South-Western Shore of Lake Tanganyika' in Page, ME, *Africa and the First World War*, pp. 186-214 (London, 1987), Roberts, Andrew, 'East Africa – The First World War, 1914-1918' in *The Cambridge History of Africa 7*, pp. 664-70 (Cambridge, 1986), Farwell, Byron, *The Great War in Africa, 1914-1918*, pp. 105-358 (London, 1986), Boyd, William, *An Ice Cream War* (London, 1982), Miller, Charles, *Battle for the Bundu: The First World War in East Africa* (London, 1974), Ward, WEF & White, LM, *East Africa: A Century of Change, 1870-1970*, pp. 78-95 (New York, 1971), Gardner, Brian, *German East: The Story of the First World War in East Africa* (London, 1963), Ingham, Kenneth, *A History of East Africa*, pp. 245-70 (London, 1963), Dolbey, Robert V, *Sketches of the East African Campaign* (London, 1918)

[10] Gewald, Jan-Bart, *Forged in the Great War: People, Transport, and Labour, the Establishment of Colonial Rule in Zambia, 1890-1920*, p. 135 (Leiden, 2015)

[11] Further Reading: Deutsch, Jan-Georg, *Emancipation without Abolition in German East Africa, 1884-1914* (Oxford, 2006), Grant, Kevin, *A Civilised Savagery: Britain and the New Slaveries in Africa, 1884-1926*, pp. 135-66 (London, 2005), Deutsch, Jan-Georg, 'Freeing slaves in German East Africa, 1890-1914' in Miers, S & Klein, M, *Slavery in Colonial Africa*, p. 109-32 (London, 1999), Sunseri, T, 'Slave Ransoming in German East Africa, 1885-1922' in *The International Journal of African Historical Studies 26/3*, pp. 481-511 (1993), Caplan, P, 'The East African Slave Trade, 1861-1895' in *The International Journal of African Historical Studies 22*, pp. 1-26 (1989), Romero, P, 'Where have all the Slaves gone?' in *Journal of African History 27/4*, pp. 497-512 (1986), Anonymous, 'Slavery in German East Africa' in *The Muslim World*, p. 437 (1917), Beech, M, 'Slavery on the East Coast of Africa' in *The Journal of the African Society 15/58*, pp. 145-9 (1916), Karstedt, F, 'Zur Sklavenfrage in Deutsch-Ostafrika' in *Koloniale Rundschau*, pp. 616-21 (1913)

cenaries. Their pay was cash and spoils after a victory. A third of these troops consisted of foreign mercenaries like Manyema, Baganda and Bemba from neighbouring British territory. The rest were local Askari of the Ngoni, Sukuma and Nyamwezi micro-nations. Until 1916, 3,007 whites and 12,100 Askari had been concentrated. If needed, German officers were able to recruit additional irregular units—with the assistance of local authorities. Normally these chiefs had to sign up after their subjugation and put men at the disposal of the Germans in case of an 'emergency'. Prior to 1918, 3,000 Askari had deserted from the army, 4,500 were listed as missing and 4,200 were held in military detention. Approximately 1,000 Askari defected to the Allies—and were fighting against the Germans.[12] Apart from the Askari themselves, their families made up a major part of the military columns. They went along with the troops and carried personal belongings, searched for food and water, collected firewood, cooked, sewed, mended uniforms, took care of the sick and the wounded. The children were used as piquets, messengers, runners and lookouts.

90 percent Africans

The Allies deployed approximately 240,000 soldiers: 80,000 whites and South Africans, 35,000 Indians and 125,000 black Africans.[13] Kenya was the operation base until 1916. There the troops and porters were gathered. The allied armies were made up of the King's African Rifles (KAR),[14] the *Force Publique* and the Nyasaland Native Force, i.e. Around 1917, the King's African Rifles reached a total of 35,000 Askari—mainly from Kenya

---

[12] This was the reverse of the situation at the start of the war when many of the Askari had previously been with the British King's African Rifles. When disbanded in 1911, they joined the German *Schutztruppe* (see Peter Charlton contribution).

[13] Koller, Christian, 'Deutsche Wahrnehmungen feindlicher Kolonialsoldaten im Ersten Weltkrieg' in *Südasien-Chronik 5*, p. 43 (Berlin, 2015)

[14] Further Reading: Adams, Gregg, *King's African Rifles versus Schutztruppe Soldier: East Africa, 1917-1918* (New York, 2016), Page, Malcolm, *King's African Rifles: A History* (Barnsley, 2011), Nunneley, John, *Tales from the King's African Rifles* (London, 2001), Parsons, Timothy, *The African Rank-and-File: Social Implications of Colonial Military Service in the King's African Rifles, 1902-1964* (Oxford, 1999), Hodges, GWT, 'African Manpower Statistics for the British Forces in East Africa, 1914-1918' in *Journal of African History 19/1*, pp. 101-16 (1978), Moyse-Bartlett, H, *The King's African Rifles: A Study in the History of East and Central Africa, 1890-1945* (Aldershot, 1956)

and Malawi. Nandi and Baganda were recruited in Kenya.[15] The Ngoni, Chewa, Yao, Lozi, Bemba, Ndebele, Ila and Tonga in Malawi, Zambia and Zimbabwe. Portugal deployed approximately 20,000 soldiers. In the Congo the *Force Publique* had been raised to 25,000 men by 1917.[16] A lot of them came from the province of Katanga or were Manyema. As a result of the white soldiers being affected by disease, the British military commander decided to let black Africans fight more intensely. The units of the KAR were raised and more reinforcements were requested. Approximately 10,000 soldiers—Hausa, Ibo, Ewe and Fulani—were sent from West Africa to East Africa. The result: from 1918 on 90 percent of all troops were black Africans.

Without porters no movement

The period between 1916 and 1918 is frequently referred to as a 'safari war'.[17] The main means of transport of the troops were their legs. The allies had to run after the Germans if they wanted to win. Therefore, one thing is clear: without tens of thousands of porters there would not have been a war in East Africa. Roads barely existed, railway lines were not developed sufficiently, and the withdrawing troops destroyed what remained of the infrastructure. Without porters a military operation would not have been possible. The men had to march six to seven hours a day—with loads of up to 30kg on heads and shoulders. They had to climb mountain passes and swamps. The sick or exhausted were left behind. At night the porters were guarded by armed personnel and were tied up in order to prevent them from fleeing. The tax lists, which had been implemented in the colony before the war, listed all healthy men. Using these lists, the porters were recruited. Recruiters moved through the villages and read names; the people were gathered and chained up.[18] From the villages they then had to march to the depots. The British recruited approximately 550,000 men in Malawi, Kenya and Uganda. From the Congo came 260,000 porters,[19] from West Africa 10,000, from Mozambique 90,000. In

---

[15] Pesek, Michael, *Das Ende eines Kolonialreiches – Ostafrika im Ersten Weltkrieg*, p. 101 (Frankfurt am Main, 2010)
[16] Van Reybrouck, David, *Kongo – Eine Geschichte*, p. 164 (Berlin, 2012)
[17] *Safari* means *journey*, ie mobile
[18] Pesek, M, *Das Ende eines Kolonialreiches* pp. 160-163 (2010)

Tanzania the allies and the Germans recruited approximately 670,000 porters. The number of porters deployed altogether amounted to 1,5 million people.[20]

Building, cooking, tracking

Most of the carriers were signed on for a certain time, only a few served through the complete war. The majority of the carriers worked behind the lines. They took care of supplies and the maintenance of communication lines. If a carrier was sent to the front, he repeatedly was at risk of attack since the respective enemy tried to interrupt the supply. The transport of goods and weapons was not the only task of the carriers, though. They had to build roads and bridges, cook and track, and were always victim of colonial bureaucracy. In Kenya, the porters had to carry an identity disc. On this their name and the duration of their service was stated. These discs were often lost during battles or the officers took them away. Furthermore, the entry lists vanished from the depots. If that happened, the carriers were not able to claim their pay. Additionally, the agreed upon wages were often not paid at all or only partially. Even if a carrier could state how long he had worked there were cases where men had to wait for their pay until the end of 1920.[21]

Entrapped like animals

At the beginning, good pay attracted many people into the service of carrier or army duty. By 1916 this motivation was no longer enough. The whites introduced conscription, normally handled by the local chiefs. They were ordered by the respective colonial government to assign carriers and soldiers. Any who refused were threatened with deposition, arrest or death. In addition, there were mobile police units which, mostly at night, recruited weapons-grade men. They went from house to house and took along any men they could find. The people were chained and carried away. A further means to recruit was to raise duties and taxes. The pressure of payment was increased so that those affected could only fulfill the outstanding debts by

---

[19] Van Reybrouck, P, p. 164 (2012)
[20] Koller, P, p. 43 (2015), Pesek, M, p. 156 (2010)
[21] Hodges, Geoffrey, *Kariakor: The Carrier Corps. The Story of the Military Labour Forces in the Conquest of German East Africa, 1914 to 1918*, p. 178 (Nairobi, 1999)

profitable work. Tardy tax payers were arrested and assigned to carrier duty. In this context there are cases known where women were taken as hostage to force men into becoming carriers. The recruitment of carriers and Askari was like slave hunting in the nineteenth century where men in the villages were entrapped like animals.[22] When the carriers fled they had to face being pursued and shot.

Starvation, disease, mismanagement

The depression caused by conscription, tax rises and seizure of food stuffs triggered a mass exodus. Whole districts became desolate. The fields lay fallow, the villages deserted. Passing military units had confiscated all available food. And in order to hinder the pursuing enemy, the existing infrastructure had been destroyed. Roads, bridges and railway lines were blown up. The result of burnt fields and villages was famine. In Rwanda, Tanzania and Uganda alone, over 100,000 people died. In total approximately 300,000 were affected by hunger. The misery was so bad that there was not even time to bury the dead.[23] Thousands of refugees wandered across the country in search of food and water. These migrations as well as the military troop movements led to the spread of diseases like smallpox and typhus. In addition, there was syphilis—mostly due to surging prostitution.[24] And that was not enough: at the end of the war East Africa was affected by the Spanish flu. Traditional agriculture changed dramatically: in the Congo the colonial administration forced farmers to plant rice in order to feed the troops. In Malawi, the produce was maize, in Mozambique, cotton. Thus, the existing agricultural structure was ended, changed or it collapsed. This immediately affected the structure of the villages, their organisation and social structure. Since chiefs often were, or had been, forced into being the 'middleman' between the colonial administration and the population their status within the community deteriorated. A lot of chiefs lost the trust which had been accorded them traditionally. The

---

[22] Pesek, M, p. 159 (2010), Segal, Ronald, *Islam's Black Slaves*, pp. 194-5 (London, 2001)

[23] Maddox, Gregory, 'Mtunya: Famine in Central Tanzania, 1917-1920' in *Journal of African History 31/2*, p. 190 (1990)

[24] White, Luise, *The Comforts of Home: Prostitution in Colonial Nairobi*, pp. 42-5 (Chicago, 1990)

result: according to European reports, 'public safety' collapsed from 1916.[25] Cattle transport was only possibly at night since during the day there was danger of regular assaults. To avoid poverty, people often succumbed to theft and begging. Human trafficking surfaced again. The sale of a boy yielded a cow, a girl that of two.[26]

Uprisings and resistance

Due to the existing reality of conscription, forced labour, price increases, tax rises, mistreatment and hunger, massive resistance rose in all East African colonies. Most of the people fled from advancing troops to wild terrain, hid or went to other colonies. Certain groups also opted for armed resistance.[27] For example, the *Mumbo-Cult* in Kenya and the *Nyabingi-Movement* in Uganda-Rwanda were at war for years with the Europeans. At the same time in Malawi a lot of people joined the *Nyau-Movement*.[28] In other cases, whole ethnic groups rose, like the Barue, Yao and Macua in Mozambique, the Gusii, Giriama and Turkana in Kenya.[29] These uprisings could only be suppressed by troops. In Tanzania, the Wahehe and Makonde sided with the Allies against the Germans. The same applied to the Massai, Wangeni and Surkuma. The Belgians in the Congo had to proceed against various uprisings: unrest in the region of Kivu as well as insurgencies by the Bashi-Lele and Luba were

---

[25] Pesek, M, pp. 222-4 (2010)

[26] Maddox, P, p. 191 (1990)

[27] Further reading: Braukämper, Ulrich, *Afrika 1914-1918: Antikolonialer Widerstand jenseits der Weltkriegsfronten* (Berlin, 2015), Herzog, Jürgen, *Geschichte Tansanias*, pp. 37-67 (Berlin, 1986), Ranger, TO, *Dance and Society in Eastern Africa, 1890-1970*, pp. 45-76 (London, 1975), Gwassa, GCK, 'The German Intervention and African Resistance in Tanzania' in Kimambo, Isaria, Temu, AJ, *A History of Tanzania*, pp. 85-122 (Nairobi, 1969)

[28] Wipper, Audrey, *Rural Rebels: A Study of Two Protest Movements in Kenya*, pp. 23-87 (Oxford, 1977), Pachai, Bridglal, *Malawi: The History of the Nation*, pp. 215-25 (London, 1973), Hopkins, Elizabeth, 'The Nyabingi Cult of Southwestern Uganda' & Rotberg, Robert, 'Chilembwe's Revolt Reconsidered' in Rotberg, Robert & Mazrui, Ali, *Protest and Power in Black Africa* (Oxford, 1970) Bessell, MJ, 'Nyabingi' in *Uganda Journal 6/2*, pp. 73-86 (1938)

[29] Pesek, M, pp. 227-8 (2010), further reading: Newitt, Malyn, *A History of Mozambique* pp. 415-21 (London, 2009), Brantley, Cynthia, 'Mekatalili and the Role of Women in Giriama Resistance' in *Crummey, Donald: Banditry, Rebellion & Social Protest in Africa*, pp. 333-50 (London, 1986); Brantley, Cynthia, *The Giriama and Colonial Resistance in Kenya, 1800-1920* (Berkeley, 1981)

crushed brutally. In addition, there were mutinies inside the *Force Publique*. In Uganda the Kiga and Tutsi rose. Chiefs of the Ganda protested against conscription: they compared work for the British with former slavery.

Bad beer, cooked seed

The carriers in the colonial armies also offered resistance. Already directly after recruitment many fled on the way to the depots—mainly at night. Also, during battles many carriers escaped, others pretended to be ill or feigned mental illnesses. It is also reported that some took deliberately poisoned food or water in order to sideline themselves. The daily, so to speak passive, resistance of the carriers is in general imbued by intentionally 'playing dumb', feigning of insanity or extra slow working. The civilian population had to find other ways of resistance: one refused to provide workers, carriers or soldiers; withheld food, hid supplies or cooked the seed, which had been distributed by the Europeans, before it was planted. When the food was then claimed the farmers showed that nothing had been growing. In Tanzania, the German recruitment patrols were poisoned by the villagers with bad beer,[30] Belgian units were attacked by the populace. In Malawi, the government representatives were chased away and beaten when trying to recruit. Some chiefs rebelled as well: they refused to report to the authorities the names of men fit for military service—and they did not let the refugees from recruitment drives be taken. There was also an increase in raids of German supply depots: the desperation of the population was too much. The Wahehe, in particular, repeatedly attacked German patrols and stole their cattle.

Unbelievably cruel

During the war in DOA the allies lost in total 10,000 soldiers and over 100,000 carriers.[31] On the German side it is estimated that 100,000 carriers also died. The outbreak of the Spanish flu cost the lives of a further 500,000 people in East Africa.[32] In

---

[30] Clifford, HC, *The Gold Coast Regiment in the East African Campaign*, p. 22 (1920)

[31] Iliffe, P, p. 250 (1979)

[32] Van Reybrouck, P, p. 170 (2012). Further Reading: Gewald, Jan-Bart, 'Die Spanische Grippe in Afrika' in *Periplus – Jahrbuch für außereuropäische Geschichte 2011*, pp. 152-74 (Berlin, 2011)

addition, thousands succumbed to the malaria, small pox, typhus, malnutrition, diarrhoea and hunger. The total number of civilian victims is stated at half a million.[33] Financially, the war cost around 300 million British pounds.[34] Territorially, the largest part of the former colony DOA went as a mandate to the British. The Belgians took over Rwanda and Burundi. A small part, the Kionga Triangle, was given to Portugal.[35] The carriers and Askaris reported after the war that few understood what they had fought for. A veteran described the war as 'unbelievably cruel': in pre-colonial times there would not have been struggles which contributed so many victims.[36]

Wage labour instead of slavery

Only a few black Africans had been working outside of their communities before the war. This changed dramatically during the war: thousands of people were now dependent on cash in order to pay for food and taxes. Then reconstruction work followed. Whole districts were not habitable anymore, the fields had been destroyed and the wells filled up or poisoned. It was also necessary to care for the wounded or invalids. Nevertheless, the colonial administration still demanded fatigue and taxes from the African population. Prices for food had increased, as had tax. From 1921 international economic crises also affected Africa: farmers became more impoverished and the necessity to work for whites increased. The respective national currencies lost approximately half their value in comparison to the pre-war

---

[33] Bayart, Jean-Francois, 'Africa in the World' in *African Affairs 99*, p. 221 (2000)

[34] Further Reading: McCarthy, DMP, 'Money and Underdevelopment in Tanganyika to 1940' in *Journal of Economic History 36/3*, pp. 645-62 (1976)

[35] Further reading: Callahan, Michael, *Mandates and Empire: The League of Nations and Africa, 1914-1931* (Brighton, 1999), Digre, Brian, *Imperialism's New Clothes: The Repartition of Tropical Africa, 1914-1919* (New York, 1990), Brett, EA, *Colonialism and Underdevelopment in East Africa, 1919-1939* (New York, 1977), Beer, George Louis, *African Questions at the Paris Peace Conference* (London, 1968), Louis, Roger, *Great Britain & Germany's Lost Colonies, 1914-1919*, pp. 117-60 (Oxford, 1967), Anne Samson, *Britain, South Africa and the East Africa Campaign, 1914-1918: The Union comes of age* (London, 2005)

[36] Pesek, M, p. 369 (2010); further reading: Greenstein, Lewis, 'The Nandi Experience in the First World War' in Page, ME, *Africa and the First World War*, pp. 81-94 (New York, 1987), Hodges, Geoffrey, *The Carrier Corps: Military Labour in the East African Campaign, 1914-1918*, p. 53 (Oxford, 1986), Page, Melvin, 'Malawians and the Great War: Oral History in Reconstructing Africa's Recent Past' in *The Oral History Review 8*, pp. 49-61 (1980)

period, with direct implication for the war veterans for example, who saved their pay to buy cattle or land. The economic system of the carriers, which had been implemented during the war, continued to have an effect: the systems continued with the registration and management of thousands of workers benefiting colonial industry. A consequence still effective to the present day: in search for work, people moved to the cities. Basically, Europeans completely transformed the societies in East Africa. Within 40 years, a host of wage-workers had been created. Whereas in 1908 the authorities in Tanzania registered only 35,000 wage workers, the number in 1926 was already 276,000. At the same time the number in the Congo was 450,000[37] and in Kenya 195,000. The army of wage workers replaced the slaves of the nineteenth-century.

The colonial powers had assured the African populations that for their military support in the European war they would receive improvements in their personal circumstances and more political influence. These promises were not fulfilled. As a result, various political organisations and trade unions were created in the years after World War One. The number of followers of Pan Africanism increased in eastern and southern Africa.[38] The main demands were protection of the African populations, abolition of forced labour and hut tax, African participation in the political power of their own countries, development of an educational system and public health. Also the natural resources would be available to the Africans themselves. For example, the *Nyasaland Native Association* in Malawi and the *Industrial and Commercial Union* in South Africa organised strikes. In Uganda the *Nyabingi-Movement* called for boycotts of work and tax paying. In Kenya it was the *Kikuyu Association*: their concern was compensation for black African families who lost their land to Europeans.

---

[37] Van Reybrouck, P, p. 156 (2012), further reading: Seibert, Julia, *In die globale Wirtschaft gezwungen: Arbeit und kolonialer Kapitalismus im Kongo, 1885-1960* (Frankfurt am Main, 2016); Higginson, John, *A Working Class in the Making: Belgian Colonial Labor Policy, Private Enterprise, and the African Mineworker, 1907-1951* (University of Wisconsin, 1989)

[38] The works by Edward Blyden, Marcus Garvey and WEB Dubois are important; further reading: Füllberg-Stolberg, Katja, 'The Controversy over Pan-Africanism as an Idea and Political Movement in the First World War Period' in Bley, Helmut & Kremers, Anorthe, *The World during the First World War*, pp. 315-29 (Essen, 2014), Geiss, Immanuel, *The Pan-African Movement* (London, 1974)

The Belgian *Force Publique* in German East Africa during World War I

Kris Quanten[1]

Introduction

Current military historiography is mainly dedicated to the centenary of the First World War. In addition, all attention goes to the European front characterised by a strategic immobility, desperate trench warfare and massacres bordering on madness. However, the First World War was not limited to Europe. There were still plenty of secondary fronts, which remain largely uncovered. Belgian troops thereby also played their part. In this chapter we will highlight one of these secondary fronts, namely the deployment of the Belgian colonial army, the so-called *Force Publique*, in German East Africa from 1916 to 1917. This commitment must be seen against the background of the large-scale British campaign against the German colonial army led by Paul von Lettow-Vorbeck. Operations began on 8 August 1914 and lasted until 25 November 1918—more than two weeks after the armistice in Europe.

It is not our intention to go into detail about the British-German campaign—this has been extensively covered in numerous other publications—but to discuss the Belgian involvement, and in particular the Belgian military contribution to this operation. At the same time, the deployment of the *Force Publique* in German East Africa cannot be seen separately from the political context. Therefore, the political decision-making process—and this at both the Belgian and the international level—is also scrutinised. The complex—and often

---

[1]Lieutenant-Colonel, General Staff, Doctor Kris Quanten is a historian and military professor in the Conflict Studies Department at the Royal Military Academy in Belgium.

divergent—interests that were at stake for the various actors after all, gave rise to different strategies. To direct our research, we posed the following questions: How did the Belgians end up in this arena? Which Belgian interests warranted such a military deployment? What was the overall Belgian contribution to the British war effort? To what extent did Belgian military intervention influence the course of the operations? And finally, what results did the Belgian military deployment yield in both military and political terms? In order to formulate an answer to all these questions, we have opted for a three-pronged approach. In the first part we discuss the general context both in the Belgian Congo and in German East Africa on the eve of the First World War. The section on the Belgian military operations has been chronologically divided into three parts: from 1914 to 1916, what we have called the defensive phase; the year 1916, which was marked by the attack on Tabora and 1917 with the attack on Mahenge. In the epilogue, we briefly outline the subsequent course of the operations, although the Belgians were no longer directly involved. Finally, in the conclusion, we elaborate on the political and military consequences of the campaign and make an overall evaluation.

For this study, we rely mainly on existing literature. However, very little in-depth research has been done on the Belgian military campaign in German East Africa and an overview that examines the military operations in their wider political and international context, is virtually nonexistent. In most cases the studies are the work of officers who were themselves involved in some of the operations and emphasize a particular aspect. One notable exception is the three-volume book *Les campagnes coloniales belges: 1914-1918*, which was edited by the Belgian Ministry of Defence in the early thirties.[2] For the political and diplomatic aspects, the studies of Ingeborg Vijgen and Guy Vanthemsche proved to be enlightening.[3] We also did our own archival research. Next to the Belgian National

---

[2] Merzbach, Libert, Peeters, Stiers, Weber, *Les campagnes coloniales belges, 1914-1918* (Institut Cartographique Militaire, Etat-Major Général de l'Armée, 3 Vol, 1927-1932)

[3] Vijgen, I, *Tussen mandaat en kolonie. Rwanda, Burundi en het Belgische bestuur in opdracht van de Volkenbond (1916-1932)* (Acco, 2005) pp. 47-71. Vanthemsche, G, *Congo : de impact van de kolonie op België* (Lannoo, 2007), pp. 103-9

Archives (BNA) with the Records of de Broqueville and Orts, the archives of the *Force Publique* (FP) in the Africa Archive (AA) of the Federal Public Service Foreign Affairs (FPSFA), and the so-called Russian archives of the Royal Museum of the Armed Forces (RMAF) in Brussels, which includes the Belgian military documents relating to the campaign in German East Africa, yielded surprising results.

General background on the eve of the First World War

Since 1885, Belgium possessed its own colony in Central Africa, the Belgian Congo.[4] At the head of the colony stood the Governor General.[5] In practice however, he had no political power; he was merely responsible for the implementation of colonial policy. The actual decision-making power was in the hands of the Ministry of Colonies in Brussels. In 1914 it was led by the Catholic Jules Renkin. The colony also had its own security forces, the *Force Publique*. This colonial army formed the backbone of the colonial system. It had to create a climate of security and peace; the necessary condition to let the colony reach its full maturity. On the eve of the First World War the *Force Publique* consisted of some 15,000 Congolese soldiers, commanded by 275 Belgian officers and NCOs.[6] Its organisation reflected the paternalistic colonial approach based on the principle of strict racial segregation between Africans and Europeans. The command functions remained firmly in the hands of white officers, while the Congolese soldiers had to be satisfied with lower, executive functions. Since its inception in 1885, the *Force Publique* was primarily a police force that was responsible for local law enforcement and the effective occupation of the territory. This is also evident from the organisation. Due to the vastness of the country (80 times the size of Belgium) and the poor road infrastructure which made rapid movements of large units virtually impossible, the *Force Publique* had a very decentralised structure. For example, each

---

[4] Congo was colonised at the initiative of King Leopold II and was initially a personal possession, called the Congo Free State. It is only in October 1908 that the colony was transferred to the Belgian State and it was named the Belgian Congo.

[5] In 1914 Felix Fuchs was the Belgian governor-general in Congo.

[6] Henry de la Lindi A, '*Les campagnes belges d'Afrique (1914-1917)*', CRAOCA, Nr. 2, (2005) p. 29

district had one company.[7] The territorially scattered units were available for the local district commissioners. The commander of the *Force Publique* had a purely administrative role. He was only responsible for the logistical preparation of the units. The effective deployment of the troops was a matter for the local colonial officials. The *Force Publique* was therefore not an army in the classic sense of the word. It had neither the resources nor the structure to carry out large-scale military operations.

In 1914 Germany was a major colonial power. It had four colonies in Africa, two of which bordered on the Belgian Congo, namely Cameroon and German East Africa. At the head of German East Africa stood governor Heinrich Schnee, who favoured a policy of neutrality and wanted to keep the colony out of the war for as long as possible.[8] However, the commander of the colonial forces, Lieutenant Colonel von Lettow-Vorbeck, had a different opinion.[9] He conducted a more expeditious policy and wanted to prepare the colonial army for possible operations from the moment he arrived in January 1914. The forces, or *Schutztruppe*, at his disposal consisted of 216 German officers and non-commissioned officers and 2,500 native troops, also known as *askaris*.[10] The territory of German East Africa was vast (twice the size of the motherland). The terrain, the climate and the existing infrastructure would have a significant impact on the conduct of military operations. In the west, on the border with Congo, and in the northwest is a mountainous region with peaks over 4,500 meters. The rest of the country consists mainly of savannah and vast bamboo forests. It is a very dry and very

---

[7] The colony was organised in 22 districts. It was only in July 1914 that the Belgian Congo was divided into four provinces: Kasai-Congo, Equateur, Province Orientale and Katanga. The organisation of the *Force Publique* was adapted to that. Henceforth, the troops were split into four groups, one for each province.

[8] In 1914 German East Africa had a population of 7,645 million natives and 5,336 Europeans. The most densely populated areas were Ruanda and Urundi. Schnee H, *Deutsch-Ostafrika im Weltkrieg* (Vero Verlag, s.l., 1919) p. 28

[9] Von Lettow-Vorbeck had previously gained a lot of operational experience. In 1900 he took part in the international expedition against the Boxer Rebellion in China. He was also involved in suppressing rebellions of the Herero and the Khoikhoi in German Southwest Africa between 1904 and 1906. In January 1914, the then 44-year-old lieutenant colonel was appointed commander in chief of the armed forces in German East Africa. Von Lettow-Vorbeck P, *La guerre de brousse dans l'Est-Africain (1914-1918)* (Payot, 1933) p. 32

[10] Merzbach, Libert, Peeters, Stiers, Weber, Op. Cit., Vol. 1, p. 40. Von Lettow-Vorbeck P, Op. Cit., p. 11

barren area. Additionally, there are several lakes—in fact, they are real interior seas—the most important of which are Lake Victoria in the north and Lake Tanganyika in the west. These lakes would play an important role in the logistic supply of the troops. The area where the operations took place is located just south of the equator, leaving only two seasons: the dry season from May to late October, followed by the wet season from November to April. During the latter successive torrential rains change dirt roads into real mud pools, rendering military operations virtually impossible. During the dry season, daytime temperatures can reach 35 degrees Celsius while the nights are very cool. In the mountainous regions night frost can even occur. In addition to these extreme temperature differences, there are also numerous diseases and infections, such as malaria, dysentery and sleeping sickness which make the living conditions very hard. In terms of infrastructure, there were very few paved roads in German East Africa. In most cases dirt roads and trails connected the main towns and villages. However, the colony possessed a well-developed rail network. The railway from Dar es Salaam to Kigoma on Lake Tanganyika ran centrally across the country. This 1,250 kilometre line of communication was vital for Germans for the rapid movement of troops as well as for the provisioning of supplies from the port of Dar es Salaam.

1914-1916: The defensive phase

On 4 August 1914 Germany invaded Belgium. With this the motherland was dragged into the First World War. Initially the Belgian government hoped to keep the colony out of the conflict. For that she relied on Article 11 of the Berlin Conference Act of 1885 which stipulated the neutrality of the Congo Basin, provided that all signatories were in agreement. Paris and London, however, refused to agree with the Belgian neutrality proposal. At that time the German troops in Africa were outnumbered. The allies saw this as an opportunity to deal with the German colonial empire as well as with the German *Mittel-Africa* ambitions once and for all. They therefore had more to gain from an offensive attitude than from neutrality as proposed by the Belgians.[11] On 8 August 1914 the British started hostilities by shelling the port of Dar es Salaam.

---

[11] Vijgen, I, Op. Cit., p. 51

The German Governor Schnee realised that an escalation of the war to Africa was inevitable. He therefore had to accept the plans as proposed by his military commander, von Lettow-Vorbeck. The top priority was the development of the colonial army. Apart from all German men in the colony, additional native soldiers were also mobilised. In December 1915, the German colonial army had already 11,367 *askaris* commanded by 2,712 Germans.[12] They were organised into 45 companies. In addition, there were 2,600 Tutsis from Ruanda, the so-called Ruga-Ruga, who had sided with the Germans and served as auxiliaries.[13] Nevertheless, von Lettow-Vorbeck realised that despite the substantial increase in forces, he was no match for the Allies' superior numbers in the surrounding countries.[14] Instead of a conventional approach, he therefore resolutely opted for a mobile guerrilla war, based on small units. Through the masterful use of manoeuvre on the interior lines and the performance of small-scale actions without letting the enemy come to grips, he wanted to force his numerically superior opponents to spread out their forces throughout the country.[15] The strategy of von Lettow-Vorbeck was clear: the more allied troops he could fix in German East Africa the fewer troops were available for the European front and therefore pressure on the German front in Europe would decrease.[16] The deployment of his force was completely in line with that strategy. He turned the bulk of his forces—about 6,800 troops—to the northeast, opposite British East Africa (present-day Kenya and Uganda) where he expected the greatest threat. A group of 2,000 soldiers

[12] Among the German officers was a certain Kurt Wahle. He was a retired general who was on holiday with his son in German East Africa at the time of mobilisation. He volunteered spontaneously and was initially responsible for the logistic supply of troops and later for all the operations in the western part of the colony. Merzbach, Libert, Peeters, Stiers, Weber, Op. Cit., Vol. 1, p. 110

[13] The Tutsis were led by mwami Musinga, who strongly favoured the Germans. RMAF, Record 185, Box 2299, Folder 5469, *Correspondance entre le vice-gouverneur Malfeyt et le commissaire général Henry*, 15 December 1914, pp. 75-76

[14] The situation for von Lettow-Vorbeck was anything but favourable: in the north, the British mobilised three divisions in British East Africa; in the east they imposed a complete naval blockade thereby compromising the supply line to the colony; in the south in Mozambique a thousand Portuguese troops were mobilised, in addition to a thousand British troops in Rhodesia. Finally, in the west, the Belgian led *Force Publique* had a similar troop strength as the German colonial army.

[15] Von Lettow-Vorbeck, P, Op. Cit., pp. 24-31

[16] Von Lettow-Vorbeck, P, Op. Cit., p. 11

guarded the coast to prevent a possible disembarkation by the British Navy. In the northwest, opposite Uganda and Kivu, he placed 3,000 troops. In the west 1,500 troops guarded the border between Ruanda and the Belgian Congo and another 500 troops were responsible for the control of Lake Tanganyika. Finally, he sent a force of 1,500 troops to the south to block a possible incursion from Rhodesia or Mozambique.[17] Von Lettow-Vorbeck personally commanded the northern forces opposite British East Africa. Because of the enormous distances between the different fronts however, he could not possibly lead all the operations himself. He therefore restricted himself to giving general guidelines. For the exact details, he counted on the sense of initiative of the local commanders who possessed a great freedom of action.

Von Lettow-Vorbeck realised only too well that time was not his ally. The Belgians and the British were busy building and reorganizing their forces and it would take several months before they were at full strength. Under those circumstances, attack appeared to be the best defense. So he decided from the start to take the initiative by performing harassing actions. These were surprise attacks against the British lines of communication in British East Africa, as well as against positions of the *Force Publique* at the border with the Belgian Congo. It is in this context that as of 15 August 1914 eastern Congo was rocked by numerous raids conducted by German patrols.[18] Most of the time these were small-scale guerrilla actions without leading to a decisive battle. Then again, the main effort of von Lettow-Vorbeck was not in the west at the border with Congo, but in the northeast opposite British East Africa where he expected the greatest threat. On 22 August there was a significant turn of events. The German warship *Hedwig von Wissmann* shelled Albertville from Lake Tanganyika, thereby heavily damaging the Belgian steamer *Alexandre Delcommune*. From then on, the Germans were masters of Lake Tanganyika and they did not hesitate to fire upon Belgian positions on the west bank of the lake. A response to these provocations was inevitable. Initially, the Belgian government had instructed Governor-General Fuchs to

---

[17] Janssens, E, *Histoire de la Force Publique* (Gesquière, 1979) p. 156
[18] Lefevre, P, Lefevre, J-N, *Les militaires belges et le Rwanda 1916-2006* (Racine, 2006) pp. 19-22

maintain a strictly defensive policy.[19] However, the border between Congo and German East Africa was more than 800 kilometers, and guarding it was hampered by the mountainous terrain. Moreover, border defense was a provincial responsibility: in the north that was the *Province Orientale* headed by vice-governor Justin Malfeyt and in the south that was Katanga where Charles Tombeur was vice-governor. Each province thereby obstinately followed its own course and coordination between the two was minimal.

It is only with the shelling of Albertville that the policy of the Belgian government toughened. In a telegram dated 28 August, the Minister of Colonies, Renkin, bluntly stated that limited offensive actions were admitted for the purpose of defending the territorial integrity of the colony.[20] But the *Force Publique* was not prepared for the conduct of large-scale operations: it possessed neither the resources nor an appropriate structure. It was essential that the *Force Publique* was reformed from a local police force to a deployable army as soon as possible. Especially vice-governor Tombeur, who was also a colonel in the *Force Publique*, would play a leading role therein. On his own initiative he decided to reorganise the different companies in Katanga into three battalions with a unified command structure. The centralisation permitted a greater flexibility to the deployment of the troops. That decision soon proved to be the right choice. When on 5 September the Germans attacked the little town of Abercorn in nearby Northern Rhodesia, Tombeur decided—at the request of the local British commander—to send a battalion. This had to buy the British the necessary time to mobilise and send reinforcements to the threatened area. Meanwhile, the Belgians had to protect the border between Abercorn and Saisi and prevent the Germans from threatening the Belgian southeast flank. Eventually two battalions—which amounted to 55 Belgians and 1,360 Congolese—were deployed during the operation. They stayed in Northern Rhodesia until November 1915. The situation in the

---

[19] Merzbach, Libert, Peeters, Stiers, Weber, Op. Cit., Vol. 1, p. 129
[20] Merzbach, Libert, Peeters, Stiers, Weber, Op. Cit., Vol. 1, pp. 130-1
Correspondance diplomatique et politique relative à la guerre en Afrique. Rapport du Haut Commandement : violation des lois de la guerre par l'ennemi (Van Oest, 1919) p. 14. BNA, Records of de Broqueville, Folder 421, *Note sur la politique de guerre suivie au Congo par le Gouvernement belge, Note de Renkin au Roi Albert*, 12 Oct 1916, pp. 1-45

Northern *Province Orientale* differed thoroughly with the one in Katanga. Vice-governor Malfeyt—unlike Tombeur—had no previous military experience and had handed over command of the troops to his deputy, Major Henry Josué who used a more cautious tactic. To defend the border he used an outstretched linear dispositive with the *Force Publique*—still organised in companies—to occupy a number of strategically important positions. From August the German offensive actions also started here. There were skirmishes at Toa, Uvira, Kisenyi, Luvungi and the island of Kwidjwi in Lake Kivu, where the *Force Publique* suffered many losses.

In early 1915 it was apparent that the attacking strategy had to be adapted; defensive actions alone did not suffice anymore. The Belgian Congo could no longer just stand by and watch the German attacks. The idea of an attack on German East Africa became increasingly acceptable: the Belgian defensive policy was exchanged for an offensive one. The Belgian government in exile (Le Havre) also supported the switch. It realised that offensive action against German East Africa, could yield not only military but political benefits as well. It counted on a territorial expansion of the Belgian colony as payment for its participation in the Allied war effort. The Belgian government was particularly interested in the left bank of the Congo River estuary.[21] The idea was that Belgium would cede the occupied territories in German East Africa to the British, who would in turn, put pressure on Portugal to relinquish the left bank of the Congo estuary to Belgium. As compensation, the Portuguese would acquire a part of the German colony on the border with Mozambique.[22] However, this was a bold calculation, and the outcome was far from certain.

At first glance, the Belgian approach in Africa looked to be in contradiction with the neutral policy the Belgian government—

---

[21] Congo, which size corresponds with that of entire Western Europe, had a coastline of 37 kilometres. The left bank of the Congo estuary was in the hands of the Portuguese, making the colony also very vulnerable. Therefore, the Belgian government had a high interest in securing control of the left bank. For that they counted on diplomatic support by the British in exchange for participation in the war effort against German East Africa.

[22] FPSFA, AA, FP 2658, *Note de Orts à Renkin*, 19 Jun 1916. BNA, de Broqueville, Folder 421, *Note sur la politique de guerre suivie au Congo par le Gouvernement belge, Note de Renkin au Roi Albert*, pp. 1-45, 12 Oct 1916. Van Zuylen, P, *L'échiquier congolais ou le secret du Roi* (Dessart, 1959) pp. 434, 446-7

and especially King Albert—had strongly defended in Europe. The reason for this remarkable turn of events was the Belgian fear that Congo would be used by the Allies—and especially by Great-Britain—as a bargaining chip to soften German ambitions on the European continent. In particular, King Albert suspected the French and British of secretly deciding to redraw the map of Africa, whereby Belgium would suffer.[23] In order to avoid such a scenario, resolutely using the *Force Publique* in the allied conquest of German East-Africa appeared to be the best strategy. Additionally, its deployment would ensure that the Belgians would become involved during the post war negotiations on the partition of Africa.

A large-scale military action required a prior reorganisation of the *Force Publique*. Firstly, the actions of the two regions had to be coordinated. In February 1915 the Minister of Colonies decided to hand overall command of the troops of the two provinces to Colonel Tombeur.[24] This brought the entire eastern front under his command. He had to coordinate the military efforts and ensure the unity of command. From Elizabethville he reorganised his forces, which he divided into two groups: Brigade North led by Colonel Philippe Molitor and the Brigade South led by Lieutenant-Colonel Frederick Olsen. Each brigade consisted of two regiments that were in turn composed of three battalions. In total, about 10,000 men. Yet the reorganisation also revealed many problems, especially in logistics. All supplies had to be brought in from Matadi, the only port on the Atlantic Ocean, a trip of more than 2,800 kilometres, which took no less than four months. For that, thousands of indigenous porters, who often lived in appalling conditions, were used.[25] The arma-

---

[23] King Albert's fear was not unfounded. In 1911 the British had already proposed to divide the Belgian Congo between the powers – Great Britain, France and Germany – to dissuade Germany of going to war in Europe. Willequet, J, 'Anglo-German rivalry in Belgian and Portuguese Africa?' in Gifford, P & Louis, WR, *Britain and Germany in Africa. Imperial rivalry and colonial rule* (New-Haven, 1967) pp. 245-73, Vanthemsche, G, Op. Cit., pp. 105-9

[24] There was a lot of envy between Henry and Tombeur. Both were hoping to be given the supreme command of the operations in eastern Congo. That Tombeur eventually got the position came as no surprise. In addition to his military career, he had a lot of political experience as vice-governor after all. He had also been the orderly of Albert I and therefore enjoyed the King's confidence. Following the appointment of Colonel Tombeur as overall commander of operations, Lieutenant-Colonel Henry – deeply disappointed – requested a transfer to the European front. Henry de la Lindi, A, Op. Cit., pp. 36-8. Vijgen, I, Op. Cit., p. 59

ment of the *Force Publique* was ill-suited for offensive operations. Therefore, in 1915 an extensive weapons pro-gramme was launched that involved new weapons and artillery pieces coming from Belgium and France.[26] It was clear though that the reorganisation of the *Force Publique*, on both the logistical and organisational level, would still take a long time to complete and held back the planning of operations. Because of this Tombeur's anticipated offensive had to be postponed three times.[27]

The measures that had been taken were situated both on the military and on the political level. For example, from 1915 onwards, the Belgian government was going to take several diplomatic initiatives. Indeed, she realised that the deployment of the *Force Publique* could only be effective if it was part of a broad international approach. She therefore started looking for allies, just like on the European front. The British colonial forces seemed to be the obvious choice. Where the unofficial contacts between the commanders on the ground were very positive, the British Colonial Office proved very reluctant towards mounting a combined military operation. The British suspected the Belgians of having territorial ambitions to the east of Congo, which conflicted with their pursuit of a north-south connection on the African continent.[28] Moreover, the British troop strength, both in British East Africa and Northern Rhodesia, was as yet too limited to launch a large-scale

---

[25] In practice, entire villages – men, women and children – were mandatorily employed to obtain a sufficient amount of porters. For the whole of the campaign in German East Africa the total number of porters is estimated at 260,000. FPSFA, AA, FP 2663, *Pertes en homes pendant la guerre*, 28 Feb 1919. Merzbach, Libert, Peeters, Stiers, Weber, Op. Cit., Vol. 1, p. 34

[26] So the old and worn out Albini rifles, which still fired with black powder, were replaced by the French Gras (in total 15,500 pieces). The artillery was renewed as well: in addition to the existing Nordenfeld- (47mm) and Krupp Guns (75mm), four batteries of four guns each were provided by Saint-Chamond (70mm). The problem was that no specific ammunition was provided for those new guns. So there was nothing for it but to use the existing stock of 75mm shells, but that meant all the shells had to be filed down by 2.5mm! Tasnier, L, Van Overstraeten, R, *Les opérations militaires* (Bertels, 1923, pp. 328-9). Merzbach, Libert, Peeters, Stiers, Weber, Op. Cit., Vol. 2, pp. 70-4

[27] RMAF, Belgian military presence abroad – Congo Free State and Belgian Congo, Papers Libert, Folder 152, *Télégramme de Tombeur à Renkin*, 6 Mar 1915

[28] BNA, Records of de Broqueville, Map 421, *Note sur la politique de guerre suivie au Congo par le Gouvernement belge, Note de Renkin au Roi Albert*, 12 Oct 1916, pp. 1-45 Louis, WR, *Great Britain and Germany's lost colonies. 1914-1919* (1967) p. 68

operation. The British military buildup was still ongoing and it would eventually take until 1916 before it was at full strength. The British dismissive attitude led to disappointment and incomprehension by the Belgian government.[29] Whereas in 1914 the British did not want to know about the Belgian neutrality proposal and were in favour of an operation against the German colony, they now suddenly appeared unwilling to cooperate on the Belgian initiative. Without British support a large-scale offensive seemed to be excluded for the time being. However, the Belgian Minister of Colonies, Renkin, did not want to throw in the towel just yet. He promptly ordered Tombeur to start developing the operational plans. The colonel wanted to launch a converging attack based on two columns, one approaching from the north via Kigali and one from the south via Bismarckburg.[30] His intention was to encircle the German forces in the west of German East Africa and eliminate them. By doing so, he wanted to put an end to the German attack on the east of Congo. However, this plan proved to be too ambitious, especially without British help.[31] In July 1915 it was modified at the insistence of the government and reduced to a smaller operation that was only set against Ruanda.[32] The northern column had Kigali—the administrative capital of Ruanda—as objective while the southern column focused on Nyanza—the political capital and the residence of the local Tutsi king, mwami Musinga. In order for the operation to be successful Tombeur set as prerequisite that Lake Tanganyika had to be recaptured.[33] The Germans controlled the entire region with their navy on Lake Tanganyika. At the same time the lake was absolutely vital for the logistical supply of Belgian troops during their advance.[34] At the continued insistence of the Belgians, the

---

[29] Vijgen, I, Op. Cit., p. 60

[30] RMAF, Record 185, Box 1569, Folder 3856, *Instructions générales du Colonel Tombeur aux commandants de groupes*, pp. 162-5

[31] RMAF, Belgian military presence abroad – Congo Free State and Belgian Congo, Papers Libert, Folder 152, *Télégramme du commandant des troupes britanniques en Rhodésie du Nord à Tombeur, 21 April 1915*

[32] FPSFA, AA, FP 2650, *Télégramme de Renkin à Tombeur*, 21 Jun 1915. RMAF, Belgian military presence abroad – Congo Free State and Belgian Congo, Papers Libert, Folder 152, *Plan de campagne*, 31 Jul 1915

[33] RMAF, Record 185, Box 21, Folder 244, *Période défensive à la frontière orientale, Note de Tombeur à Renkin*, pp. 28-32, 12 Mar 1915

[34] The German navy on Lake Tanganyika was composed of the ships *Hedwig von*

British finally proved willing to cooperate. In October and November 1915, two fully assembled British battleships were transported over land from Cape Town to Lake Tanganyika.[35] Together with several smaller Belgian ships they would have to mount the attack on the German fleet.[36] To support this maritime action, the Belgian government also sent four seaplanes as air support to Congo.[37] This first joint initiative was successful: in February 1916, the *Hedwig von Wissmann* was sunk.[38] Four months later, in June 1916, the last German warship, the *Graf von Götzen*, was disabled after a raid by Belgian aircraft. As a result, the Germans lost control of Lake Tanganyika.

In December 1915 a major reversal occurred. The British notified the Belgian Government that they would like to participate in a combined attack on German East Africa. The defeat of the British troops in Tanga had been decisive for the British change of heart.[39] The military defeat had important

Wissmann, Kingani and *Graf von Götzen*.

[35] These were *Mimi* and *Toutou*, which were 12 metre long motor boats. They had to be carried 4,800 kilometres inland, including the traversing of a 1,800 metre high mountain range. RMAF, Record 185, Box 3204, Folder 7089, *Rapport du major Stinglhamber*, 10 Nov 1915, pp. 321-322. RMAF, Record 185, Box 3204, Folder 7089, *Rapport général sur les opérations et travaux au lac Tanganyika pendant la campagne 1914-15-16*, 10 Jan 1917, pp. 3-108

[36] The first maritime action took place on 26 December 1915. *Mimi* and *Toutou* were engaged against *Kingani*, which was captured and afterwards taken into British service as HMS *Fifi*.

[37] Captain-Commander Albert de Bueger was designated by the Belgian government for this mission. As Belgium did not have any hydroplanes, he contacted London which provided the Belgians with four Short Type 827 floatplanes. The four pilots and technical personnel were all Belgian.

[38] The combined Anglo-Belgian flotilla was commanded by the British commander Geoffrey Spicer-Simson. Ironically, it was *Fifi* that engaged the *von Wissmann*, which suffered serious damage as a result of the firing and finally sunk.

[39] Tanga was a strategically important city on the Indian coast. From there a railway line went to Uganda. On 2 November 1914, a force of 8,000 Indians, supported by the Royal Navy, disembarked with the intention to conquer a bridgehead. However, von Lettow-Vorbeck had prior knowledge of the attack and he used the railway to transfer additional troops in extremis from the northern front to Tanga. The British were not informed of this and were met by fierce German resistance. After three days of heavy fighting, the Indian troops were forced to return to their ships. In addition, they had to leave all their heavy equipment behind. British losses, 360 killed and 487 wounded, were high in comparison with German losses: 61 dead and 81 wounded. The Battle of Tanga, the first large-scale confrontation in German East Africa, was therefore a humiliating defeat for the British. Tasnier, L, Van Overstraeten, R, Op. Cit., p. 333. Von Lettow-Vorbeck, P, Op. Cit., pp. 43-4.

political consequences: the British now realised that they should no longer underestimate the German colonial army, and especially that they needed the Belgian *Force Publique* for their operations against German East Africa.[40] Moreover, the situation in German South West Africa had also changed. In July 1915 the German colony had been captured by South African troops.[41] At the request of the British, these newly available troops would be used against the last German stronghold: German East Africa. So in early 1916, the 17,000 soldiers who were already stationed in British East Africa were joined by 15,000 South Africans.[42] This force was led by the South African General Jan Christian Smuts, who already wanted to start with a large-scale operation in the spring of 1916. Now nothing seemed to stand in the way of a combined operation against German East Africa. Also the planning of the operations gained momentum. The plan was to perform a double envelopment: the British, who had the most troops, would attack with three divisions from the north, while the Belgian *Force Publique* had to advance with two brigades from the west.[43]

This put an end to the defensive phase. From 1914 to 1916 the Belgians had limited themselves to defending the Congolese border. Yet this did nothing to prevent the German attacks. An offensive against German East Africa seemed inevitable. To that end, the *Force Publique* was reorganised and rearmed. It was intended to launch a limited offensive to conquer a strip east of the Congolese border and thus put an end to the German operations. The Belgian Government argued that the territories

---

Hordern, C, *Military operations East Africa* (Vol. 1, HMSO, 1941) pp. 60-170

[40] Louis, WR, *Great Britain and Germany's lost colonies. 1914-1919* (1967) p. 64

[41] In 1910 the Union of South Africa was founded. It had the status of a dominion within the British Commonwealth. The first government was led by Prime Minister Louis Botha, who would fully support Britain during the First World War. He would deploy the South African troops on the side of the British.

[42] FPSFA, AA, FP, 2650, *Note de Renkin au Roi Albert*, Dec 1915. Louis, WR, Op. Cit., p. 54

[43] Additionally, in the south there were operations being conducted by the Portuguese from Mozambique and by the British from Northern Rhodesia. Yet these were secondary operations. The intention was to force the Germans to send troops to the south, and so weaken the northern front. According to von Lettow-Vorbeck the greatest threat came from the British in the north and the Belgians in the west. Hordern, C, Op. Cit., pp. 275-93

that were occupied by the *Force Publique* could later serve as leverage for territorial expansion of the colony. Therefore 1916 was the year of the reversal in the Belgian strategy: the defensive policy was exchanged for an offensive one.

Offensive phase: the attacks on Tabora and Mahenge

On 26 February 1916 General Tombeur gave his guidelines for the attack.[44] His final plan remained roughly the same as the initial plan, with only some minor modifications. To circumvent the German defensive positions north of Lake Kivu, the northern brigade had to advance from Kivu to Kigali through Ugandan territory. The southern brigade would attack south of Lake Kivu towards Nyanza via Shangugu.[45] For his offensive Tombeur had 11,698 soldiers and 719 Belgian officers and NCOs at his disposal.[46] On 20 April 1916 the operations began. Initially the *Force Publique* met with little resistance. Von Lettow-Vorbeck had indeed moved different units of the western front to the northeast in a reaction to the large-scale British offensive that had started in March. The remaining troops in the west could only limit themselves to small-scale actions, after which they always retreated to the next defensive positions. Without too much difficulty, the Belgians captured Kigali on 6 May and Nyanza on 19 May. After the capture of the latter city, mwami Musinga, who—until then—had collaborated with the Germans, submitted to the Belgians. With this act the *Force Publique* controlled the whole of Ruanda.

The swift success of the Belgian advance came as a surprise. As a consequence, Tombeur urged Minister Renkin to continue the operations.[47] The conditions seemed favourable for wresting even more territory from the Germans without too much effort. Because the British had their hands full in the northeast, the Belgians would be able to do so virtually unchallenged. Minister Renkin was clearly on the same wavelength as the general on

---

[44] In February 1916 Colonel Tombeur was appointed general-major by Minister Renkin. Merzbach, Libert, Peeters, Stiers, Weber, Op. Cit., Vol. 2, Annexe Nr. 1, *Précisions au Plan de Campagne*

[45] The German forces north of Lake Kivu were commanded by Captain Wintgens (1,100 men); those in the south by Major von Langen (700 men).

[46] Merzbach, Libert, Peeters, Stiers, Weber, Op. Cit., Vol. 2, p. 60

[47] BNA, de Broqueville, Nr. 421, *Télégramme de Tombeur à Renkin*, 2 Jun 1916

this. He assumed that the more land area the *Force Publique* conquered, the more Belgium would be able to influence the repartition of Africa in a post-war peace conference. His goal was to put Belgium in the strongest negotiating position possible. In his eyes the conquest of vast territories in German East Africa was the best guarantee for obtaining territorial compensation at the Congo estuary. Whereas Minister Renkin initially only counted on the territory of Ruanda, he now seemed to nurture far greater ambitions: in a telegram to Tombeur he promptly gave permission for the conquest of the whole area between Lake Tanganyika and Lake Victoria, as well Urundi and a strip east of Lake Tanganyika all the way to Kigoma. This was a considerable expansion of the original objectives.[48]

Backed by the Belgian Government, Tombeur resumed his advance in early June.[49] The Brigade North marched further towards Lake Victoria which was reached on 1 July. But there the force came across fierce German resistance, by which it was held up. Meanwhile, the Brigade South had started its march toward Usumbura and Kitega, which were captured on 6 and 17 June respectively. After the fall of these cities, the local Tutsi leader, mwami Mwambusa, had no choice but to submit to the Belgian authorities. This brought Urundi effectively under control of the *Force Publique*. On 8 July, the southern brigade continued its operations in the direction of Kigoma. That city was of strategic importance: it was not only a major port on Lake Tanganyika, but it was also the terminus of the railway line from Dar es Salaam. On 28 July the city fell into the hands of the *Force Publique* without much resistance.[50] The Belgian advance seemed unstoppable. In less than three months' time, the *Force Publique* had accomplished all its operational aims. It now controlled an area three times the size of Belgium. Things looked very bad on the African western front for the Germans. Due to the rapid advance of the different Belgian columns, the

---

[48] BNA, de Broqueville, Nr. 422, *Télégramme de Renkin à Tombeur*, 9 Jun 1916

[49] BNA, de Broqueville, Folder 422, *Note pour Renkin*, 16 Jun 1916 RMAF, Record 185, Box 2312, Folder 5493, *Ordres du général Tombeur aux commandants de brigades*, 26 May 1916, p. 281

[50] The capture of Kigoma also had significant advantages in terms of logistics. Henceforth supplies for Belgian troops could be transported by ship from Albertville, which was significantly faster than over land. Merzbach, Libert, Peeters, Stiers, Weber, Op. Cit., Vol. 2, pp. 365-98

German troops were cut off from each other and threatened with isolation from their main force in the east. Therefore, von Lettow-Vorbeck decided to regroup in Tabora and have them construct a defensive position.[51]

The withdrawal had important consequences. British General Smuts wanted to administer a decisive defeat to the Germans at Tabora. For that he was planning a large operation for which he also counted on the Belgians. The British had suffered considerable losses during their offensive in the northeast and their advance had been very difficult. The climatic conditions had taken their toll and had caused a lot of victims among the South African and Indian troops. That was in stark contrast to the Belgian successes. Therefore, Smuts wanted to use the *Force Publique* for his attack on the German stronghold. In early July, the British general sent a request to Tombeur to partake in the offensive via the Belgian liaison officer Captain Raoul Van Overstraeten.[52] The aim was to attack Tabora, an important road junction and trade center, simultaneously from different directions, and subsequently eliminate the encircled German troops.

The proposal came as a surprise to the Belgians. It signified a further expansion of the war. The proposal therefore created some debate in the Belgian Government. Especially Foreign Minister Eugène Beyens opposed it.[53] He feared that the Belgians were increasingly being used by the British to do their dirty work, without receiving any guarantee from the British Government for any form of compensation whatsoever. He wanted to avoid the *Force Publique* being used purely to serve British interests. However, Minister Renkin did not agree. He especially considered the long-term advantages and therefore came back to his earlier arguments of the more territory the Belgians could conquer, the more they would benefit during the future peace talks. Moreover, it was hard to leave the British, who at that time were making heavy sacrifices on the European

---

[51] Von Lettow-Vorbeck, P, Op. Cit., pp. 166-8

[52] FPSFA, AA, FP 2653, *Télégramme de Orts à Renkin*, 5 Jul 1916. Van Overstraeten, *En ces temps-là. Carnets d'un officier de liaison dans l'Est Africain* (Cahiers Léopoldiens, 1961)

[53] Beyens, E, *Un diplomat belge au service de son pays, 1915-1917* (Centre Guillaume Jacquemyns, 1981) pp. 247-8

front, to their own devices.⁵⁴ Renkin's arguments finally proved to be decisive. On 12 July, Tombeur received permission from the Belgian government to take part in the operations against Tabora.⁵⁵ That approval had been given on one condition: the deployment of the *Force Publique* had to be restricted to the area delimited in the south by the railway from Kigoma to Tabora and in the east by the line Tabora-Mwanza, an area of no less than ten times the size of Belgium.⁵⁶ With this, the originally planned limited Belgian advance went out the window. Belgian territorial appetite appeared to be insatiable.

Mid-August, the Belgian northern brigade and the British column started with their advance on Tabora. However, they both met with fierce German resistance that caused a lot of delay. In particular, the British offensive did not get out of the starting blocks.⁵⁷ Meanwhile Tombeur had ordered Brigade South to progress to Tabora from Kigoma, on a route running alongside the railway. The aim was to take the fortified city in a pincer movement. However, coordination between the different forces was lacking. In addition, the southern brigade encountered significantly less resistance during its advance, making them progress much faster. In late August the brigade was less than 50 kilometres from Tabora.⁵⁸ It looked increasingly likely that Tabora would be taken by the Belgians and not by the British. But that liberation would have to wait until 19 September. By clever manoeuvering, forward German troops managed to temporarily halt the advance of Brigade South. That tactical defeat, however, would not affect the ultimate outcome of the battle. Rather, the delay of the western column allowed Brigade North to still achieve a timely junction, thereby threatening to encircle the German forces in Tabora. General Wahle, who commanded the German forces in Tabora, realised that the battle was lost. Instead of fighting to the bitter end against the Belgian superior force, he decided to withdraw

---

⁵⁴ To relieve the front at Verdun, the British had started the Somme offensive on 1 July 1916, in which hundreds of thousands of British soldiers would die. It would therefore be particularly difficult for the Belgians to refuse participating in the attack on Tabora.
⁵⁵ FPSFA, AA, FP 2658, *Télégramme de Renkin au Roi Albert*, 15 Jul 1916
⁵⁶ FPSFA, AA, FP 2653, *Télégramme de Renkin à Tombeur*, 1 Aug 1916
⁵⁷ FPSFA, AA, FP 2654, *Télégramme de Van Overstraeten à Renkin*, 22 Aug 1916
⁵⁸ Merzbach, Libert, Peeters, Stiers, Weber, Op. Cit., Vol. 2, pp. 419-52

his troops and join von Lettow-Vorbeck's main force. As a result, the *Force Publique* took the city on September 19 without fighting. The Belgians had won the race to Tabora. In less than five months, they had marched more than 1,500 kilometres on foot in particularly trying circumstances. The price they paid was high: 24 Belgians and 481 Congolese were killed during the fighting; another 17 Belgians and 853 Congolese died due to illness.[59]

The taking of Tabora led to great optimism on the Belgian as well as the British side. Everyone seemed to assume that German resistance would now rapidly crumble. The Belgian Government also believed that the moment was favourable to politically cash in on its military successes. In September, Minister Renkin launched a proposal to transfer the control of Tabora to the British in exchange for British recognition of Belgian rights to other territories that the *Force Publique* had conquered.[60] The purpose of the underhanded initiative was clear: by showing the necessary goodwill, the Minister hoped to receive formal guarantees from the British on Belgian claims to the conquered territories in the west. However, the attempt did not achieve anything. The British played their cards close to their chest and relegated the final settlement of ownership to a peace conference to be organised later.[61] On 25 February 1917, the Belgians had no alternative but to hand over the city and the entire region surrounding it to the British during an impressive parade.[62] The Belgians were—once again—left behind with no guarantee of territorial claims. Meanwhile Tombeur had already begun the withdrawal of the Belgian troops because the government had decided that they would no longer take part in the continuing campaign in German East Africa. Only four battalions of the *Force Publique* would stay behind in the German colony to occupy the conquered territories (Ruanda, Urundi and the area between Lake Victoria and Lake

---

[59] Merzbach, Libert, Peeters, Stiers, Weber, Op. Cit., Vol. 3, p. 438

[60] BNA, Records of Orts, Folder 433, *Memo van Orts*, 8 Sep 1916. BNA, Orts, Folder 433, *Résumé des négociations relatives à Tabora*, 20 Dec 1916. BNA, de Broqueville, Folder 422, *Observations sur l'administration des territoires occupés dans l'Est Africain allemand*, Oct 1916, 11 p. RMAF, Record 185, Box 74, Folder 163, *Négociations diplomatiques relatives à l'occupation de Tabora*, pp. 1-15

[61] Louis, WR, *Ruanda-Urundi. 1884-1919* (Clarendon, 1963) p. 230

[62] RMAF, Record 185, Box 74, Folder 163, *Rapport sur la cérémonie de la remise de la place de Tabora aux autorités anglaises*, pp. 111-9

Tanganyika to Kigoma).[63] In early 1917 many officers and NCOs were withdrawn to Belgium, where they were needed on the front on the Yser river. In February General Tombeur also left. He was succeeded by Lieutenant-Colonel Armand Huyghé.

However, the evacuation of Tabora was not the end of the Belgian deployment in German East Africa. The troops of von Lettow-Vorbeck—still some 7,500 men strong—had lost increasingly more ground because of the successive Allied offensives.[64] At the end of 1916 they were pushed back to the southeast in the vicinity of Mahenge, where they were in danger of being surrounded. General Smuts was convinced that the end of the campaign was now in sight. To eliminate this last German stronghold, he had planned a grand offensive after the wet season in 1917.[65] But it would never come to this. On 24 February, von Lettow-Vorbeck took the initiative by unexpectedly launching a counterattack. He succeeded in breaking through the encircling forces with 500 men, led by Captain Wintgens.[66] It was the beginning of a hellish journey through the colony. Not only Tabora, but also the other territories occupied by the Belgian forces came under threat again. The Belgian government immediately offered to send 4,500 soldiers of the *Force Publique* to help the British.[67] The reason why the Belgian Government came with this—quite remarkable—proposal is unclear.[68] In contrast with previous operations, a further territorial expansion was absolutely out of the question. Perhaps they hoped the proposal would create some leniency with the British with regard to the realisation of Belgian demands in Central Africa.

Throughout the summer of 1917 the Belgians and the British unsuccessfully pursued the German column.[69] Ultimately, it was not until October 1917 that the German raid came to an end. The result was that the final offensive against the main

---

[63] Merzbach, Libert, Peeters, Stiers, Weber, Op. Cit., Vol. 3, p. 13

[64] Merzbach, Libert, Peeters, Stiers, Weber, Op. Cit., Vol. 2, pp. 605-606

[65] FPSFA, AA, FP 2654, *Télégramme de Tombeur à Renkin*, 17 and 20 Dec 1916

[66] FPSFA, AA, FP 2654, *Télégramme de Van Overstraeten à Renkin*, 24 Feb 1917

[67] FPSFA, AA, FP 2654, *Télégramme de Renkin à Malfeyt*, 30 Mar 1917. Merzbach, Libert, Peeters, Stiers, Weber, Op. Cit., Vol. 3, pp. 14-17

[68] Great-Britain, lacking additional reserves for deployment in German East Africa at that time, urgently requested Belgian reinforcements.

[69] Merzbach, Libert, Peeters, Stiers, Weber, Op. Cit., Vol. 3, pp. 105-115

force of von Lettow-Vorbeck had been stalled. In June 1917 it was therefore agreed that the Belgians would leave the pursuit to the British; at that moment the German force had marched to the northeast, in the direction of Kenya. Rather than continue the chase, the Belgians would, along with the British, prepare a major offensive against the German main force in the vicinity of Mahenge. Two hastily assembled columns of the *Force Publique* were transferred to Dodoma and Kilosa from Kigoma by means of the central railway; from there they went on foot to the plateau of Mahenge. The Belgian troops got moving mid-August. Huyghé's plan was to surround the Germans. For that the columns advanced along two axes toward Mahenge. During their progression the troops met with stubborn resistance from German forward positions. However, the Germans wanted to avoid a decisive battle and thus continued to retreat after each confrontation. Once the Belgian troops threatened to encircle Mahenge the Germans called it a day and they cleared the fortified city. On 9 October, Mahenge fell into the hands of the *Force Publique*. This effectively ended the active role of the Belgians in German East Africa.[70] The pursuit of the German troops was left to the British.[71] The latter had already started with a large-scale offensive from the east. As a result, the proverbial noose tightened around the German troops. Nevertheless, von Lettow-Vorbeck would provide another major surprise: with his force he managed to break through the encirclement and escape to Mozambique, where he played a game of cat-and-mouse for ten months (from November 1917 to September 1918) with his British pursuers.[72] But

[70] During the operations in 1917, both during the pursuit of the column Wintgens and in the attack on Mahenge, four Belgians and 144 Congolese were killed. In addition, a further 13 Belgians and 417 Congolese died due to illness or accident. Merzbach, Libert, Peeters, Stiers, Weber, Op. Cit., Vol. 3, p. 438. RMAF, Record 185, Box 2823, Folder 6425, *Rapport du docteur Rodhain*, pp. 1-91

[71] In January 1918, the British would call again upon the Belgian colonial army for assistance in pursuing von Lettow-Vorbeck. The proposal went very far and amounted to nothing less than full integration of the *Force Publique* in the British forces. In practice, this meant the Congolese soldiers came under direct command of British officers. The Belgian government opposed the proposal and resolutely rejected it. FPSFA, Diplomatic Archives, Africa 1-3, *Nota van Renkin aan Hymans*, 6 Feb 1918. FPSFA, Diplomatic Archives, 1-3, *Note de Hymans au Roi Albert*, 13 Feb 1918. Scott, JB, *Official statements of war aims and peace proposals. Dec 1916 to Nov 1918* (Carnegie Endowment for International Peace, 1921) pp. 231-2

[72] Von Lettow-Vorbeck's forces consisted at that time of 320 Germans and some 2,000 askaris.

despite their numerical superiority they still failed to catch him. Cornered by his pursuers, he crossed the border with German East Africa again in late September 1918. From there he advanced to the north to subsequently invade Rhodesia. Von Lettow-Vorbeck was like a ghost. The British were at their wits' end. In late October, it even looked as if the Germans wanted to push through to Angola via Katanga. But it would never come to this. On 13 November 1918, a British courier was captured by a reconnaissance unit of von Lettow-Vorbeck. From the papers he had on him, it was evident that the war in Europe had ended: Germany had signed a truce on 11 November. Continuing the fight in German East Africa would therefore be pointless. Von Lettow-Vorbeck decided to lay down his arms. On 25 November he surrendered with his troops in Abercorn to the British. This brought an end to the First World War in Africa. Von Lettow-Vorbeck had performed above and beyond the call of duty. For four years he succeeded, with only a token force, to fix a much stronger opponent in East Africa which never managed to defeat him. German East Africa was the only front in the First World War where the Germans remained undefeated. This would contribute to the myth that would arise around the person of von Lettow-Vorbeck in the post-war period.

Conclusion

The Belgian military deployment in German East Africa, as well as the associated political objectives, saw a whole evolution during the First World War. We have labeled the period from 1914 to 1916 as the defensive phase. The objective as proposed by the Belgian government in this phase was two-fold: firstly, to assure the defence of the eastern border of the colony, and secondly to prepare a limited offensive from 1915 to put an end to the German invasions in the Belgian Congo. With this the Belgian defensive policy was exchanged for a more offensive one. Conducting offensive operations entailed, however, that the *Force Publique*—which was originally founded as a local police force—had to be transformed into a deployable army. This transformation process would take a considerable amount of time. In addition, collaboration with the British was also crucial. However, London provisionally kept its distance. The British suspected the Belgians of having territorial ambitions to the east of the Congo, which did not fit into their pursuit of a north-south connection on the African continent. For all these reasons it would eventually take until April 1916 before a combined offensive got underway. This brings us to the second phase: the Belgian offensive against German East Africa. This operation was originally only focused on Ruanda. However, as the *Force Publique* continued its advance, the territorial ambitions were adjusted. After Ruanda, Urundi soon followed and eventually the whole area between Lake Victoria and Lake Tanganyika was conquered. The line of thought of the Belgian government was that the conquered territories would serve as leverage for a territorial expansion of the colony during the post-war peace talks. The greater the occupied territory, the more weight Belgium would carry. However, the Belgian Government was not interested in an expansion of the colony to the east; rather, its sphere of interest lay in the west, on the Congo River estuary. For this, they proposed a sort of triangular exchange: Belgium would transfer the areas in German East Africa that had been captured by the *Force Publique* to the British who, in return, had to put pressure on the Portuguese to give up the left bank of the Congo estuary to the Belgians. But that reasoning was called into question from the outset. The British played their cards close to their chest and abstained from any pronouncement on possible compensations. This uncertainty would urge the Belgians—especially Minister Renkin—to an even greater military zeal. By unconditionally deploying the *Force Publique* on the British side, he still hoped for British recognition of the Belgian claims to the area between Lake Victoria and Lake Tanganyika. It is against this background that the participation of the Belgians in the subsequent operations, first against Tabora and then against Mahenge, must be seen. But that recognition failed to materialise and the proposed exchange even less so. The fact is that London did not give any consideration to the aspirations of its small ally. German East Africa was simply too important a link in the creation of the British north-south connection from the Cape to Cairo. Throughout the campaign, London would use the Belgians, without giving anything back in return. Belgium risked being left behind empty-handed after the war. During the Paris Peace Conference, where the repartition of the German possessions in Africa was discussed, the Belgian diplomats would do anything within their power to salvage territorial compensation.[73] For that they received support from an unexpected side. Pressured by the American President Woodrow Wilson, the British finally had no option but to slice up the colonial cake. In May 1919, the negotiators reached an agreement, in which Ruanda and Urundi became Belgian mandated territories under the auspices of the League of Nations.

From a military point of view, the Belgian contribution to the operations in German East Africa should not be underestimated. At the zenith of the operations, the numerical strength of the Belgian colonial army amounted to a quarter of that of the British troops. Considering the vastness of German East Africa as well as the experienced German colonial army, the Belgian military involvement was therefore of crucial importance to the British. Additionally, the *Force Publique* achieved remarkable results. In a few months it managed to conquer the whole western front and to occupy a vast area. This led to significant savings for the British: because of this they could concentrate their forces in the northeast against the German main force. In addition, the Belgians would play an important role in the follow-up operations against Tabora and Mahenge, although without decisively defeating the Germans. Yet all these military successes cannot be separated from the German strategy. For von Lettow-Vorbeck, after all, the biggest threat came from the British and not from the Belgians and therefore he directed his main force toward the northeast. This explains why the Belgians met relatively little resistance during their advance from the west. Major battles, comparable to those in Europe, did not take place there. The conflict was mostly limited to small-scale battles and skirmishes with an enemy who retreated time and time again. The biggest obstacle to the Belgian operations was therefore not German resistance, but the terrain, climate and above all the logistics that suffered from the ever longer lines of communication. This is also evident from the official list of losses of the *Force Publique*. The number of casualties due to illness and exhaustion was a multiple of the number of soldiers who were killed during the fighting.[74] Throughout the colonial war from 1914 to 1918, 28 Belgians and

---

[73] BNA, Orts, Folder 433, *Note de Hymans à l'ambassadeur belge à Londres*, 6 May 1920. Vijgen, I, Op. Cit., pp. 87-106

[74] Merzbach, Libert, Peeters, Stiers, Weber, Op. Cit., Vol. 3, p. 438

625 Congolese were killed; 30 Belgians and 1,270 Congolese died from disease and accident. Nevertheless, the highest price was paid by the forgotten group of indigenous porters. They had to drag supplies for the troops for hundreds of kilometres in appalling conditions without anyone caring for them. Few numbers on their losses are available. Clearly, the Belgian administration was not in the least interested in their fate. Recent estimates—which are still very cautious—assume some 27,000 men, women and children perished.[75] Not only the black soldiers, but a lot of porters as well, therefore paid for the Belgian military successes with their lives. They were sacrificed on the altar of Belgian colonial interests in a war that was not theirs.

---

[75] De Waele, J, '*Voor vorst en vaderland : zwarte soldaten en dragers tijdens de Eerste Wereldoorlog in Congo*', *Militaria Belgica 2007-2008* (Koninklijke Vereniging Vrienden van het Legermuseum, 2009) p. 128

"I can never say about the men..." The Jammu and Kashmir Rifles

Andrew Kerr[1]

The story I am going to tell is of my grandfather, Alec Kerr, who followed the family tradition of service to India that had started in 1760. He found himself in 1914 as the attached British officer to the private army of the Maharaja of Kashmir which was soon to be sent to East Africa as an emergency measure.

The title *I can never say enough about the men* comes from a letter Alec wrote to another officer who had returned to India to recover from wounds. This letter I found in my research in a file at the Imperial War Museum. The research had been triggered by a photograph, in a family album, of some exhausted and run down Indian soldiers and as a military man I wanted to know 'how on earth did this happen?' Of course, in true Victorian tradition, nobody had ever spoken about their war, so my father never knew anything about his father's wars apart from the medals.

Early on in this investigation, I discovered the most staggering casualty rate. The 2nd Battalion Kashmir Rifles had started with 715 men and received at least 600 reinforcements. By January 1917 there were only 218 riflemen left on the battalion roll and when the army medical board inspected them they found only twenty or so fit to soldier on and sent them back to India. They had been utterly wiped out as a functioning military body. This situation gripped my interest and I wanted

---

[1] Andrew Kerr is a management consultant specialising in strategy and personal development. His other great passion is conservation where he champions the sustainable management of the European Eel. Andrew followed his family traditions of India and Soldiering. The former through his education at Haileybury (The Old East India College) and the latter as a cavalry officer with the 17/21 Lancers and the Royal Gloucestershire Hussars.

to learn how this disaster had happened and who was responsible.

The Indian Expeditionary Force for East Africa was assembled in a great hurry. It has often been called 'scraping the barrel' and Britain had to seek permission from several Maharajas to deploy their private state forces. On the Western Front in 1914 Britain deployed 100,000 men, France and Germany each mobilised some four million. Britain had no continental-scale conscript army; it was a small colonial volunteer army for policing the Empire. Britain had invested its energy into the navy and had built a staggering fifty battle ships and battle cruisers between 1904 and 1916. What this meant for East Africa was an ill-equipped and ill-prepared force.

The Kashmir Rifles were involved in many of the battles including Tanga (November 1914), Jasin (1914/5), Kilimanjaro (1916) and the long march south. The question of supply, or its breakdown, is critical to understanding the campaign. The three railway lines in East Africa were incredibly important and these ran east-west, there were no lines of communication north-south. What is also significant is the German strategy of ambush and withdrawal, their use of machine guns using the locally recruited Askari coupled with German non-commissioned officers (NCOs) to direct and control them and a very strong medical presence which helped keep them in the field.

At Tanga, November 1914, the Kashmir Rifles demonstrated their infantry skills with disciplined fire and manoeuvre tactics so much so that they captured several German machine guns and penetrated further into the town than any other formation. They demonstrated real military competence and this is in contrast to several other Indian units that completely broke down under the pressure of battle.

The battle of Jasin, December 1914-January 1915, is particularly interesting for me as Alec arrived on Christmas Day with one hundred reinforcements. The Umba River was in full flood. Grandfather was at a camp called Samanya just a few miles north of Jasin and the troops he sent to reinforce the besieged garrison were, along with others, unable to get through. The troops at Jasin were completely surrounded: they ran out of ammunition and water, most were wounded and they were forced to surrender. It was a German victory. However, the cost, especially of officer casualties was so great to the German Commander von Lettow-Vorbeck that it led to a change of strategy and tactics. He realised that he could not win the war with one major battle and instead developed his ambush, withdraw and lay waste strategy.

The Kashmir Rifles lost several commanding officers during the campaign and the British increased the number of attached officers. This gradually developed into a dual chain of command with the British more junior officer receiving orders through the Brigade Commander and then working with the established Kashmir officers to deliver the military performance.

During the march south in 1916, Alec was often leading the advance guard of the Kashmir Rifles (up to half the battalion). The march south was characterised by acute water shortage and often no rations or food. After a few weeks supply completely broke down. The commander, General Jan Smuts seemed to have had no concept of logistics—it was as if he was still commanding a highly mobile, horse-borne column-type raid from the South African Boer war of 1899-1902. Miller's[2] description of malaria, blackwater fever and dysentery convey a picture of terrible suffering.

Smuts desperately pushed his army on trying to get behind the Germans to force them to do battle and take casualties. On one occasion he achieved this: at the battle of Lukigura. Alec led the advance guard when it made a great sweep marching through the night to attack the German fortified position coming in from the side and achieved surprise. At Lukigura holding fire power was brought onto the ridge, where the Germans were dug in, from armoured cars. The Kashmir Rifles with re-enforcements from the 25th Fusiliers charged with fixed bayonets and Kukris waving. They actually took the ridge killing many Germans and Askaris. The captured flag and machine guns sit today in pride of place at the Kashmir Rifles museum back in India.

However, if Lukigura was the high point, calamity was to follow as disease and dysentery took hold—Alec, along with tens of thousands of soldiers, was evacuated. When making comparisons of casualties between the different units the Kashmirs showed great endurance—they were in theatre for

---

[2] Charles Miller, *Battle for the bundu* (1974)

thirty months. The Rhodesians survived about fifteen months and the South Africans about ten months.

Smuts' army ceased to exist and he was recalled to London in February 1917 where he was heralded a hero in the belief that the war was won: German East Africa was occupied and surrender would soon follow. In fact von Lettow-Vorbeck was never caught and his formal surrender took place eventually, after the Armistice, on 25 November 1918.

On Call in Africa in War and Peace: with 3 East Africa Field Ambulance

Dr Tony Jewell[1]

Introduction

The focus of this chapter will be the East Africa Campaign of the First World War. It will tell the story of my grandfather's experiences in the war based on his memoir *On Call in Africa in War and Peace—1910-1932* which was published in 2016.[2] I edited the memoir which was originally written by hand in small exercise books which the family inherited after Dr Norman Jewell's death in 1974. The family resolved to bring the memoir to print as the story is of interest to many who research the East Africa Campaign, the development of military and colonial medicine in East Africa, and are interested in the first-hand accounts of people who were there at the time—to see the world through their eyes.

The risk of memoirs is that they are based on 'memories' after the events described and are subject to recall bias. It was wonderful therefore to have his account validated when our editorial collaborator Anne Samson of the Great War in Africa Association (GWAA) discovered Norman's daily army war diary stored in The National Archives. This document provides a unique and almost complete record for the period from the preparations for the attack on Taveta in October 1915 and the Eastern campaign trail down through German East Africa (GEA) to Masasi near the Portuguese East Africa border in March 1918.[3]

---

[1] Tony Jewell was Chief Medical Officer for Wales between 2006 and 2012 when he retired. Together with his siblings, they published the memoirs of Norman Parsons Jewell, a doctor who served with 3 East African Field Ambulance.
[2] Jewell, NP, *On Call in Africa in War and Peace – 1910-1932*, (Gillyflower, 2016)
[3] The National Archives, WO 95

Norman was evacuated out with malaria on occasions and had a short period of convalescence but provided leadership to the 3rd East African Field Ambulance for the duration. The account provides insight into the public health challenges during the campaign, the treatment of military wounds and casualties, as well as the greater overall impact of malnutrition and infectious diseases such as dysentery and malaria. The specific challenges in the campaign include the logistics problems, which were based on the climatic conditions, terrain and poor transport infrastructure. The high illness rates challenged the already stretched medical services and there was an adverse British Government inquiry (The Pike Report 1918) into particularly the medical leadership during the campaign.[4]

When editing the text I was struck by the 'matter of fact' way that acts of bravery were recorded. These often heroic deeds that are documented lends support to the David Winfield observation that: 'heroes are ordinary people who have achieved extraordinary things in life'.[5]

This modesty and the verification through war diaries held at The National Archives gave me confidence in seeing events through his eyes.

This paper will cover
- Dr Norman Jewell's war service between 1914-1918
- His role in leading the 3rd East Africa Field Ambulance
- Specific challenges faced such as food, water, sanitation and supplies
- Stories from the front line, leadership, lessons learnt
- Ratio of deaths from disease and war wounds in the East African theatre.

Dr Norman Jewell's engagement with the WW1 campaign started in Kisumu on Lake Victoria in December 1914 when he was involved with treating the injured from the battle of Susuni including many of Ross's Scouts who were later disbanded after an enquiry into their discipline and conduct. He was there too during the battle of Bukoba in June 1915 and experienced working with the 25th Royal Fusiliers (Legion of Frontiersmen) under the leadership of General Jimmie Stewart who at one

---

[4] The National Archives, WO 141/31 Pike Report (available on www.gweaa.com)
[5] www.brainyquote.com

point was admitted to hospital in Kisumu. In October 1915 Norman was transferred to Voi and Bura where preparations for the invasion of German East Africa were being undertaken. It was at this point that he took command of the 3rd East Africa Field Ambulance, which was distinct from the Indian Medical Services who were responsible for the Indian Expeditionary Forces. Each force had its own medical services, Norman seconded from the Colonial Service was responsible for a local Field Ambulance which often served alongside an Indian Field Ambulance.

Food, water and sanitation

The massing of troops in the Voi area immediately illustrates some of the big challenges in the East Africa Campaign. The first was the provision of accommodation for troops in this challenging African bush environment with its associated sanitary facilities such as toilet 'blockhouses'. The second big challenge was to provide adequate food and water for the multi-ethnic/multifaith British Imperial Army recruited from Hindu and Muslim soldiers from the Indian subcontinent, African soldiers from East and West Africa as well as British and South African European soldiers. Water for washing and drinking was scarce and the needs of troops and carriers in the heat of the African bush country was very trying. This area, some 100 years later, is still largely part of the Tsavo, and other National Park game reserves.

Once on the march there was competition for natural water supplies from rivers with horses, mules and oxen. Human and animal contamination of such sources was widespread and the cause of much dysenteric disease. There was also an obvious temptation to camp close to rivers or lakes which posed a high risk of mosquito bites and the consequential malarial disease. British troops often wore shorts and short sleeved shirts which provided ample skin areas for mosquitoes and other insects such as the tsetse fly which transmitted 'sleeping sickness' to both animals and humans. Mosquito nets were in short supply and there was confusion over the use of quinine as a low dose prophylactic.

An estimated 15,000 troops arrived using the Uganda railway as the main means of transport and it was the railway that began to be extended towards Taveta through hostile country with African wildlife and German Schutztruppe ambushes to cope with. Even if motorised vehicles were available there were few built roads and there was an overall dependence on mules and human carriers.

The 3rd East Africa Field Ambulance team

Dr Norman Jewell's 3rd East Africa Field Ambulance had an Indian Sub Assistant Surgeon (Zorowar Singh) and a Rhodesian Sergeant Jock Anderson and Corporal Ben Ziegler from Nairobi. These senior members of the team served throughout his time, despite them all succumbing to malaria and dysenteric disease from time to time. The stretcher-bearers were mainly Zanzibaris and the dressers were black African recruits. The Asian storekeeper and cook were also core members of the team.

This period before the advance provided an opportunity for training and drills. The training aimed at keeping the stretcher bearers close to the fighting men in the front line, so they could transfer the wounded back to the dressing station as quickly as possible using stretchers if available. Further transfer back to the field and clearing hospitals would complete the role of such mobile field ambulances. This military medical evacuation pathway was common to all theatres in World War One. However, the logistics required for the evacuation to base hospitals was much more challenging in East Africa than for example the Western Front due to the nature of the country—large open spaces with thornbush and scrub, or mud so thick nothing could move.

Transport

Transport was multimodal with marching on foot supplemented by mules, horses and ox drawn carts. Motorised supply lorries and ambulances were relatively scarce and when available were limited by breakdowns, the lack of graded roads and fuel supplies. Some of the terrain made transport a challenge with wet monsoon conditions as well as formidable mountain ranges or wide crocodile infested rivers to cross.

Building the railway extension to Taveta was of strategic importance and the subsequent use of the GEA railways and farm trolleys showed the logistical value of these local rail networks in addition to the hospital trains used for evacuation back to Nairobi.

Evacuation of the wounded from the front line

One of the principles of military medicine in theatres of war is the rapid response to front line war wounds and the speedy transfer of the wounded to places of safety such as the clearing and base hospitals where more specialist surgical treatments can be applied. Norman Jewell was responsible for the training of the teams to withstand the noise of battle and scenes of death and injury. Many of the novices had little or no prior experience of modern warfare, including the use of 4-inch battery guns, machine guns and aircraft.

The East Africa theatre has been referred to as a sideshow and the Forgotten Front.[6] However, although the death toll was nowhere near as high as the Western Front, people were still being killed and wounded in action and in need of medical support. Early in the campaign, Dr Jewell describes seeing a senior British officer (Lieutenant Colonel Graham of the King's African Rifles) walking past his stretcher team to report to HQ and then back towards the frontline at Latema-Reata, only to be killed instantly by a bullet through his head during their first battle. The impact on his fellow officers and men in this early phase of the campaign can be imagined.

Sometimes the recovery of bodies and wounded led to the risk of being in 'no man's land' as the Major Temple Harris[7] (OC Combined Ambulance Unit) incident illustrates. In this case, both doctors, Jewell and Harris, were caught in crossfire at dusk and had to cautiously find their way back through the frontline after dark when the shooting ceased. They escaped with their lives only to be nearly bayoneted by their British Army Indian troops on the front line with whom Major Harris of the Indian Medical Service was able to converse in Hindustani.

As the advance pushed on through GEA the supply lines became more stretched and subject to ambush from the 'Tip and Run'[8] strategy of von Lettow-Vorbeck, the German commander. This was manifest in the deteriorating state of British uniforms which begun to disintegrate from the 'wait a bit' thorn bushes and general wear and tear. The senior officers seemed to

---

[6] Anderson, Ross, *The Forgotten Front* (Tempus 2004)

[7] Crichton-Harris, Ann, *Seventeen letters to Tatham: A WW1 surgeon in Africa* (Keneggy West, 2002)

[8] Paice, Edward. *Tip and Run: The Untold Tragedy of the Great War in Africa*, (Weidenfield & Nicholson, 2007)

manage to be immaculately turned out which became an issue for Norman's team. This was exacerbated when they met German hospital teams and saw their kit and that they had better access to medical and other supplies. This was captured by the Punch cartoonist AW Lloyd who was with the 25th Royal Fusiliers in his series of cartoons drawn during the campaign.[9]

Basic food and supply of drinking water was a challenge to the advancing forces which resulted in malnutrition, exhaustion and a greater susceptibility to infectious diseases. The preventive measures against the mosquito, such as provision of nets and the siting of camps away from water was unsatisfactory, as was the policy toward the prophylactic use of quinine. The supplies of quinine on the German side was much better as was the medical staffing levels and training of their medical corps. The Germans were lucky enough to have nearly a doctor per column. This was only because there had been a tropical medicine conference in the German colony at the outbreak of war.

Norman recounts that while suffering from malaria with a temperature of 105 degrees he had to take over a captured German hospital in Korogwe, which had been abandoned with all its patients when the German *schutztruppe* withdrew. Luckily, the German doctor who had been left behind was co-operative and helped treat Norman's malaria and the English nurse who had been working there was able to take command while Norman recovered. There were other examples of such professional respect and co-operation between the opposing forces, such as the exchange of sick and injured.

The towns and sea transport

When the troops entered Dar es Salaam the town seemed relatively unscathed apart from the attempt to block the harbour entrance by scuttling a ship. The hospital had sustained only minor damage and was an impressive sight and useful facility for the Allied forces. Hospital ships were able to transport the sick and wounded back to Mombasa or further afield if they were being evacuated home.

Some troops were transferred up country from Mombasa by train to Nairobi or the Highlands, which were free of malaria,

---

[9] Lloyd, AW, *With Jannie in the Jungle* (African Publications, 1920)

and being away from the frontline were suitable for much needed rehabilitation. As Britain and its allies largely had naval control over the Indian Ocean the sea routes were used for transporting troops to the new front lines, as happened for Norman, at Kilwa Kisiwani and Lindi, as well evacuating troops home via Bombay to Seychelles. Norman accompanied the Seychelloise labourers on their return journey when he was given recouperative leave.

Hospital accommodation

During the campaign opportunities had to be taken to use pre-existing buildings as field hospitals and part of the medical evacuation route. The Swiss House at Mkesse was used as a hospital and later in the campaign Schaedels Farm near Lindi Bay was an example with its farmhouse and buildings and trolley/miniature railway transport. However, tented clearing stations and field hospital accommodation was common, as was the building of new bandas using local materials based on the successful German models.

Facilities for surgical treatment were limited and they had to make do with what room/instruments and medical supplies were available. Dr Jewell describes undertaking major surgical procedures on critically injured troops whose outlook in a pre-antibiotic era would have been poor. Sometimes churches were commandeered for hospital usage.

The ratio of deaths from disease v illness

The incomplete official record of casualties during the war, show the high ratio of illness and death from disease as opposed to war wounds. Of the 9,546 total deaths of officers and other ranks of the Expeditionary Army, 64 per cent were from disease as opposed to being killed or wounded in action. Of the much larger number of Indian and African Followers who helped transport supplies the deaths were much higher and estimated as 42,600 of which 99 per cent were from diseases such as dysentery, malnutrition and malaria.[10]

In an official report on medical services in the Great War, the East Africa Campaign compared poorly in terms of survival when in military medical units from both wounds or disease.

---

[10] MacPherson & Mitchell, *History of the Great War* (HMSO, 1923)

For example, on the Western Front 7.6 per cent of admissions with wounds died compared to 9.87 per cent in East Africa. Deaths from disease once admitted to military hospital on the Western Front accounted for less than one per cent while in East Africa it was 2.55 per cent.[11] The terrain, distances of supply and evacuation lines and local endemic and epidemic diseases in Africa contributed to this result.

Senior leadership concerns

However, there were adverse reports too of the relatively poor medical leadership in the campaign and the unfavourable comparison made between the German military medical organisation and the British Expeditionary Force.[12] An investigation undertaken by Surgeon General William Pike and Lieutenant Colonel Andrew Balfour were critical of aspects of the top leadership of the medical services (not the front line) as well as some sectors such as the hospital ships, and some of the hospitals such as the infectious disease isolation units. The report was published before the end of the war in Whitehall and kept secret as the findings were felt to be politically/militarily sensitive. Courts Martial of some offenders happened swiftly however and medical officers were punished.[13] Front line teams such as 3EAFA, which were visited by the investigating team, were in general praised for their work including their attention to cleanliness/hygiene and bravery. Norman for example received the Military Cross for gallantry and was cited for working nonstop for 62 hours treating the wounded.

Black African casualties

With the publication of data on war wounds and deaths the plight of the mainly black African carriers was acknowledged as were the black African soldiers in West African regiments as well as the East African regiment the King's African Rifles. The Askari war memorial in Nairobi is a token of this suffering and loss in what after all was a western imperial war whose origins

---

[11] Harrison, Mark. *The Medical War – British Military Medicine in the First World War* (Oxford University, 2010)

[12] Vaughan-Williams, HW, 'Medical Services in the East African Campaign, 1916 1917' in *South African Medical Journal* (Jan 11, 1941) pp. 9-12

[13] WO 141/31 Pike Report

lay in Europe and drew in other parts of the world along the lines of competing European colonial powers.

Conclusion

This memoir contributes to our understanding of the East Africa Campaign and is validated by transcripts from The National Archives carefully set in historical context. It adds value too in recounting in a matter of fact way the serious challenges faced in the front line throughout the campaign in German East Africa. It provides insight into how the health of soldiers depends on good nutrition and access to clean water. The particular difficulties due to climate, terrain and weather extremes such as monsoon rains stretched supply lines and logistical communications including the evacuation of the wounded and ill soldiers. Leadership in extreme conditions was of paramount importance and it is striking how the multi-ethnic 3 East African Field Ambulance team held together through adversity. In the final analysis military leaders need to be aware of the mental and physical needs of their army if they wish to command fighting men rather than disband regiments decimated by disease as happened during this campaign.

Forgotten Citizens and Servicemen: The West African Contribution to the First World War

Nigel Browne-Davies

Introduction

The West African 'home front' and the participation of West African servicemen in the First World War is a largely neglected aspect of the historiography of the conflict.[1] Although the contributions of West African servicemen in the African campaigns has featured in some scholarly works on the First World War, few, if any, have thoroughly examined the responses of West Africans from traditional societies and the British West African elite to the First World War.[2] Although some commentators have described the war as a European conflict, it was West African servicemen, largely from traditional African societies outside the British cultural sphere of influence and who may have been ambivalent towards the war effort, who served. Where the educated elite in British West Africa did not actively participate in military operations, they remained fervently supportive of the Allied war effort.[3] However, although the British West African elite supported the war effort, the deterioration in Anglo-African relations that existed at the advent of the conflict continued throughout the First World War.[4] The poor relations between British colonialists and educated black Africans contributed to the disillusionment of

---

[1] Farwell, Byron, *The Great War in Africa,* 1914-1918 (WW Norton, 1989) p. 14
[2] Ibid. pp. 14-15
[3] Turay, EDA & Abraham, Arthur, *The Sierra Leone Army: A Century of History,* (Macmillan, 1987) pp. 38-39, Osuntokun, Akinjide, *Nigeria in the First World War,* (Long, 1979) pp. 64-66, 70-1
[4] Osuntokun, *Nigeria in the First World War,* pp.64-66, 70-1

the educated black African elite and the enhancement or development of radical nationalist and political movements by educated Africans to initiate colonial policy change.[5]

This chapter shall examine the military contributions of West African servicemen in the African theatre and the responses of British West Africans to the First World War. It is the perspective of this chapter that British West Africa was a 'home front' of the First World War and that the educated British West African elite viewed black African participation in the war as an equal contribution to that of their European counterparts on other home fronts.[6] This chapter examines the responses of West Africans from traditional societies and the British West African elite to British engagement in the conflict. Finally, this chapter shall provide insight into the role of West Africans, largely from the rural or traditional West African societies, in the military operations of the war.

British West Africa in 1914

The four territories that comprised British West Africa were distinct territories with diverse ethnic groups and pre-colonial histories.[7] Although British colonial policies differed within the four territories, there were similarities that contributed towards similar cultural outlooks and administrative and political structures across British West Africa.[8] The British West African territories were divided between areas that were strictly defined as 'colonies' and the hinterland or traditional West African societies in the 'Protectorates.'[9] The colonies were

[5] Wyse, Akintola, *HC Bankole-Bright and Politics in Colonial Sierra Leone, 1919-1958* (Cambridge University Press, 2003) pp. 32-33. In contrast to East, Central and South Africa, there were few, if any, white settlers in West Africa at the time of the First World War. The term African in this chapter refers to black African unless otherwise specified.

[6] Crowder, Michael & Osuntokun, Jide, 'The First World War and West Africa, 1914-1918,' in Ajayi, JFA & Crowder, Michael, (Eds), *A History of West Africa*, (Longman, 1987, Second Edition) pp. 546-7

[7] Rathbone, Richard, 'West Africa, 1874-1948: Employment Legislation in a Nonsettler Peasant Economy' in Hay, Douglas & Craven, Paul, (Eds), *Masters, Servants, and Magistrates in Britain and the Empire, 1562-1955* (University of North Carolina, 2005) p. 481

[8] Prais, Jinny Kathleen, *Imperial Travelers: The Formation of West African Urban Culture, Identity, and Citizenship in London and Accra, 1925-1935* (University of Michigan, PhD, 2008) pp. 103-104

[9] Prais, *Imperial Travelers*, pp. 103-104

subject to British common law whilst the Protectorate was administered in accordance with British and customary West African law.[10] The differences between the administration of the colony areas and the protectorates of British West African territories was further reflected in the status of the inhabitants of each territory.[11] British citizenship was conferred upon inhabitants of the colony areas whilst the traditional African societies in the Protectorate regions were 'British Protected Persons,' and not British subjects.[12] Thus, although British West African territories were inhabited by African subjects of the Crown, there were two distinct classes of Africans. However, even among the British subjects of African descent, the educational, socio-economic and demographic makeup of the colonies created some cultural distinctions between British subjects of African descent in each colony.

Sierra Leone was the first British Crown Colony in West Africa and a haven for repatriated ex-slaves and liberated Africans rescued from slave ships. The territory comprised the 'Colony', which was mainly the Freetown peninsula, and the 'Protectorate', which was the ethnically diverse hinterland that was adjacent to the Colony.[13] The Protectorate was populated with various ethnic groups including the Temne, Mende, Limba and Sherbro people.[14] The Sierra Leone Creoles, the educated African elite of the colony, were the descendants of the various African-American, Afro-Caribbean, and African freemen and ex-slaves who were repatriated between 1792 and 1865.[15] As British subjects, the Creoles formed a cultural elite that was

---

[10] Kimble, David, *A Political History of Ghana: The Rise of Gold Coast Nationalism 1850-1928* (Clarendon, 1971) p. 532

[11] Kimble, *A Political History of Ghana*, pp. 313, 532

[12] Prais, *Imperial Travelers*, pp. 103-104. Alongside Afro-Caribbean people, British West Africans were among the earliest Black Britons or Black British people and there are several references to the term 'Black Englishmen' in colonial newspapers.

[13] Spitzer, Leo, *Creoles of Sierra Leone: Responses to Colonialism, 1870-1945*, (University of Wisconsin, 1974) pp. 70-71. Areas such as the Sherbro or the British Sherbro which was annexed to the Colony in 1861, also formed part of the Colony. However, the precise citizenship and rights of the subjects of the Sherbro were not entirely clear.

[14] Fyfe, Christopher, *A Short History of Sierra Leone* (Longmans, 1967) p. 1

[15] Fyfe, Christopher, *A History of Sierra Leone*, (Oxford University, 1962) p. 378. African-Americans and Afro-Caribbeans continued to settle into the Freetown Colony after 1865.

heavily influenced by Britain and espoused loyalty to the Crown.[16] Although historians such as Akintola Wyse have criticised the emphasis within scholarship on 'Creole power' within the colonial system, it is evident that some Creoles attained high positions within the civil service, and legal and medical fields of the colonial strata.[17]

The Gold Coast was colonised by the Portuguese, Danish, and Dutch before the British gained complete control in 1867.[18] Coastal towns such as Cape Coast and Elmina were populated by the Fante, an Akan-speaking ethnic group and Accra, another principal town was populated by the Ga.[19] After several major military campaigns, the British gained control of the Ashanti hinterland and declared it a Protectorate in 1902. Although the mixed-race elite of British descent in Accra and Cape Coast developed British mores, the coastal towns such as Cape Coast, Elmina, and Accra were also populated by Africans and Eurafricans descended from Danish, Dutch and Portuguese mercantilist companies and colonialists who had established trading forts and outposts before British rule.[20] Although these mixed-race families maintained their ethnic ties with the local Fante or Ga populations, the upper echelons of Eurafrican families of Cape Coast and the Ga Mulatofoi largely formed a distinctive social and political group that adopted aspects of British culture.[21]

---

[16] Wyse, *HC Bankole-Bright and Politics in Colonial Sierra Leone*, pp. 16-8

[17] Wyse, Akintola, *The Krio of Sierra Leone: An Interpretative History* (Howard University, 1991), pp. 41-42. That Creoles attained high positions within the colonial strata does not indicate they held some form of power that could be wielded to benefit themselves. It was the lack of qualified Europeans and high mortality, the cadre of qualified Creoles, and British policies in the middle to late nineteenth century that contributed toward the positions held by some of the Creoles. Creoles would often serve as 'Assistants' to European superiors who were sometimes less qualified than their Creole subordinates. Thus, Wyse's criticisms of perceptions of 'Creole power' is substantiated by the evidence.

[18] Kimble, *A Political History of Ghana*, pp. 1-4

[19] Parker, John, *Making the Town: Ga State and Society in Early Colonial Accra* (Pearson, 2000) pp. xxii, 33

[20] Parker, *Making the Town*, p. 33

[21] Parker, *Making the Town*, pp. 33, 67. Afro-Danish families among the Ga Mulatofoi were perhaps the most distinctive social and political group of Eurafricans. Afro-Danish families frequently intermarried and occupied Osu, or Danish Accra.

Nigeria comprised the former Lagos Colony, the Niger Protectorate and the Northern Nigeria Protectorate, territories that were formally amalgamated by Governor Frederick Lugard in 1906 and 1914.[22] Thus, Nigeria had the largest population in British West Africa. The Northern Nigeria Protectorate was largely populated by the Hausa and Fulani ethnic groups and the Niger Protectorate by the Igbo and smaller groups in Calabar such as the Efik and Kalabari. The Lagos Colony was largely populated by the Yoruba people in addition to the Amaro or Aguda, the descendants of Brazilian returnees, and the Saro, descendants of Sierra Leone Creoles and liberated Africans who settled in Nigeria.[23] The Legislative Council of Nigeria was largely dominated by the Saro and their descendants.[24]

The Gambia was the smallest of the British West African territories and comprised the Colony and Protectorate. The Gambia colony was inhabited by the Wolof people, an indigenous ethnic group and the Aku people, or Creoles, an educated African population with British citizenship imbued with a fusion of European and African mores and values.[25] The Aku served in privileged positions within the colonial strata of the Gambia and some historians have compared the status of the Aku to that of their Creole counterparts in Sierra Leone.[26]

'The Educated African': The British West African Elite

The British West African elite or 'Educated African' was an influential social and political class in the four British West African territories who agitated for and asserted their belief in equal treatment as British citizens.[27] Although British West

---

[22] Osuntokun, *Nigeria in the First World War*, pp. 3-5
[23] Ayandele, EA, *The Educated Elite in the Nigerian Society* (Ibadan University, 1974) pp. 11-12
[24] Ayandele, *The Educated Elite in the Nigerian Society*, pp. 9-12, 17-8
[25] Mahoney, Asi Florence, *Creole Saga: The Gambia's Liberated African Community in The Nineteenth Century* (Privately Published, 2006) pp. 9-10
[26] Mahoney, *Creole Saga*, pp. 9-10
[27] Crowder, Osuntokun, *The First World War and West Africa*, pp. 546-7, 575 The term 'Educated African' was a broader term encompassing the British West African elite, the Americo-Liberians of Liberia, the Metis of Senegal, the Fernandino Creoles of Bioko Island in Equatorial Guinea and other individuals or groups from the Americas who settled in West Africa during the nineteenth or twentieth centuries.

Africa comprised various ethnic groups, a British-oriented elite developed in all four British West African territories.[28] The advancement of educated Africans in the clergy, civil service and professions in British West Africa led to the apogee of the educated African ascendancy in the nineteenth-century.[29] Furthermore, in social relations, educated Africans and Europeans in the territories were on intimate terms, attending the same social events and engaging in the same fraternal activities.[30] As collaborators with British colonial authorities, educated Africans believed that their British citizenship, education and social intimacy with the colonial authorities would lead to greater opportunities and political self-determination.[31]

In all four British West African territories, professions such as law and medicine, the clergy, and the upper and lower ranks of the civil service were dominated by educated Africans.[32] In Nigeria, the Saro, originally from Sierra Leone, and the Amaros, originally from Brazil, were the principal merchants, professionals, civil servants, and served on the Legislative Council.[33] In Sierra Leone, the Creoles dominated the civil service and the medical and legal professions.[34] Similarly, some African or Eurafrican families of partial Ga or Fante ancestry in the Gold Coast and the Aku people in the Gambia were influential and prominent in commerce, colonial politics, and the professions.[35]

The highest political office for the British West African elite was an appointment to the Legislative Council.[36] Although the Legislative Councils of the four British West African colonies

[28] Wyse, *The Krio of Sierra Leone*, p. 28
[29] Kimble, *Political History*, pp. 131-141, Ayandele, *Educated Elite*, pp. 13-14, 28-36
[30] Porter, Arthur, *Creoledom: A Study of the Development of Freetown Society*, (Oxford University, 1963) pp. 106-7. Intermarriage was not uncommon among Europeans and the educated African elite in the Gold Coast and Sierra Leone.
[31] Ayandele, *Educated Elite*, pp. 14-20
[32] Kimble, *Political History*, pp. 131-41. Ayandele, *Educated Elite*, pp. 13-4, 28-36
[33] Ayandele, E.A, *'Holy' Johnson, Pioneer of African Nationalism, 1836-1917* (Frank Cass, 1970) p. 313. Wyse, *The Krio of Sierra Leone*, pp. 28
[34] Porter, *Creoledom*, pp. 109-4
[35] Kimble, *Political History*, pp. 61-70, 93-7
[36] Fyfe, *A History of Sierra Leone*, pp. 318-320, Ayandele, *'Holy' Johnson*, pp. 164-6, Kimble, *A Political History of Ghana*, pp. 404-7, Mahoney, *Creole Saga*, pp. 9-10.

provided a few prominent educated Africans with limited participation in the political process, membership remained highly prestigious in the territories.[37] Selection to the Legislative Councils was based upon a recommendation by the Governor of the colony.[38] Eminent West Africans such as James Bannerman, a prominent merchant who became the first Lieutenant and Acting Governor of African descent in the Gold Coast, and Captain James Pinson Libolu Davies, a wealthy merchant in the Lagos Colony, were selected to serve on the Legislative Councils of their respective colonies.[39] Selection to the Legislative Council recognised the achievements and status of elite British West Africans and membership was largely confined to wealthy merchants or professionals.[40]

The vibrant newspaper press across British West Africa was also the preserve of the educated African elite.[41] The press served as an instrument for political expression and allowed educated Africans to publicise their discontent with colonial officials and policies.[42] Several newspapers were founded by Afro-Caribbean and West Africans in British West Africa during the middle to late nineteenth-centuries. Leading newspapers in British West Africa included the *Sierra Leone Weekly News*, *Gold Coast Leader*, and the *Times of Nigeria*. These newspapers did not necessarily always reflect the interests and concerns of middle and working class West Africans, but largely reflected the perspective of the upper echelons of British West African society.

Thus, at the dawn of the twentieth century, some members of the educated African elite, such as Dr James Africanus Horton, cultivated the perspective that through their advancement and adherence to British mores and values, further political self-determination would be granted to educated Africans.[43] However, as British colonial policy shifted from informal to

---

[37] Porter, *Creoledom*, pp. 122-4
[38] Kimble, *Political History*, pp. 404-5, Ayandele, '*Holy' Johnson*, pp. 90
[39] Ibid.
[40] Ayandele, '*Holy' Johnson*, pp. 164-6, Wyse, *HC Bankole-Bright*, p. 20
[41] Fyfe, Christopher, *Sierra Leone*, pp. 464-5
[42] Omu, Fred IA, 'The dilemma of press freedom in Colonial Africa: the West African example' in *Journal of African History*, Vol 9:2 (1968) p. 279
[43] Fyfe, Christopher, *Africanus Horton: West African Scientist and Patriot* (Oxford University, 1972) pp. 76-7

formal empire and racial theories regarding the superiority of the Caucasian race gained support among segments of the colonial establishment, the opportunities that had been afforded to the educated African elite were significantly curtailed.[44]

'The European Armageddon': West Africa and the Great War

The outbreak of the First World War reverberated across British West Africa.[45] A headline from the *Sierra Leone Guardian* entitled the 'European Armageddon' encapsulated the apprehension and concern of West Africans of the imminent danger.[46] British West Africans also realised that their territories were geographically important to the British aim of capturing German colonial territories. Thus, although the African theatre and West Africa is perhaps accurately depicted as the periphery of the Allied campaign to suppress the Central Powers, the importance of British West Africa to the Allied Powers' campaigns in Africa cannot be understated. The West African Regiment, West African Frontier Force, and 1st Battalion West India Regiment were stationed in Freetown and the deep-water port was used to dispatch servicemen and supplies to the war front.[47] Nigeria, the most populous British West African colony, bordered the former German Cameroon and the former Gold Coast bordered former German Togoland. The strategic importance of the British West African colonies to the campaigns in Togoland and the Cameroons and the loyalty of the educated African elite, contributed to this important aspect of the Allied effort.

Furthermore, British West Africans largely supported the British war effort and were willing to express their loyalty to the British Empire despite their dissatisfaction with British colonial policies. Although Anglo-African relations were corrosive on the outbreak of war, the educated elite, without

[44] Ayandele, *Educated Elite*, pp. 21-8
[45] The European Armageddon: Notice No. 3,' *Sierra Leone Guardian*, 21 Aug 1914, 'The European Imbroglio: Notice No. 3,' *Sierra Leone Guardian*, 21 Aug 1914
[46] 'The European Armageddon: Notice No. 3,' *Sierra Leone Guardian*, 21 Aug 1914
[47] Turay, Abraham, p. 38, Wyse, *HC Bankole-Bright*, p. 32, Macpherson, *Medical Services*, p. 277. Freetown, containing one of the largest natural harbours in Africa, was the only territory garrisoned with imperial troops at the commencement of the war and used as a naval and coaling station during the conflict.

compromising their opposition to some colonial policies, willingly overlooked the state of Anglo-African relations for the sake of supporting the British war effort.[48] Ardent critics such as Dr John K Randle summarised the position of the British West African elite by stating that as British subjects, a truce between British West Africans and the British colonial authorities was in place in light of the war.[49] Randle summarised his position:

> The Fact must however, not be disguised, even here, that in recent years the administration of the government of this colony has not given the people entire satisfaction. The people see that government is not carried in their interest. But, however painfully true this is, let us not forget the wider principle that we are citizens of the British Empire.[50]

At the start of the conflict, there was genuine concern among some of the educated African elite for the well-being of the British Empire and the war effort.[51] Editorials in the British West African press consistently expressed a willingness to serve in defence of the colonies and the wider war effort.[52] However, as the conflict waged on, British West Africans became increasingly disillusioned with colonial policies that continued to discriminate on the basis of racial origin and curtailed the rights of the educated elite as British subjects.

Responses to the war in British West Africa

At the beginning of the war, British West Africans remained steadfastly loyal to the British cause and anxious that Britain should prevail.[53] Although some British West Africans perceived the war as a European conflict, some within the elite ridiculed the notion that a war, partially fought in Africa, could be a strictly European affair.[54] The British West African press

---

[48] 'Natives Under British Rule in West Africa,' *Gold Coast Leader*, 21 Nov 1914
[49] Wyse, *HC Bankole-Bright*, p. 32
[50] John K Randle quoted in Wyse, *HC Bankole-Bright*, p. 32
[51] 'Notes and Comments: Cape Coast at Intercessory Prayers,' *Gold Coast Nation*, 13 Aug 1914. An intercessory prayer was held at Cape Coast, Gold Coast, where it was reported that every creed of the townspeople was present as a result of deep concern for the welfare of the British Empire.
[52] 'Editorial Notes,' *Gold Coast Leader*, 15 Aug 1914
[53] Crowder, Osuntokun, *The First World War and West Africa*, p. 547

expressed loyalty to the British Empire and some articles stated that Britain was the most favourable colonial power for West Africans. However, British West Africans were not slavishly loyal to the British cause and educated Africans expected concessions including greater political rights and the end of racial inequality in return for their loyalty.[55]

Although colonial politics at the advent of the war differed between the various territories, educated Africans in British West Africa had similar grievances with colonial policies and expectations for recourse.[56] The lack of political concessions and Europeanisation of the civil service that excluded Africans on account of race were viewed with disdain by the educated elite, and British treatment of African soldiers in comparison to their French counterparts was equally criticised by the colonial elite. Thus, although British West Africans remained loyal to the British Empire and the war effort, enthusiasm faded as the racist British colonial policies continued and political concessions were not granted.

The response of the Gold Coast elite to the war

Anglo-African relations in the Gold Coast were probably not as corrosive as in Nigeria and Sierra Leone, yet still discriminatory colonial policies polarised relations in the Gold Coast.[57] Anglo-African relations between Europeans and the Gold Coast elite had been characterised by intimate friendship and intermarriage but the early twentieth century largely signalled a shift in these cordial relationships. The Gold Coast press responded by heavily criticising racial policies that excluded African civil servants and professionals from colonial appointments.[58] The press and members of the educated elite were

---

[54] 'Editorial Notes,' *Gold Coast Leader*, 21 Nov 1914. An editorial contributor stated in the *Gold Coast Leader*, 'this idea, as we have remarked, that the war is a white man's war is also general among Englishmen in West Africa. But West African natives like the gallant inhabitants of North Rhodesia have no such delusion in the matter. War on the soil of Africa between Englishmen and Germans cannot be an affair of white men only, and the sooner our white rulers understand this the better it will be for all concerned.'

[55] Crowder, Osuntokun, *First World War and West Africa*, p. 547

[56] Crowder, Osuntokun, *First World War and West Africa*, p. 547

[57] ''Natives Under British Rule in West Africa,' *Gold Coast Leader*, 21 Nov 1914, 'India's Aspirations,' *Gold Coast Leader*, 24 Apr 1915

particularly concerned with the blatant discrimination that precluded educated Africans, who were often educated in Britain at their own expense and earned qualifications, from equal treatment in the civil and medical services.[59] The newspapers frequently recalled the apogee of the British West Africa elite when educated Africans served in the Gold Coast administration in high-ranking positions such as Chief Medical Officer or Postmaster-General of the Colony.[60] The Gold Coast elite also compared their condition to that of other colonial subjects in the Empire such as India and encouraged unity among the Empire to formally challenge British colonial policies that were dissatisfactory to the elite.[61]

However, despite the dissatisfaction of the Gold Coast elite with British colonial policies, following the entry of Britain into the war, the educated Africans in the Gold Coast supported the British war effort with devotion. An editorial in the *Gold Coast Leader* published before Britain entered the war reflects some of the sentiments of the Gold Coast elite:

> If England is drawn into the war there [??] no doubt that the wishes and hopes of her West African subjects are that she emerges from it triumphant and victorious . . . it is true that we are subject races that we labour under great disadvantages under the present condition of government of subject races in the British Empire. England has faults and does us wrong in many things, but she has been the source the little light we have seen and known, and with all her faults we love her still, and we would not exchange for her any other European master.[62]

Thus, in similar vein to their counterparts in the other British West African territories, the Gold Coast press did not slavishly support the war effort. Editorials acknowledged the strain in Anglo-African relations but expressed a willingness to overlook these slights for the perceived greater purpose of supporting the war effort.

---

[58] Kimble, *Political History*, pp. 98-105
[59] Ibid. pp. 98-105
[60] 'The unrivalled Senegalese,' *Gold Coast Independent*, 8 Jun 1918
[61] 'Editorial Notes,' *Gold Coast Leader*, 20 Jan 1912. 'India's Aspirations,' *Gold Coast Leader*, 24 Apr 1915
[62] 'War in Europe,' *Gold Coast Leader*, 8 Aug 1914

Throughout the war, the Gold Coast elite loyally supported the war effort but also clamoured for equal opportunities such as appointment to colonial positions and demanded the eradication of racist policies.[63] Some sections of the press stated that the war would result in opening the 'gates of opportunity' for British West Africans and the end of colonial policies preventing Gold Coasters from equal opportunities based on racial prejudice.[64] As the conflict came to a conclusion, a *Gold Coast Leader* editorial outlined:

> The gates of opportunity are not open to all Imperial subjects alike, regardless of colour . . . but the war has proved our loyalty, our equal sacrifices in lives and money: in fact it has opened our eyes that both white and black have a common destiny and a common goal to be reached by all. Therefore the sooner this state of things is changed for the better, the better for us all.[65]

It was the perspective of some segments of the Gold Coast elite, who adhered to the Wilsonian doctrine of self-determination for nations, that the loyalty and service of West Africans for Britain in the conflict provided the educated elite with an even greater claim to be treated as equally as their British counterparts of 'pure' European descent.[66]

However, as the war came to an end, articles in the press reflected the increasing frustration of the educated elite regarding British colonial policies that did not offer any substantive political concessions to educated Africans. The educated Gold Coast elite sought political concessions that allowed for greater self-determination in return for their loyalty during the war and contrasted the British colonial policy of exclusion with the French colonial policy of assimilation:

> The French idea of colonisation is assimilation as opposed to segregation and is founded solely on merit and not colour . . . the experience of all serious students of the systems of government of what are called Crown Colonies . . . all are

---

[63] Ibid., 'The unrivalled Senegalese,' *Gold Coast Independent*, 8 Jun 1918

[64] 'Editorial Notes,' *Gold Coast Leader*, 6 May 1916. 'Our Native Chiefs and Their Tribunals,' *Gold Coast Independent*, 13 Jul 1918. The Gold Coast press sometimes referred to the "gate," or "gates of opportunity" that precluded African advancement in the civil and political spheres.

[65] 'The unrivalled Senegalese,' *Gold Coast Independent*, 8 Jun 1918

[66] Ibid.

agreed that the conditions existing in the French Colonial Empire are diametrically opposed to those existing in the British Empire, where there is a predominance of the native element.[67]

It was evident to Gold Coasters that the Wilsonian doctrine of self-determination did not apply to the colonial subjects of British West Africa. Thus, the perception of some segments of the Gold Coast elite that the British were the most benevolent colonial power was eroded by the treatment of educated Africans following the conclusion of the conflict.

The Nigerian educated elite and the First World War

Significant tension existed between the educated elite in Nigeria and British colonial authorities at the commencement of the First World War.[68] The educated African elite was an influential social class that dominated the higher echelons of colonial Nigerian society and asserted its rights to equal treatment as British subjects.[69] The Nigerian educated elite was dominated by the Saro, who were mainly the descendants of Sierra Leone Creoles and liberated Africans, and the Amaro, descendants of Brazilian returnees. Furthermore, there were several indigenous Nigerians from Abeokuta, Ibadan, Calabar, and Lagos, who were members of the educated African elite in colonial Nigeria.[70]

At the advent of the First World War, the terrible state of Anglo-African relations was a result of the opposition of the educated African elite in Nigeria to Governor Frederick Lugard's policies regarding the administration of the amalgamated territory.[71] The educated elite were frustrated with the policy of indirect rule in northern Nigeria that Lugard implemented which allowed for the Protectorate to be ruled indirectly through local chiefs.[72] The system of indirect rule was in stark contrast to the administration of the Colony presided over by the Legislative Council, which was replaced by the

---

[67] 'The unrivalled Senegalese,' *Gold Coast Independent*, 8 Jun 1918
[68] Osuntokun, *Nigerians in the First World War*, pp. ix, 64-9
[69] Freund, Bill, *The Making of Contemporary Africa: The Development of African Society Since 1800*, p. 52, Osuntokun, *Nigerians in the First World War*, p. 64
[70] Osuntokun, *Nigerians in the First World War*, p. 64
[71] Ibid., pp. 3-9
[72] Ibid., pp. 64-6

Legislative Council of Nigeria in 1916.[73] The educated elite viewed the policy of indirect rule as divisive, precluding educated Nigerians from participating in governing the country and hindering the political development and integration of Nigeria.[74]

Despite the controversy regarding Lugard's colonial policies, the educated African community in Nigeria largely supported the British war effort.[75] As British subjects and loyal citizens, the educated elite expected political concessions from the colonial administration in recognition of their loyalty. Thus, the Nigerian press actively supported the British war effort although Anglo-African relations had deteriorated significantly between the educated African elite and the British colonial authorities.[76] As an editorial in the *Times of Nigeria* stated:

> Knowing under God that our welfare and interest is bound up with the British Crown and Empire under whom we have enjoyed liberty, fairplay and justice, it behoves us as loyal and dutiful subjects and protected subjects to engage ourselves continually in earnest and fervent prayer to the Almighty God, that it may please Him of His great mercy and goodness to grant victory to the British Army, and that our Father in heaven may direct His Majesty's government for all their deliber-ations especially in this critical time.[77]

Articles in the Nigerian press expressing disdain of the educated elite for Germany did not necessarily include local German merchants.[78]

In contrast to other British West African territories, the Nigerian press did not heavily moderate the tone or rhetoric that railed against the colonial policies that the educated elite believed were unjust.[79] Furthermore, the Nigerian press crit-

---

[73] Onwuekwe, Chika B, 'Constitutional Development, 1914-1960: British Legacy or Local Exigency?' in *The Foundations of Nigeria: Essays in Honor of Toyin Falola*, (Africa World, 2003) p. 161

[74] Osuntokun, Akinijide, *Nigeria in the First World War*, pp. 64-66

[75] Ibid., pp. 69-72

[76] 'Troublous Times,' *Lagos Standard*, 19 Aug 1914

[77] 'Notice: Rule Britannia,' *Times of Nigeria*, 15 Sep 1914

[78] Osuntokun, *Nigeria in the First World War*, p. ix. The educated Nigerian elite favoured German mercantilist firms because the firms offered easier credit to African traders. Thus, although in Sierra Leone, local German residents were held in suspicion, the Nigerian press sympathised with the German residents in Nigeria and their plight during the war.

icised the colonial policies implemented by Governor Lugard by comparing Lugard's policies to those of German colonialists.[80] James Bright-Davies, a Sierra Leonean journalist who wrote scathing articles criticising colonial policies and the strategy of British mercantilist firms, was jailed for sedition. The elite continued to be scathingly critical of indirect rule and the treatment of educated Africans despite their loyalty to the Crown.

Discriminatory policies contributed to the disillusionment of the elite during the war effort. The refusal of British forces to enlist educated Nigerians as officers reinforced the notion that educated Nigerians, who asserted their rights to equal treatment, were second class British subjects. Thus, the war fostered the reinvigoration and development of a distinctly African nationalism among the educated African elite of Nigeria and heightened their rejection of Anglicisation. The war contributed to a distinctly Nigerian nationalism that ultimately resulted in agitation for greater political participation and ultimately the formation of the first Nigerian political parties which would eventually contribute towards the decolonisation movement that culminated in Nigeria gaining independence in 1960.

The Sierra Leone Elite and the First World War

The Hut Tax War and the subsequent colonial policy of prioritising the selection of Europeans for employment in the civil service contributed to a significant deterioration in Anglo-Creole relations at the start of the First World War.[81] The British colonial establishment blamed the Sierra Leone press for inciting the Hut Tax War and subsequent administrators sought to reduce Creole influence in the senior civil service. Thus, although Sierra Leone Creoles held eighteen out of forty civil service posts in 1892, by 1912 Creoles held fifteen out of nineteen civil service posts, and five of these posts were abolished after their holders retired.[82] Furthermore, racist

---

[79] Osuntokun, *Nigeria in the First World War*, pp. 66-9

[80] Osuntokun, *Nigeria in the First World War*, pp. 68-70. 'Natives Under British Rule in West Africa,' *Gold Coast* Leader, 21 Nov 1914. The Gold Coast press also noted that the policies in Nigeria were on 'Germanised lines' and were supported by British colonialists who adhered to 'Germanised' colonial policies.

[81] Hyam, Ronald, *Britain's imperial century, 1815-1914: a study of empire and expansion*, (BT Batsford, 1976) p. 288

[82] Ibid., p. 288

colonial policies that excluded Sierra Leonean medical officers from service in the West African Medical Staff further reinforced the abandonment of 'fair play' by the British colonial authorities and signalled to Sierra Leoneans that a new era of Anglo-Creole relations had emerged. Newspapers such as the *Sierra Leone Weekly News*, one of the leading newspapers in British West Africa, the *Sierra Leone Guardian* and the *Colony and Provincial Advocate* vehemently opposed the Europeanisation of the medical service and other civil service units.

The corrosive state of Anglo-Creole relations at the beginning of the war was further augmented by the tenure of Governor Edward Marsh Merewether who was vehemently opposed to Creole advancement in the civil service or echelons of the colonial government.[83] Merewether, subscribed to the pseudo-scientific racial theories on the supposed inherent deficiencies in peoples of African descent.[84] His refusal to invite prominent Creole citizens to Government House for social events led to further tension with the Freetown community and garnered the attention of the Sierra Leone press.[85]

However, at the outbreak of the Great War, the deplorable state of Anglo-Creole relations in Sierra Leone did not prevent the elite from expressing significant support for the British war effort.[86] As the inhabitants of Britain's 'Ancient and Loyal' Sierra Leone, the press espoused loyalty to Britain and disdain for Germany and the Central Powers.[87] Although some Sierra Leoneans expressed ambivalence towards the conflict and the Freetown press sometimes designated the conflict as a 'European' war, the editorials of Freetown newspapers reflected the support of upper class Creoles for the British war effort. The Freetown press displayed a unique understanding of the historical context of the conflict and the potential consequences of Britain's involvement in the conflict.[88]

---

[83] Cole, Festus, 'The Sierra Leone Carrier Corps and Krio Responses to Recruitment in World War I' in Dixon-Fyle, Mac & Cole, Gibril Raschid (Eds.), *New Perspectives on the Sierra Leone Krio* (Peter Lang, 2006) pp. 54-6, Wyse, *HC Bankole-Bright*, pp. 26-7

[84] Cole, *Sierra Leone Carrier Corps*, pp. 54-6. Wyse, *HC Bankole-Bright*, pp. 26-7

[85] 'The Acting Governor of Sierra Leone,' *Sierra Leone Weekly News*, 21 Feb 1914

[86] 'General News: "At Home," Government House,' *Sierra Leone Weekly News*, 3 Feb 1912. Rambler, 'Rambling Talks: Loyal Sierra Leone,' *Sierra Leone Weekly News*, 7 Nov 1914

[87] Ibid.

Articles in the press made distinctions between British liberalism in contrast to the brutality of the Germans. The *Sierra Leone Guardian* editor, wrote:

> For the past few days, harrowing, but let us hope, exaggerated accounts have been circulated in the City as to the alleged dreadful sufferings inflicted upon our countrymen and all British Subjects at the Cameroons since the outbreak of War. Some of the details given are too horrible to relate and ... is causing the Freetown public to contrast the very liberal treatment being accorded to the German detenues ... with the reports of the treatment being meted out to the Creoles in the German Cameroons.[89]

The Creole elite's disdain for Germany extended beyond the columns of the local press and encompassed a diverse range of Sierra Leoneans.[90] A special set of constables was established to patrol the streets of Freetown and to prevent German captives from escaping from where they were held at Mount Aureol and the Government Model School.[91] Sierra Leonean Muslims from the Colony, Protectorate and Algeria denounced the Ottoman Empire and condemned the Empire for contradicting the Koran.[92]

In similar vein to other British West African territories, the Freetown press expressed the sentiments of a segment of the Creole population by encouraging young Creole men to enlist. Rambler, a regular columnist for the *Sierra Leone Weekly News* opined that:

> the Creole boy love [sic] the soldier life. He loves the smart uniform and the swaggering gait of the 'so jer man.' But he wants a chance of promotion to induce him to join the colours. Give him the hope of an epaulet, a star and a sword and by Jingo! you'll see what stuff he is made of.[93]

The Freetown newspapers made frequent references to Sierra Leoneans who enlisted in the British army such as Henry

---

[88] Ibid. Some articles referred to the Napoleonic wars, in which ancestors of the Creoles had fought alongside the British.
[89] 'The European Armageddon: Notice No. 3,' *Sierra Leone Guardian*, 21 Aug 1914
[90] Turay, *Sierra Leone Army*, p. 39
[91] Spitzer, *Creoles of Sierra Leone*, pp. 152-3, Turay, *Sierra Leone Army*, p. 39
[92] Rambler, 'Rambling Talks: Muhammadan Feeling,' *Sierra Leone Weekly News*, 14 Nov 1914. Turay, *Sierra Leone Army*, p. 39
[93] 'The King's Own Creole Boys,' *Sierra Leone Weekly News*, 7 Nov 1914

'Harry' Clement Solomon and Robert R 'Bob' Collier, an amateur boxer and the son of a wealthy Creole merchant.

Although the Sierra Leone press initially displayed an almost unwavering loyalty to the British war effort, the blatant discrimination in the recruitment process received coverage during the conflict.[94] Some Sierra Leoneans initially attempted to attribute the lack of Creoles in the military to the "submissive" nature of Creoles in contrast to their indigenous counterparts.[95] However as the war continued, Sierra Leoneans began to realise that the racial discrimination that had limited their opportunities in the colonial service similarly precluded Creoles from enlisting.[96] As British subjects rejected by their colonial mentors, some segments of the Creole population began to question the futility of 'imitating' or 'aping' Western culture. As transatlantic Black nationalist efforts such as Marcus Garvey's began to establish connections with Sierra Leone, the cultural reawakening of some Creoles began to occur following Britain's rejection of its Black British subjects.

Thus, although Anglo-African relations were revitalised in the Gold Coast and Nigeria, the First World War was perhaps the signal of a downward spiral in Anglo-Creole relations that continued throughout the decolonisation era.[97] As Creole merchants were supplanted by Lebanese merchants, locally known as 'Syrians' or 'Corals', and economic hardship had an effect on working class Creoles, the frustrations of Sierra Leoneans would be exhibited in the post-war period by a resistance to colonialism that was rooted in the experience of working-class Creoles during the First World War.

African servicemen in the Great War

Although the patriotic fervour and loyalty to the British war effort was espoused by the British West African elite, it was largely Africans from traditional societies in the hinterland or territories adjacent to the British-oriented coastal settlements who served as active participants in the military campaigns.[98]

---

[94] 'The British Empire and The Blacks,' *Sierra Leone Weekly News*, 19 May 1917
[95] Ibid.
[96] Ibid.
[97] Spitzer, Leo, *Creoles of Sierra Leone*, pp. 155-156
[98] Crowder, Osuntokun, The First World War and West Africa, pp. 560-6

The Allied campaigns to capture the German colonies of Togoland and the Cameroons required the service of thousands of West Africans.[99] Although the precise number of West Africans who served in the African theatre of the First World War is unclear, it is evident that at least 68,821 West Africans served in combative and non-combative roles throughout the course of the war.[100]

West Africans from the hinterlands and Protectorates of British West Africa comprised the majority of servicemen, however, the response of traditional African societies to the outbreak of the First World War was one of ambivalence and concern over the disruption to daily life that might result from the war.[101] Thus, although the Educated Africans sympathised with the global implications of the war for the British Empire, West Africans from traditional societies were less concerned with the implications of the war outside the economic disruption to trade and commerce. The ambivalence of West Africans from traditional societies towards the war effort posed a significant dilemma for British authorities who had a dearth of African servicemen and sought to recruit West Africans for service in the campaigns.[102]

A consistent theme of British recruitment in British West Africa was the recruitment of West Africans from traditional societies and largely the exclusion of educated Africans from service as officers.[103] The British sought to recruit Mende and Temne people in Sierra Leone and the Fulani and Hausa from Northern Nigeria.[104] Africans were recruited through British collaboration with ruling chiefs who probably coerced their subjects into 'volunteering' for service with the British military.[105] The recruitment of West Africans for war service

---

[99] Ibid.
[100] Ibid., p. 557. Crowder and Osuntokun cite this figure from CO 879/121/1098, *Report on the Combatant Manpower of the Native Races of British West Africa*
[101] Ibid. pp. 560-6
[102] Kimble, *A Political History of Ghana*. The limited size of the British colonial forces compared with colonial forces in Francophone West Africa required British recruitment from the British West African colonies, particularly to serve in the Carrier Corps.
[103] Osuntokun, p. 78
[104] Moberly, *Military Operations Togoland and the Cameroons*, pp. 7-8, 31
[105] Killingray, David & Matthews, James, 'Beasts of Burden: British West African

created a labour shortage that further exacerbated the economic plight of the British West African territories and led to several revolts.

Evidence suggests that uprisings in British West Africa that occurred during the course of the war were partly the result of resistance by some West Africans to recruitment into the British army.[106] The Egba uprisings in Nigeria and the revolt led by Prophet Elijah II to overthrow the British colonial government were partly the result of the tension between British colonialists and West Africans before the war exacerbated by the British attempt to collude with chiefs to forcibly recruit men for service in the war. Furthermore, the economic conditions resulting from the loss of German commercial enterprise contributed to the dissatisfaction of some West Africans from traditional societies. Some colonial officials such as Lugard of Nigeria blamed Educated Africans for inciting rebellion against the Crown.[107] Thus, although Educated Africans in the colony-areas were expressing their devotion to the British cause, a sizeable number of British West Africans viewed the war as an inconvenience and an encroachment on their socio-economic conditions.

West Africans in the military

The British West African military units that served in the campaigns of the First World War had developed organically from militia and colonial police forces that served in the hinterlands or Protectorates. Although the West African Frontier Force (WAAF) was the primary combatant British West African military unit, the West African Regiment was also deployed for service in Cameroon.[108] The WAAF was administered by the Colonial Office in London and comprised 8,500

Carriers in the First World War,' *Canadian Journal of African Studies/Revue Canadienne des Études Africaines*, Vol. 13:1/2 (1979), pp. 13-14

[106] Crowder, pp. 560-1. Osuntokun, pp. 100-10

[107] Osuntokun, *Nigeria and the First World War*, p. 125

[108] Fyfe, *A history of Sierra Leone*, The West African Regiment, established in 1896 as an Imperial Unit and administered by the War Office, served in the Cameroon campaign. It was formed to serve primarily in Sierra Leone Protectorate although could be deployed across British West Africa. At least eight Sierra Leoneans serving in the West African Regiment received Mentions in Despatches during the Cameroon campaign. Sierra Leoneans serving in the West African Regiment were not eligible for the WAFF Distinguished Conduct Medal.

men at the start of the war, including the five battalions of the Nigeria Regiment comprising 5,000 men and a battalion of the Gold Coast Regiment (formerly Gold Coast Battalion) comprising 3,250 men.[109] Furthermore, the Sierra Leone Battalion comprised 325 men and The Gambia Company 130 men who also served in the WAAF.[110]

At least 14,200 Sierra Leoneans and Nigerians were recruited as carriers in the West African Carrier Corps during the First World War. Thousands served in the Togoland and Cameroon campaigns and at least 9,391 served in East Africa. The carriers were often given meagre supplies and hundreds died from tropical ulcers during the campaigns.

The squalid conditions of the West African servicemen, particularly the Carrier Corps, influenced some West Africans to reconsider the relationship between Britain and British West Africa.[111] Some newspapers compared the seemingly favourable treatment of French West African troops to that of British West African servicemen.[112] Isaac Theophilus Akuna Wallace-Johnson, a Sierra Leone Creole clerk in the West Africa Regiment, was deeply disaffected by his experiences in Cameroon and the treatment of the carriers. Wallace-Johnson was to become a political agitator challenging the colonial authorities and mobilising working-class members of the educated elite.[113]

The campaigns

Allied forces led by Brigadier-General Charles Macpherson Dobell formed the Cameroon Expeditionary Force to capture Togoland and the Cameroons. The Togoland campaign was relatively brief.[114] However, the campaign in Cameroon was arduous and the weather conditions and terrain contributed to a prolonged struggle and the spread of disease among the

---

[109] Haywood & Clarke, pp. 5-8. The WAFF was established in 1897 from various constabularies in the British West African territories and was the most important military force in British West Africa.

[110] Gorges, Brigadier E Howard, *The Great War in West Africa*, (Hutchinson, 1920) pp. 98-99

[111] 'Wallace-Johnson, Isaac Theophilus Akuna' in Akyeampong, Emmanuel Kwaku, Gates & Henry Louis, *Dictionary of African Biography*, Volume 6, p. 147

[112] 'The Unrivalled Senegalese,' *Gold Coast Independent*, 8 Jun 1918

[113] 'Wallace-Johnson et al', *Dictionary of African Biography*, Vol 6, pp. 147-8

[114] Moberly, *Military Operations Togoland and the Cameroons*, pp. 3-4

British forces. Thus, West African servicemen, and in particular the carriers, suffered from diseases which resulted in higher numbers of death than from combat.

The West African carriers, medical personnel, and WAFF played a significant role in the Allied victories in Togoland and Cameroon. Dobell praised the West African servicemen in the Cameroon campaign, stating that 'to them no day seems to be too long, no task too difficult. With a natural aptitude for soldiering, they are endowed with a constitution which inures them to hardship; they share...an inexhaustible fund of good humour!'[115] The contribution of West African servicemen is exemplified by the service of Alhaji Grunshi, a lance corporal in the Gold Coast Regiment, who was the first soldier in the British military to fire a shot in the war.[116]

The requirement for medical personnel in the Cameroon campaign provided Educated Africans with one of the few opportunities to serve during the conflict.[117] A small number of West Africans also served in the medical units of the British Expeditionary Force. Although British colonial policy, perhaps reinforced by the Manual of Military Law, prohibited or strongly discouraged applicants of African descent serving in positions of authority, the dearth of trained European medical staff to serve in the Cameroons led the British military to recruit Africans for service in the medical department. Ebenezer George Luke, a Sierra Leonean medical dispenser was deployed to Cameroon, receiving the three campaign medals for his service. SB Palmer, a Sierra Leonean Medical Dispenser based at the colonial hospital in the Gambia served in the Cameroon campaign alongside assistant nurses of African descent from Sierra Leone. Macormack Charles Farrell Easmon, a promising medical doctor, served as a lieutenant in the West African Medical Staff during the Cameroon campaign. Easmon received the three campaign medals and was possibly the only Black African commissioned as an officer in the First World War.

West African servicemen also participated in the East African campaign which was waged by the Allied forces to

---

[115] Ibid., p. 427
[116] Ibid., facing p. 8
[117] Patton, Adell, *Physicians, Colonial Racism, and Diaspora in West Africa* (University Press of Florida, 1996) p. 171

capture German East Africa (GEA).[118] The decision to deploy the WAFF to other theatres of war was a result of the commendable performance of West African servicemen in the Cameroon campaign. Furthermore, West African servicemen were deployed as a result of political pressure from the British press for the creation of a Black African army comprised of indigenous Africans in a similar vein to the French forces.[119] However, the most compelling basis for the service of West Africans was that the climate of German East Africa contributed to the death of hundreds of Indian and European servicemen and these casualties further reinforced to the British the need to utilise West African servicemen.

The Colonial Office decided to deploy the WAFF and the newly-formed Sierra Leone Carrier Corps to GEA in 1916. A battalion of the Gold Coast Regiment was the first West African unit to serve in East Africa, arriving in GEA in mid-1916.[120] Four battalions of the Nigeria Regiment also served in East Africa. West Africans such as Belo Akure Distinguished Conduct Medal (DCM), Military Medal (MM) served with distinction.[121] The performance of the East African porters resulted in British forces enlisting 3,500 Sierra Leoneans to serve as the Sierra Leone Carrier Corps. A contingent of 1,000 servicemen in the Sierra Leone Carriers also served as drivers, crewmen on steamers, and manned monitors with the Inland Water Transport Service in Mesopotamia.[122]

The bravery of West Africans is reflected in the honours that several servicemen received. Although West African servicemen were sometimes honoured for exceptional bravery by protecting European officers, the heroism of these men should not be over looked.[123] Musa Bauchi of the 1st Battalion of the Nigeria Regiment received the WAFF DCM and was among seventy-eight Nigerians to receive honours in battle.[124] Lance Corporal

---

[118] Crowder, Osuntokun, 'The First World War and West Africa, pp. 555-6. Modern-day Burundi, Rwanda and parts of East Africa.

[119] Ibid.

[120] Ibid, p. 556

[121] 'Foreign,' *The Crisis*, Aug 1917, p. 197, Haywood, *The History of the Royal West African Frontier Force*, pp. 198-9

[122] Turay, *Sierra Leone Army*, p. 50

[123] Crowder, Osuntokun, The First World War and West Africa, p. 556

[124] *Federal Nigeria: Annual Report 1957* (HMSO, 1961), p. 162. Forty-eight Nigerian

Sorie Kanu was among four Sierra Leoneans to receive the DCM for exceptional bravery.[125] Lance-Corporal Palkuke Grumah and Sergeant Yessufu Mamprusi were among twenty Gold Coast Regiment soldiers who received the DCM and twenty-three who received the MM.[126] Private Saljen Sidibi was one of at least three Gambians to receive the DCM.

The remarkable sacrifice of West African servicemen, who may not have fully grasped the global implications of the conflict, is perhaps best exemplified by the statistics on casualties. At least 2,000 West African carriers died from disease or were killed in action. There were ten Gambia Company troops who died during the war including two soldiers awarded the DCM. Thirty-nine servicemen of the Sierra Leone Battalion were killed or died of disease in the Cameroon campaign and 69 men were wounded,[127] 953 Gold Coast Regiment soldiers were killed in battle, 270 died of disease and 530 were wounded and 340 Nigeria Regiment soldiers were killed, 263 died of disease and 852 were wounded.

Limited exposure, if any, to British education ensured that the vast majority of West African servicemen did not have their experiences recorded or noted for posterity.[128] However, the important contribution of West African servicemen was not lost upon the educated elite of British West Africa.[129] The labour shortage that resulted from West Africans being recruited for service and the casualties and treatment of West African servicemen further reinforced to the educated elite the requirement for equality across the British Empire. It was the British colonial response to the aspirations and expectations of the educated elite that contributed to the decline in Anglo-African relations following the conflict.

---

servicemen earned the DCM, with four soldiers earning the DCM with four bars. Thirty Nigeria Regiment soldiers received MMs.

[125] Turay, Abraham, *Sierra Leone Army*, p. 48

[126] Haywood, *Royal West African Frontier Force*, pp. 298-300 Two Gold Coast Regiment Soldiers received the DCM with a clasp.

[127] Turay, Abraham, p. 48

[128] Farwell, *The Great War in Africa*, p. 14

[129] 'The Unrivalled Senegalese,' *Gold Coast Independent*, 8 Jun 1918

251

The aftermath of the Great War in Africa: The disillusionment of the Elite

The First World War and its aftermath had significant consequences for the colonies that comprised British West Africa.[130] Although the inhabitants were largely on the periphery of where the major battles and campaigns occurred, the consequences of the conflict in the post-war era were pronounced in the colonies. The inhabitants of British West Africa were impacted by political, economic, and societal changes that coincided with or were a direct consequence of the First World War.[131] Furthermore, as West Africans grappled with some of the woeful conditions following the conflict, the Spanish Influenza Epidemic swept through British West Africa bringing further misery.[132]

The economic conditions following the First World War were perhaps the most devastating aspects of the conflict.[133] The labour shortage and disruption to trade resulted in economic hardship for the educated elite and Africans from traditional societies.[134] Dissatisfaction with the economic conditions in British West Africa was reflected in various revolts that occurred following the war.[135] Thus, the Anti-Syrian Riots and the Rice Riots of 1919 in Sierra Leone were manifestations of the dissatisfaction that Protectorate citizens and the educated elite had with the economic conditions in the territory following the end of the First World War.[136]

The First World War contributed to a revival of African nationalism and provided the educated African elite with a further impetus for their political movements at the end of the war. The continuation of colonial policies aimed at displacing the educated African elite further reinforced to the educated African elite the futility of identifying and celebrating British

---

[130] Wyse, *HC Bankole-Bright*, pp. 32-34
[131] Ibid., pp. 32-36
[132] Spitzer, *Creoles of Sierra Leone*, p. 159. The influenza crisis exacerbated social tensions in territories such as Sierra Leone, where the Creole community blamed its spread on the alleged insanitary living conditions of the Lebanese community.
[133] Crowder & Osuntokun, *The First World War and West Africa*, pp. 566-571
[134] Ibid.
[135] Spitzer, *Creoles of Sierra Leone*, pp. 156-161
[136] Ibid. pp. 156-161

citizenship.[137] Educated Africans across British West Africa began to challenge the Anglicisation of the educated elite and expressed an appreciation for distinctly African culture.[138] In Nigeria and the Gold Coast, the educated African elite strongly rejected terms such as 'native' and instead advocated for the use of the term 'African' in reference to African peoples.[139] As an editorial in the *West Africa* publication outlined in 1920:

> The day is past when it was supposed that by the simple process of teaching the African to read and write, to sing hymns, and to dress like an Englishman, he could be turned into a black Englishman.[140]

The cultural introspection and the revival of African nationalism among the educated African elite further reinforced the importance of West African unity to challenge colonial policies and gain greater self-determination for British West Africa.

The emphasis on West African nationalism among educated Africans also coincided with an increasing political awareness among the educated elite in British West Africa. Although British West Africans had long agitated for greater rights and political freedoms, the First World War contributed to the political awareness of British West Africans as the conflict reinforced the inequities in British colonial policy towards African involvement in the political administration. Furthermore, British West Africans believed that the post-war emphasis on the 'self-determination' of nations should apply equally to the British colonies, irrespective of racial or cultural differences. Although the British West African elite did not necessarily serve in active operations, educated Africans were fully conscious that the African campaigns had been fought by their brethren from the hinterlands or rural areas.[141] It was on the basis that West Africans had seen active duty in war that educated Africans renewed their efforts to gain racial equality, greater political rights and self-determination.[142] Thus, the

---

[137] Kimble, *A Political History of Ghana*, pp. 545-47
[138] Osuntokun, *Nigeria in the First World War*, pp. 75-77
[139] Ibid., p. 75, Kimble, *A Political History of Ghana*, p. 540
[140] Kimble, p. 546
[141] Wyse, *HC Bankole-Bright*, pp. 31-32
[142] Osuntokun, *Nigeria in the First World War*, pp. 78-82, 90-94

continuation of race-based colonial policies following the First World War contributed to the deterioration of Anglo-African relations and confirmed to leading members of the elite that British West Africa required self-determination for Africans.

The African nationalist fervour and the clamour for a new political strategy to challenge the increasingly racialised colonial policy culminated in the formation of the National Congress of British West Africa.[143] Although the idea of establishing a Congress had been conceived prior to the war, the conflict reinforced that a distinctive form of West African nationalism had to develop for greater political freedoms to be granted to British subjects of African descent. The establishment of the National Congress of British West Africa was reflective of the realisation that political petitions or protestations through the press were not adequate methods for challenging colonial policies. Furthermore, as an organisation largely comprised of the British West African elite, the founding of the Congress reflected awareness among West Africans. Although the National Congress of British West Africa was unsuccessful in securing further political rights for British West Africans,[144] the Congress was the first of several movements that eventually contributed towards independence across the area.[145]

Conclusion

The First World War was a military conflict that had far-reaching political, social, and economic consequences for the inhabitants of British West Africa.[146] Expressions of loyalty by the educated West African elite and the participation of West African servicemen in the conflict reflected the importance of British West Africa to the First World War. West African servicemen, often from traditional societies without any stake in the war, served with honour in the conflict and without them the African campaigns could not have been successful. However, the continuation of colonial policies that discriminated against the educated West African elite and the lack of

---

[143] Wyse, *HC Bankole-Bright*, pp. 31-32
[144] Ibid. pp. 31-32
[145] Osuntokun, *Nigeria in the First World War*, pp. 78-82, 91-94
[146] Ibid., pp. 78-82, 82-94

political concessions following the war contributed to the disillusionment of the British West African elite with Empire and the possibility of equal treatment under British rule. It was disillusionment with the British Empire among the educated West African elite during the First World War that contributed to the development of the decolonisation movements across British West Africa.

The Germans and British in São Vicente Cape Verde

Célia Reis[1]

São Vicente is an island situated in the northwest of the archipelago of Cape Verde, with the city of Mindelo serving as its major settlement.

From the middle of the nineteenth century, the Porto Grande (Great Harbour) became an important base for navigation due to its geographical position in the Atlantic. In 1836 a delegate of the East India Company came to this area in search of a navigation base and decided on Baía Grande. This was the beginning of the village and the development of the island. Here, the East India Company established the first coal depot, followed by other firms, which did the same. Coal became the basis of the local economy, as many ships started visiting the island because of it. The three operating British companies were working as a cartel, not allowing competitors to establish.[2] However, competition grew from other ports near Cape Verde, such as Las Palmas and Dakar.

Another important aspect of the development of São Vicente was its influence in communications. The first submarine cable was laid here in the 1870s, and soon other cables linked this island to the rest of the world. In 1914, nine cables were laid

---

[1] Célia Reis, Instituto de História Contemporânea – FCSH/NOVA. She teaches history and has published widely on Portuguese colonialism.
This work is financed by FEDER through the 'Programa Operacional Factores de Competitividade – COMPETE' and by national Funds through the 'FCT – Fundação para a Ciência e a Tecnologia' within the project UID/HIS/04209/2013.

[2] Beside others, Prata, Ana 'Porto Grande of S. Vicente: The Coal Business on an Atlantic Island' in Bosa, Miguel Suárez (ed.), *Atlantic Ports and the First Globalisation c. 1850-1930* (Palgrave Macmillan, 2014) pp. 49-69, Pires, Francisca Gomes, 'O Porto Grande e a Urbe Mindelense na Aurora da Contemporaneidade (1850-1914)', Masters dissertation in Contemporary History, FCSH, 2014

here—eight in Praia da Matiota (Matiota Beach) in Porto Grande and the other one in Praia de São Pedro.

Coal and cables were the main elements of São Vicente in both economic and societal terms. In fact, these establishments belonged to the British, and some people from Britain settled. They constituted a separate group in society, having their own church, cemetery, sports associations and their own masonry (*British Exiles*). In fact, there were many foreigners of which the British community was the largest. Indeed, in 1879 the British constituted 86 of the 114 foreigners in the region.[3]

Despite its minor political and administrative importance (the capital of the archipelago was Praia, in the island of Santiago), Mindelo was the most developed settlement[4] and the consular delegations were established here.[5] The British consulate in Mindelo existed for a long time. During the Great War, the person in charge of it was Captain Arthur Trevelyan Taylor [1911-1921]. The German Consul used to be Augusto Vera Cruz, a local trader and politician, but he dismissed himself in September 1914 and at the start of World War I, in the same month, Eric Klinger arrived in Mindelo to represent German interests in the region.[6]

From 1914 to 1918 three Governors ruled Cape Verde. At the beginning of the war, the person in charge was Commander Júdice Bicker, appointed in 1911. He left the archipelago in

---

[3] Oliveira, João Nobre de, *A Imprensa Cobo-Verdiana. 1820-1975* (Fundação Macau, 1998) pp. 102-103, Reis, Célia, 'Cabo Verde', in Marques, AH de Oliveira (ed.), *O Império Africano. 1890-1930*, vol. XI of *Nova História da Expansão Portuguesa* (Editorial Estampa, 2001) p. 112, Medina, Lia, 'Evolução demográfica da Ilha de São Vicente. Do Descobrimento a 1950', Masters dissertation in Sociology and Demography, ISCTE IUL, 2009, p. 53, Pires, Francisca Gomes, 'O Porto Grande e a Urbe Mindelense na Aurora da Contemporaneidade (1850-1914)', mainly pp. 55-59. Descriptions of St Vincent in Routledge, Katherine, *The Mistery of Easter Island* (Cosimo, 2007) pp. 27-30

[4] http://bdigital.cv.unipiaget.org:8080/dspace/bitstream/10964/261/1/8-5-Cabo_Verde_entre_os_seculos_XIX_e_XX.pdf (consulted 21/4/2016), Barros. Marília E. Lima Barros, *S: Vicente: Prosperidade e Decadência (1850-1918)* (Centro de Estudos Africanos. Universidade do Porto) (accessed on line http://www.africanos.eu/ceaup/uploads/WP_2008_03.pdf (consulted 1/4/2016).

[5] Monteiro, Ana Rita Amaro, 'O Movimento Consular em Cabo verde nos Finais do Século XIX', *Africana*, n.º especial, 4 (1996) pp. 113-124, Pires, Francisca Gomes, 'O Porto Grande e a Urbe Mindelense na Aurora da Contemporaneidade (1850-1914) p. 38

[6] Process in Arquivo Histórico Ultramarino (Overseas Historic Archive) (AHU), 9/708 CCart002187

September 1915, when the new authority, Commander Abel Fontoura da Costa, arrived. In March 1918, because of the Revolution in Portugal and the change of government in Lisbon, now led by Sidónio Pais, Teófilo Duarte started governing the islands.

The beginning of the conflict

The Governor of Cape Verde knew about the Declaration of War in August 1914 from the Bristish Consul. In Porto Grande, there were two German merchant vessels and, Júdice Biker, feeling insecure about the right procedures on this occasion, requested guidance from the Ministry.[7] Four days later, he asked the Minister for a warship, to ensure neutrality, but the Government in Lisbon could not provide assistance.[8]

The Central Government also wanted to avoid conflict at this stage, so the Ministry ordered the colonies to ensure that if any ship of a belligerent nation entered any port, it could not stay for more than 24 hours, except in the case of British vessels.[9] In fact, some British ships remained in São Vicente, fearing the German cruisers.[10]

This order only applied to warships, not to the merchant fleet,[11] and at the beginning of the war, eight German merchant vessels docked at Porto Grande. Their names were *Beta, Burgmeister-Hachmann, Dora Horn, Heimburg, Santa Bárbara, Theoder Wille, Fogo,* and *Wurzburg.*

Besides the Consul, the crews of these ships were the only German people within the archipelago.[12] Another 14 seamen, including two officials, joined them when they were caught by the British at sea, and then handed over to the Consul's responsibility. The Consul accommodated them in the ships anchored in the port. In February 1916 they were still on board these ships.[13]

[7] AHU, 9/795 CCart 42064, telegram Governor of Cape Verde (GCV) to Ministro das Colónias (MC), 5 Aug 1914

[8] AHU, 9/795 CCart 4207, telegram GCV to MC, 5 Aug 1914, and information from Direção Geral das Colónias (DGC), 12 Aug 1914

[9] AHU, 9/765 CCart 4167, telegram MC to governors of colonies, 11/12 Aug 1914

[10] AHU, 9/765 CCart4199, telegram GCV to MC, 15 and 29 Dec 1914

[11] AHU, 9/795 CCart 4304, telegram (confidential) MC to GCV, 13 Sep 1914

[12] AHU, 9/765 CCart4199, telegram GCV to MC, 29 Dec 1914

On the ship *Wurzburg*, the Germans published their own journal, the *Kapverdische Schiffs Zeitung*. After 3 October 1914, the proceeds were given to the German Red Cross, but the appeal to national pride was perceived as a threat.[14]

When anchored in the harbour, all the ships had to respect international convention and to lower the TSF antennas.[15] The British resisted the intimidation, especially the cruiser *Carseravon*, and the Governor wrote to Lisbon, looking for guidance. The Portuguese Minister, after consideration, refused the British use of telegraphy. This situation began when the crew of the *Heimburg* attempted to hoist its antenna and the Portuguese guards objected. The Government had to authorise the marine authority to close and seal the cabin.[16]

But this was only one of many problems. The British were suspicious that the Germans would cut the submarine cables, so the Governor forbade naval navigation at night in the area and entrusted the Portuguese cruiser *São Gabriel* to monitor.[17]

The British Consul intensified his pressure over the Portuguese authority with telegrams from London, inquiring about the possibility of an attack carried out by the German crews, and seeking Portuguese protection of their interests. However, the Portuguese forces were weak, with only 56 police officers and 11 local soldiers. The Governor asked for more men and a ship and authorisation to inspect the German ships for arms.[18] Following this, the gunboat *Ibo* and the cruiser *São Gabriel* left for São Vicente, but the search for German ships was complicated. Despite the compliance of the Overseas Minister, the German Consul refused to be of any assistance and the Foreign Office gave up on the idea.[19] Thus, the Germans

---

[13] AHU, 9/967 CCart 5929, letter GCV to MC, 25 Feb 1916 Information about the capture in AHU, 9/765, CCart 4230, telegrams GCV to MC, 24 and 29 Aug 1914

[14] Oliveira, João Nobre de, *A Imprensa Cabo-Verdiana*, 293-294

[15] AHU, 9/795 CCart 4205, telegram GCV to MC, 7 Aug 1914

[16] AHU, 9/765 CCart 4231, telegram GCV to MC, 12 Aug 1914 and information from DGC, 13 Aug 1914

[17] AHU, 9/765, CCart 4203, telegram GCV to Ultramar, 30 Sep 1914

[18] AHU, 9/765, CCart 4230, telegram DGC, 10 Sep 1914, letter Direção Geral dos Negócios Políticos e Diplomáticos (DGNPD) to Diretor Geral das Colónias (DrGC), 9 Sep 1914. 9/765, CCart 4232, telegrams GCV to MC, 4 and 5/6 Sep 1914 and from DGC, 10 Sep 1914, information from DGC, 5 Sep 1914

[19] AHU, 9/765 CCart 4230, telegram from DGC, 10 Sep 1914, letter DGNPD to

posed a danger to British interests, and the local Consul intensified pressure over the Portuguese, despite Portugal's neutral position.[20]

In December 1915, another suspicion arose. A Dane called Flechtemberg arrived from America to buy the wolfram transported by the ship *Heimburg* and to carry it to the United States. However, suspecting he was German, the British delegation in Lisbon delivered a memorandum to the Portuguese Foreign Office asking for the interdiction of these transfers. In Mindelo, the Consul had already warned the Governor. However, Flechtemberg was travelling with an American passport, legalised by the British consulate in New York, and his identification was valid. In spite of the information, the Consul retained his doubts, especially because Flechtemberg was often seen with Klinger, the representative of the German Government. Flechtemberg left Cape Verde in a passenger ship, but a British cruiser captured him and transported him back to São Vicente as a prisoner on a war vessel, from where he transported to England. American interests pressured the Portuguese Government to obtain the wolfram but the British insisted that it should not be delivered.[21]

External defence was a problem for the Portuguese authorities because of its weakness in terms of arms and men. Twelve marines and an official arrived in November 1915, but it was not enough, especially when there were suspicions of submarines in the proximity. The naval forces were few and this situation reduced the Portuguese *de facto* sovereignty, given that it was the British Cruiser HSM *Highflyer* that was guaranteeing the island's defence. When this vessel left Cape Verde, the situation worsened, causing the Governor to insist upon the necessity of new ships to defend the archipelago.[22]

Meanwhile, in October, the British discovered two tanks of oil in Santa Luzia. In spite of being almost empty, they were clean

---

DrGC, 9 Sep 1914, 9/765, CCart 4232, telegrams GCV to MC, 4 and 5/6 Sep 1914 and from DGC, 10 Sep 1914, information from DGC, 5 Sep 1914

[20] This climate was also reported in Grant, Heathcoast S, *My war at sea, 1914-1916* (ebook, ed. Mark Tanner, http://warletters.net/wpcontent/uploads/2014/06/My-War-at-Sea-1914%E2%80%931916.pdf, (consulted 21/4/2016)

[21] AHU, 9/758 CC 3781, letters DGNCC to DrGC, 6 Dec 1915, 3 Mar and 3 Jun 1916, telegrams GCV to MC, 12 and 14 Dec 1915, 29 May and 21 Jun 1916

[22] AHU, 9/707 CC 2159, telegram (confidential) GCV to MC, 27 Oct 1915

and in good condition, possibly because of their use by German submarines. Given that German crews frequently used to be away, suspicions about the presence of German submarines grew. With permission from the Portuguese authorities, a delegation, with an English officer, went to Santa Luzia, to verify the situation. Afterwards, the British Minister in Lisbon thanked the Portuguese authorities for their collaboration.[23]

Portuguese cooperation occurred yet again with permission to keep the two captured ships *Kankee* and *President Mitre* in São Vicente.[24]

The local population

Whilst living in the town, the Germans established links with the locals and looked upon them with sympathy. As the Governor noticed, there was a clear feeling of hospitality favourable to the Germans[25] on an island with so many British interests. This situation was problematic because the Portuguese Government was preparing the country to enter the war. So, in order to prevent any hardships, the Governor banned a ball in a house trimmed with Portuguese and German flags at Christmas, 1915.[26]

This state of things increased British suspicions, and, even in September 1916, again through their Minister in Lisbon, they showed their misgivings about Aníbal Rocha, a Portuguese hotel owner, who had close relations with the Germans.[27] However, local investigations concluded that they were engaged in a mere commercial relationship.[28]

It was in this environment that, in January 1916, some of the workers of the coal companies decided to strike, demanding better payment considering that the workload had increased. The demands were accepted by the local authorities, but were dependent on the directors of the firms. However, there were

---

[23] AHU, 9/707 CCont. 2159, copy of letter British minister in Lisbon, 11 Dec 1915; letter (confidential) DGNPD to MC, 18 Dec 1915
[24] Process in AHU, 9/758 CC 3779
[25] AHU, ACL SEMU DGU cx 160, letter (confidential) GCV, 9 Mar 1916
[26] AHU, ACL SEMU DGU cx 160, letters GCV to MC, 19 Apr 1916, and confidential, 9 Mar 1916
[27] AHU, 9/764, CCart 4313, letter DGNPD to DrGC, 2 Sep 1916
[28] AHU, 9/764, CCart 4313, letter (confidential) GCV to MC, 6 Oct 1916

signals indicating the possibility of other strikes and, to avoid any problem, the Governor moved from Praia to Mindelo.[29]

The requisition of the ships

The Allies needed means of transportation and asked the Portuguese Government to commandeer the German ships anchored in their ports, which occurred on 24 February 1916. As mentioned above, there were eight vessels moored in Porto Grande, which were occupied by Portuguese forces during the day. A question of sovereignty was posed when the British cruiser *Highflyer* entered the harbour offering help, which the Portuguese Governor did not accept.[30]

Ships and cargo were searched and products like corn were sold to avoid its deterioration. Goods which could be used in other countries were sent accordingly.[31] These boats then received Portuguese names, as can be seen in the following table:

German name	Portuguese name
Beta	Maio
Burgmeister-Hachmann	Ilha do Fogo
Dora Horn	S. Nicolau
Heimburg	Santo Antão
Santa Bárbara	Santiago
Theoder Wille	Boa Vista
Fogo	Brava
Wurzburg	S. Vicente

Of the crews, 225 members (including 65 officials) were landed[32] and lodged in the Military Hospital and in three houses in the town. The Overseas Office ordered the Governors of all colonies with German citizens in the same situation to prevent their departure without, however, formally forbidding it. This was a response to the attitude of the German Government of restricting the exit of the Portuguese citizens.[33]

---

[29] AHU, ACL SEMU DGU cx. 160, letter GCV, 21 Jan 1916
[30] AHU, 9/758, CCart 3778, letter GCV, 28 Feb 1916
[31] AHU, 758 1H MU DGFTO, CCont. 3754, 758 1H MU DGFTO, CCont. 3777, 9/650 CCart 376, some documents
[32] AHU, 9/758, CCart 3778
[33] AHU, 9/707 CCart 2161, information from DGC, 2 Mar 1915

The British naval base

In the Atlantic waters from the Canary Islands to South America, the 9th Cruiser Squadron was responsible for the surveillance and protection of ships from German attack. São Vicente was visited many times by these ships, including the *Highflyer*.[34] The British used to cruise the area and convoy vessels, but in Porto Grande the boats were always anchored.[35]

By 16 March 1916, Porto Grande had become the base of the British Squadron. Over the next months until 19 December, there were always some ships of this Squadron, commanded by Rear-Admiral Sir Gordon Moore and later, from 30 August by Sydney R Fremantle.[36]

The British and Germans in São Vicente

The Portuguese situation changed in March 1916, with the declaration of war. After that, the preparation of the army and diplomatic relations as an ally intensified. Naturally, this moment had repercussions in São Vicente when the 225 German men became enemies and a naval force of an ally was formally established in the harbour. This last situation represented a special problem for Portuguese sovereignty, increasing pressures on its authorities, because of defence and the German presence.[37]

In April, the British Foreign Office and its Consul demanded the inspection of the German ships by a British engineer. The Governor tried to avoid this, but did not have technical personnel to do the work. The issue was discussed between the Foreign and Colonial Offices and an inspection took place, with the consequence that the ships could not sail because they needed distributors. More significantly, the Governor concluded that more demands would follow and, accepting his own

---

[34] As we can see in http://www.naval-history.net/OWShips-WW1-05-HMS_Highflyer.htm (consulted 24/4/2016)

[35] Inso, Jaime do, *A Marinha Portuguesa na Grande Guerra*, (Edições Culturais da Marinha, 2006) p. 21

[36] About this squadron, http://www.dreadnoughtproject.org/tfs/index.php/Ninth_Cruiser_Squadron_(Royal_Navy) (consulted 24/4/2016)

[37] AHU, 9/758 CC 3780, letters GCV to MC, 19 Apr and 2 May 1916, telegram MC to GCV, 22 Apr 1916, letter DGNCC to DrGC, 1 May 1916

responsibilities, started fearing the implications those demands would have on Portugal.

The danger of German presence

The presence of Germans constituted a security problem when the permanent military forces weakened—only 49 men and marines from the gunboat *Beira* were available. The Governor therefore took preventive measures by replacing the forces, looking for volunteers to watch the streets and ordering a 9 p.m. curfew.[38] But these measures did not please the inhabitants of the island and the Governor, knowing this, asked for authorisation to declare emergency rule when necessary. This happened on 25 March,[39] but was only the beginning. In fact, the presence of Germans in São Vicente continued to be a problem for the authorities. At the end of March, the American cruiser *Chester* anchored in Porto Grande and the crew established contact with the Germans, giving them money and buying them drinks. The American and German crews sang the German national anthem together. According to the Governor, he feared these contacts, because the American crews could offer guns to the Germans, and so he decided to intensify the preventive measures, inviting the inhabitants to stay at their houses after 9 p.m. and volunteers to take positions to defend foreign property, mainly the telegraph stations and the coal depots. At the suggestion of the British Rear-Admiral, the lights of the ships and of the town were turned off.[40]

All this intensified local protests,[41] even in the Portuguese Parliament.[42] As a result, the Governor considered it necessary to implement more intense measures by suspending citizens' warranties and establishing press censorship. Locally, the political situation was difficult, with some people supporting the Governor and others standing against him.[43]

---

[38] AHU, ACL SEMU DGU cx. 160, letter (confidential) GCV, 9 Mar 1916
[39] *Diário da Câmara dos Deputados (DCD)*, n. 66, 5 Apr 1916 (on line http://debates.parlamento.pt/)
[40] AHU, ACL SEMU DGU cx 160, letter GCV, 19 Apr 1916, 9/647 CCart 7222.
[41] AHU, 9/647 CCart 7222 and ACL SEMU DGU cx 160, Protest, 10 Apr 1916
[42] *DCD*, n. 66, 5 Apr 1916
[43] AHU, ACL SEMU DGU cx 160, letters GCV, 19 and 29 Apr 1916. Oliveira, João Nobre de, *A Imprensa Cabo-Verdiana*, 295-6

The warrants were issued one month later,[44] in spite of the opinion of the British Rear-Admiral.[45] In this situation, it is understandable that local opposition increased after the declaration of war, fuelled by the fact that active preventive measures were not applied to the other islands.

The authorities still needed to consider the problem of the German presence in São Vicente, given that the Germans could instigate incidents affecting British interests, start a political movement or other occurrence. In Lisbon, already in March, the service of Maritime Transport suggested the complete removal of Germans from Cape Verde, but this idea failed because all the ships passing by the archipelago had no capacity to accommodate them. For the Governor, the solution was to shift them to the other islands, and, in fact, they were transported to Santiago and São Nicolau.[46] This was a moment of change for the British sailors: to avoid any problems, they had not left their ships for nine months and now they could enter the town.

Even with the removal of the Germans, the local Governor and the British authorities insisted on their complete departure from the archipelago. The Germans finally left Cape Verde at the end of July in a Portuguese cruiser, *Pedro Nunes*, sent specifically to get them, and other Germans in Funchal, and to transport them all to Angra do Heroísmo, Azores.[47]

The German ex-Consul remained in Mindelo. After the declaration of war, when the Governor thought about making him leave the archipelago, instructions from Lisbon were given for him to stay with a provision of food and accommodation, because the Foreign Office was negotiating the exchange of German and Portuguese consular representatives. A little after, the Colonial Office forbade his departure, and he stayed under surveillance of the police. But the Governor and the British commanders requested his departure, because he was sending

---

[44] *DCD*, n. 93, 19 May 1916, 23-4

[45] AHU, ACL SEMU DGU cx. 160, telegrama 22 Apr 1916

[46] AHU, 9/758 CC 3778, letter Presidente da Comissão Administração do Serviço de Transportes Marítimos, 17 Mar 1916, copy of telegram GCV to MC, 27 May 1916. 9/764 CCart 3700, letter GCV to MC, 17 Jun 1916; CCart 4301, letter GCV to MC, 11 Jul 1916

[47] AHU, 9/764, CCart 4301, letter GCV to MC, 11 Jul 1916, telegrams MC to GCV, 4 Jul 1916, GCV to MC, 7 Jul 1916. 9/764 CCart 3700, letter GCV to MC, 17 Jun 1916. 9/765, CCart 3760, letter GCV to MC, 7 Jun 1916

information to Germany using neutral ships. Indeed, the British authorities not only pressured the local responsible, but also the central government. In Lisbon, his representative showed the Foreign Office the dangers of having the German ex-Consul in Cape Verde, however, by then, the Governor had already prepared for the departure of Erich Klingler in a ship that left São Vicente on 2 September 1916.[48]

The British squadron and local defence

As the Governor thought, the British presence meant a great pressure. The Rear-Admiral wanted better surveillance over the channel and the harbour, but in May there was only a Portuguese gunboat, *Beira*, and it was impossible for this boat to ensure all of this. Trying to avoid the use of the British vessels for this work, the Governor requested more ships, but the Marine Office did not have the means to answer his request.[49] In July, when the gunboat had to go to Dakar for repair, there was no other solution than to allow surveillance by British vessels, with a clear loss of sovereignty.[50]

It was after this event that the gunboat *Ibo* went to Cape Verde.[51] In consequence, the base was protected by the Portuguese gunboats *Ibo* and *Beira*, resulting in close contacts between their commandants, respectively lieutenants Corrêa da Silva and Cisneros de Faria, and the British Rear-Admirals. The first of them was Sir Gordon Moore, but, on 22 September, Rear-Admiral Sydney Fremantle arrived.[52]

It was this new Commandant, Fremantle, who asked for greater security. This was satisfied by using local artillery, and

---

[48] AHU, 9/764 CCart 4316, letter (confidential) DGNPD to DrGC, 20 Apr 1916. CCart 4316, telegram MC to GCV, 26 Apr 1916. CCart 3700, telegram GCV to MC, 19 Jun 1916. CCart 4301, letters GCV to MC, 11 and 27 Jul 1916 (in the same box, many telegrams about the exit of the Cônsul). CCart 4313, letter DGNPD to DrGC, 2 Sep 1916. CCart 4319, letter GCV to MC, 1 Sep 1916, telegram GCV to MC, 2 Sep 1916

[49] AHU, ACL SEMU DGU cx. 239, process 1916-18. 9/758 CC 3780, letter GCV to MC, 19 Apr 1916, letter GCV to MC, 2 May 1916, letter Major General da Armada to Diretor Geral das Colonias, 28 Apr 1916

[50] AHU, ACL SEMU DGU cx. 239, process 1916-26, letter GCV, 27 Aug 1916

[51] AHU, ACL SEMU DGU cx. 239, process 1916-26 e 28

[52] Silva, Henrique Corrêa da (Paço d'Arcos), *Memórias de Guerra no Mar* (Imprensa da Universidade, 1931) p. 58

a tugboat from a coal house with guns to police the bay. New harbour defences were established by putting up a garrison and armaments for Ilhéu (little island) dos Pássaros.

Cape Verde on the route of the submarines

On 28 September, Rear-Admiral Fremantle, Commandant of the Naval Division, conferred with the Governor because a German submarine was spotted 60 miles south of Cape Bojador. They decided to improve surveillance and other measures.[53] The proximity of the submarines showed the possibility of an attack, even to the English squadron, which left São Vicente, being redirected to Freetown, on 18 November. This was a moment of great consequence to the local economy, because, without the protection of the squadron, ships could not use the harbour. Besides this, orders from England forbade the sale of coal to ships that were not allies.

The submarines

At the beginning of December 1916 there were more sightings of submarines in the area, which were using the Canary Islands as their clandestine base. After the sightings, whether true or fabricated, they eventually appeared in the archipelago.

The gunboat *Ibo* spotted a submarine near São Vicente perhaps intending to destroy the telegraph cables. *Ibo* fired, other ships helped, but the submarine, perhaps U-47, manoeuvred and avoided being hit. This spotting alarmed the local population, who feared an attack as something similar had occurred in Funchal a few days before. Military means were despatched as soon as possible for defence; soldiers who were returning from other colonies in the steamer *Mozambique* landed to protect the island and trenches were excavated. However, this submarine did not return. Furthermore, the Portuguese ships had another task: to intercept Greek vessels in the harbour. These new ships soon totalled nine.

On 9 February, another submarine navigated into the channel of São Vicente, but moved away when fired on from Ilhéu dos Pássaros, and the presence of *Ibo*.[54]

---

[53] AHU, ACL SEMU DGU cx. 239, process 1917-10, letters GCV, 8 Oct 1916, and 16 Mar 1917

[54] Silva Henrique Corrêa da, *Memórias de Guerra no Mar*, pp. 81-112

Meanwhile, during January the material and soldiers had arrived, albeit an insufficient number.[55] As a result, other means of sea and land defence were organised.[56]

On 2 November, when Brazilian vessels arrived at Porto Grande, whilst in transit to Europe, a submarine torpedoed two of them, the *Guahyba* and *Acary*. *Ibo* pursued the submarine, and sank it.

In the following days, the *Kemmerland*, a Dutch ship anchored in Porto Grande was suspected of serving Germany. The vessel had visited before, in July, and shipped to Buenos Aires and then to Brazil, from where it left for the Netherlands, and, at the same time as *Acary*, it berthed in São Vicente to load coal. The commandant of *Ibo* suspected it because the ship was already fully loaded. Suspicions grew when their signals to the German submarine were seen. During the afternoon of 1 November 1917 part of the crew landed and a sailor told a woman that she would soon see a submarine. Other members of the crew were touring in a little boat. In addition, men from the crews of the previously commandeered ships were recognised.[57]

Because of this situation, the Governor sent a military force to the *Kemmerland* to stop them signalling. But, as the signals continued, the Commandant of the *Ibo* insisted on arresting the crew; his insistence forced the Governor to do so, accommodating the crew in a hotel and a house. After that, on the 7th, the submarine appeared near the *Kemmerland* and stayed in the area for the next few days. The attitude of Commandant Corrêa da Silva led to an enquiry which caused a diplomatic incident, with protests from the Dutch Government. The *Kemmerland* remained in Porto Grande until April.[58]

Another misgiving occurred when the Spanish steamer, *Balmes*, arrived on 6 November. Besides some signals made by

---

[55] AHU, 9/650 CCart 7493, information DGC, 23 Dec 1916. SEMU DGU cx. 239, process 1916-33, letters (confidential) GCV, 3 and 16 Jan 1917

[56] Silva Henrique Corrêa da, *Memórias de Guerra no Mar*, 77, pp. 109, 128-9

[57] AHU, 9/625, CCart 6340, telegrams GCV to MC, 11 and 29 Nov 1917, letter GCV to MC, 29 Nov 1917, testimony of lieutenant Henrique Monteiro Corrêa da Silva, copy of declarations of Brazilian consular agent, 11 Nov 1917

[58] AHU, 9/625, CCart6340, telegram GCV to MC, 29 Nov 1917, letter (confidential) GCV to MC, 11 Nov 1917, and others, telegrams MC to GCV, 24 and 28 Nov 1917, and others; p. 615 1H MU DGFTO, telegram GCV to MC, Apr 25, 1918. Silva Henrique Corrêa da, *Memórias de Guerra no Mar*, pp. 121-2, 140-91

the ship, some members of the crew dived near the Brazilian vessels. But *Balmes* departed the following day.[59]

As a result of these incidents, the defence of São Vicente was intensified,[60] but the danger did not stop, and more submarines were seen near the archipelago, obliging the Government to send a further gunboat and more armaments, albeit too late.[61]

Other questions with the British

The British raised yet another sovereignty issue. On the day the Brazilian vessels were torpedoed, the honour of the Portuguese nation was smirched during a ball, in the house of the Submarine Cable. The reason for this was the weakness of the Portuguese defence, but the British also mentioned Portuguese cowardice. In defence, Commandant Corrêa da Silva, reminded the British of his own efforts and repeated the appreciative words of the British Rear-Admirals. The Consul apologised for the situation verbally and by letter.[62]

Another problem was the lack of coal. In March 1917 there was a shortage and the Governor asked for the services of the central Government in negotiating with England. The situation was worse the following year, almost without stock.[63] Naturally, the situation was related to the abandonment of the harbour by almost every British ship, which caused a local crisis. But, if the information given by the Governor was right, it was not only the British ships abandoning the harbour, but also ships from other allied nations: according to the news, two Dutch steamers with coal heading to Cape Verde were stopped in the USA, and could only leave that territory with the compromise of returning with goods from South America instead. The Governor objected to the discriminative attitude of the Allies, because they were

---

[59] AHU, 9/625, CCart6340, copy testimony of Brazilian consular agent, 11 Nov 1917

[60] AHU, 9/774 CCart 4490

[61] AHU, 615 1H MU DGFTO, telegram GCV to MC, Apr 12, 1918, letter Majoria General da Armada to DrGC, 1 May 1918. 9/772, CCart 4285, report, 13 Apr, 1918

[62] AHU, 9/625, CCart 6340, copy letter Commandant of Gunboat, 10 Nov 1917; Silva, Henrique Corrêa da, *Memórias de Guerra no Mar*, pp. 143-147

[63] AHU, 9/761 CCart 4059, telegram GCV to MC, 5 Mar 1917. 9/761 CCart 4059, telegram GCV to MC, 5 Mar 1917. 9/625, CCart 6333, information DGC, 8 Apr 1918. 9/875 CCart 6000, telegram GCV, 17 Jun 1918

protecting Dakar and neglecting São Vicente, both in commercial and defensive terms.[64]

Later, with new means and a new attitude from the British, it was possible to organize convoys of ships from Cape Verde, alternating with Dakar and Freetown. This happened in September 1918, but there was not another convoy because, fortunately, the war ended.[65]

Local populations

The attitude of the local population of São Vicente created difficulties for local authorities, as mentioned above. Hostility was maintained during the months of vigilance and work of the gunboats, as Corrêa da Silva wrote. According to his description, except at the beginning of December 1916, when people feared an attack such as the one on Funchal, the locals never took the Portuguese manoeuvres seriously. There were even incidents between the Portuguese crews and the local residents and the British never landed.

Conclusion

Because of its locality, Cape Verde was an intersecting zone of two spaces in the same war: in the south, there was the war in Africa, in colonised space; in the north, there was the European war (and one of its instruments, the submarine, reached the archipelago).

In the four years of the war, there were different phases in Cape Verde, reflecting the politics of Portugal. at the beginning, it was neutral, in 1916 it become belligerent. The main concerns of the Governor were in accord with these diverse positions. The presence of Germans in São Vincente also changed.

However, the situation of São Vincente was special, because of British interests. Thus, the actions and intentions of the Governor sought a balance, sometimes with great difficulty, between British pressures, on one side, and the defence of Portuguese sovereign power, on the other. The last was increasingly problematic because of the combination of several conditions. The military weakness of the Portuguese in the

---

[64] AHU, 9/650 CCart 7724, letter (confidential) GCV to MC, 2 Dec 1917, information from DGC, 18 Dec 1917

[65] Inso, Jaime do, *A Marinha Portuguesa na Grande Guerra*, p. 132

island, where men and weapons were in short supply, justify British intentions to participate in its defence. But in the past, Britain had highlighted the vulnerability of the Portuguese colonies in confrontation with the great powers, and the local authorities had to refuse, until it was impossible, the contribution of the foreign military forces. Besides that, the opposition of local populations against the British and the institutional position of the colony, without the desired autonomy, reflected on the close relationship with the Germans. Another problem was the economic situation of the colony, motivated by the elementary shortages and as a result, by the removal of the main recourse of São Vincente, the navigation in its port.

The British and their economic interests in the island of São Vincente were vitally important for local life. During the Great War, the Portuguese authorities had to face its interference while struggling to keep national sovereignty.

Diversity in Adversity: The British in Egypt during the First World War

Lanver Mak, FRHS[1]

One country in Africa that was very important in safeguarding British interests during the First World War was Egypt. It was a vital launching pad for British military operations in the region. The security of the Suez Canal was paramount for the smooth passage of British ships, supplies, and troops from the Empire to the European front. Although Egypt was for all intents and purposes ruled by the British Consul-General and his officials since 1882, it was still formally under the sovereignty of the Ottoman Empire—a German ally. Thus at the outset of the war, Britain promptly established Egypt as a British Protectorate in order to secure its interests in Egypt from enemy powers. Within this context, this chapter seeks to add to the historiography of the small yet prominent British community during the war. Drawing from census and court records, private papers, and business, newspaper, military, church and missionary archives, this work examines the diverse roles and reactions of the British in Egypt to the challenges posed by the First World War. Men joined the war effort in Europe or stayed behind in key jobs while women served as volunteers, nurses and hostesses. Some opposed certain government initiatives such as the requisitioning of Victoria College while others decried the criteria to forgo retirement in Britain in order to purchase tax-free war bonds. Egypt's Britons also

---

[1] Lanver Mak, FRHS has taught in the Middle East and has been visiting fellow at the Institute of Commonwealth Studies, University of London. *Author's note*: This work is based on part a chapter in my book, *The British in Egypt: Community, Crime and Crises, 1882-1922* (IB Tauris, 2012). I thank IB Tauris for permission to adapt the material here.

experienced diverse economic realities during the war— prosperity due to the economic boom, missed opportunities in light of the restrictions on German and Austrian firms, and hardship due to inflation. It is hoped that this discussion will add to the historiography of the British Empire in Africa during the Great War.

Before launching into the crux of this account of the diverse roles and reactions among the British in Egypt during the First World War, it may help to mention the demographic challenge of defining the British community in Egypt at this time. According to the 1917 census, there were about 3,200 Britons from Britain in Cairo, a slightly smaller number in Alexandria and around 9,000 in all of Egypt.[2] Military personnel were not accounted for in the 1917 census due most likely to their temporary status and their enormous number in Egypt at the time. Figures suggest that by the end of the war, as many as 300,000 to 400,000 troops under Britain's imperial command may have entered Egypt though not all were there at the same time.[3] Also, a proportion of these troops under British command were not ethnically English, Scottish or Welsh, but were from countries under Britain's colonial tutelage such as India. The problem in determining the exact number of Britons in Egypt during the war is due to the fact that many of the newly arrived British troops and nurses became part of the community of longer-term British residents. This group of British military and support personnel were new to Egypt because the troops who were in Egypt prior to the war had almost all been sent to fight in Europe. A fair number of British officers participated in balls, dances and events and became prominent members of Egypt's British community. The lower class rank and file, though excluded from the high society events, attended British church services and were regularly invited into homes of British residents. Since the community included British civilians and new military and support personnel, simply narrowing the

---

[2] Census of Egypt, 1917, Table VII, p. 482

[3] Jeffrey, Keith, *The British Army and the Crisis of Empire, 1918-1922* (Manchester University, 1984) p. 113, suggests that about 400,000 Imperial troops entered Egypt during the First World War. Porter, Brian, 'Britain and the Middle East in the Great War' in Peter Liddle, (ed.), *Home Fires and Foreign Fields, British Social and Military Experience in the First World War* (Brassey's Defence, 1985) p. 162, estimates that 300,000 Imperial troops entered Egypt during that time.

British population to around 3,000 in Cairo and a total of 9,000 in Egypt may not be the most precise depiction of the community's size. Though it may not be possible to determine the exact population of the British community at this time, it is possible, from private diaries and memoirs, newspaper archives and other records, to observe the community's diverse roles, viewpoints and economic challenges.

Diversity of Roles for British Men

In 1914, there were two British led armies in Egypt—the Army of Occupation headquartered in Cairo and the Egyptian Army based in various posts in Egypt, the Sinai and the Sudan. The 5,000 troops of the Army of Occupation were mostly ethnically British, except for one Indian mounted battery.[4] The Egyptian Army consisted mainly of Egyptians but was primarily led by British officers. However, after the declaration of war, almost every regiment of the Army of Occupation withdrew from Egypt and returned to Britain to fight in Europe since they were already well trained and ready for battle. British officers of the Egyptian Army joined the war effort in Europe as well, though the bulk of Egyptian Army's rank and file remained at their posts.[5] This sudden exodus of British military personnel affected the British community in Egypt. Many of these officers had regularly attended the British churches, participated in British sporting and recreational activities and frequented the clubs and hotel dances of Cairo and Alexandria during the winter season. Perhaps more painfully for their families, the troops' hurried withdrawal meant that their families were abandoned in Egypt, and left to wait until they could return to Britain. One British soldier, who came to Egypt to replace the

---

[4] Macpherson, WG, *Medical Services General History*, III (HMSO, 1924), 363 and MacMunn, George & Falls, Cyril, *Military Operations Egypt and Palestine* (HMSO, 1928) p. 11, states the actual composition of the troops in the Army of Occupation just before World War I. It consisted of a regiment of cavalry (3rd Dragoon Guards), a battery of artillery ('T' Battery, Royal Horse Artillery), a mounted battery (7th Indian Mountain Battery, Royal Garrison Artillery), five battalions of infantry (1st and 2nd Battalion Devonshire Regiment, 1st Worcestershire, 2nd Northamptonshire, 2nd Gordon Highlanders) and companies or detachments of Royal Engineers, Army Services Corp, Royal Army Medical Corps, and Army Veterinarian Corps.

[5] Keown-Boyd, Henry, *Soldiers of the Nile: A Biographical History of the British Officers of the Egyptian Army* (Thornbury, 1996) p. 9

departed forces, recorded that the families of these men who were now fighting in Europe

> were left behind here ... There were 15 or 20 English folk ... mostly wives of the Northamptons (We relieved the Northampton Regiment ... [These] married women and children still occupy a large section of the barracks, and that is why some of us are in tents ... [one family] takes up quarters that accommodate 19 of our fellows.[6]

For British men in Egypt who were not part of the Army of Occupation or the Egyptian Army and were eligible to fight, they were urged to join the war effort. After Britain declared war on Germany, Lord Kitchener, who left his post as the British Consul-General of Egypt to become the Secretary of State for War, issued a call for 100,000 new soldiers to reinforce the 200,000 already in the regular army.[7] Initially, only British men with previous military experience or who were 'athletic and well-educated English gentlemen'[8] from public schools were encouraged to participate in the war effort. Many of them volunteered because 'theirs was an interest well worth protecting.'[9] The British upper and middle classes, whether made rich by tradition, London-based commerce or manufacturing in the North of England, accumulated vast amounts of wealth during the last decades of the nineteenth-century through the booming export trade and overseas investments.[10] Since many of the men in Egypt's British community belonged to the privileged classes, their volunteering for the war effort was natural and immediate. Defeat at the hands of Germany not only threatened the Empire but their wealth and livelihoods as well. Besides economic concerns, a sense of urgency, securing the well-being of their families, and the nationalistic fervour of the time motivated them.[11] They were from a diverse array of 'Government

---

[6] National Army Museum, Sergeant Harry Hopwood, Battalion orderly sergeant of the East Lancashire Brigade, later of 2nd Volunteer Battalion of Manchester Regiment, private letters to his mother, 28/11/1914

[7] Keegan, John, 'Foreword' in Ian Beckett & Keith Simpson (eds.), *A Nation in Arms: A Social History of the British Army in the First World War* (Manchester University, 1985) pp. viii, ix

[8] Egyptian Gazette, 28 September 1914

[9] Winter, Jay, 'Army and society: the demographic context' in Beckett & Simpson (eds.) p. 196

[10] Ibid.

services ... banks, and other commercial undertakings' such as policemen, journalists, businessmen, lawyers, educators,[12] and missionaries who became military chaplains.[13]

However important victory over Germany was, some Britons were not willing to join the war at all costs. Since the British authorities in Egypt did not publicly acknowledge that it would facilitate their officials' involvement in the war by retaining their jobs and giving them paid leave, many aspiring volunteers did not join the war effort at the risk of losing their jobs. They also kept quiet in fear of embarrassing the government by highlighting its perceived lack of commitment to the war evidenced by its unwillingness to guarantee their jobs. Finally, two months after Britain's declaration of war, 'the Government decided to grant leave to Anglo-Egyptian officials who wish to join the British army and will keep their posts open for them. [This] ... led to ... a rush of volunteers from Egypt.'[14] They were given full paid leave of between three and a half months to six months.[15]

Besides the government's guarantee of paid leave and postwar employment, the expensive travel also hindered the initial deployment of Egypt's Britons to serve in the war in Europe. A small number of these willing volunteers could not afford the passage to Britain and initially, 'no steps [were being] taken ... by the British community'[16] in Egypt to help, unlike the British community in Constantinople which provided a travel fund and an additional allowance for young men to return from Turkey to Britain to fight in the war.[17] However, by the summer of 1915, Mr Birley, acting President of the British Chamber of Commerce, announced that it would fund the cost of the passage to Britain for anyone who needed it.[18] With the promise of paid leave, post-war jobs and travel funding for all willing

---

[11] *Egyptian Gazette*, 1 Jun 1915
[12] Ibid., 25 Jan 1916
[13] Gairdner, Canon Temple, Secretary of Egypt Mission, *Church Missionary Review*, May, 1919, p. 70
[14] *Egyptian Gazette*, 2 Oct 1914
[15] Ibid., 2 Oct 1914
[16] Ibid., 1 Jun 1915
[17] Ibid.
[18] Ibid., 3 June 1915

volunteers, many Britons in Egypt joined the battlefront in Europe.

British men who stayed in Egypt

After Eldon Gorst became Consul-General in 1907, more opportunities were given to Egyptians in government jobs, yet certain Britons were still indispensable to the civil service. The government struggled to reconcile the requests of male staff to join the war effort 'with the imperative necessities of administration, and to hold the balance as evenly as possible.'[19] Also, certain businesses like the Anglo-Egyptian bank prevented specific personnel from joining the war effort in order to maintain its viability, as expressed by the bank's interim manager to his superior in London:

> Murray and Birch have been disputing as to which of the two has the prior right to go—I have told Birch that *he cannot possibly be spared* and I think he now understands this...As regards Moulson if you particularly wish him to go to Khartoum we will arrange to send him but we shall absolutely need someone to replace him. He is the *only* English man left on our staff, apart from the Chief Accountant and Cashier.[20]

The 1917 Military Services Act also made it possible for British men between 18 and 41 living abroad to be drafted. As a result, indispensable employees of government departments and other businesses had to be issued with consular certificates in order for them to be exempt from the draft. This exception was allowed only if their 'retention in the country in which they are at present . . . [is] considered of greater advantage to the common cause and to British commercial interests [according to] . . . His Majesty's Consular officers.'[21]

Despite this exemption, there was still a significant shortage of British workers in Egypt due to the many who had left to join the war effort. For example, the Ministry of Education was left desperately low on teaching staff since 'about fifty per cent of

---

[19] Ibid., 4 Sep 1917
[20] Barclays Group Archives, correspondences between Anglo-Egyptian staff and managers, letter from Arthur Blunt to HR Coombs, 9 Aug 1915 (emphasis mine)
[21] TNA: FO141/664/2476, letter from Robert Cecil to His Majesty's Representative in Cairo, 18 May 1917

the English staff ... served in His Majesty's forces. Most...were teachers in secondary schools.'[22] One example of this anxious search for staff was the appeal from Education Adviser Douglas Dunlop to High Commissioner Wingate for more passports for teachers from Britain to enter Egypt and also in his pursuit of a 53-year old teacher, named Charles Ashbee, who was beyond the age of military service.[23]

Besides the Ministry of Education, the Alexandria City Police was 'anxious to enlist Englishmen...owing to vacancies caused by the war,'[24] as immediate replacements. The Church Missionary Society also lost key missionaries particularly to military chaplaincies and 'these sacrifices, willingly made ... were heavy enough considering [their] none too great strength before the war.'[25] Moreover, with the potential changes in the Mixed Courts due to the possible abolition or downgrading of the Capitulations in light of Egypt's new identity as a British Protectorate, it was

> necessary to recruit more English lawyers ... However the Judicial Adviser Malcolm McIllwraith] scarcely knew how [he] could get men ... during the war [since] nearly all the best of the younger men are away from their work and in [a military] camp, somewhere or other.[26]

In spite of the effort to retain as many men as possible in key positions, the war severely crippled the British male workforce in Egypt and created job vacancies in many different sectors.

The roles of British women

Like the men, British women had various roles during the war as well. Although women did not engage in combat, they were instrumental as volunteer nurses, hostesses and organisers of events to help convalescing or restless soldiers pass their days in Egypt.

---

[22] Ibid., FO141/503/1604, letter Mr Hebard, Egyptian Education Mission, to Lloyd Lord, 4 Oct 1926

[23] Ibid., FO141/669/4394, letter Douglas Dunlop, Minister of Education to High Commissioner, 10 Feb 1917

[24] *Egyptian Gazette*, 29 Sep 1914

[25] Gairdner, Temple, 'The Nile Valley in War-Time: A Word to the Home Base' in *Church Missionary Gleaner*, XLVI, 543, May 1919, p. 70

[26] TNA, FO141/621/321, letter to Lord E Cecil from Malcolm McIllwraith, 31/01/1916

The Gallipoli campaign and Egypt's vital role as 'one big hospital'

In order to understand the significance of the work that the British women in Egypt had during the war, it is important to realise the enormity of the task that they faced as the casualties from the Gallipoli defeat invaded Egypt. Much has been written about this failed Allied effort in 1915 that consisted of regiments from Britain, Canada, Australia and New Zealand. It is sufficient to say here that the 'hastily planned, ill-coordinated, inadequately supplied, and badly led'[27] Allied campaign at Gallipoli was defeated by Ottoman forces. Casualties on both sides were staggering. The Ottoman casualties amounted to more than 250,000.[28] Out of the 500,000 men in the Allied force,[29] 45,000 Britons lost their lives.[30] More than 150,000 were wounded or captured. Many of the 90,000 sick and injured were evacuated by ship to Alexandria, turning Egypt into one vast hospital and rallying many of the women of Egypt's British community to active charitable service.

The Gallipoli casualties meant that Cairo and Alexandria became key centres for receiving ill or injured Allied soldiers.

> Few places presented greater facilities than Cairo and Alexandria for establishing hospitals in suitable buildings, and it was fortunate that this was so, as otherwise hospitals would have had to be pitched under canvas, exposed to the sand and dust of the desert, as was the experience in Sinai and Palestine.[31]

The requisition of buildings for hospital usage increased exponentially as the Gallipoli struggle raged on during 1915. In April 1915, only 200 beds were available for British officers while 3,780 were available for men of lower ranks in all of Egypt. By January 1916, there were 870 beds available for officers and 32,262 beds available for those in lower ranks.[32] A

---

[27] Adelson, Roger, *London and the Invention of the Middle East: Money, Power, and War, 1902-1922* (Yale University, 1995) p. 118

[28] Karsh, Efraim & Karsh, Inari, *Empires of the Sand: The Struggle for Mastery in the Middle East, 1789-1923* (Harvard University, 1999) pp. 144-145

[29] Ibid.

[30] Liddle, Peter, 'The Dardanelles Gallipoli campaign: concept and execution' in Peter Liddle, (ed.), *Home Fires and Foreign Fields*, p. 110

[31] MacPherson, p. 382

[32] Ibid.

similar pattern of growth occurred for the facilities available to Indian soldiers.[33] The British authorities in Egypt were trying desperately to transform nearly all suitable buildings into hospitals, acquire the services of existing hospitals, maximise the number of beds for patients and mobilise personnel to care for them. Egypt had truly 'now become one vast hospital.'[34] Though initially, 'it was evident that the estimated accommodation in Egypt for the sick and wounded off Gallipoli was far short of the actual requirements . . .in time, every wounded soldier had a bed.'[35]

Hospitals and hospitality: British women as volunteers, nurses and hostesses

Not only were the sick and injured from Gallipoli given hospital beds, they were taken care of by many of the women of the British community in Egypt. These volunteers followed the pattern of British women in Britain who joined the Voluntary Aid Detachments (VAD) and had to finance their own way through courses and exams on nursing, first aid, and hygiene. They funded themselves through the period of training in hospitals and were eventually paid only £20 per year—even less than some house servants who were paid, on average, £25 to £30 a year.[36] They learned to cram stretchers into makeshift wards; build successful rest stations; convert railway trucks into storehouses, packing-cases into furniture and condensed milk cans into mugs; and supply endless drinks and cigarettes to the dying, wounded, and ill British soldier.[37] Likewise, the British women of Egypt who volunteered and formed Egypt's VAD in the wake of the Gallipoli campaign also demonstrated this level of initiative and dedication but were unable to cope as the large numbers of dying, wounded and ill who flooded into Egypt from Gallipoli in the summer of 1915. The need to recruit more women was clearly evident.

---

[33] Ibid., in April 1915, 235 beds were available for Indian officers and 5,282 for lower ranks. By January 1916, 1,131 beds were available for Indian officers while 34, 874 were available for men of the lower ranks.
[34] Elgood, PG, *Egypt and the Army* (Oxford University, 1924) p. 170
[35] Ibid.
[36] Ouditt, Sharon, *Fighting Forces, Writing Women* (Routledge, 1994) p. 15
[37] Ibid., p. 13

When the terrible and unexpected Gallipoli casualties began to be brought back to Egypt, week by week . . . [the] Colonial and Voluntary Aid Detachment nurses . . . were far from proving sufficient. The requirements of the situation had, therefore, to be met by voluntary recruitment among the ladies of Cairo, Alexandria, and other towns and chiefly among the wives and daughters of the official and business classes. And most devotedly and whole-hearted-ly were these appeals to their patriotism and spirit of self-sacrifice responded to, though many of these ladies had plenty of domestic occupation at home.[38]

As a result of these appeals, more women of the British community in Egypt, mainly from Cairo and Alexandria, increased the ranks of the VAD to about 1,000 volunteers. Since military doctors were already overwhelmed with clinical and surgical duties, the women in the VAD were responsible for minor medical and non-medical needs of the patients from Gallipoli.[39] Instruction in Cairo and other centres was given to teach the art of bandaging and other elements of first aid. Many women, after a few weeks, became fairly proficient. Non-medical tasks included 'making beds, and serving in overheated canteens;'[40] cooking, preparing snacks and afternoon tea in the hospitals; and handing out cigarettes, writing paper, envelopes, pencils, handkerchiefs, books, pillows and walking sticks from hospital comfort stores which were managed by the British women volunteers.[41] Even 'when organisational break-downs . . . prevented the patients from receiving petty luxuries like picture-postcards and cigarettes, or basic necessities like razors, toothbrushes, and clean clothes, the . . . Englishwomen helped to supply the deficiencies.'[42] Outside the hospitals, the women worked in tea kiosks on the quays, met the ships bringing in the sick and wounded from Gallipoli, and assisted in hospital trains between Alexandria and Cairo. They provided 'tea and recreation rooms, entertainment, games, [and] literature,'[43] organised tram rides provided outings for 6,000

---

[38] *Egyptian Gazette*, Malcolm McIllwraith's comments, 4 Sep 1917
[39] Elgood, p. 144
[40] Ibid., 145
[41] Imperial War Museum Archives, Lady Rochdale, Diaries, 12 Jun 1915
[42] Brugger, Suzanne, *Australians and Egypt, 1914–1919* (Melbourne University, 1980) p. 54

patients each month in Alexandria,[44] and helped to trace the whereabouts of missing soldiers from Gallipoli.[45] In their mission 'to assist in alleviating as much as possible the suffering of the sick and wounded, and to assist the authorities in promoting the [soldiers'] well-being,'[46] the British women of Egypt served admirably and tirelessly.

Besides their hard work in the hospitals, British women were also indispensable in offering hospitality in their homes. In addition to the injured soldiers in hospitals, as many as 84,000 to 152,000 allied troops were assembled in Egypt during the war waiting to be deployed to the battlefront.[47] The first contingent of troops from Australia and New Zealand totalled 39,000 and the East Lancashire Territorials plus the Indian Army made the total count of troops around 84,000. By January 1916, after the final evacuation at Gallipoli, more than 64,000 troops from Australia and New Zealand were added, making the total force in Egypt about 150,000 strong.[48] Since there were so many idle soldiers in Egypt, hospitality was desperately needed and a fair number of British homes obliged. Some families strongly encouraged church attendance as well. For example, Mrs GMA Horsford's memoirs record the weekly Sunday dinners that were organised for a few soldiers at her childhood home in Cairo. Her eventual husband 'W.H. Horsford became one of the many wartime soldiers who were made welcome in [her] home and who were regular visitors on Sunday afternoons and evenings.'[49] Those who visited for dinner were rigorously urged to attend church too.

'There was one stipulation, whatever their denomination, if any, they were expected to go to church. This meant a long journey back into the town and then up again to the Citadel on time for 8 o'clock dinner. For many of them, these visits were their only touch of home life.'[50]

---

[43] *Egyptian Gazette*, 13 Jul 1916
[44] Ibid., 16 Aug 1917
[45] Ibid., 22 Jan 1917
[46] Ibid., 13 Jul 1916
[47] Brugger, p. 56
[48] Ibid.
[49] Imperial War Museum Archives, Mrs GMA Horsford, memoirs
[50] Ibid.

Besides Sunday dinners, some British women entertained soldiers to tea or organised parties for them at the Continental Hotel or garden clubs near Qasr el-Aini.[51] Other women opened their homes for convalescent soldiers.[52] Though Australian troops 'had few opportunities to enjoy private hospitality or develop personal contacts with [British] civilians,'[53] as British homes were more likely to welcome British officers, many British families provided hospitality for the Australians. One Australian drew 'attention to the graceful way in which the kindness...[and] hospitality [were] given' by the British in Egypt.[54] Another Australian soldier praised 'the splendid work for the soldiers'[55] carried out by the British community as a whole. Although men were involved, British women were instrumental in the task of caring, catering and providing hospitality for the British troops in Egypt.

Conflict between the British community and government policy: Requisitions

Besides the various roles of British men and women during the First World War, the conflicts between certain Britons and official government policy also reveal noteworthy diversity within the community. The British military authorities requisitioned many large buildings during the war and the Victoria College of Alexandria was no exception. Victoria College existed to import the best of English public school education into Egypt. At the outset of the war, Mr Lias, the headmaster, was adamant that the school should remain on its premises since any alternative would damage the success of the school. Even before the official request for requisition, Mr Lias, wrote to Sir John Maxwell, commander of the military forces in Egypt, to plead his case against the requisition of the college.

> I do not think it is generally understood how difficult it would be to carry on a boarding school (we have 53 boarders) in a provisional building. First of all there are the dormitory arrangements, then there is the question of a dining hall, not

[51] *Egyptian Gazette*, 18 July 1916
[52] Ibid.
[53] Brugger, p. 56
[54] *Egyptian Gazette*, 7 Jun 1915
[55] Ibid., 4 Jun 1915

to mention the difficulty and perhaps impossibility of arranging for games, which are necessary for the boys' health, and such lessons as physics and chemistry, which need special classrooms.[56]

Though Lias repeatedly argued against the requisition, Victoria College was taken over by the military. Sir Maxwell confirmed to McMahon from Army Headquarters that 'I am afraid we must take up . . . Victoria College . . . [It] is the only possible building in Alexandria which will take 1,000 beds.'[57] And as expected, the requisition was very damaging to the continued success of the school. Victoria College was moved to the Egyptian Survey Department building near the Ramleh Railway Station in Alexandria. The makeshift premises did not have enough room for the various classrooms that the school required. The college even sought the use one of the sheds outside the main building as a chemistry classroom. Yet, the British authorities refused this request stating that the sheds were needed for the storage of heavy iron and other articles.

Besides the lack of space, the school also suffered financially. By the spring of 1916, it had a deficit of £E 200 to £E 300 largely due to the reduction of student boarders. There were 64 boarders in March 1914; yet only 40 boarders in 1916. Though there was a slight increase in the number of day-only students, the resulting financial increase could not cover the monetary shortfall from losing nearly a third of the boarders due primarily to the requisition of the old building and the inadequacy of the new premises.[58] The conflict between the British government and Victoria College was an example of the diverse outlooks within the British community in Egypt during the First World War.

The issuing of tax-free war bonds

To raise money for the war effort, the British authorities issued the sale of British Government Exchequer Bonds (tax-free investments for the patriotic buyers to profit from interest accrued) which provoked conflict between members of Egypt's

---

[56] TNA: FO141/512/608, letter Mr Lias to Sir Henry McMahon, 13 Apr 1915 quoting letter Lias to Maxwell, 10 Dec 1914
[57] Ibid., FO141/512/608, letter Maxwell to McMahon, 16 Apr 1915
[58] Ibid., letter Lias to McMahon, 15 May 1916

British community with government policy. Although the government and the British Chamber of Commerce in Egypt highly recommended the purchase of these bonds, small investors among Egypt's Britons found the investment limiting and disadvantageous because the bonds were not available to them in small amounts at £5 or £10 per purchase, but were available in Britain. Investors outside Britain were only invited to buy bonds ranging from at least £50 to £100. If an investor only had £5 or £10 per month for the purchase of the bonds, he could not pay for them outside British soil. Only two arrangements were open to him. He could either pay a bank in Egypt to send his £5 home every month or he could pay a bank in England to purchase his £5 bond. Either way, he needed to pay again for postage and insurance on his bond to be sent safely to England.[59] Needless to say, less affluent investors were unhappy with the additional spending on postage and insurance and found the purchase of smaller bonds from overseas an inconvenient and expensive burden. One investor explained:

> If the 'old country' [Britain] needs money surely she could put bonds in her Dominions—Protectorates or what you will—that I and many, many thousands, and tens of thousands of individuals, may step into a consulate, a Post Office, or a Bank, and exchange cash for bonds . . . [I appeal to readers to explain how] an individual with a small monthly income (exceeding by . . . Say . . . £15 his actual out of pocket requirements)—can obtain bonds, loans or anything else that the Chancellor or Exchequer has for sale.[60]

Unfortunately, the reply that this prospective investor received from KP Birley of the British Chamber of Commerce was simply to take the trouble and invest anyway for the good of Britain's war effort. Birley argues, 'Does not the patriotic nature of the call appeal to all Britishers and encourage them to take a little trouble where necessary, in which I am sure, their bankers will help them.'[61]

Most disappointing for Egypt's Britons who hoped to invest in the tax-free bonds was the requirement imposed by the British government that if they wanted to purchase the bonds, they

---

[59] *Egyptian Gazette*, 9 May 1916
[60] Ibid.
[61] Ibid., 16 May 1916

would have to declare their intention to never return to Britain again. Only a permanent non-resident of Britain was allowed to obtain the tax exemption on the bonds. One potential investor lamented that he had to deny himself the greatest longing he had in life which was to return to Britain to reside in retirement in order to purchase the tax-free bonds. He 'must never again indulge in the hope, which ninety-nine out of every hundred Anglo-Egyptians cherish, that the happy day will come when he can spend his declining years among his relations and friends at home.'[62] To renege on permanent non-resident status in Britain meant that one had to end up paying the tax accrued over the years with interest to the British Government upon one's return to Britain for retirement or whatever reason. Therefore, to declare one's permanent non-residency and then to return to Britain was probably a fate even more punishing than not being allowed to retire in Britain. One British resident in Egypt described this frightening prospect in this way:

> ... after having invested in these Bonds, should he go back on his declaration and after many years decide to make his home in England either in order to retire or because he has obtained an appointment at home, the unfortunate and patriotic investor in such securities will, as soon as he lands on his native shores, find himself called upon to pay a quarter of his capital probably representing the arrears of income tax on these Bonds extending over years. He may have very little money and may have spent all his interest from such investments on educating his children, or he may have lost it through unprofitable business transactions, and then he will find the inexorable Income Tax gatherers selling him up and reducing him to ruin. This is the alternative to perpetual exile which will await the poor Britisher, who out of patriotism has invested his money in these Bonds. The Government will have no pity in taking its pound of flesh.[63]

The prospect of never living in Britain again was to be avoided at all costs for most Britons overseas. Even KP Birley of the British Chamber of Commerce asked, 'However patriotic we may be, are we to declare that we will never live in England again as a price for such an investment?'[64] Not surprisingly, this

---
[62] Ibid., 29 May 1916
[63] Ibid.
[64] Ibid.

predicament discouraged many Britons in Egypt from investing in Exchequer Bonds and put them at odds with the British government.

The War's economic effects on the British in Egypt: Economic boom

Lastly, the diversity of challenges and responses that the British in Egypt faced during the war resulted from the range of economic experiences they encountered—prosperity, missed opportunities and hardship due to inflation. The mass influx of Imperial troops at the outset of the war created an economic boom in Egypt. The significance of the boom, however, can be more clearly appreciated in light of the short yet severe economic depression that preceded it. At the outset of the war, there was a sudden cessation of the large influx of visitors to Egypt during the winter tourist season.

> The streets of Cairo, at the beginning of November 1914, when the early winter visitors [would normally] begin to arrive . . . and the 'Savoy' and other of the more luxurious hotels . . . [had] the mournful and deserted appearance [like] . . . the height of summer. Numbers of the best shops and hotels remained barred and shuttered, and scarcely any motors or other vehicles were observable in the streets . . . The whole town . . . seemed hushed and deadened.[65]

Almost overnight, 'the numerous large hotels of Cairo and Alexandria, the expensive shops, the principal dealers in oriental . . . rugs, and wares of various kinds...[were] confronted with the possibility of ruin.'[66] Though the Greeks, Levantines and other non-British Europeans ran many of these businesses, one can assume that British businesses suffered as well in this climate. However, just as abrupt as the economic decline was the speed and enormity of the unprecedented boom that followed. By the spring of 1915, the departed troops to Europe were replaced by two infantry divisions[67] and a cavalry brigade dispatched from India whose task was to defend the Suez Canal. At the same time, three divisions of infantry, the 42nd East

---

[65] Ibid., 4 Sep 1917, Malcolm McIllwraith's reflections
[66] Ibid., 4 Sep 1917, Malcolm McIllwraith's reflections
[67] Elgood, p. 115. The two Indian Infantry divisions were the 10th and 21st divisions of the Indian Expeditionary Force.

Lancashire Territorial Force, and two divisions from Australia and New Zealand, were given the task of undergoing training to prepare for battle. Lord Kitchener, Secretary of War, had originally intended to use the Australasian troops to fight in Europe but there was not enough accommodation for them in Britain. Thus they were assigned to train in Egypt instead and were later directed to fight in the Middle Eastern theatre of war.[68] The British 'turned Egypt into an immense transit camp, supply and training ground.'[69] Under the central command of Lieutenant-General Sir John Maxwell, who was ultimately accountable to Lord Kitchener,[70] the troops, numbering 40,000[71] by the spring of 1915, poured into Cairo, Alexandria and Port Said. Huge camps were set up for them. They not only saved hotels, shops, and tourist and transportation businesses from bankruptcy but compensated for the losses incurred in the initial months of the war.

This economic boom was accompanied by the enormous spending power of the soldiers. Egypt 'acquired an army of military tourists that [spent] £E 3000 to £E 5000 a day.'[72] Certain 'English regiments contained some of the greatest peers, and richest men in England [and] . . . wealthy Australians and New Zealanders, too squandered their money in pro-fusion.'[73] Lady Rochdale records that the Australians all seemed 'very rich, [and did] mind what they paid.'[74] An average Australian trooper was paid two shillings per day whilst the entire monthly salary of a private in the Scottish infantry was only four shillings and two pence.[75] The Australians received the 'highest pay given to privates in any army . . . [and] on top of that each man had seven and half pence over and above the

---

[68] Anglesey, Marquess of, *A History of the British Cavalry, 1816-1919: V: Egypt, Palestine and Syria, 1914 to 1919* (Leo Cooper, 1994) p. 3

[69] Porter, Brian, 'Britain and the Middle East in the Great War' in Peter Liddle, (ed.), *Home Fires and Foreign Fields*, p. 162

[70] MacMunn, p. 13

[71] *Egyptian Gazette*, 12 Feb 1915 and Porter, 162. There were 70,000 Imperial soldiers in Egypt in 1915 (including Indians and other Westerners).

[72] Ibid.

[73] Ibid., 4 Sep 1917

[74] Rochdale, 26 Jan 1915

[75] Anglesey, p. 3

British scale of rations.'[76] For all the suffering and pain that the Gallipoli campaign brought about for the British and Australasian armies, it was partially offset by the ongoing payment of large salaries for many soldiers and the subsequent spending of this money in Egypt.

> All the accumulated arrears of money that were paid out to the Anzacs [Australian and New Zealand forces] and the British troops who had been fighting for months at Gallipoli came in a great windfall to Cairo and Alexandria . . . They had come out of the jaws of death, they might be returning there at any moment, and they made the most of the present, as only soldiers can . . . Egypt must have reaped a rich harvest from the Army . . . most of the money [was] spent in Alexandria and Cairo.'[77]

The imperial troops, particularly the Australians with their free spending attitudes, filled the streets of Cairo and Alexandria with 'a good deal of spare time and plenty of money, [and] monopolised every bar, music-hall, picture palace, and dancing hall, and almost wholly replaced the civilian element.'[78] They 'squandered enormous sums on worthless "souvenirs", on trinkets and handkerchiefs for their lady-loves, and in interminable drinks and drives.'[79] They bought huge amounts of 'food for themselves and fodder for their animals.'[80] The economic boom also facilitated a rise in construction and the opening of new businesses. The new Banco di Roma building, housing the Vacuum Oil Company, and the new Imperial Ottoman Bank building were erected in Cairo.[81] Further, 'some fifty new bars and taverns were opened . . . in [just] six weeks'[82] and many new English bookshops were established during this period.

> The large quantities of English books for sale and the number of new bookshops that have sprung up, mostly stocked with light literature in English...[are] one of the most patent signs of the presence of English troops in Egypt

---

[76] Ibid.
[77] Briggs, Martin, *Through Egypt in Wartime* (Unwin, 1918) p. 27
[78] *Egyptian Gazette*, 12 Feb 1915
[79] Briggs, p. 27
[80] Nelson, Nina, *Shepheard's Hotel* (Barrie & Rockcliff, 1960) p. 76
[81] *Egyptian Gazette*, 10 Oct 1915
[82] Ibid., 12 Feb 1915

... van loads of ... novels and other popular books ... are ordered at regular intervals ... The hundred of thousands of British and overseas troops in Egypt are insistent upon a supply of light and readable literature.'[83]

To refresh the tired shopper, tea gardens such as Alexandria's New English Tea Gardens, under the management of an English lady, were established to provide a place of respite, away from the heat and dust.[84] For the British in Egypt, times were better 'than any [they had] ever known'[85] and 'for the most part, the inhabitants, both native and foreign, [made] profit out of the war.'[86]

Missed opportunities

Despite the economic boom, British businessmen in Egypt missed the opportunity to capitalise on new restrictions imposed on German and Austrian businessmen during the war. Soon after war was declared on Germany, the Austro-Hungarian Empire and the Ottoman Empire, the British authorities implemented martial law to:

> override the Capitulations ... which would otherwise have kept the [British controlled] Egyptian government as powerless as before to take effective action against European foreigners. Under the umbrella of martial law however, it could control the businesses of firms suspected of trading with the enemy [and] take over firms of enemy nationality.[87]

The imposition of martial law allowed the British authorities to sequester German and Austrian homes for military service[88] and to freeze German and Austrian assets.[89] There were also prohibitions on 'German ships entering Egyptian harbours; Egyptian ships entering German harbours; [the] import of Ger-

---

[83] Ibid., 10 Nov 1916
[84] Ibid., 2 Apr 1916
[85] *Egyptian Gazette*, 12 Feb 1915
[86] Caillard, Mabel, *A Lifetime in Egypt: 1876-1935* (Grant Richards, 1935) p. 189
[87] Richmond, JCB, *Egypt, 1798-1952: Her Advance Towards a Modern Identity*, (Methuen, 1977) p. 172
[88] *Egyptian Gazette*, 4 Sep 1917
[89] Raafat, Samir, *Maadi: 1904-1962: Society & History in a Cairo Suburb* (Palm, 1994) p. 47. For example, the German Luthy family and the Austro-Hungarian Lichtenstern and Scheynoha families had their assets sequestered and properties taken over by the British military.

man goods into Egypt; [and the] exports of all goods [from Egypt] to German ports.'[90] British forces were permitted to capture enemy ships in Egyptian harbours and all Egyptian ports were closed to German shipping.[91] These restrictions on German and Austrian business activity presented an environment where British businesses could have subsumed a far greater proportion of trade and economic initiative in the region.

However, the British sense of fairness seemed to have hindered British businesses in Egypt from accumulating greater profit. For instance, although High Commissioner McMahon's speech in 1915 stated that 'British prospects ... were very bright and ... that he was ready to render ... every reasonable assistance and support'[92] to the British Chamber of Commerce, he also argued that a fair trading environment was crucial to economic credibility and growth.

> The British Protectorate would not be used to push unduly British interests at the expense of ... other nations. It would benefit all interests by assuring a greater security and other advantages ... This would attract British capital and so give a fresh impulse to British trade in the country. Egypt, has now the advantage of an able and enlightened ruler, who was anxious to promote all industrial interests.[93]

Besides the government's commitment to fair-play, British manufacturers did not take advantage of the loss of German and Austrian trade. As one British businessman bemoaned:

> Unfortunately, English commission houses in Egypt are not numerous; therefore, no great pressure can be brought upon the British Chamber of Commerce, which is content to go on in the same old drowsy manner and does not seem to realise that German and Austrian trade, which had a very strong footing in Egypt before the war, must be substituted by British trade, and *not find the market open to them immediately after the war*.[94]

---

[90] Middle East Centre Archives, St. Antony's College, University of Oxford, Sir Alex William Keown-Boyd, memoirs, letter RH Dunn, Legal Secretary in Khartoum to Private Sec of Governor-General in Khartoum, 9 Aug 1914

[91] Ibid.

[92] *Egyptian Gazette*, McMahon's speech at British Chamber of Commerce in Egypt banquet, 26/04/1915

[93] Ibid.

[94] Ibid., 25 Jan 1916 (emphasis mine)

Due to Britain's position of power, it seemed likely that 'a preference would be given to British goods if some energy were displayed by the British Chamber of Commerce and active steps were taken to put the British manufacturer in close touch with the responsible commission houses.'[95] However, instead of turning to British firms, the commission houses began to look to America to replace German and Austrian goods.

Remarkably, though much of German and Austrian business activities and assets were frozen, some continued to engage in trade. The Government permitted certain German companies to carry on trade only if they were locally controlled by non-German partners, allowed to trade only in Egypt with Britain and its Allies, and licensed only to trade for the purpose of liquidation.[96] The Courts allowed non-German partners of companies with German owners in Egypt to continue to do business so as not to hurt the businessmen of non-enemy states—Egyptians or other Europeans.[97] Astonishingly, one such company, whose directors were mostly German, was allowed 'to make profits out of contracts with the British Army.'[98] Ironically, this may have economically benefited Germany and thus strengthened her in the war effort. When asked whether the British Chamber of Commerce in Egypt had 'taken any steps in the matter of bringing pressure to bear on the authorities on the scandal of enemy firms,'[99] one prominent British businessman replied, 'the Chamber had done nothing in this matter ... it was inconceivable that [it] would ever think of such a daring and audacious policy.'[100] Given the opportunity at the time to subdue German and Austrian businesses in Egypt, the British government (with its commitment to fair-play) and British businessmen seemed to have done little to take economic advantage of their dominant position in Egypt during the First World War.

---

[95] Ibid.
[96] Ibid., 22 Feb 1916
[97] Hoyle, Mark SW, *The Mixed Courts of Egypt* (Graham & Trotman, 1991) p. 100
[98] *Egyptian Gazette*, 14 Jan 1916
[99] Ibid.
[100] Ibid.

The high standard of living and the rise in cost of living

As Egypt prospered during the war, the standard of living inevitably rose. One British child in Cairo commented after a trip to Khartoum:

> Cairo ... was cool and fresh ... It was heavenly to get home at last ... to find a well laid table with cold ham and tomatoes for breakfast with butter in a gleaming silver dish with an ice compartment in it. Real butter! In Khartoum, it came up once a week on the mail train, was in a tin and was always semi-liquid by the time it reached us and it always tasted rancid.[101]

In many parts of Cairo, well-dressed shop owners and fashionable people in carriages were easily noticed.[102] As one visitor observed, 'of all the various war centres, [Egypt] is decidedly the safest and most comfortable ... and of all the capitals within the war zone, Cairo [is the best] for order and comfort.'[103] The missionary Temple Gairdner affirmed this by saying: 'Egypt has been one of the safest and quietest lands on earth during the war, thanks to the overwhelming nature of the defense which the British Government saw right to bestow on the key of the Empire.'[104] Good food, trendy clothes, safety and comfort, essential hallmarks of a high standard of living, characterised Egypt during the Great War.

However, coupled with a high standard of living was an unfortunate high cost of living. A report by the National Bank of Egypt claims that the cost of living index doubled from 1914 to 1918, from 100 to 202.[105] Due to the increased cost of fuel and food, the Turf Club significantly raised its prices in 1917. The Club raised the cost of its dinners by two piastres while the cost of tea rose by one piastre. A fee for use of a table was two and a half piastres charged to non-members of the Club. The Club's normal annual expenditure for coal in 1914 was £E 200,[106] but

---

[101] Imperial War Museum Archives, Mrs GMA Horsford, memoirs
[102] *Egyptian Gazette*, 10 Oct 1915
[103] Ibid., 15 Mar 1916
[104] Gairdner, Temple, *Church Missionary Review*, LXIII, 1916, letter from Cairo, 26 Aug 1916
[105] *National Bank of Egypt, 1898-1948, 50th Anniversary Report* (NBE, 1948) p. 51
[106] The value of the Egyptian pound was almost equivalent to the sterling during

by 1916, it was £E 500 and by 1917, it was £E 800.[107] During the war, rents increased from 20 to 50 per cent (in some cases by 85 per cent)[108] and food stuffs by 92 per cent in Cairo from July 1914 until May 1918, and by 116 per cent in Alexandria during the same period.[109] Did income keep pace with these increases? Salaries of government officials went up only on the average of 10 to 20 per cent.[110] After paying out all the essential costs, a government official and his family were left with little money for recreation and amusement which they deemed 'necessary for these hard times.'[111] The sharp price rise presented grave challenges for British businesses in Egypt as well. Arthur Blunt, the interim manager of the Anglo-Egyptian Bank, in his letter to his manager in London, gave a glimpse of how businesses responded to the high cost of living facing their employees.

> Our Minet el Basal staff (near Alexandria) . . . complaining of the difficulty of making both ends meet owing to the further rise in the cost of living. Some of the lower paid married men must be feeling it and I suggested that I . . . give the most deserving men up to £10 each. I have since heard that special war bonuses have been granted in several offices . . . Everything has gone up tremendously of late.[112]

Though the Great War provided Britons in Egypt with great economic benefit, many also suffered due to 'the . . . Exceptionally high . . . cost of living.'[113]

Conclusion

Among members of the British community in Egypt, there was a variety of roles and reactions to the adverse challenges posed

---

the years of the occupation. One Egyptian pound was equal to one sterling and six pence. See Roger Owen, *The Middle East in the World Economy, 1800–1914* (Methuen, 1981) p. 8

[107] *Egyptian Gazette*, 3 May 1918
[108] Ibid., 1 Jun 1918
[109] Ibid., 26 Jul 1918
[110] Ibid
[111] Ibid., 1 Jun 1918
[112] Barclays Group Archives, Wythenshawe, Manchester, correspondence between staff in Egypt with managers in London of the Anglo-Egyptian Bank, letter Arthur Blunt to Coombs, 7 Jun 1917
[113] Ibid., letter Carruthers to HA Richardson, chairman of AEB, 27 Jan 1916

by the First World War. Men joined the war effort in Europe or stayed behind in key jobs while women served as volunteers, nurses and hostesses. As for conflicting perspectives within the community, some Britons opposed the government's requisitioning of Victoria College while others disagreed with the criteria for tax-free war bonds. Britons in Egypt also experienced diverse economic realities during the war—prosperity due to the economic boom, missed opportunities in light of restrictions on German and Austrian firms, and hardship due to inflation. It is hoped that this research will contribute to the economic, social and cultural historiography of the British Empire in Africa during the Great War.

Economics and Politics

The 'other Portuguese Flanders': strategic ambition and operational disaster in the Portuguese Great War in Mozambique

António Paulo Duarte; Ana Paula Pires; Bruno Cardoso Reis[1]

Introduction

Portugal was a belligerent in the First World War in two continents, Europe and Africa, and in three different theatres of war, France (Flanders), Angola (Southern regions) and Mozambique (North and Eastern regions). Despite fighting in different theaters of war, one strategic goal unified the sending of both these expeditionary forces. Portugal, with its intervention in World War One, was hoping to ensure its position in the world system and improve its standing vis-à-vis its main ally and potentially, most dangerous adversary, Great Britain. For Portugal, an improved status in a new post-war international order was more than enough to justify a significant effort in intervening in the World War both in Europe and in Africa.

---

[1] António Paulo Duarte is Advisor and Researcher, Senior Technician Career, National Defense Institute (IDN) and Coordinator of the Research Project 'Thinking Strategically Portugal: The International Insertion of Small and Medium Powers and the First World War' (IDS-IHC (FCSH/UNL)-ICS (UL) partnership, supported by the Coordinating Committee for Centennial World War of the Ministry of National Defense, 2014-2018; Ana Paula Pires is a researcher at the Institute for Contemporary History at NOVA Faculty for Social Sciences and Humanities where she coordinates de group 'Economy, Society, Innovation and Heritage'. Pires is also affiliated with Stanford University. Bruno Cardoso Reis is an adviser to IDN and associate researcher at the Michael Howard Center for Military History at King's College. He is since 2017 an assistant professor at the ISCTE-IUL CIS.

This chapter will try to show that the very demanding intervention was the result of a very ambitious strategic goal for a small power and very young republican regime. The paper will not describe the Portuguese military campaigns in Mozambique in World War One. It will focus on the political aims and the military actions of Portugal in Mozambique with an analysis of the political purposes and strategic impact of the war. First, it looks at the political 'Weltanschauung' or vision, then, it relates policy decision-making, strategic planning and operational concept, to see, in the end, the real impact of these three factors on the ground: politics, policy and strategy.

This work seeks to connect military and political history and strategic studies. Strategy tells us that war is politically driven, but that political management is very difficult because of the action of the enemy.[2] Strategy required an understanding of what is war. History tells us that we have to understand the actions of the historical actors in their historical context, without anachronisms. History gives the historical researcher, the capability to understand historical personalities in their own language and reality.[3]

Firstly, the political vision of the radical wing of the Republican government of Portugal and its place in the role of Portugal in the World War. Then, we will see how these war aims were translated into political action and military strategic conceptions. The paper will close with some remarks on the effects of these actions on the country's international position.

The new Portuguese Republic and the Great War

Portugal became the most recent of only three republics in Europe after a victorious take-over of power in October 1910. On 9 March 1916 Germany declared war on Portugal. The paradox is that, unlike in the case of Belgium, even if it was Germany who formally declared war on Portugal, the Portuguese government did all it could for that to happen. The government was dominated by the more radical wing of the Republican Party—known as Democrats, or *Jovens Turcos* ('Young Turks') in the case of its military wing. They wanted to participate in the war, their political aims—internal as well as

---
[2] See for example, Gray, Colin S, *The Strategy Bridge: Theory for Practice* (Oxford University Press, 2010) pp. 7, 25, 131-3
[3] Pomian, Krzystof, *Sur l'Histoire* (Éditions Gallimard, 1999)

external—relied on an active military intervention in the most demanding, and it was hoped, prestigious theatre of war, the Western Front of the conflict in Europe. Portugal was divided about the intervention. This division reflected a broader political fissure between more radical republicans, on the one hand, and monarchists and Catholics and more moderate republicans on the other.[4] The main focus of division was not between Anglophiles and Francophiles on one side, and Germanophiles on the other. The latter were, if not nonexistent, politically insignificant; even the exiled former King Manuel II, after all, lived in Britain. The division was not on whether to support the Western allies, but how to do it. There was a great deal of opposition—except for the most radical wing of the Republicans to sending an expeditionary force to the Western Front. Where there was consensus, was on the African front of the war—in which Portugal had long felt threatened by Germany, its ambitious colonial neighbour to the north of Mozambique (German East Africa) and to the south of Angola (German South West Africa). No one questioned the need to send forces to deter or counter German aggression against Portuguese territories in Africa.

The main external war aim of the 'radical wing' in control of the Portuguese government in 1916 was to achieve a greatly improved international status and a more balanced relationship with its main ally, Great Britain, shaken by the Republican revolution. As General Norton de Matos, the Portuguese war minister of the belligerent governments, said many years after that event, intervention in the World War was aimed at giving Portugal a renewed and heightened 'sense of national dignity', and in his mind it had.[5] This was vital not just for external foreign policy, but also for domestic reasons, of internal prestige of the Republic that would guarantee its consolidation and the political preeminence within the new regime, of its radical wing and their policies.[6] The voluntaristic show of force in Flanders

---

[4] For a general overview on the political situation of the Republic, see, for example, Fernando Rosas, *Portugal no Século XX (1890-1976) – Pensamento e Acção Política* (Editorial Notícias, 2004) pp. 35-51

[5] Norton de Matos, *Memórias e Trabalhos da Minha Vida*, III Vol. (Tomo V) (Coimbra, Imprensa da Universidade de Coimbra, 2005) p. 16

[6] The belligerency of Portugal in the First World War is highly debated in Portuguese historiography. This perspective is a synthesis between, Teixeira, Nuno Severiano, *O Poder e a Guerra, 1914-1918, Objetivos Nacionais e Estratégias Políticas na*

was meant to elevate the radical Portuguese Republic internally as much as internationally. The problem was this could not be done if the 'other Flanders' was lost, if the African front went badly wrong, risking the colonial heritage seen by all Portuguese nationalists as a sacred endowment going back to the Golden Age of the Discoveries.

The Great War was seen by these Republican hawks as an opportunity to pursue one of the main reasons for the Portuguese October revolution of 1910: the new Republic as an end to the period of Portuguese decadence and the return of Portugal to a colonial great power recognised by other great powers, mainly France and Great Britain. To close the gap, Portugal would boldly have to pursue a very ambitious policy.[7]

Entrada de Portugal na Grande Guerra (Estampa, 1996) which stands for the purpose of internal political consolidation, and Fraga,Luís Alves *Do Intervencionismo ao Sidonismo, os Dois segmentos da Política de Guerra da 1ª República, 1916-1918* (Imprensa Universidade de Coimbra, 2010) pp. 79-93, who see the main aim as to get some sort of strategic parity with Great Britain and larger international autonomy. Our argument was defended in a conference some years ago, unfortunately never published, Duarte, António Paulo, 'O Desejo da Aliança: Os Republicanos Radicais, a Aliança com a Grã-Bretanha e a Intervenção Portuguesa na Grande Guerra', *Conference in the International Seminar: From the Trenches to Versailles: War and Memory (1914-1919)*, Reitoria da Universidade Nova de Lisboa, 22-27 de Junho de 2009, 23 June 2009, 14.00h. For an approximation to our perspective, see: 'A helvetização do Exército e a intervenção portuguesa na Grande Guerra', *Congresso Internacional I República e Republicanismo. Atas* (Assembleia da República, 2012) pp. 195-202. Also very interesting, is the article by Rui Ramos, 'A Revolução Republicana de 1910 e a Política Externa Portuguesa', in João Marques de Almeida e Rui Ramos, Coord., *Revoluções, Política Externa e Política de Defesa em Portugal, Séc. XIX-XX* (Edições Cosmos/Instituto da Defesa Nacional, 2008) pp. 55-94. More recently in a view highly antagonistic of the radical republican political wing, is the work of Telo, Antonio José & de Sousa, Pedro Marquês, *O CEP. Os militares sacrificados pela má política* (Fronteira do Caos, 2016)

[7] The idea of decadence is itself related with the concept of power. Decadence means power fall or power decline. The word derives from *fall* in Latin, *cadere, cair* or *queda* in Portuguese. The biggest problem facing Portugal at the beginning of the twentieth century was its power decline that could be regenerated by the new African Empire. Norton de Matos and Pereira da Silva, two of the most preeminent officers of the armed forces and active politicians in the First Republic also named the regeneration of Portugal by the African Empire as 'Portugal Maior', 'bigger Portugal', the restoration of Portugal to a preeminent international position by the development of its own colonies, a 'new Brazil'. Matos, Norton de, Op. Cit., III Vol., pp. 473 e ss. de Oliveira, Maurício, *Pereira da Silva, Oficial-Ministro-Doutrinador* (Editora Marítimo Colonial, 1968) pp. 130 e 135. A vivid demonstration of this idea is a book for school students, titled precisely *Portugal Maior*. Reis,Augusto, & Henriques, António, *Portugal Maior. Livro de Leituras Portuguesas para o Ensino Técnico* (Livraria Popular Francisco Franco, (s/d))

How could the Portuguese Radical Republican hawks believe in this possibility of Portugal as a potential rising power? They believed in this possibility evidently, in part, out of political doctrinaire idealism, but also because Portugal had the fourth largest empire in the world.[8] This was often mentioned in the Portuguese Republican Parliament. Indeed, it was true in territorial terms. But great territory is not the same as great power.

Many Portuguese public intellectuals and political figures, as did others in Europe, not least in Germany, believed Mahan´s navalist equation was fundamentally correct, that empire meant healthy finances and commerce and in the end a strong military (in particular naval) power.[9] Portugal seemed to the most ambitious to have all the possibilities to regain its status because it had the territorial basis to make this naval agenda come true.[10] All that was needed, the Portuguese 'Young Turks' believed was will power to do what was necessary to enter the war and show Portugal was not another dead man of Europe, by a show of effective martial power. This, Portuguese hawks believed, would imply a visible presence on the key battlefields, that would ensure the relevance of Portugal in international society after the war and strategic parity with Great Britain. For that, however, Portugal would have to turn a great territory into an effective machine to actually mobilize resources and train a reasonably sized expeditionary corps for the battlefield, something that would be very difficult given the poverty of the country and the lack of effective modern military means. The only thing that Portugal undoubtedly had to give was 'canon fodder' and German ships that had taken refuge in its ports, and both were sorely needed by France and Britain in 1916.[11]

---

[8] See, for example, the arguments of Celestino de Almeida, Navy Minister in Parliament 1911. *Diário da Câmara dos Deputados*, session n° 11, 11 December 1911, p. 4

[9] For example, in the 'Câmara dos Deputados', the Portuguese Parliament, one of the national representatives, Mr Luís Tavares, would use the Mahan trilogy as a demonstration of the advantages of the development of a merchant navy. *Diário da Câmara dos Deputados*, session n° 7, 11 December 1911, p. 12

[10] About the idea in general, see Duarte, António Paulo, 'Portugal maior', *Limes* (Rivista Italiana di Giopolitica), n° 5, 2010, pp. 72-73

[11] The armed forces were under equipped. The army did not have modern artillery, nor modern military instruction, and the navy was equipped with very old and small ships, the most modern of them, a small 'Contratorpedeiro', 'destroyer' of 700 ton, the first ship of the 'Douro' Class. Regarding the military situation, for ex-

Despite its position, the government of the so-called *União Sagrada* (Sacred Union)—in fact a failed attempt to copy the French political model of a government of national unity—was unable to include all of the Republicans, not to mention Socialists, Catholics or Monarchists[12]—decided not only to force Germany to declare war but to do so with extremely ambitious objectives and setting the level of ambition in terms of resources at an impossibly high level. Moreover, not only did the *União Sagrada* government decide to get the largest army in France that it could mobilise and train, with additional British support, *but* at the same time prepared the most significant military expedition to be sent to Portuguese Africa since the wars of occupation, with the aim not only to defend the north of Mozambique but also, amazingly, to conquer parts of German East Africa.

Portuguese war aims in World War One and the war in Mozambique

Portugal sent two expeditions to Mozambique, in 1914 and in 1915 respectively. The first was sent immediately after the start of the war. It had the military objective of defending Mozambique from German raids from Tanganyika. The first expedition had 1,540 men and 49 officers under the command of Colonel Massano de Amorim.[13] The second expedition had 1,584 men and 41 officers under the command of Colonel Moura Mendes.[14]

Things went badly wrong on both the Western European front and the East African front. The first requires little explanation. But the second is more paradoxical; the German forces in East Africa were small and isolated; and Portugal had a lot of experience fighting overseas. How did this happen?

The Portuguese elite did not believe in the martial qualities of the Africans. Part of the answer is simply imperial racial prejudice. The Portuguese elite increasingly adopted, especially

---

ample, see Fraga, Luís Alves Op. Cit., pp. 148-54, and Telo, António José, & de Sousa, Pedro Marquês, Op. Cit., pp. 187-8. For the navy situation, Telo, António José, *História da Marinha Portuguesa. Homens, Doutrina e Organização, 1824-1974* (tomo I) (Academia da Marinha, 1999) pp. 237-49

[12] Valente, Vasco Pulido, *A 'República Velha' (1910-1917)* (Gradiva 1997) pp. 89-91

[13] Duarte, António Paulo, Esboço para uma Leitura Estratégica sobre a Campanha de Moçambique (1914-1918), *Revista Militar*, n° 8/9, agosto/setembro 1998, p. 681

[14] Idem, p. 684

the Positivist-inclined radical Republicans, the pseudo-scientific racist views so common in Europe at the end of the nineteenth century and the beginning of the twentieth century.[15] Many seem to believe that Portugal's decline was due to the mixture of whites (Celtic or Lusitanian)—and blacks (Arab and African). This set of ideas meant that only white Portuguese could have the martial qualities to fight in a European war, even in tropical Africa. The Portuguese government would have to send expeditions of metropolitan soldiers to fight against the Germans in East Africa, instead of using large numbers of locally recruited soldiers like the latter did.

In German East Africa it seems to have been decided that in tropical Africa, only African troops would have the ideal physical conditions to fight, with Europeans in command. Racism was also present in the German policy option, not least in the notion of warrior races in selecting Askaris, but it better fitted the circumstances. In 1914, at the beginning of the war, there were in German East Africa 260 European officers commanding 2,472 African troops. During the war, the total has been estimated at 12,100 Askari troops and 3,007 European German troops.[16]

Indeed, the British, at the beginning of the war, had similar prejudices to the Portuguese, regarding the (lack of) quality of African troops. They decided however to use Indian troops instead of European as being better fitted to a tropical climate. They would, however, prove equally ill adapted to local conditions. The lessons learned with African troops recruited by Germany—*Schutztruppe*—led to considerable expansion of the King's African Rifles in 1917.[17]

Indeed, even if the fundamental mission of the first Portuguese expeditionary corps was strategic defence, sent in 1914, once the radical wing of the Republicans took full control of the government in 1915, they decided that they had to occupy

---

[15] See for example, de Matos, Norton, Op. Cit., 1ª vol., pp. 439-46. See also Pélissier, René, *História de Moçambique, Formação e Oposição, 1854-1918*, II Vol. (Estampa, 1998) pp. 438-9

[16] Sibley, JR, *Tanganyika Guerrilla: East African Campaign (1914-1918)* (New York, 1971) pp. 14-5 e 18-9

[17] The KAR mobilised many more troops, 114,000 men with casualties of 62,000, than the German Askari, according to their association site. For information above see the King's African Rifles Association at http://www.kingsafricanrifles association.co.uk/the-history-of-the-kar/. Accessed 29 Apr 2013

the 'Kionga' region, a small territory, half the size of Luxemburg, in the southeast of the Rovuma River that had long been disputed by Portugal and Germany.[18] The first expedition was incapable of doing so, but the second made the effort to occupy the territory, helped by the withdrawing of the German authorities, before the arrival of the very debilitated Portuguese army. After that, and with war openly declared, the second expedition tried to cross the Rovuma River. The expedition, supported by a small cruiser and a gunboat which fired on German positions, before the amphibious assault, tried to cross the Rovuma River in two large barges. One of them was machine gunned by German troops killing and wounding many of the assaulting troops and that stopped the crossing almost immediately with the retreat of the second barge and the withdrawal of Portuguese forces.[19]

The big showdown in Mozambique: Victory and defeat

In 1916, Portugal decided, following the same goals that were being pursued in Europe, to increase its wars aims and to occupy other parts of Tanganyika territory. The third expedition under the command of General Ferreira Gil was 4,642 strong, and would further incorporate the main elements of the second expedition.[20] They could rely on the support of ten colonial troop companies, between 1,500 and 2,000 men. In total, General Ferreira Gil would have around 8,000 troops under his command for the offensive.[21]

Of course, this was still about one-tenth of the Commonwealth forces in Tanganyika territory, 100,000 men strong who faced huge obstacles in their slow offensive.[22]

---

[18] Duarte (1998) p. 686. Marques, Ricardo, *Os Fantasmas do Rovuma. A epopeia dos soldados portugueses em África na I Guerra Mundial* (Oficina do Livro, 2012) pp. 59-64

[19] Duarte (1998) pp. 687-8

[20] Duarte (1998) p. 689-90

[21] Ten native companies were raised in Mozambique to support the military offensive. Martins, Azambuja, *Nevala. Expedição a Moçambique* (Famalicão, 1935) pp. 43, 45. They had, probably, between 150 and 200 men each, giving a total of 1,500 or 2,000 men.

[22] Nuno Lemos Pires, conference pronounced in the International Seminar 'Entering the War. The entrance of Small and Medium powers in the First World War', II Panel – 'Entering the War: Africa and Europe – Diplomacy, Economy and Society', 30 March 2016, Lisbon.

Initially, the main objective of the Portuguese offensive was Mikindani and Lindi, the last about 200 kilometres (120 miles) beyond the border line. Crossing the Rovuma was easy this time on 19 September 1916. The Germans did not offer any resistance.[23] The advance was, then, confronted by some resistance, from small groups of German Askari, who set several ambushes, but that did not stop the Portuguese advance towards the first main objective, Newala, about twenty-five kilometres beyond the border line and, more importantly given the importance of naval support, two hundred kilometres from the coast. The village was eventually taken on 28 October 1916.[24]

This was a consequence of the clash between very ambitious strategic goals and the realities on the ground forcing a change, but one that in line with the 'vanguard' concept of politics of the Radical Republicans almost always was to double down on the level of ambition. More specifically, the main objectives on the coast were already in the hands of the British forces, a situation known to the Portuguese command only a few days before the crossing of the Rovuma. The high Portuguese command in the north of Mozambique, pressed by the Portuguese government, felt forced to advance across the Rovuma, north towards Liwale.[25]

But after that, the advance started to stall. Further advance to the north was simply stopped by German resistance, now much stronger, given the arrival of reinforcements: about 600 German Askaris were concentrated for the counter-offensive.[26]

The Portuguese had superior numbers in the battlefield, between 850 to 1,600 men,[27] but they were in very poor condition: the result primarily of very poor logistics as well as bad military and physical training of rural conscripts, often already not in very good shape. Disease was also widespread among Portuguese troops. Both logistics and disease were always a major challenge for warfare in Africa and this was true in the First World War in all cases, but in the Portuguese case the

---

[23] Ricardo Marques, Op. Cit., pp. 106-12
[24] Idem, pp. 125-126
[25] Idem, pp. 114-114. René Pélissier, Op. Cit., p. 401
[26] Ricardo Marques, Op. Cit., P. 155
[27] Ricardo Marques give the number of 1,600 Portuguese troops in and around Newala. Ricardo Marques, Op. Cit., p. 155. René Pélissier says the Newala garrison had about 800 Portuguese troops. René Pélissier, Op. Cit., p. 402

problem was especially acute causing more the 75 per cent casualties. The problem was made worse by poor command and control. The advanced Portuguese HQ was still too far behind, in Mozambique, in Palma, 250 kilometres from Newala, far from the troops, and unable to react quickly to any crisis. All this contributed to a disaster waiting to happen.[28]

The Germans moved fast to encircle the Portuguese in Newala. Isolated, the Portuguese garrison, which had to accept many of the elements of the retreating columns, was too big to be effectively provisioned by the limited stored supplies, and the supply lines were overextended and disorganised, even in the absence of the German siege. Famine soon started, and the lack of water in the tropical summer was an even bigger problem.

During the night of 28 to 29 of November 1917, Portuguese troops in Newala managed to break the siege and withdraw in considerable disarray back to Mozambique. The retreat was badly organised and the troops soon split into numerous disorganised bands, and there were many individual runaways, many of whom were never accounted for. Some were captured by the Germans, a few were reported to have collapsed under war stress and became insane.[29]

The defeat of Newala had a large similarity, but is even less known in Portugal and abroad, to the military disaster of the so-called La Lys Battle, in which the CEP—the Portuguese Expeditionary Corps collapsed in the face of the German spring offensive of 1918, in Flanders.

True the Battle of La Lys was a much bigger affair than Newala. It took place for the most part on 9 April 1918, at the beginning of operation *Georgette*, the second major German operation of the 1918 spring offensive (or Fourth Battle of Ypres) with the aim of crushing the will to fight of the Western Allies before the new American troops started to have an impact in the war. Close to 20,000 Portuguese troops were engaged. Four German divisions, including elite storm troops, were launched against the Portuguese expeditionary division that had not been informed by British intelligence of the eminent attack. The Portuguese expeditionary corps was crushed and the main political aim of the intervention collapsed with them.[30]

---

[28] Ricardo Marques, Op. Cit., p. 137
[29] Idem, pp. 156-60. René Pélissier, Op. Cit., pp. 402-3

Our main argument is that both La Lys and Newala are decisive in two ways. First, they reflect the unwillingness and inability with existing means of the Portuguese military to carry out the goals set about by the radical republican government and a small faction of the military. As in La Lys, in Newala, the strategic goal of the intervention was defeated. Portugal was incapable of achieving the strategic goal of greater parity vis-à-vis Great Britain, by being an active belligerent. The majority of the professional officer corps of the Portuguese Armed Forces had been hostile from the start to the radical republican goal of creating a mass militia army on the Swiss model, both out of conservatism and of a genuine professional concern with the inability to properly fund and equip a mass army given very limited funding. Most officers were even more hostile to what they saw as overambitious goals in the World War. This was not a good way to start a massive war effort in very demanding theatres of operations, for different reasons, in Flanders and Mozambique.

Newala was, in fact, just the start of Portuguese troubles in Mozambique. After the Portuguese retreat from Tanganyika, German East African troops invaded Mozambique. This invasion would probably have happened, even if Portugal had not gone on the offensive across the Rovuma. But, by giving a priority to invading German East Africa, Portugal failed to better organise its defence and became more of a target in the strategy of survival at all costs of one of the most capable German generals—von Lettow-Vorbeck.

Mozambique was the target of two German invasions; one more limited and restricted to the Northeast Niassa province, between April and September 1917, the other, the bigger one, from November 1917 to September 1918, which cut across almost half of the colony affecting large areas of the Northern and Central provinces. These invasions were catastrophic for Portuguese colonial rule, with the Germans pursuing a well-known strategy of promoting subversion, sparking numerous indigenous rebellions. More than 10,000 additional troops were

---

30 Concerning the Battle of La Lys, see for example, Henriques, Mendo Castro & Leitão, António Rosas, *La Lys, 1918, Os Soldados Desconhecidos* (Prefácio, 2001) and António José Telo & Pedro Marquês de Sousa, Op. Cit., pp. 381 475. A very acute and precise description of the Lys Battle, with recourse to British sources.

sent in successive expeditions to try to stop the German invasion without success.[31] The republican government was well aware that the 'moral prestige' of Portugal was in danger but it simply did not have the means to successfully counter the threat.[32] To be fair, there was plenty of blame to go around in the East Africa campaign, and the British were no more capable of stopping von Lettow-Vorbeck from invading its own colonial territories, where it only surrendered after he was credibly informed that the First World War had ended. On the other hand, the 20,000 *Force Publique* of the Belgian Congo, under Belgian officers but mostly made up of locally recruited forces, better equipped, trained, supplied and commanded, performed much better and were able not only to defend the Belgian Congo but to perform a successful offensive into German East Africa. It was probably von Lettow-Vorbeck's strategic option at the end of the war to retreat/move into enemy territory less exhausted by the war effort, but it is hard to question the notion that Portugal by presenting a show of military incompetence made it a particularly tempting target for invasion.

This proved the Portuguese critics of intervention right— namely some of the most competent military officers—who argued that Portugal did not have the means to put in the field an army capable of fighting alongside the most modern European armies. Expeditionary warfare is always a major challenge, much more so in an impoverished and deeply divided Portugal. The Portuguese expeditionary forces included flawed tactical instruction and command and control, to major problems with crucial logistics and medical support.[33]

In the case of Mozambique, Portuguese forces suffered from a mix of lack of competent experienced commanders. When the latter were available their advice was ignored by decision-makers, over-ambitious aims that ignored the enormous distances and logistical challenges that war in Africa required. Also there was arguably, a basic mistake made by the Portu-

---

[31] René Pélissier, Op. Cit., pp. 405-36

[32] Marques, AH Oliveira, *O Terceiro Governo de Afonso Costa – 1917* (Livros Horizonte, (s/d)), p. 58 (Act of the Government Reunion of 4 May 1917)

[33] Several problems that confronted the Portuguese war effort during the First World War African campaign are very well described in Arrifes, Marco Fortunato, *A Primeira Grande Guerra na África Portuguesa. Angola e Moçambique (1914-1918)* (Edições Cosmos/Instituto da Defesa Nacional, 2004)

guese, but also to a lesser degree by the British and the South Africans, but not by the Germans and the Belgians, of refusing to rely primarily on local African troops. Racial prejudices of the wrong kind arguably had a significant military cost.

Portugal lost 2,000 dead in the Mozambique campaign. Significantly of the 2,000 dead, only about 150 were in combat. This means there can little arguing that Portuguese forces were not adequately prepared and supported to operate effectively in the very demanding conditions of Africa.[34]

Conclusions

In total, in Mozambique, Portugal engaged 20,000 expeditionary troops and probably about 20,000 local forces mostly in support roles, from 1914 to 1918. The result was a total military operational failure. Ironically the main political objectives ended being achieved—ensuring that in any peace settlement that the Portuguese empire in Africa would not be a bargaining chip, and would remain under Portuguese rule. In the case of Mozambique, there was even a small increase of territory in the north.[35] Was this show of commitment a result of the active belligerency of Portugal, or would this have happened because of circumstances beyond Portuguese control—namely British strategic interest in keeping large territories in Africa under a weak but loyal ally? The result was still very far from the affirmation of the new Portuguese Republic as a credible rising power.

Africa was a peripheral theatre in World War One. But for the Portuguese resources, it was potentially an excellent battlefield to have a significant political effect. Belgium managed to conquer parts of German East Africa by making the most of its African forces significantly more numerous than the German troops—but similar to the total number of Portuguese forces involved. A small power could have a large military

---

[34] Data from 'O Esforço Militar Português', *O Instituto*, Vol° 67, n°3, 1920 give the following elements: 143 deaths by combat, 4,668 deaths by disease or accident, of whom 2,506 were African porters. Other authors give other numbers, similar, but not equal. René Pélissier spoke of 54 deaths by combat and 2,000 by disease and accidents. René Pélissier, Op. Cit., p. 388. Marco Fortunato Arrifes gives a total, extract from the regimental sheets, of 1,898 deaths in Mozambique. Marco Fortunato Arrifes, Op. Cit., p. 331.

[35] See, for the total, data from René Pélissier, Op. Cit., pp. 388-390. In general, information about the number of troops engaged in Mozambique gives only the Europeans troops, forgetting the native contribution.

impact on the African front of World War One given the dispersal of resources and troops of the Great Powers. Portuguese political and military leaders failed to grasp this, and make the most of that possibility by focusing most of its resources in Africa and doing it effectively.

Portuguese war aims were out of all proportion with the military means the country had at its disposal. The result was, predictably, a number of military disasters.

Portuguese leaders wanted international visibility. But they got visibility of the worst kind, by the end of the war the consensus was that Portuguese military forces were too weak and incompetent to be trusted with the defence of any territory on their own. The understandable if ambitious search for greater strategic autonomy by Portugal during World War One had ended by 1918 in a show of greater dependency than ever before.

Bibliography

Arrifes, Marco Fortunato, *A Primeira Grande Guerra na África Portuguesa. Angola e Moçambique (1914-1918)* (Edições Cosmos, Instituto da Defesa Nacional, 2004)

Diário da Câmara dos Deputados, 1910-1911

Duarte, António Paulo, 'Esboço para uma Leitura Estratégica sobre a Campanha de Moçambique (1914-1918)', *Revista Militar*, N° 8/9, agosto/setembro de 1998, pp. 667-704

Duarte, António Paulo, 'O Desejo da Aliança: Os Republicanos Radicais, a Aliança com a Grã-Bretanha e a Intervenção Portuguesa na Grande Guerra', *Conference in the International Seminar*: *From the Trenches to Versailles: War and Memory (1914-1919)*, Reitoria da Universidade Nova de Lisboa, 22-27 de Junho de 2009, 23 June 2009, 14.00h

Duarte, António Paulo, 'Portugal maior', *Limes* (Rivista Italiana di Giopolitica), n° 5, 2010, pp. 67-74

Duarte, António Paulo, 'A helvetização do Exército e a intervenção portuguesa na Grande Guerra', *Congresso Internacional I República e Republicanismo. Atas* (Assembleia da República, 2012) pp. 195-202

Fraga, Luís Alves, *Do Intervencionismo ao Sidonismo, os Dois segmentos da Política de Guerra da 1ª República, 1916-1918* (Imprensa Universidade de Coimbra, 2010)

Gray, Colin S, *The Strategy Bridge: Theory for Practice*, (Oxford University, 2010)

Henriques, Mendo Castro & Leitão, António Rosas, *La Lys, 1918, Os Soldados Desconhecidos*, (Prefácio, 2001)
Marques, AH Oliveira, *O Terceiro Governo de Afonso Costa – 1917* (Livros Horizonte, (s/d))
Marques, Ricardo, *Os Fantasmas do Rovuma. A epopeia dos soldados portugueses em África durante a I Guerra Mundial* (Alfragide, Oficina do Livro, 2012)
Martins, Azambuja, *Nevala. Expedição a Moçambique* (Famalicão, 1935)
Norton de Matos, *Memórias e Trabalhos da Minha Vida*, 3 Vols., (Imprensa da Universidade de Coimbra, 2005)
'O Esforço Militar Português', *O Instituto*, Vol° 67, n°3 (1920) pp. 118-24
Oliveira, Maurício de, *Pereira da Silva, Oficial-Ministro-Doutrinador* (Editora Marítimo Colonial, 1968)
Pélissier, René, *História de Moçambique, Formação e Oposição, 1854-1918*, II Vol. (Estampa, 1998)
Pires, Nuno Lemos, Conference in the International Seminar 'Entering the War. The entrance of Small and Medium powers in the First World War', II Panel – 'Entering the War: Africa and Europe – Diplomacy, Economy and Society', Instituto da Defesa Nacional, 30 March 2016, Lisbon
Pomian, Krzystof, *Sur l'Histoire* (Éditions Gallimard, 1999)
Ramos, Rui, 'A Revolução Republicana de 1910 e a Política Externa Portuguesa', in João Marques de Almeida e Rui Ramos, Coord., *Revoluções, Política Externa e Política de Defesa em Portugal, Séc. XIX-XX* (Edições Cosmos/Instituto da Defesa Nacional, 2008) pp. 55-94
Reis, Augusto e Henriques, António, *Portugal Maior. Livro de Leituras Portuguesas para o Ensino Técnico* (Livraria Popular Francisco Franco, (s/d))
Rosas, Fernando, *Portugal no Século XX (1890-1976) – Pensamento e Acção Política* (Editorial Notícias, 2004)
Sibley, JR, *Tanganyika Guerrilla: East African Campaign (1914-1918)* (New York, 1971)
Teixeira, Nuno Severiano, *O Poder e a Guerra, 1914-1918, Objetivos Nacionais e Estratégias Políticas na Entrada de Portugal na Grande Guerra* (Editorial Estampa, 1996)
Telo, António José, *História da Marinha Portuguesa. Homens, Doutrina e Organização, 1824-1974* (tomo I) (Academia da Marinha, 1999)

Telo, António José, & Sousa, Pedro Marquês de, *O CEP. Os militares sacrificados pela má política* (Fronteira do Caos, 2016)

Valente, Vasco Pulido, A *'República Velha' (1910-1917)* (Gradiva, 1997)

War and Empire: Portuguese East Africa and economic warfare (1914-1919)

Ana Paula Pires & Maria Fernanda Rollo[1]

The African continent remains—as during the First World War—a worldwide issue of central importance, as evidenced by the 2012 EU/Africa summit held during the Portuguese presidency of the European Union. The continent throughout the twentieth century can be considered a stage in permanent mutation, where different elements arise from internal dynamics—yet influenced by realities foreign to the continent—interact and connect with each other. The observation tends toward greater accuracy and thoroughness once we focus on more specific realities, such as the situation resulting from the outbreak of World War One in the summer of 1914.

Portuguese East Africa (Mozambique) is an example of the globalisation process; as (i) an element of direct action, particularly through the exploitation of its natural resources in the widest sense possible, and also through the unique features of its political situation as regards international relations, and (ii) by the role it played as a crossroads, that is a space and passage for various material and non-material flows on a worldwide scale in relation to neighbouring British territories, in particular South Africa.

It is worth mentioning that during the 'Belle Époque' the network of transactions of goods and people had spread, thereby bringing closer to the centre of the world-economy remote and

---

[1] Maria Fernanda Rollo (fernandarollo@netcabo.pt) NOVA School of Social Sciences and Humanities and
Ana Paula Pires (asoarespires@gmail.com) NOVA School of Social Sciences and Humanities

peripheral places like the African territories. It was then that Mozambique gained a global dimension, and began, considering its geo-strategic importance in East Africa and the relevance of its natural resources, to be disputed by both Britain and Germany.

This paper aims at exploring in a critical and integrated manner, the main policies and measures (or the lack thereof) implemented during the Portuguese First Republic in the field of production development, as well as in the search for instruments necessary to boost the recovery of East African colonial markets, in an attempt—with varied degrees of success—to minimize the effects of external dependency, particularly as regards basic necessities. From a strategic point of view we will consider, questioning their role and importance, the new means of transport and communications: railways, steamboats, and particularly, the telegraph and wireless communications. We will consider their impact on Mozambique, particularly as tools of defence and safeguarding of the Portuguese Empire. The economy is thus the starting point for highlighting the international and multiracial nature of the Great War, with impacts and consequences falling vastly beyond the territories covered by European remembrance, in other words spanning across the collective global memory.

Europe and the rest of the world – Africa and nineteenth-century globalisation

In 1914 when the First World War started all major European powers, with the exception of the Habsburg Empire, ruled over territories outside Europe. In this paper we analyse the strategic importance of the Portuguese colonies in Africa namely Mozambique; understanding its importance in a comparative reading frame, and studying it from three perspectives: (i) the dispute of empire; (ii) mobilisation and strategy of the European powers toward war in Africa and (iii) the protection, preservation and maintenance of the integrity of the Portuguese colonial empire.

At a time and in a context of profound internationalisation, communications (terrestrial and 'voice') had acquired a new dimension, becoming, throughout the second half of the nineteenth century, the main instrument in the construction of an international economic model that involved and unleashed a scene of global and general mutation, prompted by the same technological leap that produced the Industrial Revolution (or the two Industrial Revolutions). The economic dynamism that marked these years thus reinforced the positivist faith in the notion of progress, while at the same time promoted the alliance between scientific research and technical development. Thus emerged a single global economy, supported by a thickening circulation network of people, capital and goods, a reality made visible by the growing and continuous interdependence between developed countries and the underdeveloped world. This connection was well illustrated by the signing of international conventions regulating telegraphic and postal services, and also train timetables.

On the eve of the war, Britain controlled about four-fifths of the trade in the Sub-Sahara region. Germany, continuing the policy initiated by Bismarck in the late nineteenth century, had a small, but strategically placed, empire extending itself from Madagascar to the entrance of the Red Sea. Both empires bordered territories under Portuguese administration, for whose political and economic interest they began to compete, particularly after the British ultimatum of 1890, and which would culminate in August 1913 in a secret agreement that aimed to share the Portuguese colonies in Africa between Britain and Germany.

War and empire

The colonies during the First World War were not mere battlefields, they were an integral part of the economic warfare of European countries, providing raw materials and food. Therefore, the strategic position occupied by the East African territories is important to understand, considering them as agents in the globalisation process, particularly through the exploitation of natural resources in the widest sense possible, but also through the role they played as a crossroads, connecting space and passage for various material and immaterial flows across the world.

We shall consider, as regards the Portuguese case, three major issues:
1. the extent to which the changes resulting from difficulties in cross-border commerce might have played a relevant role in the attempts to adjust Portuguese exports to wartime conditions, with an emphasis on the efforts towards expansion to

new markets (Africa and Latin America);
2. the Portuguese role in the strategy of conquer of commercial positions carried out by the British Foreign Office;
3. the extent to which the war altered the way in which governments and society regarded the national economic structure, acknowledging the limitations of the Portuguese productive system.

Although most of the clashes occurred on European soil, the involvement of the African continent played an essential role within the Great War: for over four years Africa provided human and material resources on an unprecedented scale to the Western Front. From the 'black continent' standpoint, it is worth noting, how the First World War contrasted in terms of objectives, impact, scale and duration with the many conflicts that erupted throughout the nineteenth century which were conducted mainly against native populations, and motivated by local and limited objectives.

Immediately after Britain's declaration of war on Germany, on 4 August 1914, one of the main priorities of London was to eliminate and/or control the strategic potential of the German colonies and possessions all over the world; a strategy that was felt with particular intensity in Latin America and in Africa and that consisted of capturing port facilities, submarine communications, cable and radio masts.

East Africa and economic warfare

For Portugal what was actually at stake, during August 1914, was not so much the direct effect of the armed conflict as the disarticulation of the economic workings and the regular distribution circuits. It is worth noting how devastating and far-reaching the consequences of the decrease in imports were to the economy and people's daily life. This reality was soon acknowledged and denounced by British Ambassador to Lisbon, Lancelot Carnegie, who, in a letter to the British Minister of Foreign Affairs, did not hesitate to identify it as the decisive factor explaining why intervention by the Portuguese government was '. . . at this early stage even more drastic than has been necessary in States that are more affected politically' by the conflict.[2]

The Portuguese government had also developed some policies

[2] TNA: FO 368/1063, Letter 26 Aug 1914 Lancelot Carnegie to Edward Grey

towards the promotion and development of agriculture in its colonial territories: as a first step a law was published, establishing a service agency responsible for the Portuguese colonies.[3] The new agency reflected the pretext and the opportunity to promote the export of agricultural products, while taking into account that these would only be viable if exported at a competitive price. Much more than the promotion of agricultural specialisation, the main goal of the agency had to do with the rigorous calculation of the price of agricultural products and the presentation of effective methods of reducing production costs.[4] For such objectives to be achieved it was required that, within a short period of time, significant improvements be introduced into the colonial infrastructures, such as building more roads and railways and completing a network of modernly equipped commercial ports to serve as mandatory connection points on the world trade routes. However, the Act failed to provide a single solution.

This story cannot be properly interpreted and understood if one does not bear in mind the impact and consequences of the vigorous economic recovery campaign launched by the Foreign Office immediately after the declaration of war, which sought to counteract German commerce and commercial strategies. In other words, the idea was to establish a policy (symbolising—more than really imposing—the will) to persuade British commerce and finance to invest in Portugal. It was one of the key points made by British Consul to Portuguese East Africa Errol MacDonell on Britain's chances of reclaiming German businesses throughout Portuguese Africa.

The concern of His Majesty's Government regarding the gathering of all essential information in the pursuit of a commercial policy, mostly focused on promoting and valuing British trade, was reinforced by a telegram sent ten days after the onset of hostilities by Foreign Secretary Edward Grey to the British consulates.[5] As the situation became clearer, the British Government established a specific strategy and put together the necessary instruments (similar to what it did in Latin America), aimed at controlling the Portuguese colonial markets, particu-

[3] Decree, no. 1 142, *Diário do Governo*, I Series, no. 226 3 Dec 1914
[4] Ibid.
[5] 'A guerra comercial' in *Jornal do Comércio e das Colónias*, 26 Nov 1914, p. 1

larly Mozambique, where the German presence was notorious.[6] For the rest, it was well known that, as the British Secretary of Commerce phrased it, 'War creates no trade, but it may correct it'.[7]

The way in which the British government welcomed pressure from British commercial agents interested in the Anglo-Portuguese trade is therefore unsurprising. British diplomacy would put its best effort into providing more favourable conditions to its commercial activity, eventually achieving most of its goals through the trade treaty entered into by both countries on 12 January 1914.[8] The British strategy grew more intense throughout the months that followed Pimenta de Castro's rise to power (25 Jan–15 May 1915). In reality, due to circumstances and the alleged pro-German standing of the Portuguese head of Government, the attitude of the British Foreign Office evolved into reinforcing trade relations between the two countries, through the adoption of specific measures aimed at persuading British trade and finance to invest in Portugal and thus take over German businesses and trade positions in Africa,[9] particularly in Mozambique. This was made necessary by the significant increase in the consumption by the German army of Portuguese colonial products, notably foodstuffs (cocoa, coffee and sugar). To access these products, the Germans had established alternative routes that enabled them to ship colonial products into Germany, while avoiding 'war zones' and

---

[6] Report of September 1914, put together by the British Secretary of Commerce, where the situation is well analysed: 'while the commercial relationship with Portugal is not perhaps of the first importance, it is one which may, even more than any other, repay a special effort to take advantage of war conditions'. Cf. TNA: FO 368/1063, Report Sep 1914 by the British Secretary of Commerce, p. 1

[7] Ibid, p. 1, 'The German conquest of the Portuguese market has been as quick and easy as the conquest of its territories by Junot, and it may be supposed that their hold may be as quickly and easily loosened'. One should recall that when the war was declared, 734 German ships had sought refuge on neutral waters, thus leaving them with only 600 ships and a total of 2,875,000 tons. Marc Ferro, *A Grande Guerra, 1914-1918* (Lisbon, 2002) p. 144

[8] On the signing of the Treaty of Trade and Navigation between Portugal and Britain, refer to, in particular, Sacuntala Miranda, *O Declínio da Supremacia Britânica em Portugal (1890-1939)* pp. 392ff

[9] TNA: FO 368/1382, Memorandum 22 Feb 1915, put together by the general consult Errol MacDonell. On the policy of conquer and acquisition of markets of raw materials by Germany, refer to Luís Manuel Alves de Fraga, *Portugal e a Primeira Grande Guerra*, pp. 38ff

taking advantage of the situation and 'goodwill' of their neutral neighbours.[10]

Nationality of companies established in the main ports of Mozambique, 1915:[11]

Place	Germany	Britain	Other Nationalties
Porto Amélia	• Wm. Philippi • Deutsche-Ost-Afrikanische Gesellschaft	• Consolidated Nyassa	
Moçambique	• Wm. Philippi		• JF dos Santos (Portugal) • Societé du Madal (France)
Quelimane	• Wm Philippi • Lüdwig Deuss		• Companhia da Zambézia (Germany, France, Britain, Portugal, USA) • Companhia do Boror (Switzerland) • Companhia do Lugela (Germany and Britain)
Chinde	• Lüdwig Deuss • Wm. Philippi • Deutsche-Ost-Afrikanische Gesellschaft	• African Lakes and British Central Africa Company	
Beira	• Wm. Philippi • Deutsche-Ost-Afrikanische Gesellschaft		

German companies clearly controlled the trade of Mozambican colonial products: a situation which contributed to the development of equipment and infrastructure (ports, railroad and

---

[10] TNA: FO 368/1383, Confidential memorandum on trade and finances of Portugal, 22 Mar 1915, Lancelot Carnegie to Edward Grey and C. Roque da Costa, 'A situação dos neutrais' in *O Jornal do Comércio e das Colónias*, 3 Mar 1915, p. 1
[11] TNA: FO 368/1382, Memorandum 22 Feb1915, drafted by general consul of Britain in Lourenço Marques, Errol MacDonell.

navigation lines) necessary to transport those products to European markets. Considering the importance of German investment in Mozambique and the level of competition between investors, MacDonell estimated that the minimum amount of capital needed by any British firm to operate in Portuguese East Africa was around £100,000 as it required adequate maritime premises, regular work schedules and one or two small cargo vessels to ship the products to minor ports.[12]

British diplomacy in Lisbon persevered in its intention to intensify Anglo-Portuguese trade relations, with the involvement of the British Chamber of Commerce and the Commercial Association of Lisbon which put efforts into studying the trade and finances of Portugal.[13] The British authorities were evidently aware of the difficulties in putting their strategy into practise, as the lack of interest of the financial milieu in investing in what was deemed 'a small market about which little is known and that little unfavourable'[14] was rather notorious; at best, the exploitation of Portuguese colonial resources might raise some interest, particularly concerning Angola and Mozambique. On the other side, Britain was starting to come to terms with the fact that it might be required to profer financial support to Portugal, as Carnegie argued 'in return for the supplies and support given us'.[15]

As results of Portugal's commercial activities started to appear and knowledge of the economic and financial reality became more apparent, the country's strategic value and potential became increasingly notorious, particularly in connection with its links between Central Africa and South America. This reinforced Britain's interest in promoting investment in a country described by the first secretary of the British Mission in Lisbon, George Young, 'as naturally and necessarily a customer

---

[12] Ibid, p. 5

[13] At the presentation of the report, the British ambassador in Lisbon, Lancelot Carnegie, evidenced commitment into uphold its publication and allow the effects in terms of investment in Portugal stand out: 'the enclosed report would, if published show British interests what conditions here really are, and it might also direct the attention of the local authorities to the advantage of seconding the efforts of the British interests in Lisbon(...)' TNA: FO 368/1383, Note 17 Mar 1915 Lancelot Carnegie to Edward Grey, p. 1

[14] TNA, FO 368/1383, Note 17 Mar 1915 Lancelot Carnegie to Edward Grey, p1

[15] Ibid, pp. 1-2

of ours as Ireland.[16]

This move was also in reaction to several signs and evidence that confirmed the continuation of German-Portuguese relations, particularly the involvement, during Pimenta de Castro's government, of an important Portuguese banking institution, Fonseca, Santos & Vianna (who maintained strong ties to the Burnay & C. firm) in a gold transaction where agents from Deutsche Bank[17] were also present. According to the British Foreign Office, this situation evidenced the influence that 'German finance still had in Lisbon',[18] though ignoring the intentions and goals behind the operation, particularly the destination of the gold. As far as the head of the British Legation in Lisbon, Lancelot Carnegie, knew the gold was either going to the United States of America, in payment for German purchases, or to Spain or Germany (via neutral countries).[19]

The British obviously feared that the gold was heading to Germany as its final destination and, facing such possibility, Carnegie made clear that any negotiations involving a loan or financial advance to Portugal should take into consideration not only the political hesitation of Pimenta de Castro's government, but also the rather unclear economic ties between Portugal and Wilhelm II's *Reich*.[20] The possibility of a British loan would also be compromised by the enactment of a bill by British Finance Minister Lloyd George introducing restrictions on loans to companies and foreign governments. As regards Portugal, this policy reflected on the shrinking investment in some territories of the Portuguese colonial empire, mostly in Africa. It caused investment plans and modernisation of sugar companies in Mozambique and Angola to be postponed, as well as mining activities in Tete and Manica, and the agricultural concessions

---

[16] Ibid, pp. 5-6

[17] TNA: FO 368/1383, Note 3 Mar 1915 Lancelot Carnegie to Edward Grey, p. 1. Also refer TNA: FO 368/1383, Note 24 Mar 1915 Treasury Chambers to Under Secretary of State, p. 1

[18] Ibid.

[19] Ibid.

[20] It was an inconvenient situation for Britain, but whose solution, as it had been made clear, should not include prohibition: '. . . it does not seem worthwhile asking the Portuguese Government to prohibit the export of gold or take measures to stop its irregular exportation; for if they do not do so in their own far more imperative interests they will not for us . . .' TNA: FO 368/1383, 11 Mar 1915 Lancelot Carnegie to Edward Grey, pp. 1-2

in Guinea, Cape Verde and Timor to be delayed.[21]

It is, therefore, no surprise that the measure was received with discontent and disappointment by some within Portuguese society, especially amidst those with colonial interests, or that it raised accusations in the Portuguese press, which denounced what it considered double standards of the British government toward Portugal:

> all that would be fine if, in spite of everything, the law was equal to all, but the authorisations recently granted to a sugar company in Cuba, the £2,500,000 just granted to Argentina Railways Ld. and another emission already promised to Java place our colonial interests in a state of development that cannot be satisfactorily justified.[22]

In reality, the real issue concerned the frustration of expectations that the British policy had raised, along with the failure to profit from opportunities that had been offered to the Portuguese colonies as a result of the war through the announcement of projects whose implementation depended greatly on the financial capacity of London:

> our colonies require a great amount of capital in order to develop and if the London market becomes closed to them, as is happening currently, with no effort from the Government to obtain the same treatment that is given to Cuba, Argentina or Java, the crisis they are going through shall grow significantly worse.[23]

In defence of this claim, the alliance between both countries was reinforced, in order to sustain the need for an exception that protected Portuguese interests.[24]

In summary, since the summer of 1914, British foreign policy had sought to profit from the wartime conditions in order to foster the expansion of British commercial interests around the world. In particular, Britain sought to conquer German commercial and industrial positions, both in Europe and in Africa, where the Portuguese colonies, notably Mozambique, played a significant role.

As far as Portugal was concerned, the impact and effect of the

---

[21] 'Relações externas' in *Revista Colonial*, Year 2, no. 29, 25 May 1915, p. 149
[22] Ibid.
[23] Ibid.
[24] Ibid.

world-wide conflict raised many difficulties beside those strictly resulting from the war. This reflected the weak development of Portugal's peripheral economy, which was based on an agricultural sector whose levels of production and productivity lagged behind the minimum necessary, was strongly dependent on foreign funding, freighting and essential goods (food stuffs, fuels and even equipment, technology and raw materials that were essential to its small industrial sector that by then had become reduced to a minimum). This was in spite of a vast 'empire' that was economically and strategically relevant, particularly in the context of the world-wide conflict. The war also raised awareness of the weaknesses of the domestic economy. This led to debate and internal pressure to introduce a programme of economic modernisation for the primary sector fostering industrialisation and intensifying of economic relations with the colonies, especially Angola, Mozambique and São Tomé e Príncipe. This intention was aligned to the British strategy regarding their position on the mainland and especially in the colonies. As a result, Britain encouraged it to an extent.

In Mozambique, in particular, a set of initiatives aimed to develop the commercial and economic relations between the territory and the mainland started appearing. That was the purpose behind the appeal, in February 1916 (one month before Germany's declaration of war on Portugal), by the Governor of Mozambique, Álvaro de Castro, to the Chamber of Deputies, inviting its chairman to organise and send a mission to the colony in order to collect information necessary to the execution of a survey that served '. . . as propaganda at the same time'.[25] On the same day, 4 February 1916, the Governor sent a note to the representatives of industrial and commercial associations informing them of the advantages of closer economic ties between Mozambique and the mainland; an option that could be justified, according to Álvaro de Castro, by the market conditions and the variety, value and wealth of the products of the territory.[26] The government pledged to invest all means available to adequately disseminate the initiative, through

---

[25] Refer to the note from the Government of Mozambique to the chairman of the Chamber of Deputies in 'Reforma das Pautas' in *O Trabalho Nacional*, no. 15, Mar 1916, p. 81. The proposition was only submitted to Parliament a few months later, in early May: *Diário da Câmara dos Deputados*, Session no. 79, 2 May 1916, p. 4
[26] Ibid., pp. 81-2

exhibitions and the distribution of all sorts of informative elements. The initiative actually raised the interest of the Oporto Industrial Association, which regarded the investment in Eastern African markets with some enthusiasm, underlining the need to join forces with the Commercial Association and the Commercial Centre of Oporto in order to pursue actions.[27]

The Governor's power to send the list of requests of exclusive industrial rights on the colonial territories to industrial associations (instead of sending them to the Minister of Colonies) was recent and reflected a decentralising policy regarding the administration that had been introduced by the First Republic and which seemed to produce positive results. Although the number of requests increased, the activities they pertained to were, with few exceptions, of an artisanal nature, resorting to techniques and equipment that were more often than not somewhat inadequate.

Shortly afterward, in April 1916, a draft bill authorising the Governor of Mozambique to enter into a loan of $500,000 to fund the construction of infrastructure to develop the colony was discussed in the Portuguese Parliament.[28] Until then, the intervention of the republican government concerning Mozambique was limited to exploiting revenue that directly depended on relations with neighbouring territories, particularly with South Africa, with no programme in place that fostered the development of the productive activities within the colony. This was a much criticised situation, as it was widely deemed 'imprudent'.[29]

Even so, the Portuguese Parliament hesitated in its answer to Álvaro de Castro's request, arguing that it lacked a structured development plan encompassing the construction works in need of funding.[30] Upon repeated enquiries from the Chamber, the drafter of the proposal, Ernesto de Vilhena, eventually put forward an explanation that convinced few of the

---

[27] Ibid. p. 82

[28] The loan at an interest rate of six per cent was to '... install a telephone line to Johannesburg, complete the telegraph and telephone lines of Zambezia and perform some works in order to prepare Lourenço Marques for the tourism season and open certain roads in the southern part of the province. *Diário da Câmara dos Deputados*, Session no. 64, 3 Apr 1916, p. 16

[29] See, particularly the intervention by unionist MP Armando Ochoa. Ibid.

[30] Further details on this discussion in *Diário da Câmara dos Deputados*, Session no. 66, 5 April 1916, pp. 8-14

proposed direction:

... one should not be required to thoroughly describe all the development works to which the $500,000 loan is intended, firstly because it is not customary to do so; secondly, it is inconvenient; thirdly, because such insertion would in no

Official list of requests for exclusive industrial rights in Mozambique[31]

Proponent	Type of Industry	Duration of the exclusive right	Place	Decision
Napoleão Luís Ferreira	Pottery	20 years	Lourenço Marques	Annulled
Lúcio Veloso da Rocha and António Correia Pinto	Noodles, crackers and cookies	10 years	Lourenço Marques, Quelimane and Moçambique	Denied
Julius Antonius Aurelius Schultz	Paper and parchment	20 years	All provinces	No information is available on the outcome of this procedure
Paulino dos Santos Gil and Francisco Maria da Silva	Soaps and candles	20 years	All provinces	Idem
José Joaquim de Morais	Hydraulic cement	20 years	All provinces	Idem
Giuseppe Cavallari and Giuseppe Miglietti	Ice	10 years	City and suburbs of Lourenço Marques	Idem
Napoleão Luís Ferreira Leão	Matches	20 years	No information available	Idem
Giuseppe Cavallari and Giuseppe Miglietti	Beer	20 years	All provinces	Idem
Manuel de Jesus Martins and Aurélio Augusto Loureiro	Vegetable fibre	20 years	All provinces	Idem

[31] 'Exclusivos industriais nas colónias' in *O Trabalho Nacional*, no. 15, Mar 1916, pp. 70-1

way increase the guarantees for the State represented by the loan in accordance with the legislation in force; and, fourthly, because the Parliament was adopting a centralising orientation that contravened its own decision.[32]

The matter was undoubtedly important. Therefore, in spite of the vaguely defined and loosely integrated goals, the proposal was eventually approved by the Chamber of Deputies.[33]

The interest and expectations of the possibility of the colonies supplying the mainland and Madeira with essential products grew as internal hardship increased. In reality, the government had 'discovered', somewhat late, the colonies as a source of provisions through which it could help supply the mainland and thus contain the general discontent and protests from an increasingly dissatisfied population suffering from the effects of war, aggravated by the route (or rather the lack thereof) undertaken by the political power in terms of wartime economy, mostly as regards subsistencies. All of a sudden, the colonies appeared on the horizon as the solution to a number of difficulties that afflicted the economy on the mainland. In addition to direct supply, there was also an interest in exploiting raw materials, attracting the investment of Portuguese capital in Africa. The colonies were regarded beyond political sovereignty, as part of the 'national economic space', worthy of investment, something similar to the idea that the State would try to assert much later. As the Member of Parliament José Barbosa claimed '(...) our colonies were never an advantage to the mainland, but rather the only market that has enabled us to maintain our trade and industrial balance'.[34] However, the economic exploitation of the colonies suffered little change in the long run and remained behind the possibilities and resources offered, even though their importance to the mainland cannot be assessed solely by the results of investments or colonial trade and these kept playing a vital political and economic role for Portugal.

---

[32] Ibid., p. 11
[33] *Diário da Câmara dos Deputados*, Session no. 68, 7 Apr 1916, p. 14
[34] *Diário da Câmara dos Deputados*, Session no. 67, 6 Apr 1916, pp. 13-4

Re-exportation of products from Mozambique (1913-1916):[35]

	1913	1914	1915	1916
Tons				
Raw materials	12	39	827	934
Foodstuffs	1 749	120	-	89
Total	1 761	159	827	1 020
'Contos'				
Raw materials	6	4	66	71
Foodstuffs	105	113	-	12
Total	111	117	66	84

The case of Angola was very different from the situation of Mozambique during World War One. On the other side of Africa, regardless of its immense resources, Angola was not targeted by a propaganda campaign or any appeal to investment in the same way that Mozambique was. Although it underwent noticeable development in 1914-1915, the Angolan economy fell into recession in 1916, as a result of the considerable plunge in the amount of food stuff exported to the mainland.

However, interest in Mozambique remained. Even when, after the takeover of Kionga and the occupation of Xivinga, the commercial and industrial mission that the Parliamentary Committee for the Colonies had decided to send to Mozambique in May 1916, had to be postponed, the impetus of industrial and commercial agents by no means weakened.[36]

Globally, one can assert that Portugal's involvement in the war marked a turning point in the way politicians and industrial tycoons regarded the need for closer relations between the mainland and the colonial space, in order to profit from opportunities and resources that had meanwhile become essential for fuelling a growing war effort. As Lisboa de Lima puts it, there was only one way Portugal could possibly face those challenges and it was by 'joining the efforts of each and every one ... both on the mainland as well as in the colonies, to work with one single goal, with no attempt to make mainland or colonial interests prevail over the others, as they are all Portuguese ...'[37]

[35] 'Ainda a reexportação colonial' in *O Economista Portuguez. Revista Financeira, Económica, Social e Colonial*, Year 10, no. 95, 8 May 1920, p. 156
[36] *Diário da Câmara dos Deputados*, Session no. 89, 15 May 1916, pp. 29-30
[37] 'Conferência na Sociedade de Geografia de Lisboa em 8 de Maio de 1916 feita

The war had ultimately proven that the time was ripe to conquer abandoned markets in East Africa. This was basically the idea made public by the Oporto Industrial Association when it declared that the industrial development achieved during the war required expansion into new markets, as well as the intensification of Anglo-Portuguese trade relations.

The centenary anniversary of World War One, in 2014, raised great interest both at domestic and international level, with multiple initiatives in many countries, and also within the scope of international dynamics. In addition to the importance of the study of World War I and its impact in Africa, in a multiple and global perspective at the national level, the evocation of the centenary, organised and studied in the international context, involves a dynamic that requires an active role by Portugal, as well as an opportunity to raise awareness among academics and the general public—both nationally and internationally—in the involvement and participation of the country in the Great War, both on the African front, from 1914 onward, as in Europe from 1917. Such evocations are still significant opportunities to stimulate the renewal and further research and historical dissemination and to raise awareness of the importance of historical memory and knowledge, the valuing and dissemination of both material and non-material heritage and the importance of its preservation.

---

por Lisboa de Lima' in *Revista Colonial*, Year 4, no. 41, 25 May 1916, pp. 120-1

The Status of the West African Sterling in Southern Nigeria in 1916

Bamidele Aly[1]

Introduction

The focus of this chapter is on the introduction of banknotes in Southern Nigeria in 1916 during World War One and is based on four texts from the British Colonial Office archives.

It is important to research the currency and monetary policy of Great Britain in its West African colonies, in particular around the issuance of banknotes in Nigeria during World War One. Money is not only the centre of all economic interactions but at the core of the economy. During the Great War, all belligerent nations encountered metal shortages, in particular silver and gold, and most of their budget was allocated to the war. Thus, whilst monetary creation is linked to taxation, during an armed conflict, it is more difficult to raise tax for fear of disenchantment when national unity is of paramount importance.

Nigeria exported to Great Britain palm seeds, palm oil and kernels, timber, tin, peanuts, cotton, cocoa, mahogany, shea products and maize, which could be easily processed for British consumers and sold on the world commodities markets at a fair price. Furthermore, looking at the differences between revenues and expenses published in the Colonial Office books, Southern Nigeria and subsequently the Colony of Nigeria recorded a monetary surplus. Colonial authorities generated revenues from the taxation of imported goods, which reduced reliance on the imperial treasury. The main currencies in

---

[1] Bamidele ALY is a French-Nigerian economic historian specialising in the monetary history of anglophone West Africa, the Nigerian diaspora in Europe and West Africa and African economic development.

circulation were coins, and the shipment of coins to Nigeria from Great Britain was becoming not only riskier but also costlier due to reduced financial resources at hand.

The texts under discussion are from Colonial Office file CO 984/5 (West African Currency Board),[2] accessible at The National Archives, Richmond in the UK. The texts are important in the context of the war, as Great Britain had no choice but to reduce the cargoes of (silver) coins to its overseas colonies. Two texts were written in English for the English-speaking population, that is foreign merchants and the educated Southern Nigerian elites.[3] Another two announcements were written in Yoruba directly addressing the traditional elites and the 'indigenous' population.

These notices are short but convey an important message to all residents of Nigeria. They are official documents stamped with the seals of the British Crown ordering the population and economic agents alike to accept the new currency as legal paper in all territories under control of the Crown British West Africa. The paper money was gradually introduced in the West African states (Ghana/Gold Coast, Gambia, Sierra Leone, Southern Nigeria and Northern Nigeria) from 1916. West African Sterling had been a stable currency used across all the colonies in West Africa from 1912 following the establishment of the coin-issuing institution, the West African Currency Board. West African Sterling was pegged to British Sterling. However, the four texts seem to indicate that acceptance of paper money was not without its pitfalls and its use was not that widespread.

Specimen of a 10s West African Sterling Note dated 30 March 1918

[2] CO984-5: 'Correspondence regarding the Issue of Currency Notes'
[3] Yoruba was only spoken in the south-west of the country, called Nigeria.

Example of a £1 Western African Note dated
30 November 1918

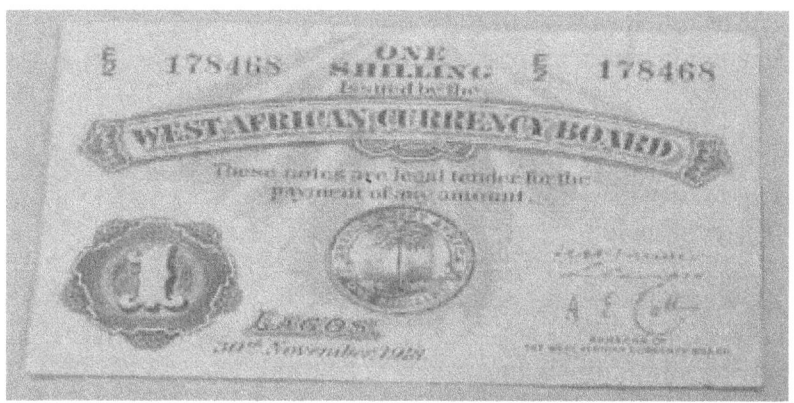

The first series of government notices in English and Yoruba were signed by Lieutenant Colonel Sir Claude Harry Moorhouse[4] (1871-1934), CMG (1914), DSO (1906), in Lagos on 8 July 1916. In July 1916, Lieutenant-Colonel Moorhouse was Secretary of the Southern Provinces of Nigeria. He started his career in the Royal Artillery in 1891 and served in Uganda in 1898, in Southern Nigeria in 1901-1902, in Northern Nigeria in 1903. He retired from the military with the rank of major and became a reserve officer in 1908. That year he served the Colonial Office as a Colonel-Deputy Chief Secretary in Southern Nigeria and as Secretary of the Southern Province of Nigeria from 1 January 1914. Then he became Lieutenant Governor of Nigeria on 1 January 1920. He returned to the army during the Great War. This explains why the second series of government notices in English and Yoruba were signed by his deputy Betram Hodges. The issue of the *Nigerian Pioneer* dated 28 July 1916 in the article 'The West African Currency' informed readers that the new banknotes would enter circulation on 1 August. It was explained that the designs and green colour for the 10s note and the green colour for the pound note were chosen purposefully for illiterate users.

Nigeria and World War One

The dates of the announcements (8 July 1916 and 3 December 1916) are significant because the United Kingdom was engaged

---
[4] Colonial Office List 1891-1921

in a military conflict with France and other allied powers against Germany, and Turkey, among others. The colonies had been drawn into the war effort to protect the Empire against the hegemonic inclinations of Germany in West Africa from the Cameroons and Togo and in East Africa from German East Africa (encompassing among others, Tanganyika, present day mainland Tanzania). Furthermore, the historian Akinjide Osuntokun[5] explains that the Germans (firms and merchants) were more popular in Nigeria than the British, for they provided generous lending facilities to their African agents and intermediaries; these agents carried into the European impenetrable hinterland German goods and reputation.[6] Germans thus dominated export and export trades of Nigeria.

In *Taxing Colonial Africa, The Political Economy of British Imperialism*, Leigh A Gardner says that Great Britain never intended to take any financial and operational risks in its empire expansion but delegated the colonial adventure to the Royal Niger Company, a royal charter company which delegated the management of the operations to local governments led by military and civilian expatriates who had become self-sufficient through the exercise of direct or indirect taxes. In the case of Nigeria, taxes were collected indirectly through import taxes and customs duties to prevent riots as was the case in South Africa and East Africa.[7]

The West African colonies had been integrated into the international trade system by reorienting the local economies towards the export of raw materials, such as kola nuts and palm oil, to support the industrial revolution; and to generate cash namely through the famous system of 'cash crops'. However, during the war, the British authorities decided to change the conditions of the circulation of money, as they were experiencing a period of strong economic growth, which was without precedent, as measured by the increase in prices of agricultural commodities on world markets.

---

[5] Osuntokun, Akinjide, *Nigeria in the First World War* (Longman, 1979) p. 336
[6] Ibid. p. 22
[7] Under British Colonial Rule of Southern Africa, hut tax riots occurred in 1880 from the Boers and in Bechuanaland in 1882.

Introduction of new currency

What were the underlying reasons for the imposition of this new fiat money[8] into areas where the population was largely illiterate? First, we will look at West African Sterling, what it was and how it was introduced. Then we will analyse why a new denomination was added in December 1916 as indicated in the second and fourth official documents written in English and Yoruba, respectively.

How did West African Sterling work?

West African Sterling was created in 1912 as the UK wanted to control the currency in circulation to eradicate competition by French traders, whose five-franc coin was very popular, and the German currency which was well appreciated in South-Eastern Nigeria. The power or authority that controls the issuance of currency also controls a society, therefore creating a common currency for all the West African colonies allowed the British Colonial Office to manage the region more efficiently and in an easily quantifiable way.

The four documents under discussion indicate that the King of England anointed by law the introduction and use of the new banknotes. In Africa, the king was regarded as the supreme ruler carrying authority. For this reason, the tone of the Government Notice is expressed differently in English and in Yoruba (see Appendices) through the choice of vocabulary. In English, the king is 'pleased to announce' but in Yoruba he orders, which recognizes this difference and yet could also signify that the UK Government and colonial authorities pre-empted that these banknotes would not be readily accepted by the indigenous populations. Some form of coercion was necessary in a time of a crisis. The design of the palm tree was expected to appeal the indigenous populations.

Cargoes of sterling silver and copper were regularly sent to the colonies and territories recognised as under control of the British Crown. This was also the case for commodity currencies such as iron bars, manillas and cowries. These transfers of fiat money and commodity currency increased transaction costs and the cost of risk to the colonial authorities, which did not want to

---

[8] The Oxford Dictionary defines fiat money as inconvertible paper money made legal tender by a government decree.

have a charge in their budgets and ledgers; they incurred transport costs (packing, carriage, insurance) due to the heavy weight and quantity of coins required in the buoyant colonial economy. On the one hand, the coins were imported from the United Kingdom, thus, the cost of production of these coins did not result in an immediate profit for the Royal Mint as the nominal value of the coins was small compared with the production costs of the coins. On the other hand, cowries (shell money or Cypraea moneta) were imported by merchants from the Indian Ocean and were not collected in Southern Nigeria. These currency transfers also reduced profits for the merchants, if the harvest of raw materials and commodities was poor or if the shipment of cowries got lost at sea or stolen.

The indigenous population was largely not directly affected by these risks, because they were largely not monetised in the modern sense of the word in the early twentieth century and could barter instead if there were insufficient cowries or other commodities and monies available for their commercial basic transactions.

In an article by Eric Helleiner entitled *The Monetary Dimensions of Colonialism: Why Did Imperial Powers Create Currency Blocks?*, we are reminded that cost reduction was the most important aim for all colonial powers in the late nineteenth and early twentieth centuries. Issuing and controlling the circulation of a new currency therefore would allow Britain not only to strengthen political and social power in a given territory but also to generate revenues from seigniorage (the difference between the face value of the currency and the cost of production of the currency). To this end, the West African Currency Board was created.

In an article 'The Paper Money' in the *Nigerian Pioneer* dated 4 August 1916, it was confirmed that the new pound and the ten shillings notes of the West African Currency Board were in circulation. It was suggested that both notes be the same size and equivalent to that of the English pound note. This comment informed the public that the unnamed journalist was not cognizant with the operations of the West African Currency Board.

West African Currency Board

According to the Cambridge English Dictionary, a currency board is a government organisation that controls the value of its

333

country's currency, often by setting a fixed exchange rate with the currency of another country. For example, a British merchant wanting to travel to Nigeria had to make a deposit at the Bank of British West Africa[9] in advance and received the equivalent money in West African sterling from the branches of the Bank of British West Africa in Nigeria. Fundamentally, the value of West African sterling was at parity with that of British sterling. The British merchant retained the purchasing power of the British sterling even if he had to exchange his holdings of British sterling into West African sterling, when he was travelling to Nigeria, the rest of West Africa or when he travelled back to the United Kingdom.

The West African Currency Board was established in London in 1912. It had similar functions to that of a central bank. However, British West African colonies were not responsible for the supply of money or the monetary policy of their (colonial) economies. It was linked to the Colonial Office via Board Representations and to the UK Treasury, as these amounts of fiat currencies were controlled centrally by the Bank of England. As West African sterling was at parity with British sterling, it was thus initially linked to the Gold Standard before the start of the war and remained so until the Gold Standard was suspended.

In Nigeria, money circulated through the presence of the Bank of British West Africa, as mentioned in the four texts. The Bank of British West Africa was founded in 1894 by Alfred Lewis Jones[10] 'to help to ease financial transactions'.[11] The bank was instrumental in the spread of West African sterling and the payment of salaries of Colonial Office staff in West Africa. It had the monopoly for banking and financial products across West Africa. In addition, owing to an agreement between the Bank and the Royal Mint, the bank received remuneration.[12]

---

[9] According to the Bank Report for 1911 published in the *Nigerian Pioneer* on 28 Jul 1916, the Bank registered as a Limited Liability Company in May 1864 with capital of £100,000 on 10,000 shares of £10 each and paid-up capital of £12,000.

[10] In *Trading in West Africa: 1840-1920* by PN Davies, Alfred Lewis Jones was born in 1845 in Carmarthen, South Wales to Alderman Charles Jones, a well-known resident of the town and to the eldest daughter of Rev. Henry Williams, Rector of Llanedi. At fifteen, he entered the office of Messrs Laird, Fletcher and Co., managing the African Steamship Company trading between Liverpool and West Africa. He eventually became a shipowner. He died in 1909.

[11] Ibid. p. 181

The new banknotes and coins had the following characteristics described by Wadan Narsey in *British Imperialism and the Making of Colonial Currency Systems*:

> i) the basis is the local silver coins as 'standard currency', ii) it is 110% backed by gold and sterling reserves in London, iii) some of the reserves are invested in securities, iv) there is an additional 10% of the reserves kept as a Depreciation Fund to guard against the depreciation of the sterling securities, and v) lastly, the responsibility for the management of currency reserves supposedly lay through the Currency Commissioners, Currency Boards and the Crown Agents, to the Secretary of State for Colonies.

The value of West African sterling was manufactured, and its purchasing value was maintained by the mechanisms described by Wadan Narsey above. Nigeria had only been in existence since 1914; the colonial authorities refused to create a central banking financial institution in West Africa. As such, West African colonies had not the wherewithal to create centrally an internationally recognised fiat currency according to Western standards of the early twentieth century.

The *Nigerian Pioneer* on 8 December 1916 in 'The Nigerian One Pound Notes and Ten Shillings Notes' noted that 'the Currency Notes may have come to stay'. The unnamed journalist seems to have developed a better understanding recognising that the monetary policy and sovereignty were retained by the Colonial Office and the UK Government.

The article 'West African Currency Notes' from the issue of the 1-8 August 1916 newspaper *Times of Nigeria* shows that most users were not satisfied with the quality of the currency notes even though the banknotes were signed by the Members of the West African Currency Board, namely GV Fiddes,[13] Under-Secretary Colonial Office, WH Mercer,[14] Crown Agent for the Colonies and L Couper, Chief Manager of the Bank of British West Africa:

---

[12] *A History of the West African Currency Board*, p. 9

[13] According to a letter to the Under Secretary of State, Colonial Office, dated 22 July 1916, Sir GV Fiddes, KCMG, CB was Chairman of the West African Currency Board until his effective resignation on 15 Jul 1916

[14] According to the same letter, Sir WH Mercer, KCMG, was appointed to be Chairman of the West African Currency Board.

The paper on which they are printed is inferior quality—coarse like cartridge paper. This may have been done on the ground of economy or in stand rough usage; but in the case of an article of such importance, vellum woven paper would have answered the purpose far better.

The new notes in circulation

In 1916, several types of currencies were in circulation: the so called traditional currency commodities, such as bars and rods made of iron and brass, and cowries, and the currencies with legal tender status such as British gold and silver coins.[15]

The commodities currencies did not allow hoarding or reduce costs of transactions daily for all parties concerned, but they had the advantage of not being as easily forged as coins and banknotes. The indigenous populations favoured the use of these traditional currencies, as they could be used for other social functions, such as religious ceremonies or ornaments. In the south-eastern part of Nigeria, the indigenous populations not only preferred brass and iron bars and irons but also bartering of palm oil and palm kernels and alcohol such as gin. In other words, they did not fulfill i) the functions of money recognized in economics such as a medium of exchange, a unit of account, a store of value and a standard of deferred payment and ii) the characteristics of money such as durability, portability, divisibility, uniformity, limited supply, and acceptability.

Moreover, residents of Nigeria were encouraged to exchange cowries and metal silver currencies against the currencies made out of aluminum, as they were cheap to produce and presented a lighter weight cargo shipment compared to the other metals. The coins made out aluminum had a catastrophic demand due to their low level of durability compared with gold and silver or copper coins; some coins were partly composed of nickel and silver, and they were to be definitely replaced by coins made of nickel.

The reason for the creation of new denominations

As seen in the historical records, new banknotes were created in July 1916 and a smaller denomination in December 1916, with the aim to replace existing coins in circulation. In June 1916,[16] banknote denominations of £1 and 10s. were designed

[15] *A History of the West African Currency Board* (1974) p. 7

and produced. In December 1916, the additional denomination of 2s was issued.

The acceleration of economic growth in Nigeria and in the Gold Coast driven by the cocoa trade had created a greater demand for currency in circulation and therefore of silver, which could not be made readily available at short notice due to the war and general shortage of silver. Indeed, the West African Currency Board in London had to send the metal money at its own costs to West Africa.

Based on the official historical records of the West African Currency Board,[17] the regulations of the Board were amended principally to provide for the issue of currency notes on 26 November 1915 through the issue of an Ordinance. The Colonial Officers were reminded in dispatches that the project of banknote issuance was discussed and foreseen at the Colonial Conference of 1914 and had to be abandoned at the outbreak of the war in Europe. The Colonial Officers and the so-called 'mercantile community' were expected to provide assistance for the acceptance of the banknotes among the indigenous populations, as they regarded the silver coinage popular. These banknotes were needed to supplement the coins due to the increased demand of money in circulation to ensure the steady growth of trade but also to reduce transportation costs. It was also important to reduce the negative effect of the silver shortage.[18] This currency was not subject to the gold standard, because the latter was suspended during the Great War.

As Ayodeji Olukoju states in 'Nigeria's colonial government, commercial banks and the currency crisis of 1916-1920',[19] the new currency appeared suddenly in February 1916 in Lagos when the Bank of British West Africa started to pay part of the wages of men in the West African Frontier Force, the colonial army and the colonial administration employees in these new denominations to accelerate their use.

Despite all efforts of the authorities, the main residents in Nigeria did not find any use for the new notes except in Lagos

---

[16] *A History of the West African Currency Board*, p. 21
[17] CO 984/2: 'The Constitution of the West African Currency Board and its Duties'
[18] Silver may have been hoarded or melted by the indigenous populations.
[19] In *International Journal of African Historical Studies* (1997) vol 30 Issue 2, p. 277

and its hinterland. These new denominations were too big for the daily transactions of the local people. Their daily purchases were mainly composed of food purchased at local markets, which did not require such large denominations. These large denominations were merely suitable for consuming goods manufactured in Great Britain or the rest of Europe, for instance. The aim to turn the indigenous populations into consumers of British goods did not come to fruition. Plus, they were not suitable for the climate as the cardboard and print could be deleted by human sweat during the dry season and washed out during the rainy season. The indigenous populations were more used to manipulating and carrying coins or commodities currencies: paper could be lost easily by people who were not used to carrying paper and did not see any value in paper compared to precious metals, which could be easily melted.

Conclusion

British colonies had to be financially independent without the support of the British authorities. One of the reasons behind the creation of a currency specifically for West Africa was to ensure control as well as economic and political exploitation of these territories vis-à-vis the competition from French and German merchants. The challenge was to create a currency that not only satisfied the British authorities but also one with which indigenous people could identify. A common currency would allow the raising of taxes in an easily quantifiable currency and provide management efficiency of the colonies in British West Africa.

The implementation of these banknotes and the colonial currency, in general, was not successful until the implementation of the Manilla Operation of 1946.[20] The indigenous population resisted the use of the banknotes, because of the quality, the fact they could be easily lost compared with the weight of coins and the quality of the paper which was perishable. The introduction of the banknotes was only a success among the communities of merchants, civil servants and the West Africa Force. The later groups would have received payment of their salaries in banknotes. Finally, we can see by the statistics

---

[20] The manillas were used in Nigeria until 1946 following Operation Manilla to permanently remove them from circulation by proposing a formalized exchange by the colonial authorities.

published in *A History of the West African Currency Board* by De Loynes,[21] that for the year 1916-1917 ending on 30 June, only £79,000 worth of notes were in circulation compared with £2,906,000 of coins and for the year 1917-1918 only £176,000 worth of notes were in use compared with £4,231,000 of coins.

References

The National Archives of Richmond, UK
West African Currency Board, file series CO 984
Statistical Blue books, file series CO 473

British Library
Lagos Standard
Lagos Weekly Record
Nigerian Pioneer
Times of Nigeria

National Archives of Ibadan, Nigeria
NC19/16: The Trading with the Enemy (Extension of Powers) Act 1915, dated 20 January 1916

Published sources

Apena, Adeline, *Colonization, Commerce and Entrepreneurship in Nigeria, The Western Delta, 1914-1960* (Peter Lang, 1997)

Ekundare, R Olufemi, *An Economic History of Nigeria, 1860-1960* (Methuen, 1973)

De Loynes, JB (John Barraclough), *A history of the West African Currency Board, London, West African Currency Board, Distributed by the Crown Agents* (1962)

Falola, Toyin & Heaton, Matthew M, *A History of Nigeria* (Cambridge University, 2008)

Falola, Toyin & Adebayo, Akanmu, *Culture, Politics, and Money Among the Yoruba* (Transaction, 1999)

Guyer, Jane I, *Marginal Gains: Monetary Transactions in Atlantic Africa* (University of Chicago, 2004)

Guyer, Jane I (ed.), *Money Matters: Instability, Values and Social Payments* (Heinemann Educational, 1995)

Helleiner, Eric, *The Making of National Money: Territorial Currencies in Historical Perspective* (Cornell University, 2003)

---

[21] Ibid. p. 41

Martin, Susan M, *Palm Oil and Protest, An Economic History of the Ngwa Region, South-Eastern Nigeria, 1800-1980* (Cambridge Uni-versity, 1988, 2006)

Narsey, Wadan, *British Imperialism and the Making of Colonial Currency Systems* (Palgrave Macmillan)

Orji, Herbert Onyekwere, *Regional banking and economic develop-ment in Nigeria* (Fourth Dimension, 1987)

Osuntokun, Akinjide, *Nigeria in the First World War* (Longman, 1979)

Stiansen, Endre & Guyer, Jane I (Eds.), *Credit, Currencies and Culture: African Financial Institutions in Historical Perspective*, (The Nordic Africa Institute, 2000)

Appendix 1 – Official Announcement of the introduction of the Banknotes dated July 1916

Appendix 2 - Official Announcement of the introduction of the Banknotes dated July 1916

Appendix 3 – Official Announcement in Yoruba and translation

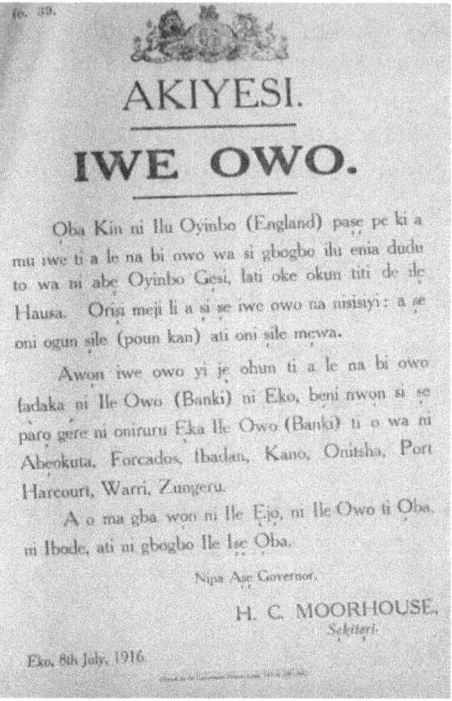

Translation

Notice

The Paper-Money

The King of England ordered that we accept these papers that we can spend our money as in all countries of blacks who are under the dominion of England from London to the Hausaland. There are two kinds now of we use as money notes: there are a twenty shillings note (i.e. a pound) and a ten shillings note.

These notes represent what we can spend at the Bank in Lagos; they also are changed exactly in various branches of the Bank, which are in Abeokuta, Forcados, Ibadan, Kano, Onitsha, Port Harcourt, Warri, Zungeru.

We can obtain them at courts, the post office, the public treasury, the customs service and all administrative buildings.

By command of the Governor,
H. C. Moorhouse,
Lagos, 8th July 1916

Appendix 4 – Official Announcement in Yoruba and Translation

Translation

Notice
The Paper-Money
We recently issued an announcement on the fact that the King of England ordered that we accept these papers we can spend as our money in all countries of blacks who are under the dominion of England from London to Hausaland. This paper represents a currency for all black people towards the direction of the sun set.
There are three kinds of notes now that we use as money: we have the twenty shillings notes (i.e. £1), that of ten shillings and of two shillings.

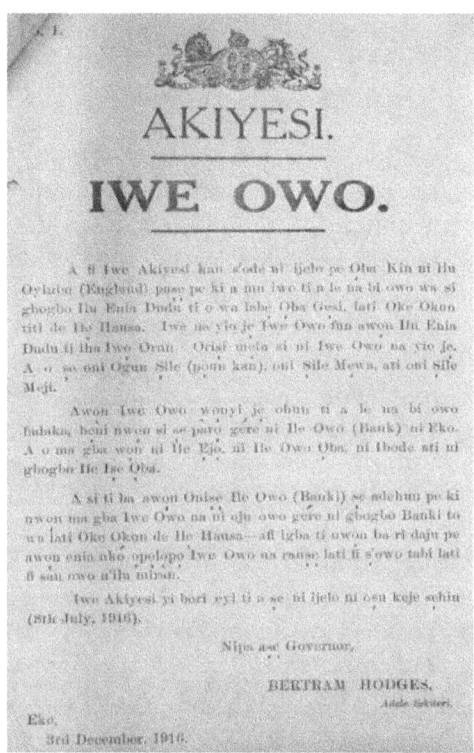

These paper currencies represent what we can spend as silver coins so that they can exactly be changed at courts, the post office and the treasury, the customs service and all administrative buildings.
And, we went to the Bank employees to make them promise they take bank notes at fair value in all banks from London to Hausaland — until they certainly bring and send many banknotes for trading or making payments in another country. This announcement covers the one we recently published in the month of July (July 8, 1916).

By command of the Governor,
Bertram Hodges,
Deputy Secretary
Lagos, 3rd December, 1916

Part 3:
Researching the African Theatre

Archival sources for the Great War in Africa are extremely diverse, encompassing, among other categories, official despatches and reports, war diaries, personal memoirs and diaries, service records, oral evidence, photographs and maps. The repositories in which these records are held are similarly extensive. The national archives of the combatant nations, including the former colonies, are key sources of information, as are the many military and regimental museums. Digitisation of records has continued apace in recent years, accelerated by the centennial commemorations and greatly increasing the accessibility of these records.

Nevertheless, many records remain difficult to access and are not catalogued in sufficient detail to enable ready identification. While it is not possible to provide a comprehensive guide to the records available, several of the papers presented at the conferences addressed these problems and reflected on the information that can be gleaned from the records. It is hoped that these papers will both point up the potential value of archival research and raise awareness of possible difficulties involved.

Because of Britain's major role in the war in Africa and the range of colonies which were drawn into the war, The National Archives of the United Kingdom provides a key resource. Three papers presented to the conference address records held principally at The National Archives, outlining problems of searching the collection and reflecting upon the information that can be gleaned about African soldiers and from medal cards and citations. A further paper shifts attention to artefacts, by outlining the collection of the Belgian Royal Museum of the Armed Forces in Brussels.

Researching the First World War in Africa at The National Archives

*Daniel Gilfoyle**

The widespread range of Britain's empire in Africa meant that it became engaged in each of the African theatres of war. While the Imperial War Cabinet had overall, if distant, control, and the War Office was generally responsible for military operations, colonial governments became deeply immersed in the war effort, providing personnel, services, equipment and food. The demands of war placed colonial societies and economies under extraordinary strain. At the same time, colonial governments were in close communication with the Colonial Office returning large volumes of records to Whitehall. The extent of Britain's colonial presence in Africa, together with the wide range of government departments involved in the war effort, means that The National Archives holds the most extensive collection of documents on the war in Africa, at least from the British perspective. Its collection comprises a unique and extensive primary resource on the history of the war in Africa. Nevertheless, the cataloguing of these records is uneven so that keyword searching may not reveal the documents, a factor which may present considerable problems to the researcher in locating relevant material.

This article identifies the major categories of relevant records, placing them within the structure of the collection, and discussing in general terms the nature of the content and the context in which they were produced. At the highest level, the records are organised according to the originating government

* Daniel Gilfoyle is Principal Records Specialist, Modern Overseas, at The National Archives, London

department, so the discussion proceeds through this departmental structure. Possible means of dealing with those records series for which catalogue detail is sparse are suggested.

Cabinet

The Cabinet has overall responsibility and control of the war effort. While the war in Africa was generally not central to the deliberations of the Imperial War Cabinet, overview situation reports were regularly submitted. These and other relevant records can be found by keyword searching the minutes and papers considered by Cabinet from 1915 through The Cabinet Papers Online website. The full text of the documents can be downloaded through The National Archives online catalogue.

In addition, Cabinet Office series now held at The National Archives include a wealth of material collected by the Historical Section of the Cabinet Office for the production of official war histories. In the case of East Africa, only the first volume of the official history was published. However, drafts chapters of the second volume were written and can be found at catalogue series CAB 44. The material collected for producing the official histories have been placed in series CAB 45. The 69 files and volumes at references CAB 45/6-74 include reports on specific phases of the East Africa campaign by prominent officers (including a report by one of Smuts's senior staff officers Colonel C P Fendall, who published a book on the East Africa Force) and on specific phases of the campaign. There is a good deal of material here on ordnance and logistics, including a report by Major-General George Giffard on the requisitioning of labour, such a prominent feature of the campaigns in tropical Africa, where motor vehicles and draft animals had very limited utility. The series incorporates a number of files on the various Rhodesian forces involved in the East Africa campaign, the British South Africa Police and Rhodesian Native Regiment, but also eleven volumes of a personal diary kept by the Colonel Ronald Ernest Murray who led the Southern Rhodesian contingent into German East Africa (CAB 45/59-69). The diaries provide a unique account of events by this authoritarian and idiosyncratic commander.

An interesting feature of the production of the official history is that during the 1930s, drafts of the chapters were sent to officers who had served in the East Africa campaign. The responses can be found at CAB 45/30-37. In many cases, these introduce a more personal voice into the official archives as some of the respondents relate their memories and the campaign. Lieutenant–Colonel Anderson, for example, provides a hard-hitting account of the difficulties faced during the attempt at capturing the port of Tanga near the beginning of the war in November 1914. These Cabinet Office records are also revealing on the processes of producing official histories, from the selection of evidence and the choice of witnesses through to the editing of drafts and the process of publishing (or not publishing).

War Office

The War Office was responsible for running the military campaigns in Africa and its files contain large volumes of correspondence, reports, war diaries and maps on the campaigns in West, East and North Africa. They are essential sources for the military history of the war. The War Office material has not been collated in a single records series and relevant documents may be found within several series. Nevertheless, the files have been given titles which appear on the catalogue, making keyword searching a reasonably effective means of locating relevant material, although the researcher may need to employ a degree of lateral thinking in devising search terms.

The registered files of the War Office at series WO 32 are an important source of high-level reports on the campaigns. Searching the series using search term "Africa AND East" produces some 22 files. They include reports by Smuts, Wapshare, Tighe and Hoskins, as well as an appreciation of the situation in East Africa by Smith-Dorrien. Jan Smut's account of Malleson's attack on Salaita Hill, remarkable for the positive gloss which it put on what was effectively a defeat, can be found at WO 32/5820. General Cunliffe's reports on the campaign in Cameroons are similarly easy to locate. While this is "history from the top", these are important records for the military history of the campaigns.

A larger volume of operational records can be found in series WO 158, the records of military headquarters during the First World War. This series has been arranged into subseries by regional campaign, including subseries of records for East Africa and Cameroons. This makes it possible for the read to browse through the titles for these regions or to search by keyword. The documents here are more detailed operational records, for example, a set of fifteen files of road and patrol reports from East Africa. A further informative source on operations in Africa is series WO 106, the correspondence and papers of the Directorate of Military Operations and Intelligence. Again the file titles are searchable by keyword.

A major source of information on the activities of individual battalions during the campaigns in west and east Africa are the unit war diaries in series WO 95. The commanding officers of units (usually battalions) used these diaries to record daily events. The British forces assembled in East Africa were extremely diverse, with units drawn from Britain, India and virtually all of Britain's African colonies. The catalogue entry for each individual diary includes the name of the battalion or unit, the date range covered and the theatre of war. This information makes it relatively easy to locate individual diaries by keyword searching the catalogue. Coverage is quite comprehensive, though by no means complete, with around one thousand diaries relating to the campaign in East Africa. The King's African Rifles, drawn from Britain's east and central African colonies is particularly well represented, with around one hundred diaries. All of the diaries from the east and west African campaigns have been digitised as part of The National Archives' World War One 100 project and can be downloaded through its online catalogue. All in all, the digitised diaries probably represent the most extensive online resource of primary documentation on the campaigns in Africa.

The war diaries have a set format and were usually written on pre-printed pages. These include a column for the date and time, a second in which the diarist wrote an account of the events recorded and a third column for further observations, which may include lists of casualties and recommendations for awards. Occasionally, the war diaries include muster lists of the troops who made up the battalion. However, mention of individual soldiers other than British officers is unusual and individuals are, generally speaking, identified only in exceptional circumstances. When something particularly noteworthy happened, perhaps a skirmish or encounter with

German forces, an account was typed or written up in detail and inserted as separate pages into the diary. There are generally entries for every day, so the war diaries reveal the many days of uneventful marching and the routine of camps and exercises, as well as encounters with the enemy. The diaries tend to be arranged in a hierarchical structure. Above the battalion diaries there may be a column diary and a headquarters diary, which take a wider overview. There are also several field ambulance unit diaries, which add detail about military medicine. Different battalion war diaries may cover the same events and may therefore provide different points of view. In this context, they may include observations about the actions of other units.

While they purport to be factual accounts of the experiences of the unit, sometimes the diaries assume a more personal tone. This is particularly the case when extreme hardship had been experienced or when officers felt they had been let down, for example, when supplies failed to appear or other units failed to provide support. The diaries contain much information about transport, supply and communications, relations between officers and men and the changing role of the African soldier. Diarists were often in an unfamiliar locale and to some extent dependent on natural resources (water, for example). For this reason they often include much landscape description and detail about the physical environment.

While war diaries are official records, written by army officers, they often sometimes incorporate a more personal viewpoint and therefore provide an important counterpoint to other types of operational records. In the absence of written accounts of the war by African soldiers, they must constitute a key primary source on the soldiers' experience of the war and indicate possibilities for a social history of the African regiments and for an environmental history of the First World War in Africa.

Admiralty and Air Force

While the First World War in Africa was very much a land war, there was also a significant naval involvement on Lakes Tanganyika and Nyasa and on the west and east coasts. This means that there is a significant amount of Admiralty material on the First World War in Africa to be found in various

Admiralty records series.

The correspondence of the Admiralty's African station during World War 1 can be found in ADM 123. The series includes material on naval action on the African lakes and off the East Coast, as well as South West Africa, but many of the volumes in the series are not described in detail, and the reader would have to look through these to establish content. Another useful source of information is the extensive material extracted by the official historians and catalogued in series ADM 137. Included in this series are several volumes of correspondence on operations off Cameroons, South West Africa, East Africa and Zanzibar. This includes material on the sinking of HMS Pegasus and the subsequent pursuit of the Konigsberg, coverage of Geoffrey Spicer-Simson's expedition to Lake Tanganyika over 1915 and 1916, and operations on Lake Nyasa. A few of these volumes have been catalogued in detail and can be searched effectively by keyword, but the most reliable way of finding relevant volumes is to browse the series on the online catalogue. Catalogue searches using keywords, for example, "Konigsberg", will produce results from the major Admiralty correspondence series, ADM 1, though there are also manuscript contemporary finding aids available to the researcher.

The Royal Navy Air Service and Royal Flying Corps also participated in the East African Theatre. RNAS planes played a key role in the sinking of the SMS Konigsberg, carrying out aerial reconnaissance and bombing.[1] The official historians collated documentation on this early use of air power, which can be found at catalogue reference CAB 45/218. Records relating to the 26 South Africa Squadron in East Africa, including a number of squadron war diaries, were collated by the Air Historical Branch. They can be located by keyword searching the papers of the AIR Historical Branch in series AIR 1.

Colonial Office

It would be difficult to exaggerate the importance of colonial governments to the pursuit to the war in Africa. While the War Office had responsibility for the conduct and pursuit of the campaign, colonial governments, among other functions, raised

---

[1] Willis, M., The National Archives blog, 9 July 1915, "Sinking the German cruiser Konigsberg"

troops, conscripted labour and provided infrastructure and supplies. Without these commitments and activities, the pursuit of the war by British forces would have been impossible. In turn, the demands of the campaigns in west, east and southern Africa had profound effects upon African and colonial societies and their economies and politics. In some colonies, the demands of the war produced both co-operation and resistance, the war effort becoming an engine for change in all aspects of colonial life. Such impacts and responses were undoubtedly uneven. Unlike the crown colonies, the Union of South Africa, for example, was effectively a self-governing nation, where policies and commitments had to be decided in the context of a limited democracy.

Throughout the war, colonial governments were in constant communication with the Colonial Office, so that its records provide an overarching account of the involvement of the British African colonies in the war. Unfortunately, Colonial Office records for this period are not described in detail on The National Archives online catalogue and only the name of the colony and the date range can be used to identify relevant volumes. It is therefore not possible to use keyword searches to identify relevant documents. Fortunately, however, the original finding aids used by the Colonial Office registry clerks survive and are still available for the researcher to use.

The Colonial Office records at The National Archives are organised into four or five categories for each colony, usually:

- Original correspondence:
- Sessional papers
- Acts and government gazettes
- Blue Books of Statistics[2]

The original correspondence is the unpublished correspondence received by the Colonial Office from colonial governors, from other government departments and from institutions and people from outside of government. The content of the Colonial Office correspondence is very wide-reaching and could touch on virtually any aspect of colonial administration, making in difficult to generalise about what the researcher might expect to find in these documents. Generally speaking, colonial

---

[2] See Banton, M., *Administering the Empire* for detailed information on the different classes of Colonial Office records

governments had a good deal of autonomy in running routine aspects of colonial administration and were responsible for all aspects of running the colony, other than foreign relations.

At times of crisis, however, they drew closer to the Colonial Office and the flows of information increased. Such crises might include conflict, expansion or circumstances in which expenditure greatly increased. The war years were by definition a period in which all of these circumstances pertained and there was accordingly a considerable increase in the volume of the correspondence. It may concern any aspect of the 'home front' in a colony, the recruitment of labour, conscription, the raising of supplies, relations with the indigenous population, economic production and so forth. The breadth of subject matter covered, together with its range across all of the British African colonies make the correspondence a key source on the history of the war in the colonies, as well as providing entry to comparative approaches.

The Colonial Office correspondence is bound into volumes with a separate series for each former colony, with the individual items in chronological order irrespective of topic. The details on the catalogue are very sparse, giving only the date range of the volume and a broad indication of the source (e.g. colonial governor or other government department). The amount of this correspondence is substantial, for example, a search of the catalogue reveals 75 war-time volumes for Nigeria, 98 for Kenya, 66 for Gold Coast, and so forth. Examining these documents entails a considerable, perhaps excessive, investment of time for researchers interested in tracing a particular topic. The situation is somewhat complicated by regional series for West Africa (CO 544) and a general series (CO 323), which contains matters relevant to the colonies generally, rather than to a specific colony or region. Additionally, the correspondence from the government in South Africa which related specifically to the war has been extracted and placed in a dominions series CO 616. This series is a key source on the considerable contribution which that colony (along with the other dominions of Canada, Australia and New Zealand) made to the war effort.

The lack of cataloguing detail for Colonial Office volumes is a considerable obstacle for researchers. It means, for example, that such an import document as the Pike Report on medical services during the war, which in volume CO 691/19, is concealed by the description Tanganyika: Original Correspondence, Offices: War, May-December 1918. This merely indicates that the volumes relates to Tanganyika and was received by the War Office. The most effective method of overcoming these difficulties and locating material in the correspondence series is to consult the registers of correspondence which the Colonial Office registry clerks used to record and find items of correspondence. There is a separate set of registers for each former colony, which list in chronological order the correspondence received and indicate the previous and following item on the same subject. Registers can therefore speed up the research process but they also record the fate of documents. For example, they may have been forwarded to other departments, typeset for parliamentary papers or even destroyed. They therefore indicate the totality of items received by the Colonial Office.

A further significant research resource is the sessional papers of each former colony. These are sets of printed papers of colonial legislative and executive councils and assemblies – in other words, a kind of colonial parliamentary papers. The amount of material varies considerable. The Crown Colony sessional papers usually incorporate a set of department annual reports and possibly the papers of commissions of enquiry and the like, as well as summary records of the meeting of councils and assemblies. In the case of the Dominions, there are quite elaborate sets of sessional papers, covering many aspects of administration.

Only the sessional papers for South Africa have been catalogued in detail and browsing the catalogue enables the researcher to see the type of material that is available in the these series. The papers (over 1,000 for the war period) cover many aspects of wartime government and administration during the war period, including very extensive material on African administration and the Native Lands Commission, infrastructure and expenditure. Notably, there is substantial material on the Afrikaner rebellion against the Union government immediately after the outbreak of war, including reports of the commission of enquiry and the select committees which were set up to investigate in the aftermath of the rebellion. Such reports record ostensibly verbatim evidence given by witnesses.

The sessional papers are supplemented by more detailed statistical information which can be gleaned from the annual blue books prepared in each colony (again there is a separate catalogue series for each one). The blue books contain detailed information on population, production, imports and exports, government expenditure, government institutions and all aspects of the economy. Legislation can be followed though series of colonial acts and the government gazettes, the local official newspapers, in which colonial governments published legislation, regulations and notices.

The Colonial Office was also responsible the administration of two African colonial regiments, the West African Frontier Force and, in East and Central Africa, the King's African Rifles (KAR). The West African Frontier Force, which was drawn from Nigeria, Sierra Leone and Gold Coast (Ghana), played an important role in the conquest of Togoland and Cameroons. Following the defeat of the Germans in West Africa, the Nigerian Regiment was despatched to East Africa in 1916, where it participated in the invasion of Tanganyika. The King's African Rifles, which was greatly expanded during the war to around 30,000 men, was drawn principally from Kenya, Uganda and Nyasaland. The KAR was a major component of the diverse British forces assembled in East Africa and played an important role throughout the campaign there. Both regiments have associated correspondence series in the Colonial Office records. Neither has been catalogued in detail, but the King's African Rifles correspondence (CO 534) can be downloaded through The National Archives' website as digital microfilm. These correspondence files contain material on administration, recruitment, discipline, observations on tribal characteristics and so forth. They provide context for the unit war diaries (see above), which can be found in catalogue series WO 95.

Overall, the Colonial Office records at The National Archives, consisting as they do a combination of policy correspondence and printed records of colonial governments, provide an overview of home fronts in former colonies and on their relations with the metropolitan government. Because of there wide-ranging nature, they provide a unique starting point for comparative approaches. They are on the whole relatively high level policy documents and the Colonial Office correspondence has a close relationship with the internal records of the governments of the former colonies.

Foreign Office

The pursuit of the war in Africa against Germany required negotiation and co-operation with the allied governments of France, Belgium, Portugal and Italy. France played its part in the West Africa campaign, while Belgian forces in Congo participated in the invasion of German East Africa and assisted with Spicer-Simson's expedition to Lake Tanganyika. In Libya, the British government negotiated with the Italians in dealing with the threat posed by the Senussi, while in the Portuguese government the British hoped to find allies who could put pressure on German East Africa from the south.

While War Office and Admiralty staff had direct connections with their opposite numbers, negotiations with foreign powers were generally conducted through the Foreign Office and embassies. The Foreign Office received correspondence from foreign governments, its own embassies and consulates abroad, from other government departments and from various institutions and individuals. This political correspondence was given a country identifier and placed in a single records series, FO 371.

However, British embassies (and sometimes consu-lates) in foreign countries kept their own archives which were later returned to the Foreign Office and ultimately to The National Archives, where they were placed in individual series. This complicates the business of researching communications between the British and foreign governments, as there may be several records series in which to look. If a researcher were interested in locating communication on Portuguese involvement in the East Africa campaign, the researcher might search the main series of Foreign Office political correspondence (FO 371), but also the records of the British Embassy in Lisbon.

Foreign Office records contain much detail on international relations and strategy, the negotiations between Britain and its allies and observations on the policies and politicians of foreign countries. It is also worth keeping in mind that British consuls were present in the colonies of allied countries and in other African states, where they routinely passed information back to the Foreign Office about enemy activity. In Abyssinia, for example, the British Consul-General at Addis Abba, Wilfred Thesiger (father of the famous travel writer) was a keen observer of German attempts to encourage anti-British activity. Despatches from Thesiger may be found in the Foreign Office political correspondence and in the correspondence of the Embassy and consulates in Egypt. In Portuguese East Africa, the consul, Errol MacDonnell, kept on eye on German infiltration of the porous border with German East Africa.

As with the Colonial Office, Foreign Office records for this period are sparsely catalogued, with only the country and date range indicated. To return to the example of Wilfred Thesiger,[3] in February 1916, he reported that enemy agents were active in Abyssinia and had provoked a number of border incidents. This brief report is filed among the political correspondence of the Foreign Office and can be found at catalogue reference FO 371/2593. The catalogue reference merely records that the correspondence concerns Abyssinia and is from 1916, together with some file and paper number. The more determined researcher will again need to consult original finding aids.

The Foreign Office clerks used a card index to record incoming correspondence before filing it. The individual card included an alphabetical keyword, a code to denote the country, a brief summary of the content of item of correspondence, together with other information which enables the identification of the file in which the correspondence has been filed. The index cards have been digitised by The National Archives and they can be downloaded through the online catalogue at series FO 1111, enabling initial research before a visit.

Maps, plans and photographs

The National Archives' collection includes many military maps relating to the various African campaigns. Maps which show the progress of the campaigns in West and East Africa can be found in records series WO 153. Many of these are printed maps that have been annotated by hand. They include a series of detailed situation maps illustrating the vain pursuit by British troops of Von Lettow-Vorbeck's through Portuguese East Africa

[3] Pace, E., *Tip and Run The Untold Tragedy of the War in Africa* (Phoenix, London, 2007)

during 1917 and 1918. A set of contemporary topographical maps, which were used by the official historians of the African campaigns, can be found at series WO 300.

However, while these maps have been collected into these series, many maps both printed and hand-drawn may be found in any of the categories of records discussed above, including war diaries, manuscript and typescripts reports in Colonial and War Office correspondence and in sessional papers. Such maps and sketches are not catalogued and can only be found in the course of examining files and volumes.

Similarly, photographs relating to the war in Africa have been collected into some specific series. The official historians collected an album of 68 photographs from the East African campaign into an album at CAB 45/11. There is a substantial photographic record of Spicer-Simson's expedition to Lake Tanganyika, with 66 photographs illustrating the overland transportation of the gunboats Mimi and Toutou, at ADM 137/268.

The photographic collection of the Colonial Office was recently transferred to The National Archives as series CO 1069. The collection contains a significant amount of images from Africa during the war period, though not specifically to do with the campaigns. The album at CO 1069/133, however, includes a photograph showing von Lettow-Vorbeck with British officers before his surrender at Abercorn, Northern Rhodesia together with other subjects from the East African campaign. Many of these photographs were digitised as part of The World through a Lens project and can be viewed on Flickr at Africa through a Lens.

Conclusion

The National Archives holds a unique and extensive array of records on the First World War in Africa, including material on the campaigns against Germany in Togoland, Cameroons, German East Africa and South West Africa and against the Senoussi in Egypt and Libya. The great extent of Britain's empire in Africa means that there is much material on the home front in the former colonies and on the impact of the war there. All of this enables at least an initial exploration of the involvement of the British Empire in the war and its social, economic and political impact upon individual former colonies.

This material is likely to be useful to researchers working in areas which have not yet received comprehensive treatment by historians, such as the military history of the campaigns in West Africa, social histories of British African regiments, the social history of the war in some colonies and the environmental history of the war in Africa.

The material is, however, widely dispersed throughout the collection as a whole. Documents on the military pursuit of the campaign are likely to be found in Cabinet (CAB), War Office (WO) and Admiralty (ADM), series, while Colonial Office (CO) and Dominions Office (DO) series are prime sources for the impact of war on colonial societies and inter-imperial relations. Foreign Office (FO) records series include much material on the international relations aspects of the war in Africa.

Searching The National Archives' online catalogue is likely to produce relevant results, but the researcher should always keep in mind that of the more important records series (and this is particularly true of Admiralty and Colonial and Foreign Office series) are not catalogued in detail. Generally, the catalogue does not have details of individual items or files and the researcher will have to use original finding aids, rather than relying on online searching by keyword.

The National Archives (London) Collection

William Spencer[1]

As one might imagine, the Archives has a wealth of information on the Great War in Africa. As technology and cataloguing improves so it is getting easier not only to identify the records relating to East Africa in the World War but also to access them as they are being digitised. The amount digitised is determined by the funding available.

I was going to start off with a connection to this physical site. There was no National Archive here during the First World War but *Mimi* and *Toutou* were built in Twickenham and in order to start their journey to southern Africa they would have sailed a hundred yards near the Archive, going through the lock, past Kew Gardens, this institution and onto the ship to take them to Africa; so a very tenuous link to the war.

Records relating to the war in Africa are not solely stuck among records of the War Office. As you can imagine, we have a large amount of material relating to the war in the Colonial Office and a lot in Foreign Office records. Wars cost money so there are papers in the Treasury, decisions need to be made relating to the Cabinet and executed so material by the War Office, Admiralty and Air Ministry needs to be consulted as well.

Unlike the Second World War where record keeping has made it a little easier to access because it is broken down into smaller chunks, during the First World War you are stuck with consulting a large amount of material. To give you an idea of the subtlety of catalogue descriptions, I want to start off with a War Office military personnel file. The first thing is the spelling

---

[1] William Spencer was Principal Military Specialist at The National Archives, London between 1993 and 2018. He is now an independent researcher.

mistake—this is the personal file of Brigadier General Aitken who commanded the operation at Tanga in November 1914. It is a military personnel file so the title itself is sufficient, but the sub-heading written on the file says, 'Censure and subsequent exoneration re conduct of operations at Tanga'.[2] Now it is not really a personal file about him as an individual. It is more about him and how the War, India and Colonial Offices tried to apportion blame for the failure of the Tanga operation of 1914. So, subtlety of title can hide absolute gems.

Key-word searching our catalogue will produce lots of document references. I always add a year onto the years. Just using the term 'East Africa' for 1913-1919 produces close to 5,000 catalogue references, around 4,500 of which are at The National Archives. Many of these, though, turn out to be individual medal cards and putting 'medal' in the 'don't find' box immediately reduces the number of results to almost half. In other words, computers are like Royal Marines—they are only as good as the information you punch into them. When you are searching our catalogue looking for material, if you use a term which is not used to describe a document, it does not mean that we do not have anything, it means that you need to expand, contract or change the term to suit your needs. So, when I talk to undergrads and postgrads at the University of Birmingham, I always say create a thesaurus of likely terms. This will make you much more adept and successful at identifying material in the catalogue. If we add 'van Deventer' to our search term the number of records hit is nine and we are starting to be a bit more specific. The results are mostly military headquarters papers (stuffed full of awards) and papers submitted to the War Cabinet.

Military historians tend to stick to the War Office and Admiralty files. But say you have manpower coming from East and West Africa and India, then the Colonial Office might have been writing letters. You are not necessarily going to find the records where the troops were fighting but rather where they came from. So, if you looked in the records for Nigeria and searched on war, you would identify all the correspondence between a given colony and a given organisation. Cast a wide

---

[2] TNA: WO 138/41 Brig. Gen. AE Atkin

net and think of where people come from, where they go to and what they do, in order to identify likely sources.

One of our most popular series is the unit war diaries in WO 95. Now there are some 5,500 war diaries by piece but there are over 30,000 individual diaries. As one might imagine they are very popular and they are in many cases very tired. Most of these have now been digitised and are available through The National Archives' website.[3] Not all diaries contain information about the fighting. A lot contain information about the non-combatant troops and the rear-echelon activities to support the men doing the fighting. The Adjutant Quartermaster diaries contain lots of statistical information, routine orders, data relating to awards—core routine orders may also appear. You will get information relating to casualties, appointments, orders saying do not do this and do not do that—orders which need to be disseminated to vast parts of the African continent for the attention of the addressee.

One of the projects that was completed a couple of years ago, called the Caribbean Heritage Project catalogued a vast amount of material relating to the Caribbean and you might think Caribbean—East Africa?[4] Whilst not necessarily producing results relating to people as named individuals, you do get details of groups and units going elsewhere. There is another West Indian series which produces quite a few results. This is Colonial Office material and has manpower going elsewhere.[5] CO 445 relates solely to Nigeria and the West African Field Force (WAFF) and CO 534 to the King's African Rifles (KAR).

People might think that the war in East Africa was confined to German, British and Portuguese East Africa but British manpower was prosecuting various other military operations, minor ones which might normally be considered peace time operations, in other parts of the African continent. The most significant is the Chilembwe uprising in 1915 followed by the Igbo revolt in 1918 in Nigeria and then you have got minor altercations in Jubaland. If you look at War Office East Africa command papers created in 1941, it has got a file created in 1902 and then a file called 'Operations in Jubaland 1902-July

[3] The African diaries were digitised in 2016
[4] The West India Regiment was from Jamaica; The British West India Regiment was made up of troops from other islands, Imperial troops.
[5] TNA: CO 318

1918'. Do not be tied to the idea that the record series only provides information to a given period of time to a given place. As things are discovered hidden in the archive, or turn up in odd cupboards in the Ministry of Defence, or new departments are created and they discover files which have been squirreled away, material keeps coming into us. So although you would think that The National Archives has everything relating to the First World War, it does not. There is a significant chunk still to come, including the records of service of those personnel who continued to serve in the army after 1920 which are still with the Ministry of Defence. We still, for example, await records of the Health and Safety Executive, a new Department—amongst its records are some of the accident reports relating to ammunitions factories in the First World War.

The National Archives' catalogue also produces data relating to material kept elsewhere. However, read the catalogue description carefully and note where the information is held. Down in Sussex for example, at the Regimental Museum, is W Downes' file. There is also the AIM 25 containing archives within the M25 mostly at the Imperial War Museum, some at The National Archives, and a little collection at King's College London. We also constantly keep updating research guides as we discover material which is not mentioned in the catalogue.

Additional notes

Catalogue series CO 1069 contains a couple of photograph albums relating to material in East Africa. This is an unusual collection for the Archive. There are loads of records containing photographs but not usually photos on their own. Some photos are in AIR 1.

The Archive is strong on maps—WO 153 military headquarters.

German material in the archive—Schnee's diary is in TNA, captured enemy documents—there is no single consolidated series. It depends on the department. The IWM has a large collection of captured enemy documents. We sometimes have the translation of the enemy document but not necessarily the original. We have German maps which are quite informative. It is about picking up pieces of information which people have left behind.

Bringing African soldiers to life using The National Archives (London) record collections

Martin Willis[1]

The Great War in Africa was fought mainly using black African soldiers with European officers. This chapter will look at what records held at The National Archives can tell us about the Nigerian Regiment soldiers from the West African Frontier Force (WAFF) who were serving in Cameroon, West Africa, between August 1914 and February 1916. To start, we will look at records that can give us an idea of who these African troops were and where they came from, before looking at records that give us an idea of what the conditions and terrain were like during the campaign and finally consider a number of case studies to see what the records can show about the soldiers' service and experiences.

The West African Frontier Force was made up of the Nigerian Regiments, Sierra Leone, Gambia and Gold Coast Regiment. For these regiments, we can use the surviving nominal rolls contained within the unit war diaries, to get a list of names of the African troops that served during the campaign.[2] These nominal rolls give the specific unit the soldiers were in at the time, list their rank and service number and are annotated with dates of killed in action, wounded and invalided.

Looking at the nominal rolls and the names listed, leads to the first possible problem; or it can be seen as a help when trying to research individual soldiers. That is the individual soldiers did not have or did not use their surname. Instead,

---
[1] Martin Willis is Quality Manager at The National Archives, London and has an interest in West Africa during the First World War.
[2] TNA WO 95/5387 & WO 95/5386 contain surviving nominal rolls for the different units of the four West Africain Frontier Force regiments.

> TNA WO 95/5387 Nigerian Regiment,
> A company, no 2 section

their surnames were recorded as the place, town or the tribal area they were from.[3] This format can be helpful as you can track an individual to the specific area they are from and build up a picture of the make-up of the units, some having more troops from the South or North of the country. Where the naming can be a hindrance is when you have multiple names listed, such as Adegbite Offa, who is listed a number of times, albeit with different regimental numbers. Historian, Akinjide Osuntokun saw this as 'One of the most unfortunate elements in the history of the West African Frontier Force as far as the African Serviceman was concerned was that they were not allowed to bear their proper last names, so that those who distinguished themselves during the war were remembered with such names as 'Sambo Kano', 'Gama Bida', 'Usman Yola', 'Adegbite Offa', 'Asuma Ibadan', 'Musa Bauchi', 'Tanko Zaria',

---

[3] This is not the same for East, Central and South Africa.

'Oke Modakeke', 'Agbe Owo' and 'Umoru Bornu'. Since these last names were the names of the towns where they came from and not their proper names, their outstanding performance was merged in the names of their towns'.[4] For the purpose of modern research it does enable us to track troops back to their specific areas or their tribal heritage, and is the first step of building a picture of individuals serving.

Looking at the map we see that Sokoto is a town in the North West of the country, Kano a town in the North (central), Ibadan

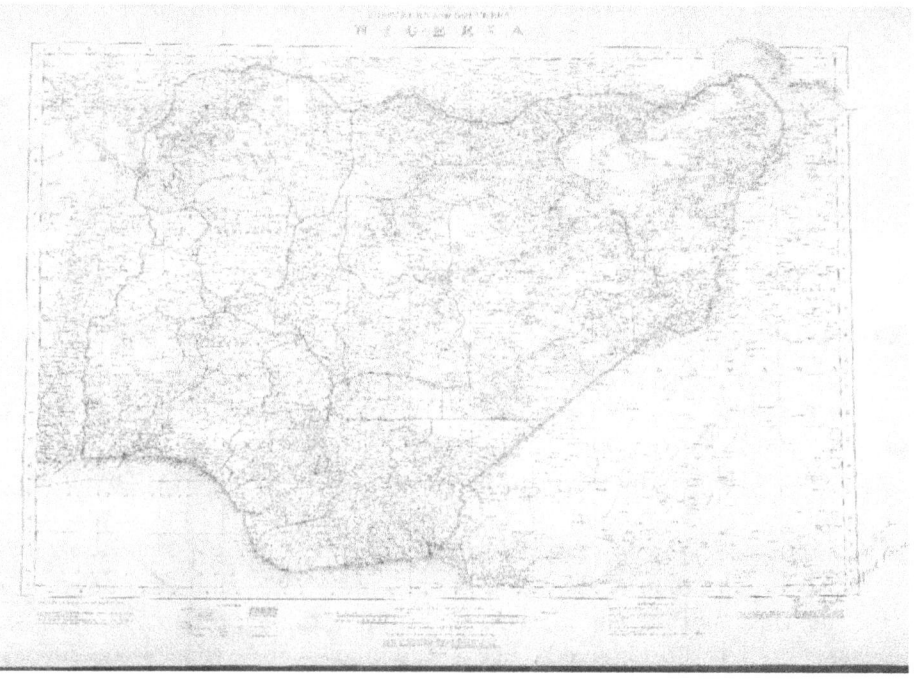

TNA MPG 1/1103 Northern and Southern Nigeria' (now Nigeria). Map showing administrative boundaries, communications, and tribal names. Signed by Charles Alfred Vaux, consultant engineer to the South Nigeria Exploration Syndicate

& Offa are in the South West, close to Lagos. With the absence of formal service records, these clues as to the origins and heritage of the troops are important.[5]

---

[4] Akinjide Osuntokun, *Nigeria in the First World War* (1979) p. 198

[5] TNA CO 641 445/42 & CO 657/3 for example, contain statistical information

The other West African Frontier Force regiments used similar naming conventions, and we can look at examples from their nominal rolls to show this. The Gold Coast Regiment used town and tribal based surnames, 'Salako Ibadan' (place) and 'Labari Dagarti' (The Dagaaba/Dagarti people—modern day Burkina Faso and Ghana). The Sierra Leone troops also used their tribes and places as their surname. 'Bundu Kissi' (Kissi people is an ethnic group living in Guinea, Sierra Leone and Liberia), 'Momo Kamalu' (Kamulu is a small town located roughly 40 kilometres from Nairobi). Gambia Regiment also used their tribes and places as their surname.

What were the conditions and terrain like and what can the records show us?

The British commanders' thoughts about the conditions and terrain are a useful start. Major General Dobell KCB, who was commanding the Allied Forces in Cameroon, was aware that the conquest of the colony would be no light task. Cameroon covered around 306,000 square miles of mainly uncharted territory, which was defended by a well-led and well-trained African force, who were plentifully supplied with machine guns. Allied forces amounted to around 4300 West African troops, which was boosted in November 1915 to 9,700 with the arrival of Indian troops.[6] Hew Strachan records the number of troops available in August 1914 from the four West African Frontier Force regiments as 7,552 troops, so we have between 4,300 and 7,552 troops available at the start of the campaign.[7] Dobell pointed out 'that neither the climate nor the character of the country favoured the offensive, officers and men were exposed to the most trying conditions—incessant tropical rains, absence of roads or even paths, a country covered with the densest African forest'.[8]

---

on the breakdown of the tribal and religious make up of units that allows more detailed analysis of the structure of the units to be carried out. CO 445 series contains the West African Frontier Force original correspondence for 1914-1918, and is a good source of information when researching. Registers of correspondence are in CO and can be used to find specific subject matters within the correspondence.

[6] TNA WO 32/5320 Operations (Narratives of): General (Code 46(A)): Reports by Brigadier General F Cunliffe and Major General Sir C Dobell on operations in the Cameroons with list of officers and men for mention.

[7] Strachan, H, *The First World War in Africa*, (Oxford University, 2004) p. 22

Dobell goes on to point out that the country in the immediate vicinity of Duala is perhaps typical of the greater portion of Cameroon in which troops have operated.

The map of Duala can give us pointers as to the terrain in Cameroon and also demonstrates some of the factors that com-

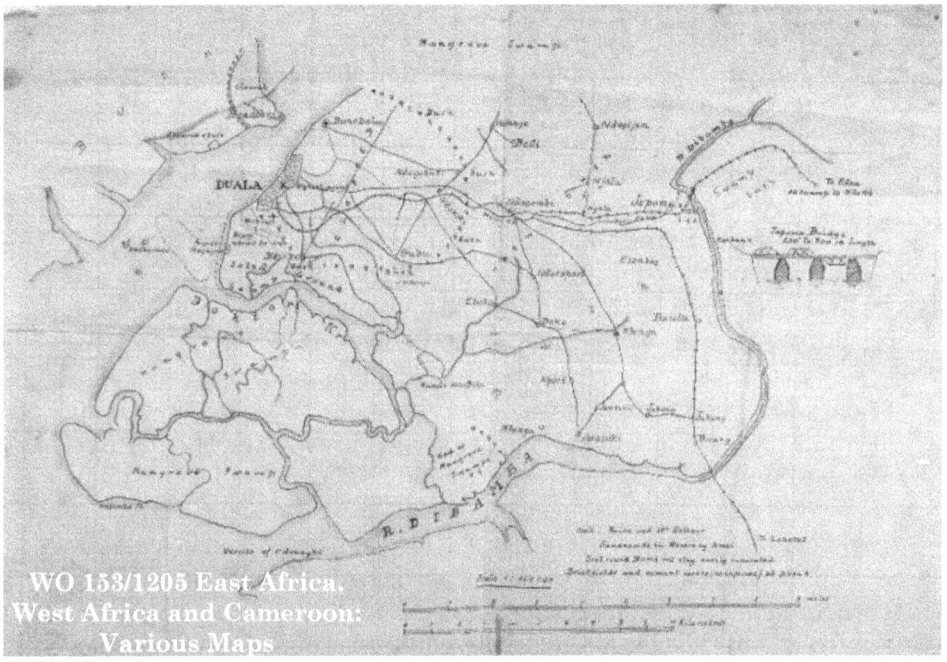

manders had to be aware of when planning operations. The map details the terrain, areas of mangrove swamp, bush lands that comprised long grass, trees and other vegetation, thus allowing us to get an idea of what the environment was like in Cameroon, which was as Dobell suggested. The map points out that 'rains end October' and 'sandbanks in river by Xmas',[9] environmental factors would be a major factor for operations. During the rainy season, it could be impossible to navigate swollen rivers, or travel distances through the terrain to engage the enemy, especially when commanders were relying on transporting people and equipment by river or on foot using African porters. The sand bank would hinder shipping accessing Duala to move troops or carrying supplies.[10]

---

[8] TNA: WO 32/5320
[9] WO 153/1205 Map dated 1914 Sep 1914, Nov 1918 and undated

War diaries, which record the day to day activities of a unit can also give us an indication of how good intelligence gathering was; the environment that operations were being carried out in; and give us a glimpse into the experiences of the troops. A good example of a recorded operation is detailed in a report of the operation against the enemy entrenched near Gazabu on 16 and 17 November 1914.[11] Lieutenant Loch, 2nd Nigeria Regiment (Ibi Column), was accompanied by Mr Glenny (political service), Sergeant Harvey (RAMC), Sergeant Morris (land contingent), 30 rank and file and carriers. Leaving Bakundi at 0600 hrs and making their way down the Bakundi—Gazabu road, at about 0900 hrs the patrol came under fire from two snipers who were in the trees. Between 0900 hrs and 1120 hrs they were periodically sniped at and watched—one of the men in the patrol was shot in the leg. Loch recorded that he had received reports that the enemy was covering the main ford at Gazabu from the eastern bank of the river, which the patrol needed to cross. The decision was taken to cross at a ford about two miles upstream and attack the enemy in the rear, thus preventing them escaping to Beli. At 1130 hrs the patrol left the road around five miles away from Gazabu, heading in a south westerly direction through the bush, arriving at the ford at 1515 hrs. The carriers and wounded man with five guards were left in a deserted farmhouse, while the rest crossed the ford, the current was very strong and the water about five feet deep, at 1625 hrs they came in to sight of the entrenchment.

CO 1069/65 (1) Nigeria Regiment crossing a river, Cameroons campaign

---

[10] WO 153/1205 East Africa, West Africa and Cameroon: Various Map.
[11] WO 95/5382 Cameroon, Headquarters and Troops: Headquarters Allied Force

The entrenchment took the form of a rectangular fort with breastworks of earth and a deep trench on the outside, within which were poisoned stakes on two sides. The ground around the fort had been cleared to about 250 yards and was to a breadth of around 150 yards either side of the road, leaving patches of seven-foot long grass on the right and left of the clearing. Loch intended to make a frontal attack across the open ground using the 24 men in the ordinary extended line, with Mr Glenny taking the right hand squad, Morris the left hand and Loch taking the centre. The strength of the enemy force was reported as between four and 16 strong; on arrival about 15 men were seen in front of the fort cooking. They advanced to about 50 yards of the clearing using the long grass as cover; the order was given to double for the opening; and the hope was to get everyone out of the grass before they were fired upon. Loch was leading the party and got about 25 yards out before giving the order to extend, when the first shots were fired from the men, who had run in to the fort. Eight to 10 men were with Loch, the rest had run back into the long grass on either side of the road. He learnt afterwards that neither flanking troops had advanced. Morris and his eight men were not seen and Glenny was seriously wounded, his men staying with him. Harvey, who had been in the rear, came forward to try and get the troops moving and found them firing into the air and in all directions, even though they could not see through the grass and were 40 yards from the clearing.

CAB 45/11, p. 7 One of SMS *Konigsberg* guns in long grass, German East Africa

As Lock advanced, a storm broke and the light started fading, but he pushed on to within 150 yards of the fort. One of his men had been killed and three were wounded, leaving six of them attacking what he later described as a fort and earthworks that required half a company to take.[12] With the merging of North and South Nigeria in April 1914, the previously two regiments were formed into one regiment and a company's strength had been set at 139 men throughout, meaning they really needed at least 70 men for the attack.[13] With fire being taken from the fort and from his own troops at the rear, Lock decided to withdraw, taking no more casualties, which was probably due to the heavy storm and bad light. They picked up the wounded and headed back to the grass, finding Glenny in a bad way. He sent the wounded on and he and three men sounded the rally and headed back up the road, which was now safe of fire owing to the bad light and weather conditions. As they went, Morris and others started to come out from either side of the road and join up with the patrol. Loch states that 'Morris was a volunteer and had never been under fire before or dealt with local troops. Morris's 'state' had an unsteadying effect on the men, who had been shaken by the action. When a flare was sent up, the men were reduced to a state of lunacy, and Loch needed to get from the rear to the front to stop the men panicking and running. As he did this the rear guard started firing back down the road, at what turned out to be Harvey and three men. Further panic attacks broke out as the darkness was now so dense that you could not see a man one yard ahead.

On arriving back at the ford, Loch tried to control the troops and ensure the wounded were safely transported, as trying to cross the ford a foot or two to the left or right meant being in six to eight feet of water. Most crossed safely but a number lost their head and jumped in and were swept away. The remaining party joined up with the men who were left at the ford before halting for the night, setting off for Bakundi at 0430 hours. The party arrived back at 1715 hours, the number of casualties on arrival were, one European wounded (later died), local troops one killed, four wounded and six missing (these were the men who were swept away and later re-joined). The report gives us

---

[12] Ibid.
[13] CO 657/3 Colonial Office: Nigeria: Sessional Papers – details of company strength with the merging of North and South Nigeria

an indication of the environment and climate that the troops were operating in. We can see the problems faced in operating over large distances, encountering rivers, working through bush lands and how quickly the weather could change. The lack of intelligence and experience meant that an under-strength attack went ahead with inexperienced men, against a well-defended entrenchment and ultimately failed.

WO 95/5384—one of a number of sketches of Ekom on the Cameroon/Nigerian border and the surrounding landscape

Another diary entry gives insight into the treatment and problems faced by carriers in the early days of the campaign. Number 4668 Lance Corporal Alabi Ibadan, F Company, 3 Nigerian Regiment was in charge of 231 carriers with military loads. They were moving from Ikom to Ogoja, which is still in Nigeria and around 100km from the Cameroon border. On arrival at Ogoja he approached the District Officer to report their arrival and arrange feeding of the party. The District Officer said that as he had no book with him, he would have nothing to do with them, refused to supply food and told him to go away. Alabi went and opened five bags of rice from the load that they were carrying to feed the carriers, thus allowing the party to continue onto Obudu with all the officers and other military loads for the column.[14] This account, supplied by Captain Lawder F Company, demonstrates some of the problems faced by African soldiers and carriers, whilst carrying out the vital work of supplying the Column. With the conditions and terrain as they were, the use of carriers was vital and the main way to move supplies over large distances, supplying the columns as they advanced.

CAB 45/11/54 African carriers in German East Africa carrying loads

Likewise, another diary entry gives us further evidence of what the conditions were like:

> 5 to 7 August 1914, Right section No1 Battery, Artillery Nigerian Regiment. 5th August, left Sokoto 0515hrs, 1 officer, 30 rank and file, 32 gun carriers and 153 hired carriers, weather fine. 6th August 1914 departed Riji 0200hrs, tornado at 0300hrs, heavy rain all day until 1500hrs, roads terribly slippery and nearly all under water. 1600hrs—35 hired carriers missing many picked up in dying condition from cold and want of food, as no food had been obtained since leaving Sokoto. 7th August 1914, 0945hrs tremendous downpour until 1645hrs, roads again under water, and 21 hired carriers fell out exhausted, many seeming in a bad way with pneumonia. [15]

---

[14] WO 95/5382 – report by Captain Lawder 'F' Company, 3 Nigerian Regiment
[15] WO 95/5387/1 War Diary No 1 Battery Artillery Nigerian Regiment

This entry graphically demonstrates how not having sufficient quantities of food supplies and the weather were a threat to health and hampered operations. When added to the other accounts we can paint a picture or get an idea of the landscape they were operating in, the changeable weather conditions and a feel for what they were experiencing.

Case studies – what can the records show us about the careers and experiences of Black African troops

The National Archives has a large collection of records that relate to the First World War in Africa. The important record series in the following case studies are WO (War Office) and CO (Colonial Office). Other useful records series for researching the wider conflict are CAB (Cabinet Office), ADM (Admiralty), PIN (Pensions and National Insurance) and FO (Foreign Office). Some of the records are keyword searchable via Discovery, The National Archives' online catalogue. Others need to be accessed via card indexes or registers of correspondence and then the original correspondence.16

CO 1069/71/128 Nigerian Regiment troops

---

16 FO 111 card index 1906-1920 is now an online card index that can be accessed and downloaded via Discovery (by year and alphabetically). WO, CAB, PIN and ADM mainly keyword searchable and CO mainly accessed via registers of correspondence, original correspondence and other series like Government Gazettes, sessional papers (Administering the Empire, 1801-1968: A Guide to the Records of the Colonial Office in the National Archives of the UK, is useful for identifying the series for different regions and types of records).

To start we are going to look at 6310 Adegbite Offa. From his name we can tell that he is from Offa, a town which is around 274km north east of Lagos, the Nigerian capital. There were several Adegbite Offa-s in the rolls, so the service number is key in identifying the correct person when exploring records that may relate to an individual's service or experience. I first came across 6310 Adegbite Offa when I started researching the campaign in Cameroon and was looking at WO 32/5320, reports by Brigadier General Cunliffe and Major General Sir C Dobell on operations in Cameroon, August 1914 to February 1916. Within the record there is a detailed narrative of the operation and the officer's recommendations for good or brave service. These are in draft form, for publishing in the London Gazette and official histories. Helpfully the draft version details the service number, rank, name, unit and has remarks. The remarks section details what the man did to be listed, in this case 'for coolness and bravery displayed by him during the action at Otu on 11th December 1914'.[17] So we now know his unit, the date of the action and where it took place, so we can look at the unit war diaries to see if anything is recorded. Adegbite is recorded as serving with the 3rd Nigeria Regiment and a search of Discovery gave the reference WO 95/5387, which only covers up to October 1914. So it appeared that there was no surviving diary covering that event. I looked at some of the Headquarters diaries in WO 95/5382 and found that there is a section of war diary for the 3rd Nigeria Regiment that covers December 1914. This you could see was separated from the other diary and demonstrates the value of working up the echelons to see if any information has been sent up the line.[18]

The diary records that on 11 December the Cross Rivers column was camped near Mfamyen, at around 0630 hours British troops on the Ekok Road fired on the enemy, who were advancing on the camp in force. They held them off, before the enemy charged the camp again at 0830 hours. There were further attacks carried out through to 1100 hours. At around 0900 hours all of the carriers ran away from the camp fearing injury, but were retrieved and kept calm. These multiple attacks failed as the commander had placed three maxims to

---

[17] WO 32/5320 reports by Brigadier General F Cunliffe and Major General Sir C Dobell on operations in Cameroon with list of officers and men for mention

[18] Diaries are recorded from the level of a battalion to a division

cover the clearing leading to the camp. Further fire was taken at the camp between 1230 and 1330 hours, and at 1400 hours the commander moved the camp to a higher hill. Fire was again taken at 1730 hours and the carriers again stampeded. The enemy strength was recorded as six to eight Europeans and 250 African troops. Point 12 of this diary page mentions 6310 Adegbite Offa and that he was cool and brave under trying circumstances, not a detailed account, but with the descriptors of the engagement we get a flavour of what was happening. Finally, the diary records that the column was proceeding to Ikonemana and that the patrol would have to travel light due to the commander not trusting the carriers. Initially another camp move saw them a quarter mile south west of the town, which the Germans had burnt out and looted eight days prior. The diary also records that food was exceedingly scarce, so we get further insight into environmental factors and the tactics of the Germans.[19]

Most importantly it records the events and gives us an idea of what Adegbite was doing during the protracted engagement. Adegbite was awarded the West African Frontier Force medal for Distinguished Conduct in the field (DCM), which is confirmed in WO 102/25—the register of West African Frontier Force and King's African Rifles Good Conduct, Distinguished Conduct and Long Service Medals.[20] There is also a Service Medal Index Card in WO 372/1/23773 which confirms his rank as Company Sergeant Major and records that he entered the African theatre of war on 9 August 1914, just after war was declared. It also records that he was issued the campaign medals: Victory, British and 15 Star, but does not record the awarding of the Distinguished Conduct Medal.[21]

There is one other set of records that I have found Adegbite recorded in, that is CO 658/4 Nigeria Government Gazettes. The first entry is dated 11 November 1915 and details the award of the Distinguished Conduct Medal as recorded in WO 32/5320—the draft copies of the London Gazette which

---

[19] WO 95/5382 Headquarters and Troops: Headquarters Allied Force – Column operation reports and orders to column commanders
[20] WO 102/25 West African Frontier Force and King's African Rifles: register of Good Conduct, Distinguished Conduct and Long Service and Good Conduct Medals, 1904 Jan 01 – 1941 Dec 31
[21] WO 372/1/23773 – Medal card of No: 6310 Company Sergeant Major Adegbite, Offa Corps: 3rd Nigeria Regiment

detail the reason why the medal was awarded.[22] The published London Gazette entry does not carry that information, just the name, rank and unit served.[23] It is worth noting that the colonial gazettes appear to publish the details some months after the event, in this case eleven months later. Adegbite is recorded again in the same record on 23 December 1915, when a notice is published detailing that he was promoted to Company Sergent Major, due to his conduct on 11 December 1914. This gives an insight into his career, in the absence of service records. This may not be every record that relates to his service, but what we have found helps us understand some of his experiences and service.

Next we look at three individuals who were serving with the 1st Battery, Artillery Nigerian Regiment. Two of the men came from the North of Nigeria—Kano and Gimba. Sangalla, however, is just recorded with a single name and it is hard to be sure if he comes from the same area. The war diary WO 95/5387 contains the nominal roll for the unit and the three names stood out as they were annotated with being wounded on the same date. '13 Sangalla wounded 3/2/15—died 11/2/15, 23 Moma Kano V wounded 3/2/15 and 34 Tanko Gimba wounded 3/2/15'.[24] This made me curious about what happened on that day. The diary records that on 2 February, '400 troops from 1 Nigerian Regiment and 1 Artillery Nigerian Regiment attacked the German entrenchment at Mburuko and Hermans Farm.' At around 0315 hrs on the 3rd they ran in to the German Picquet[25] who opened up with heavy fire from guns and around 300 men. The Nigerians' two guns also opened up and at around 0630 hours the Germans retreated. The large camp they vacated was taken. It is recorded that three gunners were wounded and are listed as Sangalla, Moma Kano V and Tanko Gimba, which ties in with the nominal roll.[26] Sangalla is listed as dying on 11 February 1915 on the nominal roll, the Commonwealth War

---

[22] CO 658/4 Nigeria: Government Gazettes – 1915 July-Dec (p. 593 & p. 683)
[23] London Gazette, supplement to the London Gazette 31 May 1916 (p. 5435) https://www.thegazette.co.uk/London/issue/29604/supplement/5435/data.pdf
[24] WO 95/5387 PART VII: EAST AFRICA, AND CAMEROONS, WEST AFRICA Cameroons
[25] Picquets were sections of men placed in front of the main body – It was their job to resist an attack and enable the main force to deploy efficiently.
[26] WO 95/5387 PART VII: EAST AFRICA, AND CAMEROONS, WEST AFRICA Cameroons

Graves Commission records that he was killed in action on 3 February 1915[27] and was a corporal, so which date he died is not clear and other records, when discovered may help answer that question. This does highlight possible problems when researching individuals as lone records may not be correct or tell the full story. There are other entries relating to these three men that highlight some of the problems faced when researching. Sangalla has a Service Medal Index Card in WO 372/17/163221, which records that he entered the theatre of war 23 September 1914; his rank as corporal; and that he was issued the following campaign medals: Victory, British and 15 Star, but does not record that he was killed in action.[28] If you only accessed the medal card you would not know he was killed in action. Number 34 Tanko Gimba, I could not locate a Service Medal Index Card for. There is however a Number 3 Sergeant Gimba who has a medal card,[29] but he is not listed on the nominal roll. So the question is, is 3 Gimba an error in the record and should actually be 34 Tanko Gimba; is the nominal roll complete? Tanko was wounded on 3 February 1915 and Gimba is recorded in WO 32/5320 as follows, 'he has throughout the whole campaign been the right-hand man of Captain Cumming, who, for the greater portion of the time was without the assistance of a European. He is the most reliable non-commissioned officer and especially during the attacks on Mora and Banyo mountains'.[30] So there is no hint of any wounding and recovery to 3 Gimba, 34 Tanko's rank is recorded as a gunner in February and Gimba's during the attack about seven months later as sergeant. It is unlikely that these are the same people, but will need further research to try and be sure. Mamo Kano V has a Service Medal Index Card which records that he entered the theatre of war 23/9/14; his rank as gunner and records that he was issued the campaign medals: Victory, British and 15 Star, which fits with the nominal roll and diary entry.[31] Again we do not get a detailed account of how the three were wounded from the record, but do get a feel for the

---

[27] Sangalla: http://www.cwgc.org/find-war-dead/casualty/2963701/sangalla
[28] WO 372/17/163221 Medal card of Sangalla Corps: Nigeria Regiment No: 13
[29] No 3 Gimba – WO 372/8/26282
[30] (Ibid) WO 32/5320 reports by Brigadier General F Cunliffe and Major General Sir C Dobell on operations in Cameroon with list of officers and men for mention
[31] No 23 Mamo Kano V – WO 372/13/98218

engagement. We also find that it is not always easy tracing records that expand our understanding or the records that you expect to find details recorded in.

The next case study looks at 5861[32] Manu Zozo 1st Nigerian Regiment. From his name it is hard to place where he originates from, so far, I have not located a town or tribe that fits in Nigeria. There are towns called Zozo in modern day Sierra Leone and Ethiopia though. He is recorded in WO 32/5320 as 'he showed conspicuous gallantry and set a fine example during the attack by Banyo Mountain, especially on 4th November 1915. He was also the first man to reach the summit of the position when the final assault took place'.[33] CO 445/36 paper 60660 discusses his recommendation and the fact that he was left off Major General Cunliffe's list (as detailed in WO 32/5320). Cunliffe's letter dated 20 November 1916, apologises that he was inadvertently omitted for a special reward in the list supplied, and goes on to describe that 'Manu behaved most conspicuously in the attack on Banyo Hill 4th & 5th November 1915. By his excellent example, he steadied the men of this section, when in a most difficult position and under heavy fire and was the first man of his company to reach a crest of the hill'.[34] Cunliffe strongly recommend his being awarded the Distinguished Conduct Medal. WO 102/25 lists 5681 Manu Zozo as being awarded the Distinguished Conduct Medal. He is also recorded as receiving a further Distinguished Conduct Medal 29 October 1917 for gallantry and devotion to duty at Bweno-Chini, East Africa, on 22 September 1917.[35] There is a report on the action in WO 95/5347/8.[36] Manu has a Service Medal Index Card in WO 372/13/111822 which records that he entered the theatre of war on 11/9/1914; his rank as Company Sergeant Major and that he was issued the campaign medals: Victory, British and 15 Star, but again does not record that he received

---
[32] Medal card lists two service numbers 5861 & 652
[33] WO 32/5320 reports by Brigadier General F Cunliffe and Major General Sir C Dobell on operations in Cameroon with list of officers and men for mention
[34] CO 445/36 – Despatches 1916 paper 60660 Sergt Mamu Zozo conspicuous gallantry recommendation Distinguished Conduct Medal
[35] WO 102/25 West African Frontier Force and King's African Rifles: register of Good Conduct, Distinguished Conduct and Long Service and Good Conduct Medals, 1904 Jan 01 – 1941 Dec 31
[36] WO 95/5347/8 3 East African Division Nigerian Brigade; 2 Service Battalion Nigerian Regiment – not Manu's specific unit

two Distinguished Conduct Medals.[37] This would be down to the fact that the African Distinguished Conduct Medal was a colonial award specifically for the WAFF and KAR. As the Medal Index Cards were compiled in the United Kingdom they would record the 'Imperial' version of medal only, Imperial DCMs are recorded in WO 372/23.

The final case study looks at 2897 Regimental Sergeant Major Belo Akure. From his name we can tell that he is from Akure, a city which is around 280km north east of Lagos, the Nigerian capital. There is an identifiable picture of Belo in the book *The African DCM* by John Arnold. This publication is a great resource for researching DCM awards and contains information and references to Belo's service.[38] Belo is recorded on the nominal role of A Company 4th Nigerian Regiment, which is annotated with 'wounded 14/4/1915'.[39] So far, I have not been able to find out how or why he was wounded. He is not listed in WO 32/5320[40] so we do not get any narrative from there, but another WO 32 general correspondence file does contain a template draft detailing the action, but without the dates recorded.[41] This appears to be a draft for the Nigerian Gazette entry,[42] which is almost identical to what is recorded in the unit war diary.[43] These documents record that 'The NCO is already in possession of the Distinguished Conduct Medal for bravery in the field. He has now been awarded a clasp for the services set out below:

> At Mbongo on 4th November 1914. His behaviour was particularly cool and courageous. He received orders to conduct the retirement of an advanced post which was being heavily attacked by the enemy. The post was separated from the main position by an unaffordable river 35 yards in width. Sergeant Major Belo Akure got his men into the only

---

[37] WO 372/13/111822 Medal card of Manu Zozo Corps: Nigeria Regiment No: 5861
[38] *The African DCM* by John Arnold
[39] WO 95/5387
[40] WO 32/5320 reports by Brigadier General F Cunliffe and Major General Sir C Dobell on operations in Cameroon with list of officers and men for mention
[41] WO 32/4977 DECORATIONS AND MEDALS: African Distinguished Conduct Medal (Code 50(Q)): Extension to all eligible natives in African units 1915-1918. General file with details recorded for a number of men.
[42] CO 658/4 Nigeria: Government Gazettes 25 November 1915, p. 623
[43] WO 95/5386/6

available canoe and, finding it would flounder if he entered it himself, with great self-devotion he lay on the bank and covered its retirement being all the time submitted to heavy fire, one bullet penetrating his sleeve. When the canoe landed he ordered the men into their trenches and then jumped in and swam the river to join them. Belo, is also mentioned for handling his section with coolness and judgement at the attack on Fondola on 29 December 1914.[44]

Reading that Belo was already in receipt of the DCM, I looked back through the register in WO 102/25 and found an entry in 1910 as well as in 1914.[45] Arnold's book confirms that this was won 'for gallant conduct during operations in Southern Nigeria 1908-09', and was issued on 4 January 1910.[46] Belo also has two Service Medal Index Cards, one in WO 372/2/92634[47] which records that he entered the theatre of war on 29/9/1914; his rank as Warrant Officer 2 class and then Regimental Sergeant Major;[48] and records that he was issued the campaign medals: Victory, British and 15 Star. The second card WO 372/23/78890 is for the award of a Military Medal that was gazetted 28 July 1917 for service in East Africa whilst serving with the 4th Nigerian Regiment.[49]

Other records that are helpful when researching

Some of the same records focused on above can be used when looking at the other West Africa Frontier Force Regiments. The Governmental Gazettes for Sierra Leone are held in CO 271, the Gold Coast in CO 99, Gambia in CO 460 and Nigeria, which we have seen examples of, within CO 658.

There are three Pension records in the PIN 15 series, which relate to the West African Frontier Force. PIN 15/2145, which contains some pension details for the Nigerian Regiments;[50]

---

[44] CO 658/4 Nigeria: Government Gazettes 25 November 1915, p. 623

[45] WO 102/25 West African Frontier Force and King's African Rifles: register of Good Conduct, Distinguished Conduct and Long Service and Good Conduct Medals, 1904 Jan 01 - 1941 Dec 31

[46] Ibid.

[47] WO 372/2/92634 Medal card of Belo, Akure Corps: 4th Nigeria Regiment.

[48] Warrant Officer 2nd class is a Sergeant Major, Regimental sergeant Majors Warrant Officer 1st class

[49] WO 372/23/78890 MM Medal card of Belo Akure Corps: Nigeria Regiment

[50] PIN 15/2145 West African Frontier Force and Nigeria and Gold Coast Regiments: claims against the Ministry in respect of service in East Africa and the

PIN 15/2146 contains details on cases relating to mainly European troops;[51] and PIN 15/1040 contains details of the investigation of apparent excessive awards and the visit of Mr WH Whiteley to the Gold Coast and Nigeria, this record contains pension details for the Gold Coast Regiment.[52] PIN 15/2145 is helpful as it recorded what payments the troops received and gives another source of information to compare with the other records highlighted. This is another source of information that helps build up the picture relating to black African soldiers. It also allows us to see what kind of payments were being made and could form the basis for a comparative study.

The West African Frontier Force has its own correspondence series: CO 641—West Africa Frontier Force Register of Correspondence 1900-1926; CO 642—West Africa Frontier Force Register of Out-letters 1900-1926; and CO 445—Niger and West Africa Frontier Force Original Correspondence 1898-1926. CO 701—contains miscellanea from the Accounts Branch and successors and includes accounting documents connected with the West Africa Frontier Force. Correspondence relating to individuals can be found within these correspondence files. One example found in CO 445/36 is the death of No 3762 Private Ojo Ibadan, E company 4th Nigerian Regiment. Ojo reportedly jumped in to a river and drowned. The record gives details from the court of enquiry that was set following the death on 10 October 1916. The record details evidence given by colleagues who were present at the time of the incident. Number 1491 Sergeant Major Alowa Ibadan stated that at 1410hrs he saw Ojo jump in to the river. 6938 Private Ngonde states that he was lying on his mat next to Ojo, aboard the *SW Raven*, when he suddenly sprung up and jumped in to the river. The master of the vessel stated that he was informed that someone had fallen overboard and Captain CH Green 4th Nigerian Regiment stated that he was informed that someone had fallen overboard, when he looked he saw the person in the water, with three men swimming towards him. Before they could reach him he

---

South Cameroons

[51] PIN 15/2146 West African Frontier Force and Nigeria and Gold Coast Regiments: claims against the Ministry in respect of service in East Africa and the South Cameroons, and also for education grants

[52] PIN 15/1040 West African Frontier Force: investigation of apparent excessive awards: visit of Mr WH Whiteley to the Gold Coast and Nigeria

disappeared, as the river was in a swollen state and had a swift current at the time. The three men, 4530 Private Ali Lokoja B company, 6818 Private Mumuni Sai A company and 7025 Private Imoru Doso of E company were mentioned for their courageous conduct in trying to rescue him. The court's opinion was that he had deliberately jumped in to the river Niger and committed suicide by drowning. At the end of the report, the commandant's opinion is recorded. Lieutenant Colonel Francis Jenkins said that he saw little justification for the conclusion that the man committed suicide—he may have been dreaming.[53] The reason for this death may never be known and it could have been an accident or intentional.

Accounts like this and the others we have looked at bring out the human story of black African troops and carriers which are trapped within the records at the archives, giving us a snapshot into their lives and experiences during the First World War in Africa. We can get a feel for the landscape, the changeable weather, the effects of the conflict on everyday life and the character of the troops.

Photographs

TNA WO 95/5387 Nigerian Regiment, A company, no 2 section

TNA MPG 1/1103 Northern and Southern Nigeria (now Nigeria). Map showing administrative boundaries, communications, and tribal names. Signed by Charles Alfred Vaux, consultant engineer to the South Nigeria Exploration Syndicate

WO 153/1205 East Africa, West Africa and Cameroons: Various Maps

CO 1069/65 (1) Nigeria Regiment crossing a river, Cameroons campaign

CAB 45/11, p.7 One of SMS *Konigsberg* guns in long grass, German East Africa

WO 95/5384—one of a number of sketches of Ekom on the Cameroon/Nigerian boarder and the surrounding landscape

CAB 45/11/54 African carriers in German East Africa carrying loads

CO 1069/71/128 Nigerian troops

---

[53] CO 445/36 – Despatches 1916, the record is indexed. CO 641/6 is the register of correspondence that covers 1913-1916

Let the collection tell its own story: Artefacts of the war in German East Africa in the collections of the Royal Museum of the Armed Forces and of Military History[1] in Brussels

Jan van der Fraenen

Between 1914 and 1918 war raged over the world. The fields of Europe were torn by artillery shells and were soaked with the blood of men from all over the world. But it was not only in Europe that the fighting parties fought their harsh and persistent battles. Africa, too, became a battlefield in Europe's war. Unlike the Belgian forces on the European battlefields, who faced an immobile and static front, the Belgian colonial forces battered their way into German territory in Africa. Here, warfare was mobile. At the same time, although large distances were covered by both advancing and retreating troops, the war became a war of attrition. In addition, it was a logistical nightmare. While in the end the Allies triumphed over the Germans in Africa, it is the German commander Colonel von Lettow-Vorbeck who is credited as the only German Great War commander who did not lose a single battle,[2] fighting in retreat with limited resources. Warfare on the African continent was very different from warfare on the battlefields of the Somme and Passchendaele. Imagining this difference and translating it to a visual and accurate presentation is a challenge for a museum whose permanent exhibitions aim to cover an entire world at war.

---

[1] The Royal Museum of the Armed Forces and of Military History is since May 2017 part of the War Heritage Institute. For more on this institute, see www.whi.be

[2] John M Bourne, 'Lettow-Vorbeck, Gen Paul Emil von' in Richard Holmes, *The Oxford Companion to Military History* (2003) p. 503

After 1918, the Royal Museum of the Armed Forces and of Military History, in short the Royal Military Museum, located in the heart of Brussels, saw its collections grow exponentially. Governments, veterans, and families, all donated souvenirs and material to the Museum. Today the Museum possesses one of the largest collections of First World War memorabilia, artefacts, uniforms, weapons, archives etc. A small number of these pieces relate to the Great War in Africa.

This chapter gives an overview of the Museum's collection and archival resources related to Africa. Each collection piece carries a specific history and tells a remarkable story. Some pieces are on permanent display, others are still waiting to be rediscovered.

A Colonial Police Force: the Force Publique in 1914

Originally founded as a colonial police force, the *Force Publique* quickly became the Belgian Congo's army at the outbreak of the war. In light of the vast territory of the Belgian Congo—about the size of Europe—it operated with very limited human resources—about 14,000 troops at the outbreak of the war. The attempts and hopes to keep Africa neutral during the war on the European continent were rapidly smashed. From the *Force Publique* a new expeditionary corps was created which saw its ranks filled with 10,000 new recruits. Before being engaged in German East Africa, these troops participated in the campaign in German Cameroon and the defence of the borders of Rhodesia. A typical uniform of a *Force Publique* soldier with equipment is present in the collection. The uniform consists of a black shirt with red lining, a pair of short black breeches and is completed with a red fez.[3] A Belgian non-commissioned officer or officer's uniform is to complete the set. It consists of a linen jacket, breeches, leather boots and a sun protecting pith helmet.[4] It was dressed in this kind of uniform that the *Force Publique* entered war in 1914. As with practically all combating

---

[3] Brussels, Register of acquisitions Royal Museum of the Armed Forces and of Military History, Inventory Number (hereafter referred to as: Brussels, Register of acquisitions, inv. nr.): 507485-507491. For more on this uniform: Philippe Jacqui, Pierre Lierneux, 'La tenue des soldats et gradés de la Force publique de 1888 à 1914' in *Militaria Belgica 2007-2008 Jaarboek over uniformologie en krijgsgeschiedenis* (2008) pp. 134-160

[4] Brussels, Register of acquisitions, inv. nr.: 801891-801894

nations in the war on all fronts, the contrast with later uniforms is large. As such, both uniforms symbolise the outbreak of the war in Africa and the first engagements on the continent.

A maritime battle on Lake Tanganyika

Soon allied attention became focused on German East Africa. In order to facilitate the logistical support for the allied troops, naval control over Lake Tanganyika had to be ensured. From the beginning of the hostilities, German ships attacked Belgian vessels and raided coastal villages and by doing so secured supremacy over the lake. The Belgians were very much aware of these problems and with the arrival of new British and Belgian ships on the lake the supremacy started to shift.

The collection contains a number of objects referring to this maritime campaign and illustrates Belgo-British relations. In February 1916 one of the German ships on the lake, the *Hedwig von Wissmann* was attacked and sunk by a reduced Anglo-Belgian flotilla of only four ships, *Fifi, Mimi, Dix-Tonnes* and *Vedette*.[5] Lieutenant Georges Goor was the commander of the Belgian vessels. He had the trying mission of organising the defence of the lake with hardly any resources, but he managed to overcome a lot of criticism. Even the eccentric British commander Spicer-Simson, known for his lack of respect towards the Belgians, had on one occasion some praise for the Belgian troops when referring to one of the Belgian vessels: 'The vessel was worth nothing, the engine was nothing special and the artillery was less than all the previous, but the men were sturdy fellows'.[6] After some days of instruction, Spicer-Simson added the following details about Goor in a report on military exercises:

> Goor, being a seaman has rapidly assimilated such knowledge as I was able to impart with him and I would feel that he would fight his ship with at least as much skill as the enemy has shown in the recent fight, and with little more practise I believe I will be able to give him points.[7]

---

[5] Section de l'Historique de l'Armée, *Les Campagnes Coloniales Belges, Tome I* (1927) pp. 250-3, George Moulaert, *La Campagne du Tanganika (1916-1917)* (s.d) pp. 37-9

[6] Henri Anrys, 'Kommandant Goor, Achtervolging op het Tanganikameer' in *Soldatenpost*, Jan 1958, pp. 4-7

[7] Brussels, Royal Museum of the Armed Forces and of Military History, Documentation Centre (hereafter referred to as: Brussels, KLM-MRA) Moscow Archive,

But in the same report Spicer-Simson is not very positive on the capabilities of other Belgian officers and men:

> Of the other members of the Belgian Division of the flotilla I do not think that there is much to say for two reasons, one being that their abilities have not come under my notice and the other that where they have come under my notice I do not consider them sufficiently startling to merit mention.[8]

As a commander, Goor was unable to participate in the confrontation with the *Hedwig von Wissmann*, as his ship was being repaired at the time. However, he joined the British commander as an observer. When the battle started Goor actively participated in the sinking of the *Hedwig von Wissmann*. The survivors were picked up by the flotilla. Wounded German soldiers were given medical care and they were sent to a prisoner-of-war camp. The wreckage was searched for intelligence and to salvage material. Inside the wreckage a field diary of a killed German officer was found, but more importantly: 'a small closet where enemy flags were kept was saved, in which we found a naval flag and a mooring flag, while the ship fought under the colours of the merchant navy'.[9] It is probably one of these flags that commander Goor kept as a souvenir and took with him in June 1916 when he became ill and had to return to Europe. The flag brought back from Lake Tanganyika is now one of the exhibits on display. Although the exact date of the donation remains unknown, the acquisition registers show that the flag was donated by commander Goor and originates from the *Hedwig von Wissmann*.[10]

Flags being treasured trophies, another example was registered in the collection in November 1920. It is the flag of the German vessel *Wami* and was given to the museum by Captain Jules Anthone. At the outbreak of the war 26 year old Anthone volunteered with the Belgian army as a private. He quickly rose through the ranks, was wounded on one occasion on the Western Front and was subsequently transferred to Africa where he received a commission as a 2nd Lieutenant of the

---

185-14-1238, *Notes on the general state of Naval and Military matters on and near Lake Tanganika*, Spicer-Simson, 3 Apr 1916 to the Governor General in Boma
[8] Ibid.
[9] Brussels, KLM-MRA, Moscow Archive, 185-14-1238, *Rapport de la destruction de la cannonière allemande Hedwig von Wissmann*, by Spicer-Simson, 10 Feb 1916
[10] Brussels, Register of acquisitions, inv. nr.: 1001050

Belgian Navy at Lake Tanganyika.[11] The *Wami* was scuttled by the Germans after a short pursuit by the *Netta* on 28 July 1916. At first the Allies thought they were in pursuit of the vessel the *Graf von Götzen*, but it soon became clear that this was the *Wami*.[12] During the engagements between the Anglo-Belgian flotilla and the German ships, the Allies were helped by seaplanes which bombed the *Graf von Götzen* and the coastal town of Kigoma at the end of July 1916.[13] The *Graf von Götzen* had its guns removed to be shipped east to the troops of Colonel von Lettow-Vorbeck and replaced by wooden dummies.[14] The *Wami* had just evacuated men and material from the town, when it was scuttled.

Other valuables probably taken from one of the three German ships, are two 3.7 cm revolver guns, one of them made by Krupp. Unfortunately, the only information provided in the acquisition registers is that it was donated by the Ministry of Colonies in 1925 and that is was taken from the Germans in Africa.[15]

The advance into German territory

With naval supremacy starting to shift in favour of the Allies, the Belgian troops divided into *Brigade Sud* and *Brigade Nord* started their advance into German territory. Between April and September 1916 the Belgian colonial troops conquered and occupied a large part of German held territory. Special mention will of course be given to the carriers who played a vital role in the advance. Without their logistical support, war in Africa would have been impossible.[16]

When the troops of *Brigade Sud* reached the outskirts of the railroad town of Kigoma, they quickly discovered that the Germans had just evacuated the town and left it undefended. The troops had no problems whatsoever entering and occupying

---

[11] KLM-MRA, Register file *Jules Anthone*, D3547

[12] KLM-MRA, Moscow Archive, 185-14-1238, *Rapport sur la croisière de la canonnière "Netta" sur la rive allemande*, by Leenaers, 29 Jul 1916, Moulaert, *op.cit.* pp. 117-8

[13] Section de l'Historique de l'Armée, *Les Campagnes Coloniales Belges 1914-1918*, Tome II (Bruxelles, 1929) pp. 401-2

[14] Edward Paice, *op. cit.*, pp. 230-1

[15] Brussels, Register of acquisitions, inv. nr.: 1000010

[16] Jan De Waele, 'Voor Vorst en Vaderland: Zwarte soldaten en dragers tijdens de Eerste Wereldoorlog in Congo' in *Militaria Belgica 2007-2008 Jaarboek over uniformologie en krijgsgeschiedenis* (2008) pp. 113-32

the railroad town of Kigoma, which was taken on 28 July.[17] The occupation of the town was quicker than anticipated, the last German train having left town only two hours earlier. Six Germans were taken prisoner, and although railroad material had been destroyed by the retreating Germans, the Belgians found 'a considerable amount of material, nearly all intact'.[18] Some of this material was confiscated or taken as a souvenir by the Belgian soldiers. One of the soldiers was Warrant-Officer Nestor Hannon, a 38-year old woodworker and aeroplane mechanic. After a brief spell on the Western Front Hannon had been detached to the Belgian seaplane squadron on the African front in early 1916, where he was involved in the occupation of Kigoma. By the end of the year he had returned to Europe and served the rest of the war at the seaplane base at Calais.[19] The souvenirs he took with him included a German pattern 1871 Mauser rifle. This is a single shot bolt-action rifle which still uses black powder. This weapon, dated 1875, is even by First World War standards very old and inadequate for modern fighting. When Hannon donated the rifle to the Museum, in October 1923, he told the curator that the rifle had been left behind at Kigoma during the bombardments by the seaplanes in July.[20] Hannon also donated a Belgian colonial bayonet for an Albini rifle which he 'found at the battlefield at Kigoma'.[21] The Albini rifle is even more obsolete than the Mauser pattern 1871 rifle. Hannon was however far from the only one who got his hands on German material lying about at Kigoma. Four very lights were taken and donated to the museum by a certain Courroble[22] in 1924 and by the Ministry of Colonies at an unknown date.[23] These very lights date from around the 1880s and can light up an area extending 900 metres.

---

[17] Moulaert, op. cit., pp. 118-9, *Les Campagnes Coloniales Belges 1914-1918*, Tome II (1929) pp. 371-3

[18] Section de l'Historique de l'Armée, *op. cit., Tome II*, p. 373

[19] Brussels, KLM-MRA, Register file *Nestor Hannon*, 3335

[20] The registers mention 29 July 1916. This is erroneous, for the Belgians already occupied the town. Hannon has probably confused dates and most likely referred to one of the air raids from July, the last one being 23 July. Brussels, Register of acquisitions, inv. nr.: 1001073

[21] Brussels, Register of acquisitions, inv. nr.: 801958

[22] I have been unable to identify Courroble

[23] Register of acquisitions, inv. nr.: 1001053, 1001054; 1001199, 1001200

Before *Brigade Sud* reached Kigoma, *Brigade Nord* had already taken the village of Biaramulo on 24 June. In the boma they installed their General Headquarters. Here the troops found weapons which had been left behind by the Germans. Two of these weapons are in the museum's collection. One pistol is a very rare 9mm semi-automatic Dreyse pistol. The Dreyse 7.65mm is not rare, but the 9mm was not produced in large quantities, as it was not popular among officers. It was not used by the German army, but officers could purchase it for private use. At the outbreak of the war, all weapons available and especially privately purchased arms were put into service by the Germans.[24] Unfortunately the Museum has no details of its acquisition, but presumably it was given to the institution in the early twenties. A similar weapon, a semi-automatic C96 Mauser, was also found in the boma of Biaramulo by the Belgians and subsequently donated to the Museum by the Ministry of Colonies.[25]

Immediately after the capture of Biaramulo on 26 June, the Belgians of *Brigade Nord* tried to cut off the retreat of the German group led by Hauptmann Eberhard Gudowius. Gudowius was a civil officer at Tabora at the outbreak of the war. He was given the rank of Hauptmann and transferred to the Mwanza and Bukoba area in September 1915.[26] This attempt resulted in a harsh confrontation between units of the 4th Regiment led by Major Rouling and the men of Gudowius at Kato on 2 and 3 July. The Germans put up a fierce fight and managed to decimate the Belgian troops, but in the end had to give way to the Belgians.[27] One of the colonial soldiers being credited with saving the Belgian day, was corporal Bopome. According to Rouling he 'fired his weapon unceasingly and assaulted the Germans. His weapon produced more noise than useful effect, but thanks to him the Germans did not get any closer and did not take us prisoner'.[28] During this confrontation

[24] KLM-MRA weapons specialist, Patrick Vandepoele, Jul 2011
[25] Register of acquisitions, inv. nr.: 1001180
[26] KLM-MRA, Moscow Archive, 185-14-5220, Intelligence supplement N°10, Notes on Officers serving with the enemy forces in German East Africa, Dec 1916, Intelligence section, General Staff East Africa Expeditionary Force, p. 10
[27] For a detailed description of the battle, see Section de l'Historique de l'Armée, *op. cit., Tome II*, pp. 324-34
[28] Brussels, Royal Museum for Central Africa, archives and historical collections,

both commanders got wounded. One Belgian wrote that Rouling and Gudowius were involved in hand-to-hand combat with each other, another one wrote that Gudowius shot Rouling.[29] Rouling does not mention any hand-to-hand combat in his report.

> All of a sudden a bullet ripped off one of my gaiters, another bullet passed between my legs tearing my trou-sers. After this I took cover behind a rock a bit to my right. The scars I have on both my hands and my face prove I was firing my Browning the moment I was hit by a ricocheting bullet.

Rouling was seriously wounded and had to be taken out of the firing line together with other wounded men. His wounds being provisionally dressed with his handkerchief, he disappeared with others into the thick African bush in search of a doctor—one was found at Busirajembo.[30] In the meanwhile the Belgians claimed victory and rounded up the Germans, taking fourteen Germans prisoner, amongst them the wounded Gudowius and his medical staff.[31] His sidearm, a Luger P08 with holster was taken from him and came into the hands of Major Rouling. Rouling finally arrived at a hospital in Kampala in Uganda and eventually in Nairobi. Later that year he was shipped back to Europe for surgery. From his left eye several shrapnel pieces were extracted.[32] He ended up in Paris and later in a Belgian

---

(hereafter referred to as: RMCA) La mémoire des belges en Afrique central, Papers of Rouling Jean, 51.39, *Commentaire sur le Combat de Kato – 3 juillet 1916 par le Colonel Honoraire Rouling, 1 juillet 1933*

[29] Pierre Daye, 'Les belges dans l'Est-African allemand' in: René Lyr (red), *Nos héros mort pour la patrie* (Bruxelles, 1923) p. 209; J. Bührer, *L'Afrique Oriental Allemande et la guerre de 1914-1918* (1922) pp. 167-8

[30] The Field Diary of Colonel Molitor mentions on 4 July that Rouling was missing: 'Le camp ROULING serait pris, le major blessé, serait introuvable'. KLM-MRA, Moscow Archives, 185-14-1373, *Copie du Journal de Campagne personnel duc colonel Molitor, Cahier I*; RMCA, La mémoire des belges en Afrique central, Papers of Rouling Jean, 51.39, *Commentaire sur le Combat de Kato – 3 juillet 1916 par le Colonel Honoraire Rouling, 1 juillet 1933*

[31] Out of seventeen Belgians, four were killed and five wounded. Out of 157 black soldiers, 35 were killed, thirty were wounded and five missing. Losses were between forty and fifty per cent, which is enormous. Four Germans were killed and 14 taken prisoner. RMCA, La mémoire des belges en Afrique central, Papers of Rouling Jean, 51.39, *Commentaire sur le Combat de Kato – 3 juillet 1916 par le Colonel Honoraire Rouling, 1 juillet 1933*. Gudowius was wounded in his abdomen and his right eye. He had to wear a monocle for the rest of his life. (Information on the nature of his wounds emailed by his son, Eberhard Gudowius to the author, 15 Jul 2012)

[32] RMCA, *La mémoire des belges en Afrique central*, Papers of Rouling Jean, 51.39,

hospital in France. At the end of 1917 he again made the journey to the colony where he arrived in January 1918.[33]

Gudowius, after helping to bury his fallen men,[34] was taken to the boma of Biaramulo where he was briefly interned by the Belgians. He was not liked by his captors, because he 'kept the arrogant and fragile attitude of the Prussian officer, despite his humiliating defeat at Kato'.[35] Gudowius spent the rest of the war in a British prisoner-of-war camp in India, together with his wife. There, their daughter was born. He returned to Berlin in 1920 where he died in December 1945.[36]

In January 1922, Rouling donated Gudowius' sidearm to the Museum, just after his retirement. A little plaque has been fixed to the weapon, presumably by Rouling himself, saying: *Combat de Kato 3-7-16*. It is a fascinating acquisition with a complete history.[37]

After the battle at Kato a large number of German weapons were picked up from the battlefield. Eleven of them found their way through the Belgian Ministry of Colonies to the Museum. They are all very obsolete weapons, one example being produced in 1876, and although this is already a bolt-action rifle, it can only hold one round and has to be reloaded after a single shot, just as the one found in Kigoma by Nestor Hannon.[38]

During the German retreat towards Mwanza, and subsequent chase by Belgian and British troops, the Germans left behind a mass of arms, which were picked up by Belgian troops.[39] The weapons they gathered include English Tower flintlock rifles. These weapons are even more obsolete than all the previous examples the Belgians found. This English rifle uses black powder and has to be muzzle-loaded after each shot.

Notice relative aux d'éclats de plombe ci annexé. The shrapnel pieces are held in the collection of this institution.

[33] KLM-MRA, Register file *Jean Rouling*, 12796

[34] RMCA, *La mémoire des belges en Afrique central*, Papers of Rouling Jean, 51.39, *Commentaire sur le Combat de Kato – 3 juillet 1916 par le Colonel Honoraire Rouling, 1 juillet 1933*

[35] Pierre Daye, *Avec les vainqueurs de Tabora, notes d'un colonial belge en Afrique oriental allemande* (Paris, 1918) pp. 155-6

[36] Information emailed by his son, Eberhard Gudowius to the author, 11 Jul 2012

[37] Register of acquisitions, inv. nr.: 1001176, 1001177

[38] Register of acquisitions, inv. nr.: 1001204

[39] Section de l'Historique de l'Armée, *op.cit., Tome II*, pp. 379-90

It probably dates back to the 1840s. To illustrate the variety of weapons left behind by the Germans the museum also possesses two hunting rifles used by German troops.[40]

This clearly illustrates how different fighting in the African bush was from the fighting on the European front.

The capture of Tabora

The Belgian objective was Tabora, a central town linked by railroad to Kigoma. In September 1916 the Belgian columns finally reached the outskirts of the town. The German troops were determined to fight for the town, but when several of their counterattacks failed they decided to raise the white flag and surrender the town to the Belgians.

A company was sent into town for reconnaissance. They found the town seemingly empty, but soon everywhere allied civilians and military prisoners appeared.

> [The Belgian Army] found the town en fête; everyone was in his best clothes making holidays, and the display of flags in every direction surprised us, though we had known of the wholesale way in which people had been getting them ready for the previous fortnight. Freedom was in the air; the dwellers in the prison camps—Europeans, Indians, and Africans—bore witness to it, as they walked about the town, congratulating one another on their changed condition . . . [41]

Amongst them was the Belgian Lieutenant Gendarme, who had been taken prisoner nearly two years earlier. He was in possession of a huge Belgian flag, which was meant to be raised in the Belgian pavilion at the Colonial Exhibition at Dar es Salaam in August 1914. He had kept the flag with him during his captivity.[42] Gendarme gave the flag to 29 year old captain Paul Jacques, officer with the General Staff of *Brigade sud*. Jacques, who had previously served on the Western Front and witnessed the first gas attacks at Steenstrate in 1915 only arrived in the colony in June 1916.[43] With a small ceremony the

---

[40] Register of acquisitions, inv. nr.: 1001075-1001078, 1001080, 1001082, 1001085-1001088, 1001097-1001101, 1001214-1001216

[41] Ernest F Spanton, *In German Gaols, A narrative of two years' captivity in German East Africa* (1917) pp. 99-100

[42] Emmanuel Muller, *Les troupes du Katanga et les campagnes d'Afrique 1914-1918* (1935) pp. 96-7

[43] KLM-MRA, Register file *Paul Jacques*, 14507

white flag was lowered and given to one of the officers and Jacques 'slowly raised the Belgian colours to the top of the pole'. Tabora was firmly in Belgian hands and the flag became 'The Flag of Tabora'.[44]

The Museum's collections hold two German flags found in Tabora in September 1916. One was donated by the family of Jacques in June 1980.[45] The other one was donated by the curator Duchesne in January 1982. This last one is accompanied by a photograph of non-commissioned officer Hingeon 'who took the German flag at Tabora'.[46]

Tabora was now officially and firmly in Belgian hands and the Germans were on the run. When the Belgians occupied the town and installed their administration, they again found material that the Germans had left behind. In the Museum's weapon depot they found a German Mauser hunting carbine, made from an official army weapon—a Mauser gew. 98—but converted into a private hunting rifle.[47] Again, this clearly illustrates what kind of weapons were used on the African front, often characterised by a certain degree of improvising and including a wide range of fire arms, from officially distributed, to privately purchased, and from obsolete to modern.

Not only firearms were among the war bounty. Artillery pieces were taken as well. The most interesting artillery piece that was captured at Tabora by the Belgians is a German field artillery gun 8cm, model C 73. It is a rather unusual piece because few 8cm guns were produced. It can be easily recognised by the shield protecting the gunners. In the Museum's collection a similar gun has been found, which was actually captured by the Belgians in Africa.[48] It is not certain whether the gun in the photograph depicting a captured gun in Tabora is the actual gun we have in the Museum's possession, although there is every reason to believe so. The gun is presently displayed in the Royal Military Academy.

---

[44] Muller, *op.cit.*, p. 97; JJDC, '*Sur le "drapeau" de Tabora*', in *La Belgique Militaire* (1938) 68, nr. 2447, pp. 262-3

[45] Register of acquisitions, inv. nr.: 1007225

[46] Register of acquisitions, inv. nr.: 1007234; KLM-MRA, photograph collection, 201070271

[47] Register of acquisitions, inv. nr.: 1001222

[48] Register of acquisitions, inv. nr.: 1000022

The end of the campaign?

When the Belgians had reached their objective, they did not intend to advance further into German East Africa. Moreover, the British took a clear stance towards the Belgians, refusing further Belgian support. This statement was led by political and not military objectives. The Belgians remained in Tabora for a couple of months, but by mid-November cooperation with the Anglo-British Force came to an end. Both sides were more interested in discussing the administration of the occupied territories than in actually beating the Germans. In addition, the difficult personal relationship between Generals Tombeur and Smuts did not help towards having a constructive alliance.[49]

In February 1917 Tabora was officially handed over to the British Forces in East Africa. During a large-scale and festive ceremony the Belgian flag was lowered and replaced by the Union Jack. Following the ceremony the Belgians embarked on a train and left Tabora, under the salute of the British. The British requested that the flag be handed over to them as a souvenir, but the Belgians firmly refused, as the flag had already been promised to the Royal Army Museum in Boma.[50] A document accompanying the Belgian flag was drawn up stating that this flag was the very one that had been raised over Tabora. In 1922 this document and the flag were handed over to the Museum in Brussels. Unfortunately, the flag got lost, probably due to bad conservation before the eighties, but the document and the history of the flag have been preserved.[51]

To illustrate the different occupations of the town by the Germans and the British, two train tickets are on display. Both tickets allow the passage from the Tabora Market to the Tabora train station. One is in German, the other in English. Colonial occupation did not end with the capture of Tabora. The town stayed under European colonial rule.

After handing over the town to the British, the Belgian *Force Publique* returned to Congo where it was demobilised.[52] In this

---

[49] Ross Anderson, *The forgotten front, the East African front, 1914-1918* (2007) pp. 152-3; Edward Paice, *Tip & Run, the untold tragedy of the Great War in Africa* (2007) pp. 242-4, 316, Section de l'Historique de l'Armée, *op.cit.*, Tome II, pp. 594-6

[50] KLM-MRA, Moscow Archive, 185-3-163, *Négociations diplomatiques relatives à l'occupation à Tabora*, written by Cpt Wéber, 14 Sep 1927

[51] Register of acquisitions, inv. nr.: 801950, 804680

[52] Section de l'Historique de l'Armée, *op.cit.*, Tome II, pp. 600-1

period an interesting little booklet was published in London. It was entitled: *The Belgian Campaigns in the Cameroons and German East Africa*. It was written in October 1916, but published by the Belgian Government in English, French and Dutch in 1917. It is clear that the writer of the brochure was convinced that the capture of Tabora by the Belgians marked the end of the hostilities for the *Force Publique* in Africa. In its last chapter—in what is actually a glorification and justification of the Belgian presence in Africa—he wrote: 'The East African campaign may now be considered as virtually ended'.[53] The booklet is an evident piece of propaganda for the Belgian government and its claims in East Africa.

A new advance

However, the war was far from over. Again, the British sought help from the Belgians in Africa.[54] Belgian Colonel Armand Huyghé now led the Belgian troops. He had previously fought on the Western Front where he had quickly risen in the military ranks.[55] This time the Belgian troops advanced towards Mahenge, which was captured in October 1917. To illustrate this part of the war, the Museum possesses a complete uniform of a Katangese unit, with the Mills equipment, dated to 1918. Another European uniform completes the set, all donated by the Ministry of Colonies in January 1921.[56]

Next to these uniforms some smaller items can be found in the Museum's collection, such as a set of playing cards used by NCO Scheyvaert, who was a clerk with the court-martial during the second part of the campaign. The ace of hearts of the American set has been stamped by the Customs in Dar es Salaam 27 September 1917.[57]

A German piece of bandage, which was taken from a German hospital in Liwale in November 1917[58] by the Belgian officer

---

[53] *The Belgian campaigns in The Cameroons and German East Africa* (1917) p. 20
[54] Edward Paice, *op.cit.*, pp. 316-23
[55] Paul Van den Abeele, 'Huyghé de Mahenge', in *Biographie Coloniale Belge*, Tome IV (1955) pp. 415-6
[56] Register of acquisitions, inv. nr.:801896-801904. For more information: Philippe Jacqui & Pierre Lierneux, '*Les gradés et soldats de la Force publique pendant la guerre de 1914-1918*' in *Militaria Belgica 2007-2008 Jaarboek over uniformologie en krijgsgeschiedenis* (2008) pp. 161-75
[57] Register of acquisitions, inv. nr.: 1001052

Jean Cayron[59] after the occupation of the town by the Belgians, can very accurately illustrates the shortages experienced by the German troops in Africa. Medical supplies were very low at all times and a variety of products—not only medical supplies— had to be produced locally. This particular item is made from the bark of a tree.[60]

Even items related to prisoners-of-war in Africa are present in the collection, such as a small map illustrating a Belgian prisoner-of-war camp in Elizabethville in Congo, photographs or a small booklet on the treatment of prisoners in Africa.[61] These items demonstrate how much camps in Africa differed from those in Europe. They are real propaganda instruments, used by both parties.

A complete uniform of General Tombeur is present in the collection. He was knighted by king Albert and became a baron. He was allowed to add Tabora to his name and so became Tombeur de Tabora. Huyghé, who led the second campaign, was also knighted and became Huyghé de Mahenge.

The Museum possesses a collection of paintings of Belgian generals made by Jacques Madyol in the early twenties, including a portrait of Tombeur.

Archives

The Royal Military Museum is a research centre as well. It keeps a wide variety of sources, such as the archives from the Ministry of Defence up to May 1940; a rich collection of private papers; tens of thousands of photographs; posters and proclamations; journals; newspapers; personnel files and maps. It also keeps the so-called Moscow Archives. These consist of a very disparate mass of documents looted by the Germans in 1940 in Belgium and transferred to Berlin. There they were subsequently taken by the Soviets and moved to Moscow, where the Cold War made sure nobody gained access to these files. In the early nineties they were rediscovered by Belgian researchers and after a long diplomatic process, the complete archive

---

[58] Section de l'Historique de l'Armee, *Les Campagnes Coloniales Belges 1914-1918*, Tome III (1932) pp. 222-4
[59] KLM-MRA, Register file *Jean Cayron*, 14996
[60] Register of acquisitions, inv. nr. 1001052
[61] This booklet is *Le traitement des civils allemands ramenés de l'Est-Africain par des Belges – Réponse documentée aux accusations allemandes, 22 juillet 1917*

was shipped to Brussels. The bulk of the archives on the military operations by the Belgian forces in Africa can be found in the so-called Moscow Archives. It contains extremely detailed war diaries of many different units, reports on actions, encounters and skirmishes in the African bush or on Lake Tanganyika. Daily orders, telegrams, maps, correspondence, notes, personal diaries from officers on the African campaign are all to be found in this archive. Noteworthy are the reports of interrogations of German prisoners, road reports and intelligence reports on German troops. No less than 169 files can be consulted on the war in German East Africa.[62]

Files on German prisoners can also be found in the section on prisoners-of-war. They contain lists of German prisoners and the places where they were held. Furthermore, correspondence and demands of the prisoners can be traced in this rich archive, as well as records of the transfer of prisoners from Africa to France. A file on Ada Schnee, wife of the German colonial administrator is available in this archive.[63]

One important source on Belgian participation in the war in Africa, is a three-volume study published by the Historical Section of the Belgian Army in the 1920s. These volumes represent official history, are enormously detailed and are available through the library in the Documentation Centre.[64]

Conclusion

Using obsolete and outdated weapons, improvised materials, hardly any artillery, only sporadic air support and with overstretched communication lines in a tropical and sickening climate, the war in German East Africa was something special, almost unreal. But there are plenty of collection pieces that can tell interesting stories on the history of these African campaigns. They clearly illustrate how different the fighting in the African bush was from the fighting on the European and western front.

---

[62] The inventory can be consulted in the Documentation Centre reading room

[63] Erik Janssen, *Inventaris van het archief van de Dienst voor de Duitse Krijgsgevangenen van de Belgische Middendienst voor de Krijgsgevangenen, 1914-1921 (1922-1926)* (Brussel, 2011) 229p.; Erik Janssen, *Inventaris van het archief van het Korps van de Krijgsgevangenen [1914] 1918 -1921* (Brussel, 2011) 63p.

[64] Section de l'Historique de l'Armée, *Les Campagnes Coloniales Belges 1914-1918* (1927). www.klm-mra.be for information on visiting the Documentation Centre

Citations for military awards

Harry Fecitt

This chapter is about citations, not medals. Medals are interesting but they cannot be issued without citations. The chain of events was that after a particular action, or a long period of service (depending on what the award was for) a commanding officer would submit a recommendation to his Brigade Headquarters for the issue of a medal to a soldier or an officer, and this recommendation would have to be accompanied by a citation.

The citations are very interesting. As the recommendation for the award was approved, if it was, and moved to the next headquarters, officers fiddled around with citations for various reasons. By the time it got to the *London Gazette*, it could be totally changed. It might have started quite long and been reduced to a couple of lines. The trick is to find the citation, if you can, in the unit war diary because that is the purist form. Next come the East African General Routine Orders which are in The National Archives (London),[1] and those are quite illuminating. They also tell you where the action occurred, which the *London Gazette* does not as it is pressed for space. So the EAGROs, as the East African General Routine Orders are called, are very useful for people who want to plot awards alongside specific actions.

Over the last few years I have been collating every citation I can find for every gallantry or service medal that was issued in the East African theatre, and I have tabulated at some length. But I have not got them all as every month I find another tucked away. The newly discovered medals are very often listed as being not related to East Africa at all. If they appeared in the *London Gazette* it is often under Birthday Honours lists or just

[1] TNA: WO 123/289 and WO 123/290

the title Distinguished Service. But by trawling through the war diaries, I can spot a name. I then have access to what are called the Medal Index Cards (the official records of the authorities for the issue of individual medals). If you subscribe to the *Ancestry* website you can have access to all the Medal Index Cards for World War One (excepting for the Military Medal, see note below), so most times you can find your man and check which theatre he was in. If he is in the campaign in the time-frame you are looking at, you can then make the assumption that he is the man who was awarded the medal.

What I want to focus on is not just the gallantry aspect of these medals, it is the other information about the campaign that you can find which helps enhance narratives that you are writing. This information is also a lot of use to medal collectors who want to enhance the value of the medals they sell.

I am going to point out how half a dozen or eight citations tell me something about the theatre. First, a Lance Corporal, a Distinguished Conduct Medal.

> For conspicuous gallantry and devotion to duty. He proceeded fifty miles from our nearest post to a point on the enemy's line of communication, tapped the enemy telegraph line and returned across the river with his cable.

If you saw that citation today, what kind of unit would you think the chap was in? Special Forces! But we did not have Special Forces until I was born to be honest. During the Great War, we had men who did the work that Special Forces do today. I came upon this one when I was walking around the Dar es Salaam war cemetery taking photographs. I saw this Lance Corporal, Argyll and Sunderland Highlanders, DCM, died in theatre 1918, buried in Dar es Salaam and I thought, 'What is he doing here? His unit was not here. Perhaps he brought his DCM from France and Flanders where it had been awarded.' I discovered he was from the 2nd Battalion of his regiment which was stationed in India. His Medal Index Card showed me he was in the theatre at the time the medal was awarded. This was a medal I stumbled upon purely because the recipient had died, probably from disease. There must be scores more of similar medals waiting to be discovered. He was in a Special Signals Unit. Many of the regular battalions in India had men who volunteered and came to East Africa even though their regular regiments did not come, and he was one of those chaps. So I was very pleased to find this, but very sad he had died.

The next is my favourite citation of the whole campaign. It is so descriptive of the theatre. It is for a South African Service Corps Conductor attached to the King's African Rifles Mounted Infantry.

> Whilst in charge of the King's African Rifles Mounted Infantry remounts on 26 and 27 June 1918 at the crossing of the Lurio River, Portuguese East Africa, he swam this crocodile infested river five times with horses, narrowly escaping seizing capture by a crocodile the third time, and swimming twice across the next day and getting all his animals over. During the whole operation, he showed great courage and devotion to duty.

What a citation! What a guy! And it shows you the daily risk lads had to take when watering mounts or getting them across rivers. There were no bridges; somebody had to swim first with a rope.

The following citations provide examples of bush tactics that can be identified. This is a Company Sergeant Major, a Nigerian.

> Conspicuous gallantry and devotion to duty. He set a fine example for coolness and courage to his men throughout the action, continually exposing himself in controlling fire particularly when his trench was exposed to heavy enfilade as well as frontal fire. [Enfilade means it was coming in from a side so the forward and backward trench defences did not stop the fire.] He continuously visited two piquets which owing to dead ground had to be kept out close to the enemy's line of advance. He rendered great assistance . . .

The interesting thing is the piquets. This citation is telling us how dead ground was controlled. Dead ground from an infantry point of view is, if you are observing from a trench, there is a dip in front of you which you cannot see into. It is called 'dead ground' but the enemy can advance up it using it as cover from view. So the tactics were to put extremely courageous men out as piquets, which is a name for a little standing patrol, who had to look into the dead ground and raise the alarm if the enemy was advancing.

Another Distinguished Conduct Medal for a Sergeant Tom, really tells us a lot about bush warfare: both the difficulty and the way you could take advantage of circumstances. It is a King's African Rifles citation.

> Whilst in charge of a standing patrol of ten rifles he went forward with one man to investigate some talking which he had heard ahead of him in the bush. He came upon an enemy party passing along a winding path which would eventually lead them to his standing patrol. He counted an enemy party of three German whites and seventy German Askari. He then hurried back to his party by a short cut and arranged his men to receive the enemy. He opened fire at close range and knocked over one German white and two German blacks. He was then forced to retire one hundred yards by the enemy out flanking him. Just at this time, his relief of ten rifles arrived. He thereupon advanced causing the enemy to retreat, capturing three rifles, sets of equipment and four hundred rounds of ammunition.

That is very illuminating. Not just the way the sergeant behaved, but his use of bush craft. He had already worked out relative positions in the bush as only the black Africans could do. The white men struggled to do this, to have a bush sense, But Sergeant Tom made it work.

A Nigerian Sergeant:

> When in charge of flankers which he led with pluck and boldness over most difficult territory, he contributed largely to the defeat of the efforts of the enemy at delaying our advance.

Here we discover how the British advanced to contact against an enemy who was trying to delay them. The British used flankers. They had people on the extremities, left and right. Their job was to get round the back; the encircling position. Every time, if you can achieve this, the enemy will consider breaking contact and withdraw.

This one introduces a heavier type of warfare. A British Sergeant with a Nigerian Regiment at the big battle at Mahiwa, October 1917.

> When his company was forced to evacuate their trench owing to heavy shell fire, he rendered great assistance in restoring order by his personal example. He led the men back himself to reoccupy the trench when the German infantry attacked and carried a machine-gun back himself at a most critical time.

This tells us something that compares with the conditions in France and Flanders. Mahiwa, was one of the few occasions where a lot of artillery was used and so what the British were doing, and doubtless the Germans too, was that when artillery was targeting the trenches the men withdrew to a safe distance and as soon as the artillery lifted, the men ran back into the trench to occupy it.

British, King's African Rifle and Nigerian citations tend to mention the location of the action. South African ones do not. This may be due to a lack of professionalism as the South Africans did not have a professional army with staff officers who understood the need for certain processes.

Some of the Military Crosses and Distinguished Service Orders are sometimes difficult to pin down as there were so many issued without citations on the King's Birthday List or New Year Honours List. There is a very large book[2] which lists all the awards of the Distinguished Service Orders and Military Crosses etc that appeared in the *London Gazette*, but very often citations did not appear alongside the notification of the award of the medal; they might have appeared eight months or so later or never at all. Therefore, you often have to make a separate search through the *London Gazette* on its website to discover relevant citations.

South African Intelligence citation:

> For conspicuous gallantry and devotion to duty he boldly attacked and destroyed an enemy food and munitions' store meeting a superior enemy force on the return journey which he dispersed. He obtained much valuable information and has done good work consistently throughout.

This shows that intelligence officers in the field were expected to destroy targets that they and their African scouts could successfully attack.

There were two kinds of Distinguished Conduct Medal for black Africans: the King's African Rifles, Nigerians and every-one from West Africa qualified for an African Distinguished Conduct Medal, but as the war developed there were blacks in other units who qualified but were not in the bracket for the African Distinguished Conduct Medal, so they got the Imperial Distinguished Conduct Medal along with white and other

---

[2] Michael Maton, *Honour the Officers* (Honiton, 2009)

Imperial troops. Private Masumbuku Mbinganga got an Imperial Distinguished Conduct Medal.

> For conspicuous gallantry and devotion to duty. He [Private Mbinganga] was one of a party under an NCO sent to obtain water which was urgently needed (as it always was) from a post held by the enemy. Though the rest of the party failed to procure any water, he, by the skilful use which he made of the local natives succeeded in obtaining some. On the following day, when in charge of an outpost station, he handled his men with great judgement on the approach of an enemy patrol. He also skilfully disarmed two natives of the enemy patrol who approached him at the post.

An officer:

> For conspicuous gallantry and devotion to duty. He remained continuously behind the enemy's lines and made valuable use of the enemy's natives. He burnt several of the enemy's food depots causing considerable havoc among their supply arrangements and killed or captured several of the enemy. His personal courage and initiative are quite exceptional.

He was a very famous South African with the name Phillip Pretorius, who was Smuts' leading scout. This was for the Bar to his Distinguished Service Order.

This shows that in those days, Intelligence men went along fighting for their information; they did not just sit down and intercept enemy signals traffic to obtain it. A good intelligence officer with his scouts could be more productive in destroying enemy supply dumps than a much stronger infantry force could be. This is because the intelligence party lived off the land without the logistical support that the infantry needed.

The Indian Mounted Batteries were key units in the war. Their guns were called screw guns because you could unscrew the jointed barrel into two pieces to make acceptable loads that individual mules could carry. Because the batteries were Indian Army you tend to think that the personnel were all Indian apart from the British officers. But here is Fitter Staff Sergeant Mason:

> On 1 May 1918 at Karonji, Portuguese East Africa, the battery was attacked on line of march at short range by a field company with two machine-guns. He, with two Indian Non Commissioned Officers, went out under heavy machine-gun fire and successfully brought in the breech of a howitzer which had been bucked off by its mule between the escort

and the enemy. An act of great gallantry as they were under fire from both sides and the enemy was very close. But for these three men the breech might have been captured.

I certainly had not realised there were men like Fitter Staff Sergeant Mason with the mountain gunners, but it makes sense. Because the British Army units had armourers attached to supervise weapons maintenance, the mountain batteries had the equivalent to look after their guns.

Now, here is an example of ordinary life in an Infantry Battalion. There were certain protocols with certain problems as you progress in rank, and certain difficulties when you get moved to a new unit. Here is a citation which admirably sums it up. It is a bar to a Distinguished Conduct Medal to a Nigerian Company Sergeant Major.

> Taking up his present duties on 17 September 1917 in succession of a Company Sergeant Major with an exceptionally fine record, and in addition to having the disad-vantage to being a new comer to his present company, he had a difficult position to fulfil during an important period. But by constant disregard of personal risk and by sound judgement in action and by continual firm handling of the men he rapidly established himself and his services have been of the greatest value.

Now that citation is nothing really when you read it as there is no blood and guts, but it is a typical example of infantry life and how good units, by choosing good people to succeed, maintained their proficiency.

When I was a lad, the man who was responsible for the battalion's supply of ammunition was the Regimental Sergeant Major. Lately, this has fallen into a bit of disrepute in the British Army as the RSM seems to walk around with the CO acting as his personal body guard. But back in the days of the Great War the battalions were practising the system properly. This is about Sergeant Hendry, a Territorial Sergeant attached to the King's African Rifles battalion.

> On 31 August 1918 after Lioma he was conspicuous for cool gallantry, while acting Regimental Sergeant Major, for steadying his ammunition porters who were shaken by heavy machine-gun fire and so maintaining a constant supply of ammunition to the firing line. On 6 September 1918 at Pere, he controlled and maintained a supply of

ammunition under heavy fire. He has consistently shown initiative and courage.

That is a job where there are no heroics, there is no glamour, but get it wrong and you lose the battalion and you lose the battle.

Another askari who got an Imperial Distinguished Conduct Medal, another intelligence person, tells us about transporting cash in the field.

> He displayed marked courage and coolness in action when with the baggage guard, having rallied some armed troops together from other units, he succeeded in beating off the enemy and by his resource saved some baggage and in particular a regimental chest containing silver from falling into enemy hands. He has consistently performed fine work.

The battalions needed money to make local purchases and to pay the troops in the field, and someone had to carry this around. In the Dar es Salaam Museum there is a German coinage chest that would have needed four men to carry it.

On the distribution of medals amongst the forces: If you were a black soldier in a Rhodesian unit, you did not stand much chance of getting a medal; and very sadly after the war in Southern Rhodesia it became government policy that blacks awarded medals for gallantry were dissuaded from wearing them. The black Rhodesians at least were allowed to have their medals, whereas the South African government would not allow its African Labour Corps men (who had served in France and East Africa) to receive medals.

Note: *Ancestry* does not have all the Medal Index Cards. They lack the cards for the Military Medal. The only place all can be accessed is at The National Archives, Kew either online for a fee or free of charge by visiting Kew. It is quite important with regards to honours and awards to know that the most common gallantry award is lacking on the *Ancestry* site. The reason for this situation is that when the decision was made for the Ministry of Defence to withdraw from West London, decisions were made about the cards (kept in fifteen eight-foot cabinets). Now the individual campaign medal cards are in the care of *The Western Front Association* (WFA), along with the cards for Meritorious Service Medal and Distinguished Conduct Medals, Mentions in Despatches and Territorial Force Efficiency

Medals. The index cards for the women are held by the Imperial War Museum.

The index cards for the Military Medal are part of an indexing project to create a definitive list of the 115,000 or so recipients of the Military Medal during the First World War. The results of this project are going to be published in time for the centenary of the Great War. Once the cards were in the possession of Western Front Association (WFA), they entered into an agreement with *Ancestry* and digitised the cards once again; so unlike The National Archives cards which were digitised from microfiche and are therefore monochrome, the cards which are on the *Ancestry* site are digitised from the original and so are in colour. But the *Ancestry* cards lack the Military Medal which of course is quite significant. The plan is to produce a roll of the names along with statistical analysis. Individuals who are researching the list have sourced in excess of 30,000 citations for the Military Medal for British, African, Australian, New Zealand, and Canadian forces but they are as yet undecided as to how they will create the list and citations. It is work in progress. The Military Medal cards are annotated with a stamp, or hand writing, indicating the operational theatre in which the award was won—the same applies for the Meritorious Service Medal cards. thank you for your attention, i now hope that you can appreciate the value of using and interpreting gallantry citations when you wish to describe a particular military action in detail.

Sources:

Arnold, John (compiler), *The African DCM Awards of the King's African Rifles and West African Frontier Force Distinguished Conduct Medal* (Orders and Medals Research Society 1998)

Arnold, John (compiler), *The Award of the Military Medal to African Soldiers of the West African Frontier Force and the King's African Rifles from 1916 to 1919* (Self-publication 2010)

Dorling, H Taprell, *Ribbons and Medals* (George Philip, 1974)

Hayward, John; Birch, Diana & Bishop, Richard, *British Battles and Medals* (Spink, 2006)

Mussell, John W (ed.), *Medal Yearbook* (Published annually in softback by Medal News)

RW Walker, *Recipients of the Distinguished Conduct Medal 1914-1920* (Midland Medals 1981)
Journals of the Orders and Medals Research Society
London Gazette notifications

www.ingramcontent.com/pod-product-compliance
Lightning Source LLC
Chambersburg PA
CBHW051624230426
43669CB00013B/2168